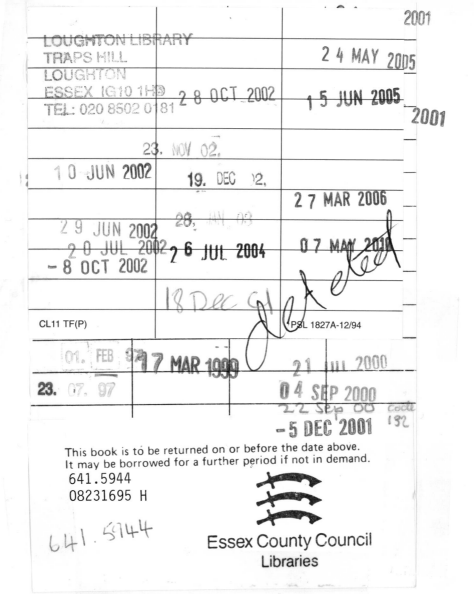

MIREILLE JOHNSTON'S
COMPLETE

French Cookery
Course

MIREILLE JOHNSTON'S
COMPLETE

French Cookery
Course

BBC BOOKS

To my daughter Margaret Brooke, *'fine mouche - fine bouche'*, to my daughter Elizabeth, *'le moineau pensant'*, and to my husband Tom, all of whom have steadily gone, in the course of these books, from tentative *'petites mains'* to thoughtful testers and are now reliable partners in our kitchen.

Published by BBC Books, a division of BBC Enterprises Limited, Woodlands, 80 Wood Lane, London W12 0TT

First published in two volumes in 1992 and 1993
This revised omnibus edition first published 1994
© Mireille Johnston 1992, 1993, 1994

ISBN 0 563 37014 9

Designed by William Mason
Photographs by Graham Kirk and James Murphy
Styling by Helen Payne
Home Economists: Allyson Birch and Maxine Clark
Maps © Eugene Fleury
This edition copy-edited by Wendy Hobson
Recipes tested by Wendy Hobson and Hilaire Walden
Printed and bound in Great Britain by
Butler and Tanner Limited, Frome
Colour separations by Radstock Repro Limited, Midsomer Norton
Jacket by Lawrence Allen Limited, Weston-Super-Mare

Title page: Salade au Chèvre (see p.234)

CONTENTS

ACKNOWLEDGEMENTS 6
FOREWORD 8
INTRODUCTION 9

The Regions

Ile-de-France 15, Brittany 18, Normandy 21,
The North and Champagne 24, Alsace-Lorraine 26, Burgundy 29,
Lyonnais, Savoie, Franche-Comté and Dauphiné 32,
Provence 35, Languedoc-Roussillon 38, The South-West 41,
The Atlantic Coast 45, Auvergne and Limousin 48, Val de Loire 51

The Recipes

SOUPS 55
STARTERS 74
SAUCES 90
EGGS 103
FISH AND SHELLFISH 118
POULTRY 148
MEAT 167
CHARCUTERIE 210
SALADS 225
VEGETABLES 235
CHEESE 260
DESSERTS 274
HOME BEVERAGES 336
LA RESERVE 339
MENUS 341
INDEXES 345

ACKNOWLEDGEMENTS

*T*his book was prepared in connection with the BBC television series filmed by Clare Brigstocke and her merry crew in France. I want to express my gratitude to Clare whose indomitable energy and vision kept it and us all together.

Many thanks to Jenny Stevens for her confidence, Diane Hadley for her ever-present support, Tricia Bowker for her infectious good humour, Clare Hughes for her endurance and energy, David South, Eric Fever, Michael Whitehouse, and Mal Maguire for their superb work and their good spirits all along. Working with such a crew transformed hard work into a true pleasure.

I want to thank affectionately Suzanne Webber, my editor who has been constantly generous and attentive, Deborah Taylor for her patience, Hilaire Walden for her precision, Frank Phillips for his eye, and Khadija for her grace under pressure. I want to thank Wendy Hobson, it was a delight working with her.

In the making of the television series I want to acknowledge all the help we have received from SOPEXA, London and particularly from Gabrielle Allen who provided so many contacts and gave so much of her time. I also want to thank Gillian Green of Air France Holidays and the many regional Chambers of Commerce and Tourist Committees, both regional and departmental, for their invaluable help during the research trips, and most expecially the Pont l'Abbé Tourist Office.

I would also like to thank Eric du Chatellier and Patricia Rio at the Château du Kernuz, Quimper, and Carole Handslip and Sarah Pope for their kind cooperation during the demonstration filming.

And finally I want to thank all the people who during the filming welcomed us so warmly in their restaurants, in their homes, and shared with us their love for their region and its cooking.

Restaurant Auberge Nantaise, St Julien-de-Concelles

Thierry and Chantal Baldinger, Lapoutroie

Raymond and Simone Bonnot, Verdun-sur -Doubs

Adolphe Bosser, Audierne

Federation of Cantal Hunters

Helene Charrasse-Moinier, Entrechaux

Marie-José Cosssec, Pont l'Abbé

Hotel d'Europe, Morlaix

The Faldy Family, Roscoff

Jenny Fajardo de Livry, Fontvieille

Collet Faller, Klentzhelm

The Gardot Family, Damvix

Sylvie Kersabiec, Moustoir-ac

The Lajudie Family, Château Chervix

Bernard Loiseau, Saulieu

Comte and Comtesse du Manoir de Juaye, Champagne-
la-Rivière

Restaurant la Marée, La Rochelle

Jean-Pierre Michel, Fontvieille

Michel Mioche, Chamalières

René and Marcelle de Miscault Lapoutroie

Jean-Pierre Morin, Aurillac

The Pellissier Family, Peymeinade

The Perrin Family, Sainte Croix en Bresse

Lulu Peyraud and her family, Bandol

Armand and Monique Pionsot, Arnay-le-Duc

Jean-François Richin, Louhans

Restaurant la Salamandre, Noirmoutier

Claude Siegrist and her Family, Beaune

Jean Bardet, Tours

Martine O'Jeanson, Tours

Jacqueline Pilloy, Crottes-en-Pithiverais

Monique Lansard, Chambéry

Daniel Boujon, Thonon-les-Bains

Claude Dubouloz, Anthy-sur-Léman

Royal Club Evian, Evian-les-Bains

Raymond Fulchiron, Lyon

Jacquotte Brazier, Lyon

Pierre Sautet, Paris

La Coupole, Paris

Fatma Maziani, Paris

Paul Bocuse, Collonges-Mont D'Or

Joël Robuchon, Paris

Monique Piat, Pierre Sitte-en-Auge

The Camut Family, La Lande St Léger

Daniel Gaslin, Bas-Courtils

Pierrette Sarran, St Martin d'Armagnac

Lydie Dèche, Nogaro

Marie-Claude Gracia, Poudenas

André Daguin, Auch

Brasserie Noailles, Bordeaux

The Cano Family, Fontcouverte

Eliane Thibault-Comelade, Perpignan

Ann Majourel, Tornac

Les Templiers, Collioure

FOREWORD

*M*any people are still convinced that a French meal is a theatrical display, based on overwhelming techniques and priceless ingredients. Cooking the French way evokes a tour de force, an acrobatic prowess. It may be seductive but it is beyond most people's grasp.

I would like to offer an antidote to this trend. In this book I only refer to the French cooking I practise in my kitchen today and enjoy at my friends' tables. I have gathered together a medley of my favourite recipes. Side by side, you will find old and new, classic and regional dishes. Most have been passed from generation to generation, with additions and improvements on the way. There are classic recipes as well as more recently created ones, but the bulk of this book has its roots in regional home cookery, the patrimony of all serious food in France. I have been sure to omit both the dazzling extravaganzas and all those dishes requiring a brigade of thirty apprentices to prepare, because clearly that type of exercise does not apply to most of us. And my idea of a good and reliable recipe is one that I can prepare alone in my kitchen to make a dish I never tire of serving and enjoying.

Cooking for me is, of course, a necessity. But it is also a precious and gentle ritual which helps gather and hold families and friends together against all the tugging and pulling of changing times. These dishes are at the core of an art of living which is French, but which everyone can master. They are inspiring but based on common sense and a reliable tradition. A good meal should not try to amaze or awe. It never needs to be a fussy affair. So, choose the ingredients with an attentive eye, read the recipe carefully, and cook with confidence and appetite without taking it all too seriously. The following recipes reflect the art of the possible; they make the most of even the simplest ingredients: cabbage, a pint of mussels or a basket of pears.

Many of the dishes in this book can be prepared in advance so they are perfect for entertaining and for all those of us who have to juggle our time. There is time to remove the fat congealed on top of a stew or a sauce, trim a piece of meat, organize a table, dress yourself calmly, and bring forth the meal with grace and without pressure. One of the assumptions about entertaining at home is that the hostess — like a duck paddling along — remains calm and unruffled on the surface but is truly frantic underneath. This does not apply to the kind of cookery we describe. Both hostess and guests have the time to enjoy the process and the sharing of a meal.

INTRODUCTION

I am with my owl-like uncle at the end of a meal. He wets his lips with a sip of armagnac, stares at the ceiling and ponders: 'In life, there are three things that truly count. One is dining well … and I can't recall the other two just now.'

The French have always taken their pleasures seriously. Food – earthy, intense, subtle, or simply reassuring – is among those we cherish most. We love to sit together with friends around a steaming *Soupe Gratinée*, contemplating its fragrant broth and the fact that, on the whole, man tends to be a wolf to man except when he prepares a good meal or shares one.

The truth is there are only three basic rules that one needs to know about cooking. It is a civilizing force. It must not be intimidating. It is a source of true pleasure.

As for civilization, there is no question that cooking is among its most vigorous, sustained sources of energy, and in France it is a regional affair. Indeed, French civilization as a coherent entity does not exist outside bureaucrats' offices. For all their power, Paris officials will never manage to persuade a major French region to renounce its version of civilization, with its own locally accented culture and cooking. Over the centuries, regional culture and cooking have worked hand in hand as recipes were passed like precious poems from generation to generation until they began to appear in books.

Each region has evolved in step with the times – many enriched by Celtic, Greek, Roman or Moorish invasions – blending together local specialities with what arrived from the Crusades and the rest of the world. Yet much more powerful than external forces in shaping regional character and cooking has been the unique way cooks in each region have responded to their local products.

This is the secret of good French cooking: passionate respect for local products. If you have even the slightest doubt that passion is the right word, please consider this: there are 250 ways to cook chestnuts in Languedoc, over 100 ways to prepare tomatoes in Provence, and apples in Normandy, and at least two dozen ways to use walnuts in Périgord. Each of the regions we visit in this book has specific products and individual ways of preparing them. A fish *à la normande*, steak *à la bordelaise*, omelette *à la basquaise* are instantly evocative of their birthplace. The strong affinities between a product, the spirit of its place of origin, and the way it is prepared locally transform each dish into a journey into the region. A pear tart is our quickest link to an orchard in the Loire Valley; a bowl of mussel soup is a breath of air from the ocean in Trouville; a platter of mushrooms transports us to the thick of Rambouillet forest.

But the old suspicions between the various provinces – why so much garlic in Languedoc; why are potatoes sautéed in goose fat in Périgord; why is watercress soup enriched with cream and butter in Normandy; why are meatless *farcis* made in Provence? – are less sharply defined than in the past.

The mutual give and take between the scholarly and the sensual, between Paris and provinces, which exists at every level of French life yields more positive results in gastronomy than perhaps in any other area. Most city dwellers in France still visit their relatives in the country regularly and remain in touch not only with their family but also with their village and its ways of cooking. This constant dialogue between local products imaginatively prepared and the influence of classic cooking to sharpen them is often invigorating. A gratin of raspberries may be fresh and delicious, but if we cover it with a pungent *Sabayon* sauce (see p.286) it acquires a new dimension. A fruit tart prepared with *Pâte Sucrée* is good, but if *Pâte Sablée* or *Pâte Feuilletée* is used, it rises to another level (see pp.296 and 276-77).

Although in France fashions and fads – with their litany of truffle or codfish ravioli, the inevitable trendy purslane, rocket, or raw salmon dishes – keep popping up, French cooking remains anchored in a sensible tradition. As Gertrude Stein observed, 'The French change completely, but all the time they know that they are as they were.' *Bon gré, mal gré*, willy nilly, real food reigns supreme.

Yet, if civilization supports us with the strength of the past, it also bombards us with the future's unsettling changes. To deal with them, we are lost without the second basic rule of cooking: it must not be intimidating. Stores are full of items providing health, slim silhouettes and freedom from time-consuming chores. In this mix of quick fixes, some are sensible, others range from distasteful to dangerous. Trendy food diets, ersatz butter, sugar or chocolate products, manipulated food substitutes, chemically hyped flavours, eggless mayonnaise, crab patties made with fish left-overs and soya are just a hint of what the future holds for us if nothing changes. Clearly, we all prefer good food to bad or indifferent food. But what are we prepared to do about it? As we tend to be a little distracted, a bit lazy, often entirely too adaptable, we may, with the best of inten-

tions, find ourselves turned into robots with passive palates, nibbling bland composites from bright containers.

We have marvelled at the variety of exotic fruits and vegetables available throughout the year. We trusted and praised technological progress. Now we are beginning to realize that what was a cause of wonderment may prove to be a threat, as we bite into a perfectly formed, utterly tasteless tomato. Now is the time to choose our products carefully, to take a minute to look, touch, smell and decide which green bean, which potato, which cheese we are buying, to select a fresh whiting rather than a frozen lobster if we can, and a plain but crisp cabbage rather than limp asparagus. No amount of Mornay Sauce is going to transform an inferior industrialized chicken into an acceptable dish.

In France, we now have labels to protect the quality of our cheese, poultry, wines and meats, naming their place of origin and their precise content. This trend is happily developing in Britain. We must use vegetables, fish, meats, cheeses that belong to a recognizable place. If we select a product with care, we can be sure that it will have flavour, be fresh and healthy, and that we are also preserving a rural system and a region.

Today, everybody from home cooks to chefs agrees that as we want lighter dishes, more intense flavours are also what we crave. We use marinades, reductions, herbs and spices to replace unctuosity and quantity. Curiously, all this is as healthy as it is tasty. After a meal with true flavours, pudding binges are few and far between.

The process of cooking need never be intimidating. It is, on the contrary, one of those happy spaces where, with a little effort, our taste and imagination can yield reliably life-enhancing results. Cooking has been for me a solid bridge over turbulent waters. Like an

exceptional poem, I find it keeps us close to many things in life that we need to be constantly reminded to see and feel again. That is why a real dish could never appear to us full-blown from outer space. The recipe for a real dish has been nurtured in the soil of past moments of pleasure. It has sustained others who kept it alive for us, and we in turn both take and give life to it as we use it.

After visiting Paul Bocuse, Joël Robuchon and André Daguin in their kitchens, it is clear that, as with many of us who cook at home, the rallying cry of these chefs is for food with real taste and texture, food with character. '*Faut de la mâche*!' – 'give us something we can get our teeth into!' they say, as they carry a whole fish, or a whole chicken to the table.

Some dishes are more immortal, more irresistible than others. I have gathered in this book a mixture of wholly regional and some more classic recipes, all of which have been adapted for a cook working alone in the kitchen using readily available produce in season. There are variations to many dishes, alternative fillings, choices of accompaniments and garnishes, so each of us can decide what works best for our schedule, budget and what products are available. McDonald may prize itself on the consistency of its Big Mac. We do the very opposite.

As for the preparation of a meal, here too we must free ourselves from any lingering intimidation. As we start to cook we must remember Napoleon's strategy: divide and conquer. A meal is made up of dozens of small victories, and a few decisive steps. Read the recipes you have chosen calmly, and write a reliable shopping list. Choose the products carefully. Then change gear as you transform the kitchen, temporarily, into a battlefield in the spirit of 'fire when you see the whites of their eyes'. You wash, peel, chop and cook many dishes at once. While the stew simmers,

and the vegetable gratin and caramel custard bake in the oven, you are free to trim the salad and blend the dressing. But no matter what happens, remember that nothing can go totally wrong. This is not a circus act you are performing in front of a hostile audience. As Julia Child said, bending to scoop a roast chicken accidentally dropped on the floor, 'You are alone in the kitchen!' To make life easier for yourself, cook as many dishes in advance as possible so you can degrease, season and garnish them and be rested and relaxed when it is time to serve them. A stew, a soup, a pâté, a fruit compote, most dressings and many sauces will keep refrigerated for a week, ready to be called upon when you need them.

There are no hard and fast rules in the realm of cooking, except perhaps in pastry-making, which does rely on simple chemistry. As for the rest, some combinations will work better than others, but it's for each of us to choose what we like. We all have our own ideas on how far we can go with shortcuts. One cook will insist on grinding meat by hand for a pâté, another will happily rely on a food processor. One will use a microwave, the other a steamer, the third a pan. A friend recently served me the most fluffy couscous, and I learned that it had been prepared … in a microwave.

And now, *à table*! In France, some families still sit in a formal way, host and hostess opposite each other, with the honoured guests to their right. Mine is a round table because I find that most convivial. A formal tablecloth may be replaced by mats, a king-size coloured sheet, a light printed bedspread, but large cotton napkins always add a feeling of comfort and luxury to the table. I use large serving dishes, casseroles, ovenproof dishes wrapped in a tea towel so I can bring them straight from the oven to the centre of the table or stand them on a trolley beside the table. And finally, in our house, everyone is always welcomed as fully-fledged participants in the whole meal.

Then there is the question of what is best to prepare for your guests. As it is not easy to answer formally, I would like to quote my great aunt's advice. She was, in fact, talking to me about clothing, but it applies equally well to cooking and entertaining. 'Darling,' she said, 'three well-chosen outfits are all you ever need in a wardrobe. The first – *tout venant* – simple and easy; the second – *pour faire bellotte* – to cut a pretty figure; and the third – *pour être triomphante* – to knock them out'

All we need to entertain at home with no help and a limited budget are a few reliable dishes which fall into the same three categories. There are dishes *à la bonne franquette* when we entertain simply. We may choose to serve *Courgette Omelette* (see p.112), *Soupe aux Légumes* (see p.60), *Salade Lyonnaise* (see p.231) or perhaps *Hachis Parmentier* (see p.190). For a slightly more important occasion, it might be *Mouclade* (see p.71), *Cassoulet* (see p.204) or *Paupiettes de Bœuf* (see p.184). The dessert will always be something prepared in advance, like *Flans Caramel* (see p.312), fruit compote (see p.281) or a fine cheese served with fruit. And finally, *pour être triomphante*, for a major event when one needs, as we say, to put 'the little dishes into the big ones' – a large family meal, an important birthday, the return of a special friend – we may prepare *Jambon Persillé* (see p.222), *Bisque de Crabes* (see p.66) or Stuffed Shoulder of Lamb (see p.174). And to crown the meal, *Marquise au Chocolat* (see p.306), *Bavarois* (see p.310), or a fragrant pile of *Crêpes Normandes* (see p.300).

Finally we have, thank goodness, the third rule, cooking's ultimate obligation: it must be the source of true pleasure. Somehow, anything prepared at home seems fresher, better; *c'est frais, c'est bon, c'est maison.* Seductive aromas floating through the house and the tangible measure of love you have given the preparation of the meal arouses the best in everyone. The dishes are a faithful bridge to palates and hearts. They transmit what at our best we do best: enjoying ourselves together. Give us real food. Bring the garden, the forest, the ocean, the orchard to our plates and, as we say in Provence,

'Régalez vous!' ... 'Enjoy!'

The Regions

Ile-de-France

It all started with Paris as a privileged centre. Later came Ile-de-France, spreading like a rich belt around the city. And then slowly Burgundy, Normandy and all the other autonomous regions joined and gathered in concentric circles. Finally, a little over a hundred years ago, France – as we know her today – was born.

From a forest inhabited by spirits, Ile-de-France has developed into one of the most powerful urban regions in the world. Over the centuries, major historical events have taken place in this plain and on these hills, filled with princes' and kings' hunting parties and accompanied by extravagant festivities. Less noticed, but no less important to those who pursue them, are the region's simpler pleasures. Workers, farmers, shopkeepers, artists and students have long enjoyed fishing along its river banks, dreaming under its majestic trees, picnicking in its woods, hunting for wild strawberries in spring and mushrooms in autumn. In the *guinguettes* of Châtou and Robinson, they danced until they dropped, revived themselves with fried fish and chilled white wine to dance again, and today we have added our own touches to keep this sense of pleasure alive.

This is a painter's country, a region of soft, subtle colours. Corot, Monet, Seurat, all the Impressionists have been inspired by the translucent light, the skies of Bourgival, Barbizon and Argenteuil, and by the innumerable rivers which cross the region, encircling it like an island.

Ile-de-France is also Paris's cradle and provider: its market garden, bread basket and dairy farm. Man's sense of order and measure are as tangible here in its perfectly tended gardens, beet fields and orderly rows of corn as they are in Versailles, and Fontainebleau's palaces, Le Nôtre's gardens or its majestic cathedrals.

This fertile plain with its lush valleys and large plateaux like Beauce and Brie is an extraordinarily productive region and, despite the overflow from Paris and creeping urbanization, Ile-de-France manages to offer a commuter territory side by side with a pastoral countryside. There are many historic towns – St Germain, Versailles, Senlis, Fontainebleau – as well as industrial suburbs and new cities. There are huge forests and peaceful villages, fortified castles and grand manors, formal parks, wood-beamed covered markets, modest vegetable gardens, as well as the formidable Rungis, the largest wholesale food market in the world.

But for some, in spite of its grace and majesty, Ile-de-France's size and its diversity translate into blandness, a lack of the specific character that distinguishes other regions in France. And there is a concern about the impact of the area's immense wealth and political power on the rest of France. Michelet, the historian, worried that Ile-de-France, 'the least original part of the country, [had] taken over the rest of the country'. Yet it might be its combination of diversity and gentleness which best explain its success as a political and administrative centre.

In its cooking, Ile-de-France reflects the same complexity and profusion. The roasted meats, silky watercress and sorrel soups, velvety sauces enriched with butter and cream — these dishes and many others reflect both the aristocratic and rural traditions of the region as well as a light, modern Parisian touch.

But the very mention of Parisian food raises the issue that concerned Michelet. Has the presence of Paris at its centre destroyed rural Ile-de-France's regional dishes? Can one speak

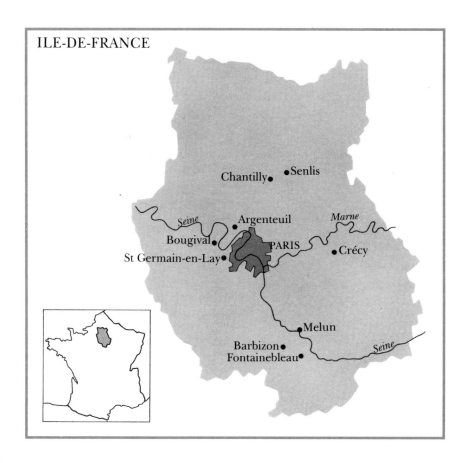

ILE-DE-FRANCE

Senlis
Chantilly• •Senlis

Seine   Argenteuil   *Marne*
Bougival•
St Germain-en-Lay•   PARIS   •Crécy

•Melun

Barbizon•
Fontainebleau•   *Seine*

of a Parisian cooking? Paris and the provinces have, over the centuries, danced together in a vivacious gastronomic *pas-de-deux*. It is true that Parisian chefs have had a tendency to extrapolate and transpose recipes, but they have always – and today more than ever – drawn their energy and their inspiration from regional cooking. It is a two-way process from the regions to Paris, where a recipe is appreciated for its provincial qualities, then refined and returned to its birthplace with a new twist. Paris's calculated chic and sophisticated appetite makes its own the earthiness of the provinces. Southern herbs – basil, savory, fennel, sage, marjoram and thyme – find themselves mingling with local parsley, chervil and tarragon. Vigorous Provençal, Gascon or Lyonnaise dishes are served along with smooth *grande cuisine* creations. Local dishes revisited by Parisian chefs emerge stronger, more forceful.

Craft, competition, a certain nostalgia and a sincere aim to emulate the best in regional cooking are highly instrumental. Often the best *choucroute*, the best *gratinée*, the best *brandade* are served in the capital. The simple potato purée is elevated to another level when Joël Robuchon prepares it. Lyonnais or Auvergnat *plats canailles* – rough, potent dishes – still attract the most refined Parisian palates.

Paris and its region are naturally more open to fashions, fads and trends than the rest of the country. Spring rolls, couscous, paella, curry, carpaccios, Indonesian satay and sushi find their place here easily, but there is still an abundance of room – and appetite – for the patrimony that draws on the Ile-de-France's own products. The region's rich orchards, vegetables and dairy products; the Brie, Melun and Fontainebleau cheeses; Chantilly's cream; mushrooms grown in the quarries along the

Seine; the bream, perch and minnows in the rivers remain such essential ingredients in all home and professional cooks' repertoires that although a town like Crécy no longer grows carrots, the carrot purée soup named *Potage Crécy* (see p.72) still reflects its roots. The region's split pea soup is called *Potage St Germain*; while Argenteuil means a dish is made with asparagus, and Montmorency one that features local cherries.

When it comes to specifically Ile-de-France or Parisian dishes served today, we find few long-simmered dishes. Many are quickly grilled or sautéed and seasoned with a touch of mustard, lemon juice, or a dot of parsley butter. There is also the traditional roast chicken garnished with a few sprigs of watercress, the ever-welcome pile of sautéed, fried, puffed or souffléed golden potatoes, the fresh vegetables, with the omnipresent mushrooms sprinkled with parsley. And then there is grilled Châteaubriand steak and calves' liver seasoned with shallot-wine-parsley-lemon Bercy Sauce; the *onglet* steak covered with a mellow layer of browned shallots; the generous offering of Robert, Gribiche (see p.101) and Mornay sauces (see p.96) and finally there are the wild duck, partridge, eel and all kinds of traditional Ile-de-France pâtés. The baguette is at its crispest in Paris, the brioche its lightest, and the pastries – Saint Honoré, Chantilly tartlets, Opéra, Pithiviers (see p.316) or fluffy fruit mousses – the most refined in France.

Ile-de-France has been called a national park of fine living. In fact, its inhabitants – the Franciliens – are realistic. They demand the impossible: the convenience of an urban space and the charm of country life. And if cooking is like music and politics, the art of mingling voices, Ile-de-France's happy people can be said to have succeeded in having their cake and eating it, while at the same time expressing what may be the region's true distinctiveness – its pleasure in sharing that pleasure with others.

*The Recipes of
Ile-de-France*

∽∾

POTAGE CRECY 72

POTAGE A L'OSEILLE 58

POTAGE AU CRESSON 58

VICHYSSOISE 62

SOUPE A L'OIGNON 68

BISQUE DE CRABES 66

NAVARIN D'AGNEAU 178

CREPES SUZETTE 301

Brittany

Brittany, with its silvery light and clouds scudding in from the open sea, is a mysterious, dream-like province softly coloured in greys and blues. But while those soft hues are the colours of dreams they are also those of the granite which this region is founded on and which symbolizes the endurance of its people. Like their houses, their churches and monuments, Bretons are made of granite. Between waves of invasion and plundering by barbarian tribes, medieval pirates and modern armies, nature has regularly dealt brutally with Brittany's farmers and fishermen. After each new catastrophe couples have joined together to salvage what they could of their livelihood, thus forging solid bonds. There is a Breton saying which reflects that solidarity between men and women: 'If the man earns the bread, it is the woman who churns the butter.'

Brittany's calm setting conceals great energy and powerful spiritual forces. Elaborate rites took place at Carnac as early as 200 BC when worshippers recreated the precise patterns, based on astronomy, in seven-metre-high granite stones. Today, Bretons are the most serious believers in all of Catholic France with hundreds of local saints. Brittany's dark dimension, its fascination with happenings beyond life's grey appearance, has spawned fertile legends of King Arthur, Merlin the Sorcerer and Viviane, and doomed Tristan and Isolde as well as a host of other magicians, demons and saints.

BRITTANY

ENGLISH CHANNEL

Roscoff
Morlaix
Brest
Audierne
Quimper
Pont-l'Abbé
Guilvinec
Rennes
Vilaine
Nantes

ATLANTIC OCEAN

Sculpted like a proud ship's bow, this lonely peninsula at Europe's western extremity has moved for centuries to the rhythms of the sea. Brittany's stubborn and independent character makes it seem even more remote from the rest of France than it is. Hunters first settled in the area around 5000 years ago, but it was only when the Celts came from Britain that it became known as Little Britain, later Brittany. A powerful Duchy in the Middle Ages, Brittany formally joined the kingdom of France following a rapid succession of three royal weddings to French kings.

This misty peninsula yokes together powerful but contrary tendencies that fire the distinctive Breton energy. Divided culturally between French-speaking upper Brittany to the east, and lower Brittany, 'Bretagne Bretonnante', in the west where Breton dialect and traditions prevail, the region is also split into two geographically, between Armor and Argoat.

Armor is the 'country near the sea' with cliffs of pink and violet rocks high above the fishing villages and harbours. Every Breton is said to be born 'with sea water flowing around his heart'. St Malo, Roscoff, Brest, Quimper, Concarneau – every big city except for Rennes – is on the coast. There are 1200 kilometres of coastline with sandy beaches, steep pink and blue granite cliffs, peaceful bays and small islands.

Inland is Argoat, 'the country near the woods', with its melancholy moors and woodlands, fields of ferns, old stones, soft hills and fresh green pastures. Here, the tidal rivers carry life-giving water to inland pastures and villages where camellias, mimosas, hydrangeas, apple, fig and palm trees stand in striking contrast to Armor's wind-battered coasts.

Brittany is France's most important fishing region, and everyone who lives near the coast is involved with it. Early in the morning, the return of the commercial fishing boats is fol-

lowed by armies of optimistic seagulls and in ports such as Concarneau or Guilvinec most of the village attends 'la criée', the daily fish auction.

Typical of the region's cookery is *Crabes à la Mayonnaise* (see p.144), the *Assiette de Fruits de Mer* (see p.137), and *Moules et Palourdes Farcies* (see p.140). These recipes are a simple response to ingredients with such freshness and flavour that they need little elaboration. Noirmoutier's freshly gathered sea salt flavours the local fresh butter, and this *beurre salé* enhances everything in local cooking from a platter of little grey prawns to a *Gâteau Breton* (see p.315) as well as the beloved *Crêpes and Galettes* (see pp.116-7) which still play a large part in meals in Brittany.

The Recipes of Brittany

LOTTE A L'ARMORICAINE 138

CRABES A LA MAYONNAISE 144

MOULES ET PALOURDES
FARCIES 140

FLANS DE LEGUMES 241

CREPES AND GALETTES 116-17

OMELETTE AUX POMMES 291

GATEAU BRETON 315

One of the most famous and indeed, controversial, of Brittany dishes is *Lotte à l'Armoricaine* (see p.138). The origin of this atypical dish is a topic of endless discussion which will probably never be resolved to everyone's satisfaction. But the debate adds to the charm of the dish.

Chestnut and mistletoe have been Brittany's symbols for many centuries – chestnuts because before cereal crops grew in the region they were the basis of most meals, mistletoe because it is sacred and represents persistence.

Despite several oil spills on the coast, fierce tempests, and failed economic ventures, the new generation of Bretons no longer passively accepts a legacy of hardship and poverty. There is now a feeling that Brittany has entered the modern world without either betraying her past or selling short her future. She has elegant seawater spas in Quiberon, Roscoff, and St Malo; a proliferation of small industries harnessing native resources; Roscoff's efficient vegetable cooperative, a computerized 'Wall Street of Vegetables' sells and delivers the region's artichokes, cauliflowers and onions internationally.

Mysterious, traditional, bittersweet Brittany. No matter where I look – prim ladies with their lace and starched coifs turning crêpes on their griddles, fishermen pulling in their nets, dancers in the village square weaving their delicate steps – I see the same quiet, cheerful determination. But my favourite vision of Brittany today is the one that links the two lands of Argoat and Armor, the past and the future; a flight of graceful seagulls winging their way inland over fields of silvery artichokes.

Normandy

Blessed with green valleys and cliffs over-looking the pounding waves below, Normandy is a province often described by novelists and painted by Impressionists. And yet it is a difficult region to define, for Normandy is quiet and self-effacing, happy to remain among the most discreet of celebrated places. Even its own poets find it hard to encapsulate its charms. When they verge on the edge of definition, they proclaim, 'the fragrance of my country is in an apple', but in the next breath they are questioning themselves: 'is our Normandy a gift from the sea?'

Napoleon used to declare: 'Le Havre, Rouen and Paris are one town, and the Seine river is its main avenue.' This is not the only occasion on which the Emperor's zest for simplifying the complex got the better of him, for Normandy comprises two main regions which have little in character to compare with Paris. Normandy is essentially a rural province along the English Channel coast, divided by the Seine into two quite distinct areas: Upper Normandy, with Rouen as its capital, and Lower Normandy, with Caen as its main city to the west.

From the edge of the Paris basin to Brittany, the rich murmur of the past can be heard throughout this lush, pastoral province. Pink and white blossoms, camellias, hydrangeas … for every cloud in the sky, they say in Normandy, there is a flower. They could also add a gallon of milk, since the rain falls gently and regularly, the grass grows faster and thicker throughout the year, and the cows give the richest milk in the greatest quantity in all of France. This region also has a special place in the hearts of gourmets everywhere as the source of calvados, an elixir some find so divine they claim it should be reserved exclusively for the gods – with a little set aside for

them and a few close friends.

Yet Napoleon was at least partly right in his definition of the region, for there are strong links with Paris. Etretat, Honfleur, Trouville and Deauville are today a short enough journey for many Parisians to own cottages, farms and châteaux in the region. Visitors enjoy the casinos, races and film festivals. Nearby, there is the Pays d'Auge with its thoroughbred horse farms, manors, half-timbered houses and thatched cottages – occasionally topped by a line of blue irises.

Here also, you will find bustling ports, for Normandy is an important maritime region. High chalky cliffs command wind-swept views of yellow sandy beaches stretching for miles at low tide, and reminding us that this is where sea bathing was invented and first practised. *Les planches* – the wooden plank promenades flanked with brightly coloured tents – invite visitors to stroll along by the shore.

To the west, the Cotentin peninsula marks the boundary with Brittany where you will find the celebrated medieval Mont-Saint-Michel. This 'wonder of the west', visited by multitudes of pilgrims and tourists, rises majestically from the sands or the waves – according to the tides – and for the last 900 years has been protected by the golden Archangel Michel atop his steeple.

Yet the region has not always been so peaceful. Invaded by the war-like Vikings in 911, it was given by King Charles the Simple to the Viking leader Rollo, who was made the first Duke of Normandy. In 1066, Rollo's descendant, William the Conqueror, took his forces across the Channel to fight for and win the English crown, thereby uniting Normandy with England. The English and French fought for supremacy in the region throughout the Middle

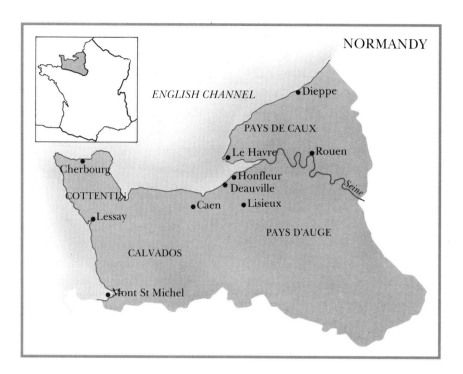

NORMANDY

ENGLISH CHANNEL

● Dieppe

PAYS DE CAUX

Le Havre ● ● Rouen

Cherbourg ●

Honfleur ●
Deauville ●

COTTENTIN

● Lessay

● Caen   ● Lisieux

Seine

PAYS D'AUGE

CALVADOS

● Mont St Michel

Ages until the Hundred Years War was finally brought to an end in the mid-fifteenth century by King Charles VII of France, due in no small measure to the intervention of Jeanne d'Arc. Since that time, Normandy has enjoyed a peaceful existence, with the notable exception of World War II, when it played such a vital part both in the evacuation of Allied servicemen, and in their successful return in 1944.

In this now tranquil province, today's descendants of Viking warriors shy away from conflict. They seem content as they greet one another with a generous four kisses. Their traditional response to most queries is a gentle, 'Well, perhaps yes … perhaps no … who's to say?'

Yet in spite of both its resources and its apparently relaxed demeanour, economic hardship has hit the region, affecting not only dairy farmers but also fishermen and those working in the ports. In an effort to adapt to modern challenges, efficient co-operatives are increasingly replacing the old craft industries. On my last trip I visited, in the most bucolic of set-tings, a spotless, automated wonder of aluminium and tiles producing 20 000 tons of excellent Camembert each year.

To catch the true flavour of the region, one must sit at a Norman table and observe the magic interaction of food and people. Normans are solid eaters, gourmands by birth who, with their large necks and plump hands, have satisfaction clearly etched in their ruddy faces. Their cooking reflects the region's opulence. It is an honest, no-nonsense exercise that could run the risk of being monotonous, if it were not for that splendid Norman trilogy of cream, butter and apples.

Cream thickens and enhances most dishes from soups to fish and meat dishes, and even salads. Butter, the second secret weapon, makes for the lightest brioches and finest *sablés*. And, of course, the finest cheeses in Normandy – creamy, pungent Camembert, tangy Pont l'Evêque, superb Livarot – are sumptuous and matured to perfection. Some are so potent that no wine or dry cider can be served with them; only calvados will do.

Apples are to be found everywhere. Unpeeled, browned apples garnish roast meats and sausages. Compotes of onions and apples are flavoured with vinegar or cider to enhance fish and meat dishes. Apples are served instead of vegetables, for which, with the exception of the potato, Normans have little appetite. Apple purée sometimes even replaces the traditional cream to thicken cooking juices.

Apples also yield 'Normandy's sun', the irresistible calvados. Most inspired cooking uses calvados – to enhance a dish of tripe, a veal chop, a chicken, a sorbet, or a simple cup of coffee. It is most famous as the *Trou Normand*, when a tiny glass is served between the courses of a rich meal, preferably after a roast, to offer a cleansing pause.

While they use their exceptionally good local fish in many light dishes, Normans are by tradition great meat-eaters. They have splendid beef and pork, fine *charcuterie*, pré-salé lamb, plump chickens and ducks to honour the celebrated *Canard à la Rouennaise*, with the crushed juices of the carcase stirred into the sauce.

Desserts have a strong presence in Normandy, whether it be a moist *teurgoule* rice pudding, delicate Mirliton almond tart, apple cider fritters or Bourdelot apples. There is an immense variety of apple tarts ranging from thick and creamy to light as a Normandy cloud.

This discreet province conveys a feeling of continuity and well-being in our changing times. Ask the seagull, ask the apple tree.

The Recipes of Normandy

BISQUE DE CRABES 66

MOUCLADE 71

GIGOT ROTI AUX HARICOTS

BLANCS 170

ROTI DE PORC AUX POMMES 193

TARTE AUX POMMES

NORMANDE 291

LES CREMETS 314

CREPES NORMANDES 300

The North and Champagne

Whether it is because, over the centuries, many wars have been fought on their soil, because they have suffered many invasions and therefore too many influences, because the local industries have known difficult times or perhaps because they are overshadowed by neighbouring Paris, it is a fact that the northern regions of France are not famous for their gastronomy.

Flanders, Picardy and Artois stretch between the Belgian border and the Channel just north of Ile-de-France. They are monotonous, flat provinces with some vegetable gardens, busy fishing towns and important cities like Calais, Lille and Boulogne. It is a cider and beer drinking country and most of the food is hearty. The region grows a great quantity of potatoes which are served in all forms but especially as chips:

les frites with mussels and light beer. Today, as we crave for pungency, the tangy flavour of the local light beer and cider in cooking tends to make some of the local dishes quite enticing. There is a soup made with beer, eggs, sugar and cream; *Hochepot*, the local sautéed beef version of *Pot au Feu*, slices of toasted bread covered with cider-flavoured, puréed onions; chicken simmered in beer and juniper brandy; *Carbonade* (see p.192); gratin of beer-flavoured mussels; *waterzoi* fish stew; some savoury-sweet dishes such as rabbit cooked with prunes and juniper berries, lamb fed on the coast's salty meadows, some delicate pies like *Flamiche* (see p.250); lots of wonderful root vegetables and chicory dishes (see pp.244-5); fine *charcuterie*; an interesting accompaniment of red cabbage, apples, chestnuts and spices cooked in red wine;

and a few good cheeses like Maroilles or Rollot. Throughout the region there is a bounty of fresh, smoked and salted herrings marinated in milk or oil, and served with hot beetroot or potato salad. Because of the local cultivation of local sugar beets, and because these provinces have a cold climate, there is also a great appetite for sweet dishes.

The Champagne region stretches on the west of Ile-de-France. It has pretty vallées, forests, vineyards and beautiful churches, but it is mainly known for its wines. Curiously, it is the only wine-producing region which offers such a bland and undistinctive cuisine. The problem comes from the Champagne wine which does not exalt nor even mingle particularly well with most food. It is grand but not very sensible to cook with this expensive wine. It is also grand but not truly food-enhancing to serve Champagne during a whole meal. In fact, Champagne is at its best when it is drank chilled – never iced – as an aperitif or with dessert.

Most of Champagne's local dishes are also found in Normandy, Burgundy or Ile-de-France. There are terrines seasoned with local Marc de Champagne brandy, stews, *potées*, eel, pike and bream *matelotes*, fresh cheese fritters, delicate biscuits and gingerbreads. But what stands apart, unique and world famous, is the sparkling Champagne wine which gloriously transforms any event into a celebration.

The Recipes of the North and Champagne

ᕫᕐᕫ

FLAMICHE AUX POIREAUX 265

PAIN D'ENDIVES 245

GRATIN DE NAVETS À

LA CHAMPENOISE 268

CARBONADE DE BOEUF 192

Alsace-Lorraine

At first sight, one is struck by the picturesque, fairy story, folksy charm of Alsace. There is an abundance of wrought-iron signs, grey-cobbled streets, covered bridges, half-timbered stucco houses and steepled roofs. It is a prim, quaint region exuding warmth and comfort. The houses all have window boxes and wooden balconies which overflow with brightly coloured geraniums. Inside, the rooms are dominated by the huge porcelain stoves, while brass and copper pans on the walls and majestic grandfather clocks all give a cosiness which is more than good enough to help its inhabitants face the bleakest of winter days.

More than any French region, Alsace's geography is the key to its past and future. Squeezed between the Rhine river and Vosges mountains, Alsace has been fought over by Germany and France since 300 BC when the Teutons first drove the Celts out of the area. It became part of Charlemagne's empire in the seventh century AD when his sons divided his empire and was Germany's until the 1500s. France's growing presence met resistance from a population accustomed to German rule until the French Revolution moved them to become so French in spirit that more than 50 000 Alsatians chose to settle in France when Germany took their land in 1871. The extraordinary life of a friend's grandfather illustrates this shifting of nationality between France and Germany which Alsace has experienced. He was born French in Alsace, became German in 1871, French in 1918, German in 1940. When he died in 1950, a citizen of France, he had changed nationality four times in his life.

Yet, as Alsace confronts the future, its geography and history, a curse for so long, may turn out to be a blessing that permits it to take full advantage of today's European, rather than national, perspective. With many trade and legal barriers disappearing, the only obstacles that will remain will be those of differing cultures and languages – obstacles with which Alsatians are at least equally familiar as any people in Europe.

Alsace's rich plain, nourished by the Rhine's alluvial soil, is the source of a wide variety of resources. It has oak and pine forests, orchards, pastures, cattle and game. There is the 'wine road' with its rows of perfectly tended vineyards, charming villages, ramparts and medieval castles perched on hilltops, and old churches of both the Catholic and Protestant denominations. The region has several large towns such as Colmar, Mulhouse, Ribeauville and of course Strasbourg, with its pink-stoned cathedral, which is both the home of the European Parliament and the region's capital.

With such a chaotic past, the Alsatians might have long ago lost their centre of gravity had they not drawn on their traditions to affirm the values they share. A multitude of traditional fairs and feasts are celebrated with elaborate pageantry. At these events women wear lavish costumes with huge black or red bows in their hair and parade through the streets accompanied by colourful bands, adorned carriages and the ringing of bells. Enthusiastic crowds flock to village festivals honouring patron saint and local produce: asparagus, trout, herring, walnuts, frogs, chitterlings, snails, gingerbread, beer, the grape harvest and, of course, the French version of Sauerkraut, la Choucroute (see p.197).

Keeping Alsatian traditions alive has necessitated keeping storks alive. A few years ago, storks, the bearers of good luck in Alsace, were placed on the endangered species list. Since then a sustained effort has been made throughout the region to make sure that storks were

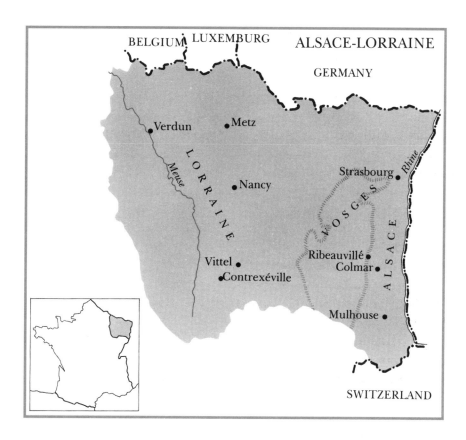

carefully bred, fed, and kept warm in winter. In their huge nests on top of chimneys, the proliferating storks are symbols for Alsatians not only of continuity with the past but also of the importance of working together today.

Gatherings, most often 'en famille', take place in bustling Tavernes on long wooden tables around a hearty *Baeckeoffe* (see p.202), a pyramidal *Choucroute Garnie* (see p.197) enriched with six or nine different dishes of meats or fish. But they also gather in Winstub bistrots where Riesling, Gewürztraminer, Sylvaner wines are served with herrings and cream, twisted egg noodles or crisp potato cakes *Galettes de Pommes de Terre* (see p.257). Of such abundance, they are proud to say, 'In France food is good, but there isn't much of it, in Alsace it is good, and there is plenty of it'.

Cookery in Alsace is based on local produce and recipes held in a collective memory which have been passed down through the ages. Even

if freshwater fish, pork, wild berries and game are no longer all to be found in Alsace itself, they are nevertheless imported, and these basic ingredients are still prepared according to traditional recipes. Winemakers, bakers, pastry cooks, butchers, *charcutiers* – all these food artisans infuse new energy into the region's patrimony. In Colmar, I met the Helmstetters, father and son who are still following the recipes written down a century ago by Helmstetter the elder's great grandfather. The recipe book is beautifully adorned and written in gothic German. When we met they were baking some 500 different breads a day.

In Kayserberg, I met a butcher curing his fresh hams with coarse salt and spices, preparing more than fifty kinds of sausage with garlic, caraway seeds, aniseeds, cumin and pepper and smoking his *charcuterie* in a fragrant mixture of fruit woods.

In Lapoutroie, I sipped pear, mirabelle, holly berry, winebud, quince and wild berry brandies as well as Kirsch. I was told that this type of brandy is called *eau de vie blanche* — white life water — because, unlike cognac, it ages in crockery rather than oak.

Everywhere I went I ate breads and cakes of all sorts: freshly baked pretzels; rye, wheat, barley and 'Miesel' breads; apple, blueberry, raspberry and the local quetsche plum tarts (see p.296); *Kugelhopf* (see p.321), Stollen, spicy Bireweck, Anisbredle, Schwonebredle, Mandalbaebbe; and brightly decorated little gingerbread figures topped with crisp icing.

Alsace, on the threshold of being European, is perhaps the most environmentally sensitive and technologically oriented of regions. People here work hard in every field and in terms of food Alsatians are among the most innovative and competitive of chefs. They have transformed traditional hearty cookery recipes into an ambitious and refined cuisine and earned the region's restaurants a large number of highly-rated Michelin stars. But excellence in that field is also a part of their tradition. Alsace inspired France's most celebrated gourmet, Brillat Savarin, to declare, 'It is one of the regions of France where I salivated the most'. Were he to return today, he would not change his mind.

Only the gentle Vosges mountains separate Lorraine from Alsace. Lorraine is bigger, there are wild mushrooms, bilberries, game-filled forests, the famous thermal spas of Vittel and Contrexeville, a tradition of beautiful Baccarat glasses and fine knife-making. Jeanne d'Arc was born in Lorraine and yet the region has always played second fiddle to its picturesque neighbour.

Its cooking is heartier than that of Alsace and less distinctive. A dish prepared *à la lorraine* generally means it is served with a red cabbage-red wine accompaniment. There are some interesting lorraine dishes like pork with quetsche plums, *potée lorraine*, quiches and chestnut-stuffed cabbage. But in reality the fruit brandies and the pastries are Lorraine's foremost claim to fame. There are mellow macaroons from Nancy, the capital, mirabelles, wild cherries, quetsche tarts, Commercy's plump madeleines sold in their pretty chestnut wood boxes, and mostly there is *Baba au Rhum* (see p.322) which was invented by Stanislas Leczynski, Louis XV's father-in-law, which has remained throughout the centuries one of France's favourite desserts.

The Recipes of Alsace-Lorraine

POTEE 194

TARTE FLAMEE 88

QUICHE LORRAINE 115

OIE AUX POMMES ET AUX

PRUNEAUX 165

BAECKEOFFE 202

CHOUCROUTE GARNIE 192

GALETTES DE POMMES

DE TERRE 257

MOUSSE AU KIRSCH 309

TARTE AUX QUETSCHES 296

KUGELHOPF 321

MADELEINES 333

Burgundy

It is easy to fall in love with Burgundy. From the vantage point of its gentle green slopes, you look down on creamy majestic Charollais cows, romanesque churches, brilliantly coloured tiled roofs, lazy canals and lively rivers. And in the midst of it, best of all, are the 'salty Burgundians' themselves with sparkling eyes, pink cheeks, accents that leave an 'rrrrr' lingering in the air, and their outrageous appetite for life.

A stream of irresistible energy runs through the region. Burgundy has more abbeys, castles, statues, restaurants, vineyards, freshwater fish, game, and more rivers and canals — 1200 kilometres in all — than any region in France. But even so, in Burgundy such abundance never seems excessive.

Touching the regions of Ile-de-France, and Lyonnais, bordered by the Alps and the Seine, Loire and Rhône rivers, Burgundy is shaped by its four main cities: Sens in the north, Nevers to the west, Mâcon in the south, and to the east the 'sacred market', Dijon, its capital since the fourteenth century.

For centuries Burgundy has been both the physical and spiritual heart of France. Body and spirit have always walked hand in hand here. The good fortune Burgundy has received from nature has made it a desirable acquisition for many peoples. Over the centuries, Celts, Romans, Greeks, Germans and a multitude of others have inhabited Burgundy as merchants, traders, pilgrims, crusaders and settlers, each contributing to the tumultuous history and also

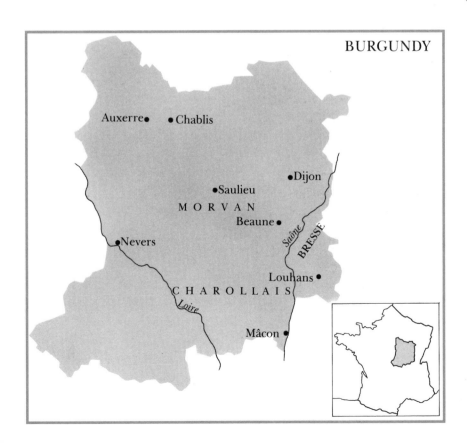

adding something to the personality of this glorious province.

At the centre of the vital network of waterways and roads linking the Mediterranean with northern Europe, Burgundy has been both a cross-roads and a meeting place throughout the ages. Excavations in Solutré show man was here as long ago as twenty-five thousand years and it was in Burgundy, at Alésia, that Caesar defeated the Gauls. By the fourteenth century, Dijon was the capital of the Duchy of Burgundy, Europe's most powerful state and a strong rival to France's royal court. As monks, artisans and farmers cleared forests and built houses, churches and castles they also tended pastures, nurtured vineyards and bred livestock. In doing so, they laid the foundations of Burgundy's cooking, and today the whole province lives under the spell of food.

Burgundy has some of the world's best beef cattle which are reared in Auxois and Charollais, its renowned poultry is bred near Bresse, and there are forests full of game and mushrooms – mousserons, girolles, cèpes and morilles. The region abounds with fish in its many rivers and springs and it seems to produce almost everything else, from honey to snails to the tastiest of berries. Patient artisans transmute local ingredients into traditional regional products such as mustard, cheese, gingerbread, and the wonderful liqueur of cassis that is used in *Sablé aux Pommes et au Cassis* (see p.332).

But, as full of promise as these ingredients and products are, what matters is knowing how to turn them into lusty, full-bodied dishes, and this often means drawing on Burgundy's medieval tradition of mingling the sweet and the salty which also happens to be very much today's taste. There are sumptuous and celebrated stews such as *Boeuf Bourguignon* (see p.191) and *Coq au Vin* (see p.154), redolent with mustards, spices, cream, garlic, onions

The Recipes of Burgundy

LA PAUCHOUSE 120

BAR AU VIN ROUGE 135

ESCARGOTS A LA

BOURGUIGNONNE 147

POULET AU FROMAGE 152

POULET A LA CREME ET

AUX MORILLES 150

BOEUF BOURGUIGNON 191

BOEUF A LA FICELLE 186

LES SABLES AUX POMMES ET

AU CASSIS 332

TARTE AUX PRUNEAUX 280

PAIN D'EPICES 325

and wine. But there are also a great variety of simple meals such as *gougères* to enhance a good wine, fresh dandelion leaves seasoned with warm vinegar and cured ham as in *Pissenlit aux Lardons et à la Vinaigrette* (see p.79), fragrant meat pies, mustard and chive omelettes and snail and herb dishes such as *Escargots à la Bourguignonne* (see p.147). There are superb fish dishes like *La Pauchouse* (see p.120), and for dessert, pears cooked in spicy wine such as *Poires, Pruneaux, et Oranges au Vin Rouge et aux Epices* (see p.282). The much cherished regional dish 'raisiné' is made up of crushed grapes reduced to a pasty syrup in which pears and quinces are turned – a dish that would have made the eyes of the most difficult Duke of Burgundy sparkle with pleasure.

More than just a part of stews and *meurette* sauces, wine is an equal partner in Burgundy's ongoing love affair with food. Proud as they are of their renowned Pinot Noirs and Chardonnays, Burgundians see wine not as a privilege of the happy few but as a birthright for all to enjoy together. In a region of boundless energy and appetite, wine should be approached gently, without haste or abrupt excesses. True Burgundians believe wine is best enjoyed from a large glass with a narrow rim so that the air can get into the glass as it is slowly swirled but so the bouquet cannot get out.

Each of us has our own idea of heaven. Some of my friends in Burgundy tell me that theirs would be to have throats in the form of a corkscrew so each swallow of wine, each bite, might be enjoyed longer and better. Following in the footsteps of their illustrious Ducal ancestors, today's Burgundians want both quality and quantity. Here more than anywhere else, happiness, like the ripe fruit on a tree, is there for anyone who is willing to take it.

Lyonnais, Savoie, Franche-Comté and Dauphiné

Lyon is a beautiful, discreet city which spreads along the banks of the Rhône and Saône rivers. The turbulent Rhône – crowded with boats transporting horses, people, grain, olive oil, salt and vegetables – has been tamed here, and is today a peaceful link between the north and the south. The city, standing at the heart of a strategic intersection, commands the roads to the Alps with connections to Switzerland, Italy, northern Europe and the Massif Central, as well as opening the gateway to the Mediterranean.

With its bustling trade fair which has remained active since the Middle Ages, with its silk industry, printing firms and quality craftsmen, Lyon has been a centre of wealth since the time of the Gauls. During the Renaissance, it was a more important city than Paris.

Savoie, Franche-Comté and Dauphiné, the Alpine districts east of Lyon, are fascinatingly diverse, with their thriving valleys, orchards, chestnut and walnut groves, lakes, soaring snow-covered mountains, steep passes and vast skiing and mountain-climbing playgrounds. Much of what used to be cultivated land only a few decades ago is now pasture sprinkled with blue gentian, thistles, silver and yellow flowers, where cows graze to the north, and sheep and goats to the south. Each summer they are joined by Provençal herds in search of good grass and cool air. The region is graced with lovely resort towns like Annecy, Chamonix, Mégève, and thermal baths and health spas like Aix-la-Chapelle and Evian.

The network of communications through this alpine region was started even before the

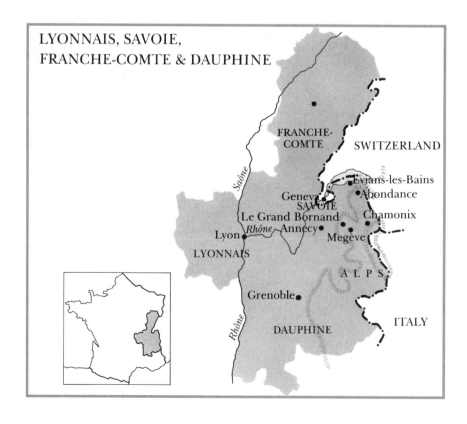

coming of the Romans when donkey tracks wound their way through the mountains. Since that time, roads and tunnels have been carved through the mountains, bridges span the valleys, railways and motorways cross the region, all strengthening the finances of the Counts of Savoie, the original 'gate-keepers of the Alps' who grew rich extracting tolls from alpine travellers.

The Court of Savoie, Lyon's rich notables, the visiting popes, princes, merchants, generals, pilgrims and travellers have for centuries set a high standard of entertaining centred around food. So much so that even today, Lyon is held as the gastronomic capital of France. Local products are consistently of the highest quality. Whereas in Paris, fashionable trends in food come and go, Lyon's chefs remain solidly anchored to their traditions and the products of their soil. They accomplish daily miracles with Bresse chicken, plump pike, a piece of Charolais meat or a handful of morel mushrooms. Celebrated chefs of the past, such as Point or Chapel, and modern chefs such as Troisgros and the indomitable Bocuse, famous *mères* (female chefs), and the chefs at *bouchons* — bustling bistros which offer substantial snacks and wines all day — gastronomic clubs, guilds and *confréries* all work equally hard to perpetuate this tradition of a hearty, spirited, serious cooking. Local wines must not be forgotten, and indeed Lyon is said to be washed by not two but three rivers: the Rhône, the Saône and Beaujolais wine.

Because pigs were traditionally fed on whey left over from cheese-making in Savoie, pork has always been produced in large quantities, and today both the Alpine regions and Lyon still prepare the finest and most abundant *charcuterie* specialities in France. Apart from the wonderful pâtés, terrines and pigs' trotters, the range of sausages is vast. There are sausages enriched with truffles, pistachio nuts or garlic, sausages cooked in brioches, warm *cervelas* served with hot potatoes, and sausages made with tripe.

Savoie, along with Piedmont, Sardinia and Nice, was once part of the Italian states, and as a result many Mediterranean products such as pasta, *morue* (dried salt cod), olive oil — which is used along with local hazelnut and walnut oil — oranges and candied fruit, have been an intrinsic part of the local cuisine for centuries. The Italian influence remains even today in the small goat cheese and parsley-filled *raviole*, corn dishes including polenta, *crozets* which belong to the gnocchi family, a curious bittersweet jam called green compote, and rosemary blossom jam which has been made here since the twelfth century.

Also from the Rhône valley and Savoie comes an abundant supply of fruit and fresh vegetables, of which potatoes and onions are the local favourites.

The variety of cheeses is superb, whether they are made on farms, in co-operatives or factories. One finds fine goat cheese like Chavignol, creamy Vacherin and St Marcellin, Reblochon, Tommes, and hard mountain cheeses like Beaufort — the prince of Gruyères — Comté and Emmenthal.

There are lake and river fish — trout, pike, crayfish and also the beloved *féra* and *omble chevalier*, members of the salmon family.

At home and in restaurants, cooks prepare invigorating dishes which clearly know and speak their own minds: luscious pumpkin soups and rich onion gratins, pike dumplings, chicken liver *gâteau de foies*, morteau sausage baked with shallots in white wine, sautéed *morue* and onions flavoured with vinegar. Another pungent local dish is *Boeuf à la Marinière*, beef and onions enriched with a paste of anchovy, garlic, mustard and wine. Savoyard and Dauphinois may be the most famous of gratins, but there are all kinds of variations made with onions, *morue*, cardoons, wild mushrooms, leeks or courgettes cooked under a crust of fragrant mountain cheese. Fondue, once eaten by villagers at night as they shelled the walnuts, is now enjoyed by everyone after a day of skiing.

As for desserts, the choice is vast, and the local nuts and fruits feature heavily. Walnut, hazelnut and chestnut cakes delight the palate, bilberry cakes and jam tarts – once made with dried fruits – covered with a lattice of pastry, biscuit de Savoie, *farcement* made with potatoes, raisins, prunes and brandy, Mont Blanc – a fluffy dessert of chestnut purée topped with cream – are to be found in abundance. Finally there is the delicious *Triple Crème*, a rich blend of thick cream, lemon juice, lemon rind and orange water.

Beaujolais is not the only drink to make the region famous. There are all kinds of delicious gentian vermouths, genepi and walnut aperitif wines and, most famous of all, the local green or yellow Chartreuse liqueur made with over a hundred medicinal plants gathered from the nearby hills.

All these invigorating elixirs are glorious reaffirmations of the principle that what tastes good may – if you are lucky – also be good for you. And that is a firmly held conviction here.

The Recipes of Lyonnais, Savoie, Franche-Comté and Dauphiné

SOUPE A L'OIGNON 68

SALADE LYONNAISE 231

SALADE AU GRUYERE ET

AUX NOIX 234

FONDUE SAVOYARDE 272

CERVELLE DE CANUT 273

GATEAU DE SAVOIE 318

GATEAU DE FOIES DE

VOLAILLES 108

PATE CHAUD FAMILIAL 215

Provence

Provence seems to need hardly any introduction. Its purple hills of juniper and lavender, its sleepy villages perched on the hillsides, its honey coloured 'mas' and whispering fountains have been rediscovered many times over. Following on the tracks of the hunters who discovered the region a million years ago, visitors like Cézanne, Van Gogh, Picasso, Dufy, Cole Porter, Colette, Somerset Maugham and Pagnol have made this among the most celebrated of places.

Provence, bordered by the Mediterranean coast in the south, the Rhône river to the west and the Alps in the east, has several quite distinct personalities. To the north there is a secret hinterland where flowers, trees and rocks, heated by the sun, exhale their heady fragrances. From here, the River Rhône winds its way south to the coast past lively cities, Roman arenas and aqueducts, and fields of fruit and vegetables. Provence's coastal region stretches from Marseilles' bustling harbour through vineyards and olive groves to the glamorous Riviera with 225 kilometres of coast running from St Tropez to the Italian border. Finally, there is modern Provence with its universities, electronics and pharmaceutical plants, computer and marine-biology research centres, and a highly developed transportation network.

The question about this region today is how much of what has made it unique is still here to discover and enjoy. Can we still blend into an open marketplace and share the fun of a village *festin*, a game of *pétanque* and a pastis in the shade?

The truth is that much of Provence is every bit as beautiful today as it was when Renoir and Matisse first painted it. It is not, however, a quaint museum. It is a vigorous and lively region

moving, as we all are, into a new century. So, while the three-hundred-year-old olive oil mill near my house in Grasse keeps turning our tiny harvest of olives into the most precious of oil, trucks have replaced donkeys at the mill and a fax and computer keep track of account details.

As Provence grows and changes along with the rest of the world, what remains unchanged and continues to make it irresistible is its extravagant range of colours, architectural forms and dazzling fragrances. As for its two most celebrated assets – the sun and the carefree disposition of the natives – the usual clichés don't always apply.

Provence has more hours of sunlight than any other region in France, and there is no doubt the sun is part of its magic. The motto of Provence is still the words of the cicada's song, *le soleil me fait chanter*, 'the sun makes me sing'. However, Provençaux and Provençales like to sip the sun with infinite precaution as if it were an intoxicating potion, drop by drop. The elaborate game of hide and seek between shade and light is played on many keys in Provence. Shady trees, narrow streets, small windows with wooden shutters, beaded curtains on the doors to screen out the heat, parasols, vine-screened terraces, bamboo beach-parasols and jasmin-covered gazebos, all reflect the ambiguous welcome given the sun.

As for the carefree and good temper of the villagers, it is mingled with an impetuous streak that is often blamed on the Mistral wind blowing fiercely down the Rhône Valley bending giant cypress trees and exciting the temper of those in its path.

In the villages of Provence with their ochre and peach houses and blue and green shutters, beyond the fountain, the church and the ancient trees there is the strategically placed Bar-Tabac.

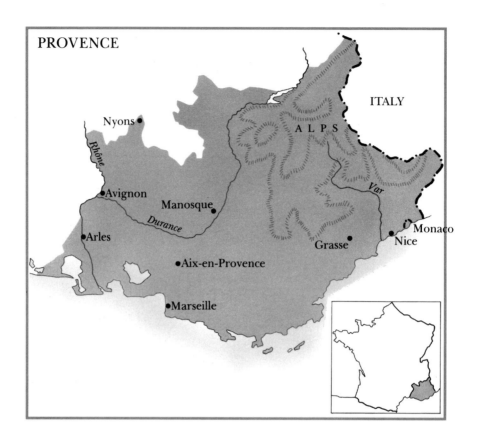

PROVENCE

Nyons•

Rhône

•Avignon

Manosque•

Durance

•Arles

•Aix-en-Provence

•Marseille

ALPS

ITALY

Var

Grasse•

Monaco
Nice

People stroll by, observe one another, sit on a low wall in a shaded square watching the activity of the pizza truck, eyeing the market's goods, making the most of every encounter. They kiss, shake hands, exchange jokes, tips and thoughts, and tease each other with bittersweet memories.

With snow-capped Alps only an hour from the coast, grey pebbled rivers, flower-strewn islands, sand and rock beaches, the turquoise sea, rich plains, exotic suspended gardens and oriental villas, the region feels and often looks like paradise on earth. But it is the men and women of Provence who have turned a *gueuse parfumée*, a poor but fragrant region, into fertile orchards, vegetable farms and luscious flower gardens thanks to irrigation, railways, lots of imagination and hard work. Everywhere, it is this ever-present heritage, the intricate honey-coloured stone walls, the dainty campaniles, the mossy fountains which best reflect Provence's graceful union of man and nature.

Cookery here is a vital part of daily life. Provençal cuisine is pungent, spirited and built around seasonal produce. The region around Cavaillon and Nice is sometimes referred to as the market garden of France. Everyone here tries to grow a row of green beans, a few tomatoes, a courgette plant, and a few pots of basil and mint. *Ratatouille* (see p.237), *Beignets de Courgettes* (see p.83), *Salade Niçoise* (see p.80) and the wide range of vegetable sauces, gratins and soups express this appetite for fresh, inexpensive local products. Near the coast, fish is a cornerstone of the cookery. The most famous regional fish soup is *Bouillabaisse* (see p.125). *Soupe de Pêcheurs* (see p.124) is made with the humblest fish from the day's catch and enhanced by the fiery red peppers *Rouille* sauce (see p.77) while *Bourride* (see p.121) is a more refined fish soup which uses lean white delicate fish and is enriched with spoonfuls of *Aïoli*, the

The Recipes of Provence

CRUDITÉS 76

FROMAGE DE CHEVRE À L'HUILE D'OLIVE 79

SALADE NICOISE 80

BEIGNETS DE COURGETTES 83

PETITES COURGETTES ET TOMATES FARCIES 84

PETITS FARCIS 85

PISSALADIERE 87

BOURRIDE 121

SOUPE DE PECHEURS 124

DAURADE AU FOUR 133

ROUGETS GRILLES AUX FEUILLES

DE VIGNE 129

BRANDADE 136

SUPPIONS FARCIS 140

PIGEONNEAUX AUX OLIVES 157

DINDONNEAU AUX MARRONS 161

AGNEAU AUX HERBES 170

DAUBE AUX OLIVES 188

RATATOUILLE 237

AUBERGINES AU COULIS DE TOMATES 238

ARTICHAUTS A LA BARIGOULE 242

GRATIN DE COURGETTES 243

GRATIN DE TOMATES, COURGETTES

ET OIGNONS 254

garlic mayonnaise (see p.76).

Tapenade, Pistou, Anchoïade , Aïoli, Rouille (see pp.76-78), all these potent sauces are used as dressings for boiled vegetables, grilled meats and fish as well as for dips for *Crudités* (see p.76), the region's favourite starter. They are also wonderful when simply spread on toasted bread for a snack.

People in Provence turn away from rich, elaborate preparations. They prefer spirited little dishes such as plates of small stuffed vegetables called *Petits Farcis* (see p.85) or *Rougets Grillés aux Feuilles de Vigne* (see p.129) that use the anise-scented herb, fennel, to flavour grilled fish. What matters here is not quantity but the intensity of each flavour; olives, saffron, herbs, lemon, garlic, vinegar, capers, bitter almonds and, of course, virgin olive oil are all used to give character and zest to a variety of dishes. Meats especially lamb (see p.170), poultry, fish and vegetables are all enhanced by the addition of a few herbs and spices and served crisp and fragrant with all their natural juices absorbed.

Like the legendary lizard on the sundial which only counts the sunny hours, people here know that, as in politics, happiness is about reaching for what is possible. They count the world's blessings, they laugh, they turn a meal, a chat, a mindless game into a shared

Languedoc-Roussillon

The largest of France's southern regions, Languedoc-Roussillon finds itself contained along a portion of the Spanish border within natural limits imposed by the Pyrenees mountains, the Rhône river and the Mediterranean sea.

Within those limits there is a rich abundance of sights, fragrances and resources, from lagoons and marshes along the coast-line to the *garrigues*, scrublands, covered with juniper, lavender and thyme extending north towards the Cévennes mountains, crowned with chestnut trees, and beyond them to the austere Causses plateau where goats and sheep graze as Roquefort cheese matures in rocky caves beneath. Punctuating the landscape are gifts to the region from antiquity: the majestic Roman Pont-du-Gard aqueduct, the Roman theatres of Orange and Nîmes, Romanesque churches, and Carcassonne's medieval fortress.

In the Middle Ages, Languedoc-Roussillon created a world and civilization of its own as artful as its antique legacy. It is here that the refined, spiritual approach to love known as *amour courtois* was perfected. Troubadours like Jaufré Rudel wrote ballads and *pastourelles* to their ladies, ensconced in the exquisite rituals of medieval court life, as pilgrims streamed into what became a main departure point for the Crusades. These were heady, prosperous times, as described in texts like Bertrand de Bar's, celebrating the large ships loaded with goods in local ports, and the wealth of a city like Narbonne. It was a confident society able to tolerate the forces of dissent, including explosive political satire.

But Languedoc-Roussillon's power and autonomy were seen by those in Paris as threats to the unification of France. For five centuries, northern France tried to impose its rule on this feisty province until it got its way in the sixteenth century and the region joined the entire kingdom of France.

As often in France, a matter of major importance was linked to the outcome of a linguistic dispute. There were two ways of saying 'yes' in medieval France: *oil* and *oc*. It is the victory of the *langue d'oil* – spoken in the northern provinces – as the official written language over the *langue d'oc*, rooted in the Latin traditions of southern Gascony, Limousin, Languedoc and Provence – that confirmed Paris's administrative control throughout France.

This represented a significant setback for the south in general, and for Languedoc-Roussillon in particular. It perhaps explains why this region has traditionally been home to many dissident elements. This is the region where the chaste, vegetarian Cathare religious group settled, converting not only aristocrats but artisans, shopworkers and peasants. It is here that Protestants were offered places of safety, as were other dissidents – Sephardic Jews from Spain, political refugees, rebellious Catalans and, most recently, North African *pieds noirs*. It is a region encumbered by history and familiar with recurrent persecutions from the Catholic clergy as well as the central power from Paris.

Today, the rich and varied elements of the region's cooking are among the most spontaneous and authentic expression of its singularity.

There are large cornfields in Languedoc-Roussillon, corn grown to feed the precious geese and ducks which will become *Confit* (see p.218), *Magrets* (see p.162) and *foie gras* (see p.227). There are orchards of apricots and peaches, rows of melons and fields of tiny purple artichokes and delicate pink garlic. There is also an abundance of anchovies, squid,

LANGUEDOC-ROUSSILLON

CEVENNES

Rhône

Tarn • Albi

Nîmes •

• Toulouse

Montpellier •

LANGUEDOC

Castelnaudary •

Carcassonne • Narbonne

ROUSSILLON

MEDITERRANEAN
SEA

Perpignan

PYRENEES

Collioure

SPAIN

---

red mullet, oysters, mussels, *palourdes* clams, tiny *clovisses*, both wild and farmed.

The vineyards yield the largest quantities of wine in France. In the last twenty years, due to European competition, wine-growers have succeeded in upgrading their table wines. As for the fruity sweet Banyuls and Muscat wines so popular as aperitifs or dessert wines, they are now served as a delicate counterpoint to goose liver, oysters or Roquefort cheese.

The cooking of Languedoc-Roussillon is as remote from elaborate *haute cuisine* as it is from tasteless fast food. It is a rustic cooking with a lot of character, bold and high spirited in Roussillon, milder in Languedoc, bursting with originality. There are eleven ways to cook snails, at least three ways to prepare Cassoulet, and 250 ways to use chestnuts in the region. Cooking here is a tool in the fight against the levelling effect of Paris, as it 'gives a rich taste

to misery'. Festive dishes like *Cargolade*, *Bouillinade*, *Cassoulet* (see p.204), *Gardiane* and *Ouillade* prepare the way for long evenings of dancing and singing.

But the secret weapon of the region is in the light touch – a drop of aniseed liqueur or a square of chocolate in *Civet* (see p.208), a sprig of wild fennel in a snail stew, a sprinkling of *persillade* on a roast chicken, a spoonful of goose fat in a bowl of *Garbure* (see p.62).

As in Mediterranean cooking, *farcis* and *hachis* are all-important here, with a litany of stuffed vegetables, chicken and lamb, meatballs, or a handful of chopped ham, shallots and garlic stirred into a stew, transforming the simplest dish into a redolent delight.

When a dish is *à la languedocienne*, it usually involves a combination of aubergines, tomatoes, and garlic. Sauces are rare, except for the beloved *all y oli (aïoli)*, garlic and oil sauce, the *all cremat*, a sauce of sautéed garlic, peppers, saffron and wine, as well as *sauce Catalane* made with garlic and bitter oranges. And finally there is the heady *beurre de Montpellier*, prepared with fresh herbs, greens, olives, capers, anchovies, mustard and lemon juice thickened with … both butter and olive oil.

For dessert, we might be offered a piece of Roquefort cheese, a honey and almond pastry or a caramelized *Crème Catalane* custard flavoured with aniseed, lemon and cinnamon.

But if I had to remember my two most cherished meals in the region, I would evoke the *goûter* I shared with little Nicolas on a sunny afternoon after his day at school. We ate warm slices of crisp country bread rubbed with garlic and spread with dribblings of goose fat and, for good measure, we picked a handful of freckled apricots. A far cry from the buttered *tartines* covered with grated chocolate which have always been the fare of my daughters' snacks. It was one of the most heady of afternoon breaks.

The other meal took place on an autumn day when the local *tramontane* wind was blowing on the hilly slopes overlooking the harbour of Collioures. After a morning spent harvesting grapes, we all gathered around a roaring fire of vine trimmings, sipping Banyuls and waiting for strings of sausages and the *cargolade*, platters of snails sprinkled with melted goose fat roasting on the barbecue. The table was loaded with dry pork liver sausages and sliced artichoke hearts, red peppers and anchovies, and a large bowl of *all y oli*. We ate, we drank, we danced the *sardane* – hands linked, arms lifted, dainty steps,

light jumps – to celebrate this day, this glorious world still at man's measure, the winding lanes leading to the coloured boats under us and the blue and white shifting skies above.

The Recipes of Languedoc-Roussillon

SOUPE AUX POIS CHICHES 61

LA GARBURE 62

SAUCE AILLADE 98

SALADE DE POIVRONS ROUGES AUX

ANCHOIS 228

CASSOULET 204

EPAULE D'AGNEAU FARCIE AUX

LEGUMES ET AUX FRUITS 174

AGNEAU A L'AIL 169

LAPIN EN CIVET 208

The South-West

Once upon a time, the Sud-Ouest bore the glorious name of Aquitaine, the 'country of waters'. Blessed with thermal springs, marshes, rivers and an ocean, the presence of Cro-Magnon man's skeleton and the frescoes of Lascaux are eloquent evidence that three million years ago human beings inhabited this vast province.

Myths abound. Some are whimsical, such as powers attributed to bears in the Pyrenees where a notice in front of a church reads: 'Bears have helped build it and will fight for it.' Others mine the region's rich vein of boastfulness, expounding the exploits of Cyrano de Bergerac, Jacquou-le-Croquant and of course, d'Artagnan and his Gascon musketeers who heedlessly defended the weak against the powerful. The region's passion for the larger-than-life often blurs reality when it comes to the derring-do of local rugby teams, the secret powers of the new Concorde being built by Aérospatiale in Toulouse, or the grand lifestyle of Bordeaux's gentry with their celebrated vineyards.

History has moved forward in fits and starts in this region, which runs from Bordelais, Landes and Pays Basque to Gascony and Périgord, with its two largest cities – Bordeaux and Toulouse – at either end. While all these areas share a common past and future, each views itself first and foremost as Bordelais, Gascon, Périgourdin, Landais or Basque. 'All for one and one for all!' cry the musketeers, but as each area insists on its individual differences, there is little of the strength that comes from unity, a phenomenon that proved decisive as the region evolved over the centuries.

From the day in the twelfth century when Aliénor of Aquitaine married Henri Plantagenet and he became King of England, the region allied itself with England for 300 years, until it was eventually absorbed into the kingdom of France. When Paris moved to take administrative and political power from the Sud-Ouest, the disorganized region acquiesced and fell into a drowsy somnolence, dropping out of the movement of most of France towards modernization and the industrial revolution.

Energy and curiosity in the region turned inward with what were often quite interesting results. The contributions of painters, writers, scholars, artisans and farmers made for a satisfying life. There were successful efforts to encourage the planting of new crops, cereals, tobacco, and a vast forest of pine trees in the Landes, which stabilized the dunes and still yield lumber and resin. But the least homogeneous of all French regions, the Sud-Ouest, did in fact preserve its unique charm by staying out of the mainstream of activity.

And although we smile as we read the words of Henry Miller: 'I believe that Cro-Magnon man settled there because he was extremely intelligent', the genuine quality of life of the region is not exaggerated, nor part of a politician's rhetoric. It is tangible everywhere you turn. Bordeaux, nestling by the estuary of the Garonne river, succeeds with elegance in being both a port and a well-bred city with rows of fine eighteenth-century houses, and broad public spaces like the Esplanade de Quinconces – the largest square in France. Here, wine is the blood of the people and the cellars, the wine shops and the glorious Chatrons warehouses, all celebrate proudly the 'blood of the vine'.

Further south, we find the thick pine forests of the Landes, its huge 114 metre high dune, and the well-sheltered triangular Bassin

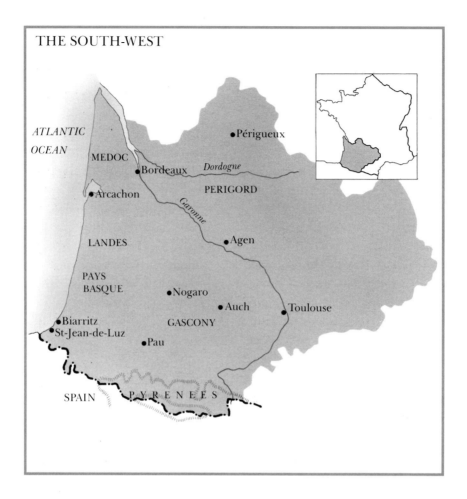

THE SOUTH-WEST

ATLANTIC
OCEAN

•Périgueux

MEDOC

•Bordeaux   *Dordogne*

PERIGORD

•Arcachon   *Garonne*

LANDES

•Agen

PAYS
BASQUE

•Nogaro

•Auch   •Toulouse

•Biarritz
•St-Jean-de-Luz   GASCONY

•Pau

SPAIN   P Y R E N E E S

d'Arcachon where oysters and mussels are bred. Just before the Spanish frontier, we reach the Basque country. People there are rather secretive, dour in spite of colourful berets and bright canvas espadrilles. But the region has a pampered, festive air with white-washed houses, fishing villages like Saint Jean-de-Luz, and resorts like Biarritz.

Travelling slowly between Bordeaux and Toulouse through fertile fields of corn, sunflowers, tobacco patches and ranks of legendary wine and armagnac vineyards, we encounter few people, fewer cars, more cows and many ducks and geese. Climbing through the narrow cobblestoned streets of a perched village, bicycling past walnut oil mills and golden-stoned farms, chatting over a glass of Floc d'Armagnac, it is so calm, poised and peaceful

that sometimes it all seems too good to be true.

Nearby Périgord – home of Cyrano de Bergerac's descendants – also seems to have been waiting for us for hundreds of years. It stretches along the wild Dordogne river between cliffs scattered with old castles and manors. Towards the Pyrenees, Gascony – whose capital, Auch, still lives under the spell of d'Artagnan – rolls with gentle hills. Perched atop these hills rest about 300 *bastides* – fortified, medieval towns with arcades, shaded squares, churches and cultivated *potagers*, clinging to the top like eagles' nests.

Finally we arrive at the pink city, Toulouse, with its lovely brick buildings, its sumptuous town hall, which has witnessed the ancient grandeur of former counts of Toulouse, and the modern glory of Europe's Aérospatiale.

The cooking throughout the Sud-Ouest is consistently reliable. Kitchens here function under the spell of duck, geese and the magic powers of armagnac. This is hearty regional cooking performed at home by generations of women who have always depended on good local ingredients. Even when some of the recipes are adapted and turned into lighter renditions by chefs like Daguin or Guérard, they retain their essential rustic charm.

Bordeaux is the exception. There are few culinary inventions here. For too long this rich town cut itself off from the neighbouring countryside and its local produce. Things are better today. Shallots and red wine lend a personal touch to the local cooking; shellfish and *Confit* (see p.218) are well used. But still only a few dishes stand out: *Entrecôte Bordelaise* (see p.183), *Lamproie Bordelaise*, *Pilades*, or *Civelles*, which are eels the size of a matchstick, sautéed *al dente* in garlic and oil. They also make a *beurre rouge* which is a *beurre blanc* variation made with red wine. When a dish is cooked *à la bordelaise*, it may mean several things: served with *cèpes*, sautéed in goose fat with garlic and parsley, or else coated with a bordelaise sauce made from wine and shallots. Another custom of the region, *faire chabrot*, means adding a glass of Bordeaux wine to the last spoonful of soup or broth and drinking it from the dish (see p.56).

In Périgord there are sumptuous dishes based on goose and duck *Confit*, *foie gras* (see p.227) and the local truffles. Périgord is famous for its wild black truffle (the white ones here are inferior to the Piedmontese ones). They are sniffed out by trained dogs or pigs. Golden flies, which are attracted by the intense smell, lead the truffle hunter to his goal. Truffles may be cultivated although they are not easy to grow and colour and size vary. Truffles are gathered from autumn to spring, brushed

The Recipes of The South-West

∽∾∽

SAUCE DE SORGES 98

SAUCE BORDELAISE 93

COULIS DE TOMATES 99

PIPERADE 107

ENTRECOTE BORDELAISE 183

MAGRETS DE CANARD 162

CANARD AUX PRUNEAUX ET À L'ARMAGNAC 164

GRILLONS 212

CROUTE AUX CHAMPIGNONS 263

POMMES DE TERRE À LA SARLADAISE 269

GATEAU BASQUE 320

GLACE À L'ARMAGNAC ET AUX PRUNEAUX 330

CROUSTADE 293

TARTE AUX NOIX 302

FLAN A L'ARMAGNAC 313

to remove the soil and then preserved in cognac brandy, fat or sweet wine. They may be canned, but a great deal of their size and taste is lost in the process. Truffles are eaten in omelettes, baked in a salt crust or '*sous la cendre*' (under a bed of charcoals). They may be wrapped and cooked in a pastry shellor used to flavour a terrine. A dish prepared *à la périgourdine* implies that it is garnished with truffle or *foie gras*, or both. Wild mushrooms – mostly ceps and chanterelles – tangy sorrel, crisp dandelion and purslane leaves are served in abundance to balance the rich texture of duck and goose. Walnuts enhance salads, main dishes and cakes. Walnut oil is sprinkled on warm *Cassoulet* (see p.204) and tossed greens, cornmeal is used in polenta-like *broye* or *millas* which, once fried in goose fat, becomes a *Cruchade* to be served with *Civet* (see p.208) or eaten as finger food. And a sip of old plum brandy is the glorious touch to complete a meal in Périgord.

Basque dishes echo Spain's cooking with an abundance of tomatoes, seafood, cured ham, and red and green peppers. There is the spirited *Piperade* (see p.107), the *ttoro* fish soup enriched with mussels, shrimps and red peppers, and squid in all guises including cooked in their ink.

The people of Gascony have imagination in the kitchen; they do wonders with every last bit of duck or goose. They flavour a *gasconnade* leg of lamb with ham, anchovies and garlic. They garnish sautéed *fois gras* and *Magrets* (see p.162) with grapes and armagnac. They fill ethereal, flaky *Croustade* (see p.293) with luscious Agen prunes. But if duck and geese are the pillars of the cooking, armagnac is the local magician. Prunes and walnuts are macerated in it, dry goat cheese and Tourtisseaux pancakes fried in goose fat are sprinkled with it. *Pousse-rapière*, the local aperitif, is made with oranges marinated in armagnac and served with local sparkling wine and, simplest of all, armagnac can turn ice-cream into the most inspiring of desserts (see p.330).

Cookery here begins with exceptional local products. Farmers have learned a lot in the last twenty years about maintaining a steady level of quality in their offerings, whether they are local craftsmen or semi-industrialized. Today the region eloquently sustains its culinary tradition. South-west cuisine may confidently claim to be not only seductive but also, as tradition suggests, part magic and part medicine. We know all about the French paradox: goose and duck products plus wine preventing cardiovascular diseases. Whether or not it turns out to be the case, with the help of the pink garlic, savory, verbena, armagnac, brandy, prunes and the gentle, sunny disposition of the people – by far the most easy-going in France – it is easy to relax with the absolute certainty that we are in good hands.

The Atlantic Coast

LOIRE-ATLANTIQUE, CHARENTES-MARITIME, DEUX SÈVRES, VENDÉE

Stretching from flat Atlantic beaches towards the heart of France, Loire-Atlantique evokes the best of provincial life, a blending of measure and pleasure. People here have always shared their land with water; draining marshes, digging canals and setting boulders to control the floods of the Loire. Marshes of the Marais Poitevin – Green Venice – have been converted into fertile gardens and pastures, and as we enter it we find ourselves in an enchanting world of narrow waterways lined with reeds, willows, elms and poplars. Punts and narrowboats with cows and sometimes an occasional plough on board, glide silently by on the green,

sun-dappled water, beneath a canopy of trees.

Calm today, the region's past is filled with all manner of mayhem from plagues to bloody, religious wars to major battles as in AD 732 when Charles Martel turned back the Saracens' invasion of Europe. Yet, for violence and emotion none of these matched the Vendée revolt that ripped the country apart in the French Revolution pitting Royalists against Republicans with columns of soldiers burning and looting the countryside. Typical of its passion is a short speech General de la Rochejacquelein made to his forces just before he led them into battle.

If I advance, follow me!

If I retreat, kill me!

If I die, avenge me!

Serenity has replaced such turbulence. All along the Atlantic coast are golden beaches and gentle cliffs, beautifully tended oyster beds, and inland, just a few kilometres away, pastures enclosed by hawthorn hedges. There are moors and creeks, canals sheltered by trees, and vineyards on the banks of the Charentes river. This peaceful place is blessed with wild geese, ducks, woodcocks, dairy cows, goats, freshwater fish, and also more elusive creatures like eels, snails and frogs.

In this region, single-storey white houses abound. They usually have two main entrances – one for the back leading to the pasture, the other opening on to the front where a flat bottomed boat, a *bachot*, is often anchored on the waterway. Southwards are beautiful limestone houses, manors, castles and abbeys of granite all of which seem to grow out of the hills as if they were part of them.

The island of Noirmoutier, just off the coast, is linked to the mainland by a causeway and offers mountains of sea salt, fields of potatoes, an array of delicate windmills, and pretty white houses with pink, blue and green shutters which often complement the colour of the owner's boat. The island sits at the mouth of the estuary of the Loire river. River banks have always belonged to fishermen, to bicycle riders, to couples lost in dreams and mostly to the celebrated *guinguettes*. Many of these small bistros where farmers, city dwellers and fishermen used to gather to drink local Muscadet wine, dance, sing and eat platters of frogs and eels are still there. Music and dancing have been replaced by the energetic bustle of winegrowers, businessmen and families enjoying salmon or pike served with the famous Beurre Nantais, a deliciously delicate butter, shallot,

The Recipes of the Atlantic Coast

⁗

SARDINES EN BROCHETTES 143

MOULES ET PALOURDES FARCIES 140

HUITRES CHAUDES 145

MOJETTES AU JAMBON 253

and vinegar sauce that can transform any plain fish or vegetable into one of France's most tempting dishes.

Cookery on the Atlantic Coast draws on exceptionally fine products. This is the home of celebrated and glorious brandy, cognac. Pineau, the local charmer, is a cognac wine which is served as an aperitif. Here, you will find a great variety of spring vegetables including Charlotte potatoes, orange-fleshed Charentais melons and Marans chickens, as well as ducks, frogs, eels, snails (called *lumas* or *Cagouilles*), and Bulot mussels. Above all there are exceptionally luscious Marennes oysters, and the nutty-flavoured local butter, one of France's finest, as well as the local Gros Plant and Muscadet wines enhance it all.

The cookery of the region is slow – sometimes called *cuisine de cagouillard*, as if prepared at a snail's pace. The Chaudrée is a local white fish and garlic soup. Oysters may be served raw with crisp sausages and a glass of sweet Pineau or baked with cream and chopped leeks as *Huîtres Chaudes* (see p.145). Mussels are often stuffed, *Moules et Palourdes Farcies* (see p.140), or prepared as *Moules Marinières* (see p.143), or seasoned with wine and cream to become the glorious stew, Mouclade. Snails are cooked with garlic, wine, shallots, bacon and mushrooms and duck is flavoured with apples, fresh grapes and Muscadet. Pike is stuffed with pork, ham is cured with sea salt, spices and brandy cider, and *mojettes*, white haricot beans, are cooked with herbs, tomato and ham (see p.255). Farci Vendéen or Pouti is made with all a garden offers in the way of sorrel, Swiss chard, fresh herbs and cabbage. The delicate Crémets Nantais and Caillebotte are the lightest of milk desserts.

Patience is expressed in this region's pace of life whether it is in the breeding of lambs, mussels and oysters or in the cookery of traditional dishes. With the shimmering waters of the sea and waterways reflecting a pale sky, with fields of rich cereals and fresh vegetables and its orderly vineyards, the Atlantic Coast has definitely turned away from the temptations of her tumultuous past. It has taken to heart the poet Aragon's praise of the flowers' quiet refusal to bend to the winds of panic. Thus it is in the Loire-Atlantique that a flowering plant, a rose bush, is traditionally placed at the end of each row of cognac vines to protect the precious crop from whatever might assail it.

Auvergne and Limousin

Here we stand in the very centre of France, 'La France Profonde'. The volcanic landscape of the Massif Central with its quiet winding roads, serene medieval villages, sparkling creeks, and bounty of wild flowers is perhaps the most isolated, least spoiled region of France. It is also one of the most sparsely populated areas in Europe. Limousin has, in fact, more lambs than people.

Throughout this rugged province one finds a solid architecture of squat fortresses, sturdy castles and Romanesque churches topped with petal-shaped tiled roofs. Like its buildings, the extraordinary energy and character of Auvergne's people has been shaped by the region's austerity.

Here the truth of the old proverb 'The most important thing parents can give their children are roots and wings' is still observed as the motto of the region. In Auvergne parents endow their children with a sense of realism, independence and the courage to strike out on their own to make their fortunes. As a result, for centuries, Auvergnats left their homeland to seek a better life in Paris. Each autumn, after the herds had been driven down to the valleys, the wood cut and stacked, villagers would walk the hundreds of kilometres to Paris and work all winter at jobs no one else would do, carrying hot water to the top floors of hotels and apartments or selling and delivering coal and firewood. Stone masons from Auvergne, known as 'white sparrows', built such monuments as the Royal Palace of Versailles and the Louvre. In May, many of them would return home to take the cattle into the open fields and prepare for the summer crops.

In Paris, the most industrious of the Auvergnats stayed on to start small restaurants in the tiny rooms where coal and barrels of wine were usually stored. They began by serving their customers simple food: country-cured ham, dried sausages and an occasional cabbage soup. Over time, many turned their little shops into simple cafés and bistros which have since grown into brasseries and restaurants. Many of the most formidable establishments in Paris, Le Dôme, La Coupole, le Flore, and Lipp were founded and run by Auvergnats and today Paris is still said to be Auvergne's largest village.

Marie and Baptiston, the traditional Auvergnat characters, frequently appear in stories and songs inspired by the region's fierce determination to survive. These two figures are courageous, penny-pinching and depicted as always straining upwards on steep roads that never seem to turn into easy downhill paths. But, along the way, solid Auvergnat friends stand ready to support them if they falter: '*Si tu glisses, tends la main*', 'If you slip, stretch out your hand.'

An extraordinary passion for agricultural excellence has always distinguished Auvergne and Limousin, and today the people of the region raise some of France's best lamb, veal and beef. Breeders and butchers have long been among the most powerful forces in this region. A single street in fourteenth-century Limoges had fifty-eight butchers with their own patron saint, St Aurelien, and a chapel which still belongs to their guild. Both the pale-caramel coloured Limousin cattle and the tall longhorned Salers cows (which look as if they just stepped out of a prehistoric engraving) from Auvergne are superbly bred. In a highly competitive industry, farmers, breeders and butchers close ranks whenever it is necessary to preserve a standard that justifies the label Blason Prestige, a symbol of quality authenticating where and how each animal has been raised.

Because the winters are hard and the country is rugged, regional cookery relies on heart-warming dishes seasoned with cheese, pork fat and walnut oil. Potatoes are known here as 'the truffles of the poor' and are the foundation of the beloved *Truffade* (see p.255) which blends them with fresh local Tome cheese and to make a highly satisfying and fragrant dish. When garlic is added and the mixture is cooked so it is crisp, like a pancake, it becomes an Alicot, another favourite.

Other traditional dishes are also hearty, such as robust, warming soups, fragrant Potées and rich stews, especially of game such as *Chevreuil en Ragoût* (see p.206). Wild mushrooms, like cèpes, are popular when seasoned with sautéed garlic and parsley (see p.263 for *Cèpes Sautés*).

One delicate product of the region is a tiny green lentil from Le Puy which Michel Mioche combines in his *Saumon aux Lentilles* (see p.130) with the freshwater salmon from local rivers.

Apart from its fine meats and robust *charcuterie*, the region is proudest of its cheese. The cows graze on the steep hills covered with grass but also gentian, wild pansies and liquorice which give a distinctive flavour to the celebrated Cantal cheese. Cantal with its thick crust and crumbly texture is made in stone houses perched on the hills or in efficient cooperatives and then nurtured and aged for years in moist cellars. Some weigh up to 36 kilos. The region also produces high quality *tommes* and luscious Saint Nectaire. Blue cheeses such as Bleu d'Auvergne and Fourme d'Ambert are usually served with bread and either fresh pears or a handful of walnuts. One of the most interesting

AUVERGNE & LIMOUSIN

Vichy

Aubusson

Limoges

Puy de Dôme

Clermont Ferrand

LIMOUSIN

AUVERGNE

Monts du Velay

Dordogne

Le Puy

Aurillac

dishes I tasted in Clermont-Ferrand was *Poires à la Fourme d'Ambert* (see p. 285). Favourite desserts in the region are the wild bilberry creamy custards and tarts and a large variety of walnut and chestnut cakes.

Auvergne is one of the rare regions in France which cannot boast any great wine but curiously it is a major supplier of bottled spring mineral waters. Rain water, filtered through rock and volcanic soil, springs forth in sources yielding more than 400 million bottles a year. Badoit, Vichy and Volvic are just three names from a great variety of different types of bottled waters, countless springs and spas. There is at least one mineral water for every ailment involving the liver, obesity, kidneys, skin and arteries.

The superb Aubusson tapestries, fine Limoges porcelain, Laguiole knives and of course Michelin tyres are also produced in the region. In addition to all this, Clermont-Ferrand, the capital, is the birthplace of the famous *Guide Michelin*.

In 1900, André Michelin decided to offer each of his customers a little red book with precious addresses of approved restaurants, accommodation and reliable garages for car repairs. A century later it has become the gourmet's bible. Every year, twelve Michelin inspectors anonymously visit restaurants throughout France keeping notes on each one and sharing impressions with their colleagues. At the end, a new hierarchy of excellence is announced; an event awaited with intense hope and anguish by chefs in every corner of France. Only nineteen restaurants in the whole of France are currently blessed with the three stars, Michelin's ultimate accolade.

What matters for Michelin is that restaurants demonstrate a sustained commitment to quality. In recent years boutiques, swimming pools, helicopter pads, exquisite cutlery and gazebo-like dining rooms seemed to have priority over food. There is now a return to more culinary values

signalling that the *Guide Michelin* has remembered that it is a child of Auvergne.

It is often said that the region can be characterized as a place which offers 'volcanoes, cheeses, prime ministers and presidents of the republic'. Many volcanoes, at least seven great cheeses, and recently two prime ministers and two of France's last three presidents have come from this region, and today on Clermont-Ferrand's main square, the statue of Vercingetorix, a native son and the leader of the Gauls, is mounted on his galloping horse, moustache bristling, sabre in hand, as a reminder to all who pass that no one here has betrayed either their roots or their wings.

The Recipes of Auvergne and Limousin

LEGUMES SECS EN SALADE 82

SAUMON AUX LENTILLES 130

FOIE DE VEAU A LA MOUTARDE 182

CHEVREUIL EN RAGOÛT 206

CEPES SAUTES 244

TRUFFADE 253

CAROTTES VICHY 238

POIRES A LA FOURME

D'AMBERT 238

Val de Loire

Le Val de Loire is *la douce France* at its most graceful. Lined with orchards, vineyards, gardens, and rows of poplars and willows, it stretches like a majestic boulevard along the Loire river from Ile-de-France to Brittany's border. Blessed by a climate and way of life that are equally gentle, it is here that France's purest French is spoken and its most delicate cuisine prepared.

Scantily populated and with little industry, Val de Loire is a secluded, quiet world of its own dotted with small, lively cities such as Blois, Orléans, Tours, Saumur and Angers. Jeanne d'Arc expressed the feeling of many when she said that if the head of France is Paris, her heart is Orléans.

Val de Loire is also the garden of France, an enclosed place where civilized achievements are visible in the smallest details of espaliered pears and apple orchards trained against trellises, tidy vineyards and beautiful rose gardens. Poets, artists and kings have left their mark on the region, but in the most discreet of ways. People here take life easily. The fishermen who perch along the calm waters look for peace and solitude … and eventually a trout, carp, pike, shad, *sandre*, or a few eels. As the hours pass they become one with the peaceful, golden river itself.

In Val de Loire, there are lovely white houses with blue slate roofs, farms, mills, monasteries, churches. Mushrooms are grown and wine is stored in chalky caves in the cool of the earth. A profusion of châteaux is scattered across an elegant pastoral setting: Blois, Chambord, Chenonceaux. Many hunting lodges were built during the Middle Ages when game was abundant, and were later transformed into châteaux. Today, about two thousand châteaux remain in the region. Some have been made into luxury homes, some are hotels, others historical monuments, and some have been abandoned to return to the landscape as ruins.

Val de Loire is the nurturing ground of classic, measured, finely-tuned French cooking. The medieval tradition of festive, courtly extravaganzas – roasted meats, staggering pâtés, every sort of game and elaborate dessert – has left fingerprints here and there, but what prevails is regional bourgeois cooking. Relying on local ingredients, the cuisine steers clear of preciousness and extravagant complications. Refined, confident as it is, its weakness is a tendency to be too tame. However, when we want to enliven dishes from this region, we can simply turn to natural allies such as its spicy grey and golden shallots, fresh sorrel and Orléans' potent wine vinegar.

The only foreign elements date from an Arab presence in the eighth century. Goats and know-how left by the departing *Maures* were assimilated by the locals, yielding the well-named Sainte-Maure goat cheese. Another exotic product is the meaty plum brought back from Damascus after the Crusades. Carefully cultivated and dried, *pruneaux de Damas* are now part of many traditional dishes and, as in the south-west, they perpetuate some of the local medieval sweet and sour dishes. A taste of honey is sometimes added for a stronger, bittersweet effect.

Farmers grow a profusion of traditional vegetables and fruits that include varieties once discarded. Vegetables are prepared in soups, gratins, salads, and as accompaniments. Château Villandry, with its sumptuous formal vegetable garden punctuated by flowers and trimmed trees, embodies the local cult for vegetables. Thanks to the temperate weather and

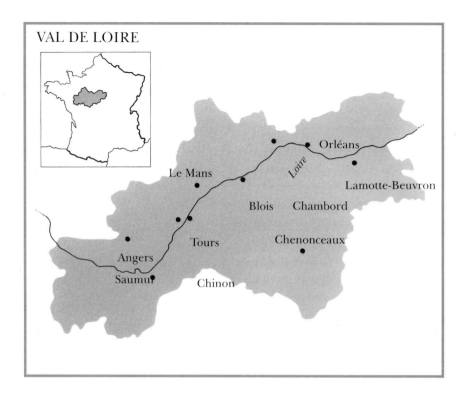

VAL DE LOIRE

Orléans
Le Mans
Lamotte-Beuvron
Blois Chambord
Chenonceaux
Tours
Angers
Saumur Chinon

Loire

the Loire valley's fertile soil, these *primeurs* are shipped to the markets two weeks before produce from Paris. Vast quantities of wild mushrooms are available all year, including the *rosé des prés*, pink and yellow *pleurottes* and the newest arrivals, shiitake mushrooms.

Game – now mostly in Sologne – has long been a favourite of the region. In medieval banquets, they even ate deer's antlers. Today, pheasants, partridges, quails, deer and wild ducks abound. They are sautéed in butter and flavoured with redcurrant jelly, juniper or white grapes if the flesh is tender. Tougher cuts may be braised with wine or turned into fragrant terrines.

Chickens from Loué, fed on grain and running free, are prepared according to one of the region's oldest recipes. Garnished with bacon and onions and cooked with red wine, their sauce is bound with the chicken blood.

Pork is turned into *charcuterie* in small factories that use the traditional techniques that vary from town to town. *Rillettes* are browned first in Tours, while in Le Mans they are simmered and served with fresh walnuts steeped with vinegar for a sharp counterpoint of flavour. They also prepare *Rillons* (deep fried meat chunks), tripe sausages (both the soft *andouillettes* and hard *andouilles*) – black *boudin* blood pudding made with greens, and white *Boudin* filled with chicken, mushrooms and truffles. And artisans still offer a curious dish of chicken and wild boar legs simmered in red wine to be eaten sliced as a fragrant ham.

River fish are abundant, while trout and salmon are successfully farmed. A treat each year between March and June is the 'springtimes': young salmon served with a spirited *beurre blanc*. *Matelote* – a fish dish made with wine and onions – has been enjoyed here since the days when the Loire was used as an important route and there were inns all along its shores. Among the most popular dishes is *La Petite Friture* – known locally as a *Buisson de Goujons* – a mound of tiny whitebait, none longer than five centimetres, dipped in milk, coated in seasoned flour and served crisply fried and hot with lemon wedges or warm wine vinegar. You will also find marinated shad, a type of herring, grilled and garnished with a creamy sorrel purée, as well as stuffed bream and carp, and rich stews of eels cooked in wine.

The region's wines find their way into many of the local dishes as they are splendid for cooking and, of course, the perfect accompaniment to the local cuisine.

The traditional habit of sautéeing most dishes in butter remains – whether it be shellfish, meat, potatoes or mushrooms. Even the local *Pot au Feu*'s vegetables and meats are browned in butter before they are cooked in the broth. Just before serving, they are once more sautéed in butter to reinforce their taste. Sauces are few; salad dressings are prepared simply with walnut oil, cider or wine vinegar.

Because the region's exceptionally rich land is primarily devoted to fruit and vegetables, there is little pasture and few cattle. Goat cheese prevails and is sold in all degrees of maturity and shapes as small as Crottins de Chavignol, Valençay Pyramids, Pouligny St Pierre, flat and round Chabris and, of course, the father of them all, the cylindrical-shaped Sainte-Maure, pierced by a blade of straw.

Fruits abound in Val de Loire. They appear in the delicate pear crêpes flavoured with local Cointreau, as narrow firm pears cooked in red wine and spices and sprinkled with pear brandy, in exquisite fruit tarts with custard, or simply packed with greengages, cherries, raspberries or peaches and mostly in the irresistible *Tarte Tatin* (see p.288). Finally, there are the

traditional *Crémets d'Angers* (see p.314), prepared with stifly beaten cream and egg whites and served with a pile of fresh berries.

Poets have a word for this region, *nonchaloir*, an old term which best describes the cultivated indolence of Val de Loire where nature, man and cooking whisper, contrasts are gentle, opposites are balanced, and harmony prevails. Pleasure is not always in the unexpected.

The Recipes of the Loire

∽⌒∾

POTAGE À L'OSEILLE 58

POTAGE AU CRESSON 58

SOUPE D'ASPERGES VERTES À

L'OSEILLE 57

SYMPHONIE DE CHAMPIGNONS DE

COUCHE 232

GRILLONS 212

RILLETTES 219

LES CRÉMETS 314

PITHIVIERS 316

The Recipes

Soups

LES SOUPES

France is a country where soup has always been an integral part of the menu, and until recently, was the best part of every meal: breakfast, lunch and dinner.

Soups are truly seasonal, made with whatever vegetables, fish or meat are available, and they remain open to everyone's individual ideas and tastes. They are healthy, economical, easy to prepare in advance and invigorating. It sounds like something that should be embroidered on a sampler since most people tend to neglect them these days.

Regional soups like *Bourride, Pochouse,* pumpkin soup – in which a whole pumpkin is filled with cream, cheese, garlic and parsley and cooked in the oven – are spectacular productions. Soups like *Bouillabaisse* or *Soupe au Pistou* are a meal in themselves. Some are rich, like onion soup; some are light, like Consommé; some are elegant, like Crab Bisque; some are simple and refreshing, like a vegetable soup. The variety is staggering.

Soups may be thickened with flour, cornflour, cream, egg yolks, *Beurre Manié* (see p.100), a handful of fine vermicelli or the addition of dried or fresh vegetable purées.

Garnishes include grated cheese, Croûtons (see p.233), fried onions, *persillade* – a pinch of parsley and garlic – finely chopped cured ham, fresh herbs, slivers of bacon and herb omelette, a spoonful of cream or a drop of olive oil. Traditionally, a mixture of butter, parsley and chives makes a subtle soup seasoning while olive oil, basil, thyme, sage and coriander give a more pungent flavour. Sage, bay leaves and parsley enhance the flavour of soups made with duck or goose. But in the end, the choice is individual; there are many regional variations and there are no rules.

Here are just two interesting traditions which you may like to try. In south-west France, *faire chabrot* means that when just two spoonfuls of soup are left, diners pour a little red wine into the soup and raise their bowls to drink the invigorating mixture. While in the Alps, a little cold goats' or cows' milk is often added to a thick vegetable soup to enrich the children's portions.

THE LOIRE

Soupe d'Asperges Vertes à l'Oseille

ASPARAGUS SOUP WITH SORREL

The Loire Valley is known as the garden of France. In spring and summer, both the large market gardens and the small allotments burst forth with a wonderous profusion of vegetables. One of the best places to witness this bounty is at the Château of Villandry near Tours, which has one of the most magnificent kitchen gardens in the world. The vegetables are grown more for their beauty than for their taste, but they show the importance of potagers in the intricate garden design of the French Renaissance.

Jean Bardet, the celebrated restaurateur of Tours, is completely enamoured of vegetables. He has a *potager* behind his elegant restaurant, the produce from which inspires his imagination. Although he serves this soup cold, he says you can heat it gently, and if you find the lemony taste of the sorrel too strong, just add a little more cream.

SERVES 6

900 g (2 lb) green asparagus
4 large handfuls of sorrel
25 g (1 oz) butter
2 tablespoons plain flour
1.5 litres (2½ pints) chicken stock
salt and freshly ground black pepper
120 ml (4 fl oz) double cream
2 egg yolks
juice of ½ lemon
freshly grated nutmeg

If the asparagus stalks are woody, peel them with a vegetable peeler. Lay them flat on your chopping board with the stalks overlapping the edge of the work surface. Snap the asparagus at the point where they become less rigid, taking care not to break off the tips completely. Put them into a large pan of salted water and bring to the boil. Drain immediately then plunge them into iced water or place them in a colander and hold them under cold running water for a few moments. Cut off the stalks 5 cm (2 in) from the tips and chill the tips to use as a garnish.

Wash the sorrel carefully and remove and discard the stems. Reserve 12 small leaves for garnishing and roughly chop the remainder with scissors.

Melt the butter in a large pan and add the sorrel; it will reduce down quickly. Add the asparagus stalks and stir well. Sprinkle in the flour and cook over a low heat, stirring continuously, for 3 minutes. Gradually pour in the stock, stirring continuously to avoid any lumps, then season with salt. Bring to the boil, skim off any impurities, then turn down the heat and simmer for 10 minutes until the asparagus is soft. Purée the soup in a food processor or, for a finer texture, force through a *chinois* or a food mill. Leave the soup on a low heat. Whisk together the cream, egg yolks and lemon juice in a small bowl. Pour this into the soup and heat gently for about 3 minutes, whisking all the time, without allowing the soup to boil. Remove from the heat and season to taste with nutmeg, salt and pepper. Cool then refrigerate until ready to serve. To serve, place some of the reserved asparagus tips and two leaves of sorrel into each bowl and pour over the soup.

Potage à l'Oseille
SORREL SOUP

The sharpness of the sorrel with its light and cleansing taste makes this potage a perfect start to any meal. The chopped sorrel leaves give a more interesting texture to the dish than when they are puréed, but all options are acceptable. You may even like to roll a few sorrel leaves into a cigar shape, slice them into thin ribbons and drop them into the boiling soup before serving.

SERVES 4

250 g (9 oz) sorrel
2 tablespoons butter
1 large onion, thinly sliced
3 leeks, white parts only, thinly sliced
a pinch of freshly grated nutmeg
salt and freshly ground black pepper
2 medium potatoes, thinly sliced
1.2 litres (2 pints) chicken stock or water
a pinch of sugar
5 tablespoons single cream
1 tablespoon snipped fresh chives or chervil

Discard the sorrel stems and shred the leaves. Melt the butter in large pan and fry the onion over a low heat until soft. Add the leeks and sorrel and season with nutmeg, salt and pepper. Cover and simmer for 5 minutes until the sorrel has softened and the volume diminished. Add the potatoes and simmer for a few minutes. Meanwhile, bring the stock or water to the boil in a separate pan. Add the hot stock or water and a pinch of sugar and salt to the vegetables, cover and simmer for 30 minutes.

Use a wooden spoon to crush the ingredients against the sides of the pan. If you prefer a smoother consistency, purée the soup in a food processor or rub through a sieve.

Stir the cream into the soup and return to the boil. Check and adjust the seasoning to taste. Serve sprinkled with chives or chervil.

NOTE

Two egg yolks may be added to the cream and stirred into the hot soup for a richer version, but do not let the soup boil.

Potage au Cresson
WATERCRESS SOUP

Watercress is a favourite vegetable in the Loire and around Paris, although this soup is also frequently prepared in Normandy. Spring is the best time to serve it as the watercress is not yet bitter. If you have cooked some vegetables, use the cooking water to prepare the soup, or use chicken or beef stock for a stronger flavour.

SERVES 4

225 g (8 oz) watercress
4 tablespoons butter
1 onion, sliced
3 leeks, white part only, sliced
3 large potatoes, sliced
1.2 litres (2 pints) water or stock
5 tablespoons single cream
a pinch of freshly grated nutmeg
salt and freshly ground black pepper
2 tablespoons fresh chervil leaves

Reserve a handful of watercress leaves for garnish. Discard the stems and coarsely chop the remaining leaves with scissors or a knife.

Melt the butter in a large pan and cook the watercress, onion, leeks and potatoes on a low heat for 10 minutes, stirring gently. Meanwhile, heat the water or stock until lukewarm. Add the water or stock to the pan, bring to the boil, cover and simmer for 25 minutes.

Purée the soup in a food processor. If it is not smooth enough, rub it through a sieve. Return the soup to the heat, stir in the cream and simmer for 2 minutes. Taste and season with nutmeg, salt and pepper. Add the reserved watercress leaves then pour into a warm soup tureen. Serve sprinkled with chervil leaves.

NOTE

You may like to scatter a handful of Croûtons (see page 233) covered with a little grated Gruyère on top of the soup just as you are ready to serve. When I make watercress salad, I keep the stems with the coarser leaves and use them in the soup.

THROUGHOUT FRANCE

Potage aux Champignons
MUSHROOM SOUP

Whether you choose to serve a homely version, façon ménagère, or one in the grande cuisine style, a mushroom soup is always delicious. Remember that iron or aluminium tend to discolour mushrooms so choose stainless steel or enamel pans.

SERVES 4

1.75 litres (3 pints) water or chicken stock
1 bay leaf
1 sprig of fresh parsley
1 sprig of fresh thyme
salt and freshly ground white pepper
225 g (8 oz) mushrooms
4 tablespoons butter
1 tablespoon vegetable oil
2 shallots or 1 onion, coarsely chopped
3 tablespoons rice flour
3 tablespoons cold water
4 tablespoons single cream
2 tablespoons finely chopped fresh chervil or parsley

Place the water or stock in a large pan with the bay leaf, parsley, thyme, salt and pepper, cover and bring to the boil.

Meanwhile, slice a handful of mushroom caps. Melt 1 tablespoon of butter in a frying-pan and sauté the mushroom caps for about 5 minutes, tossing constantly with a wooden spoon. Sprinkle with salt and pepper then transfer to a side dish. Coarsely chop the remaining mushroom caps and stems. Heat 2 tablespoons of butter with the oil in the frying pan until it foams then add the mushrooms and shallots or onion and cook for about 5 minutes, tossing with a wooden spoon.

Pour the mushrooms into the hot water or stock and simmer, stirring, for about 15 minutes. Remove the parsley and thyme. Blend the flour and water to a paste, stir it into the soup and simmer, stirring, for 2 minutes until the soup thickens slightly. Stir in the cream and simmer for 2 minutes. Add the reserved mushrooms, dot with the remaining butter and serve sprinkled with chervil or parsley.

Soupe aux Légumes

VEGETABLE SOUP

This is France's favourite soup and it varies according to the season and the region. Pumpkin, fennel, garlic, celeriac, turnips, watercress, sorrel, green beans or cabbage can all be used along with the basic trilogy of leek, carrot and potato. I use courgettes, fennel or potatoes to impart a velvety texture to the soup.

In the south of France, the vegetables are often sautéed in olive oil, in central France they use pork fat, while around Paris they use butter. Sometimes for a true *potage de santé*, a healthy soup, the vegetables are simply boiled in water and seasoned with herbs.

The vegetables can be puréed, diced, sliced or coarsely grated. Sliced onions sautéed in butter, minced parsley and garlic, chopped cured ham, fresh basil or chives, grated cheese, a spoonful of cream, a dot of butter or a drop of olive oil can all be added just before serving.

SERVES 4

2 onions
1 stick celery
2 courgettes
1 leek, white part only
2 potatoes
2 tablespoons butter and 1 tablespoon vegetable oil or
3 tablespoons olive oil
900 ml (1½ pints) water or vegetable stock
1 bouquet garni
salt and freshly ground black pepper
1 tablespoon chopped fresh parsley, chives, basil or tarragon

TO SERVE

50 g (2 oz) Gruyère, finely grated
1 tablespoon butter or olive oil

Peel and trim the vegetables. If you are going to purée the soup, chop them coarsely. If you don't purée the soup, dice or slice them evenly.

Heat the butter and oil or olive oil in a large pan, add the vegetables, cover and cook over a low heat for 10–15 minutes until soft, stirring occasionally. This will seal in all the flavours.

Meanwhile, bring the water or stock and herbs to the boil in a separate pan. Pour the vegetables into the stock and simmer, uncovered, for 30 minutes at the most. Discard the bouquet garni. Purée in a food processor or rub through a sieve for a smooth soup. Pour into a warm tureen, season to taste with salt and pepper and serve sprinkled with parsley, chives, basil or tarragon. Grated cheese, butter or a tiny bottle of olive oil can be passed around the table.

Soupe aux Lentilles

LENTIL SOUP

Lentil soup is one of winter's pleasures for me. I often sauté a handful of sorrel and add it to the soup just before I bring it to the table.

SERVES 4–6

450 g (1 lb) lentils
2 tablespoons groundnut or olive oil
2 onions, chopped
1 leek, chopped
2 carrots, chopped
3 garlic cloves chopped
1 clove
2 teaspoons dried thyme
2 bay leaves
3.4 litres (6 pints) water
salt and freshly ground black pepper

TO SERVE

1 tablespoon chopped fresh parsley, chives or tarragon
Croûtons (see p.233)
1 tablespoon butter or olive oil

Soak the lentils, if necessary, according to the directions on the packet. Heat the oil in a large pan and cook the onions, leek and carrots over a low heat until soft. Add the garlic, clove, thyme, bay leaves, lentils and water, bring to the boil, cover and simmer gently for about 2 hours until the lentils are soft.

Purée the soup in a food processor then pour into a warm tureen. Season to taste with salt and pepper. Sprinkle with herbs. Float a few Croûtons on top, drizzle a little butter or olive oil over the soup and serve.

LANGUEDOC AND PROVENCE

Soupe aux Pois Chiches
CHICK PEA SOUP

This hearty dish is prepared in Provence and also in Languedoc-Roussillon.

SERVE 4–6
200 g (7 oz) dried chick peas or 450 g (1 lb) tinned
1 teaspoon bicarbonate of soda (if using dried peas)
3 tablespoons olive oil
1 onion, coarsely chopped
2 garlic cloves, coarsely chopped
1 large tomato, skinned, seeded and coarsely chopped
1 small lamb's lettuce, coarsely chopped
2 bay leaves
1 teaspoon dried sage
1 sprig of fresh rosemary
salt and freshly ground black pepper
100 g (4 oz) piece of streaky bacon
pinch of ground coriander
1.2 litres (2 pints) chick pea cooking liquid, water or stock

TO SERVE
Croûtons (see p.233)

If you are using dried chick peas, soak them overnight in lukewarm water with the bicarbonate of soda. Drain and rinse, then place in a pan and cover with fresh water. Bring to the boil, boil for 10 minutes then cover and simmer for about 2 hours until soft. Leave them to cool in the cooking liquid for 1 hour then drain, reserving 1.2 litres (2 pints) of the liquid. If you are using tinned chick peas, rinse them in cold water and drain well.

Heat 2 tablespoons of the olive oil in a large pan and cook the onion, garlic, tomato, lettuce, bay leaves, sage, rosemary, salt and pepper for 10 minutes over a low heat, stirring occasionally. Add the bacon, coriander and chick peas. Warm the water or stock and add it to the pan. Bring to the boil, cover and simmer for 1 hour.

Remove the bacon and chop it finely. Discard the bay leaves and rosemary. Purée the soup in a food processor or rub through a sieve for a thick purée. Return the bacon to the soup, pour into a warm tureen and serve sprinkled with the remaining olive oil and the Croûtons.

Vichyssoise

COLD LEEK AND POTATO SOUP

Leek is one of the most popular vegetables in France, along with the potato. Vichyssoise soup is, in fact, not a French invention – French soups are always served warm or hot. Many believe it was created by an American chef. However, this celebrated recipe is based on the traditional French leek and potato soup and is served cold, enriched with a little cream.

SERVES 4

50 g (2 oz) butter
225 g (8 oz) potatoes, chopped
4 leeks, white parts only, sliced
2 shallots, coarsely chopped
1.2 litres (2 pints) chicken stock or water
300 ml (10 fl oz) single cream
salt and freshly ground black or white pepper
2 tablespoons snipped fresh chives or chervil

Heat the butter in a large pan and sauté the potatoes, leeks and shallots for about 5 minutes. Meanwhile, heat the stock or water in a separate pan. Add the stock to the vegetables, bring to the boil and simmer over a high heat, uncovered, for 30 minutes.

Purée the soup in a food processor then pour into a bowl. Stir in the cream and season to taste with salt and pepper. It should be highly seasoned since it will be served cold. Leave to cool, cover and chill for a few hours then serve sprinkled with chives or chervil.

NOTE

I have eaten Vichyssoise served with a spoonful of salted, whipped cream on top of each portion.

La Garbure

CABBAGE SOUP

Curnonsky, the scholarly gourmet, once declared there were four great regional dishes in France: *Choucroute garnie, Bouillabaisse, Cassoulet* and *Garbure*.

Like Henry IV, the gallant king, *Garbure* comes from Béarn. Although there are many interpretations, it is always started with onions cooked in goose or duck fat and prepared in a terracotta or enamel casserole. It can then be made with freshly hulled haricot beans, when they are in season, or small, grilled chestnuts and red pepper strips. Cabbage is essential, of course, but a handful of shredded Swiss chard is sometimes included. Goose or duck *Confit* (see p.218) are traditional, and fresh herbs add a lively note to the soup. It may be topped with a thick layer of breadcrumbs and grated cheese seasoned with a sprinkling of parsley, garlic and slivers of streaky bacon.

In her beautiful farm kitchen, Pierrette Sarran, the owner of the Auberge de Bergerayre, St Martin d'Armagnac, prepared a simple *Garbure* for us with just a few ingredients: green cabbage and potatoes in equal quantities, a few garlic cloves and some left-overs she found after she had prepared her *Confit* – a duck carcase, wing tips and necks. She simmered the soup uncovered for 2 hours, stirred in a tablespoon of duck fat at the end and served us a deliciously hearty soup.

Because duck preserve is hard to find, this is my own recipe for *Garbure* which I prepare regularly, especially on wintry evenings. Only a spoonful takes the chill out of adults and children alike and warms their hearts.

SERVES 6

1.4 kg (3 lb) dried white haricot beans
1 onion stuck with 1 clove
900 g (2 lb) piece of lean streaky bacon
1 thick slice of cured ham
2.25–2.75 litres (4–5 pints) cold water
225 g (8 oz) lima or shelled broad beans (optional)
3 carrots, chopped
1 turnip, chopped
2 leeks, white and pale green parts only, sliced
450 g (1 lb) long green cabbage leaves, shredded
100 g (4 oz) pumpkin, chopped
1 bouquet garni
salt and freshly ground black pepper
675 g (1½ lb) potatoes, diced
5 garlic cloves, crushed
1 ham bone (optional)
a few titbits of meats and bones of preserved duck or goose (see p. 218) (optional)
2 tablespoons chopped fresh basil
2 tablespoons chopped fresh mint

TO SERVE

Garlic Croûtons (see p. 108)

Soak the beans overnight in cold water. Drain then rinse. Place in a large pan, cover with fresh water and add the clove-studded onion. Bring to the boil and boil vigorously for 2 minutes then remove from the heat and leave to cool in the cooking liquid.

Place the bacon and ham in a large pan and add the water. Bring to the boil, partially cover and simmer for 1 hour. Add the lima or broad beans, carrots, turnip, leeks, cabbage, pumpkin and bouquet garni and season with salt and pepper. Return to the boil, partially cover and simmer for 30 minutes. Drain the haricot beans and discard the onion. Add the beans to the soup with the potatoes, garlic, and the ham bone and duck or goose, if using. Simmer for a further 40 minutes.

Remove the meats, slice them and discard the bones. Return the meats to the soup, pour it into a warm tureen and season with salt and pepper. Sprinkle with freshly chopped herbs. Place the garlic Croûtons in the bottom of each soup plate and pour the hot soup over them. Or sprinkle with grated cheese and grill briefly.

SOUTH-WEST, MIDI AND PROVENCE

Soupe à l'Ail

GARLIC-FLAVOURED SOUP

Whether it is enriched with olive oil or goose fat, called *Aïgo Bouïdo* or *Tourain*, garlic soups are served throughout southern France.

In Provence it is eaten the day after a particularly rich meal since '*l'aïgo bouïdo sauvo la vido*' – garlic soup will save your life. In the centre and the south-west, the *Tourain* is made with onions, tomatoes and garlic seasoned with vinegar and enriched with eggs.

A delightful friend of mine, twelve-year-old Benjamin Cano who lives near the medieval city of Carcassonne, prepared a delicious soup for me. He set soup bowls on a table, placed a Croûton in each and delicately slipped in some fresh egg yolks while he kept an eye on the pan of hot water into which he had thrown a handful of garlic cloves. He energetically whisked some beaten egg whites into the water and poured a little of the hot broth with its delicate egg threads into each bowl as he vigorously stirred the broth into egg yolks. I felt his was the very best garlic soup I ever tasted and I told him so. More soberly, now that I stand alone in my kitchen, I shall give you what I consider *the two* very best versions I know. Not a word to Benjamin.

Le Tourain
GARLIC SOUP

This uses goose or duck fat and it was customary for friends and relatives to bring it to newly-weds about 4 a.m., then go down to the kitchen to share a bowl of *Tourain* and a fresh omelette.

SERVES 4

1 tablespoon lard, goose or duck fat or groundnut oil
2 onions, sliced
6 garlic cloves, crushed
1.2 litres (2 pints) water
1 sprig of fresh thyme or 1 teaspoon dried thyme
salt and freshly ground black pepper
1 egg, separated
1 tablespoon red wine vinegar
2 slices stale rye or coarse-grained bread

Heat the lard, fat or oil and fry the onions and garlic until soft but not browned. Add the water, thyme, salt and pepper, bring to the boil, cover and simmer for 30 minutes. Strain the soup through a sieve, pushing the garlic and onion against the metal with a wooden spoon. Return to the heat, bring back to the boil and stir in the egg white, whisking steadily for about 2 minutes. Then turn the heat to low. Blend the egg yolk with the wine vinegar, stir in a ladleful of the hot broth then stir the mixture into the pan. Remove from the heat and season. Spread the bread in the bottom of a warm tureen, pour over the hot soup and serve at once.

NOTE

In Bordeaux, *Tourain* is prepared with tomatoes, onions, garlic and preserved duck and with-out egg whites. Sometimes, thin noodles are added to the soup, and it is served with sliced bread spread with goose fat, sprinkled with ground pepper and grilled until crisp.

Aïgo Boüido
PROVENÇAL GARLIC SOUP

SERVES 4

1 tablespoon olive oil
10 garlic cloves, crushed
1.2 litres (2 pints) water
7.5 cm (3 inch) piece orange rind
2 bay leaves
3 fresh sage leaves or ½ teaspoon dried sage
1 sprig of fresh thyme or 1 teaspoon dried thyme
salt
2 egg yolks (optional)
2 teaspoons red wine vinegar
freshly ground black pepper
2 tablespoons grated Gruyère or Parmesan
1 tablespoon olive oil

TO SERVE
4 thin slices bread made into Croûtons (see p. 233)

Heat the oil in a large pan and sauté the garlic for 3 minutes until barely golden, without letting the garlic burn. Add the water, orange rind, bay leaves, sage, thyme and a pinch of salt, bring to the boil and simmer, uncovered, for 15 minutes.

Beat the egg yolks in a bowl, stir in the wine vinegar and a ladleful of hot broth. Stir the mixture into the pan, lower the heat and simmer for about 2 minutes, stirring gently, until the soup becomes creamy. Do not let the soup boil or the eggs will curdle. Remove the orange rind, bay leaves and herbs and season to taste with salt and pepper. Pour into a warm tureen, sprinkle with the cheese and olive oil and serve with thin, crisp Croûtons.

NOTE

This soup is sometimes served poured over a few slices of oven-dried bread sprinkled with olive oil.

PROVENCE AND RIVIERA

Soupe au Pistou

RICH VEGETABLE SOUP FLAVOURED WITH A
GARLIC, BASIL AND CHEESE PASTE

The most exhilarating of soups, *Soupe au Pistou* is also the ultimate *potage de Santé*, or health soup. It is generally served as the major part of a meal during the summer when there is an abundance of fresh vegetables; but in autumn or winter, leeks, dried haricot beans, pumpkin or turnips offer interesting alternatives and since the basil and cheese paste can be frozen (I always add the garlic at the last moment), *Soupe au Pistou* makes a fragrant and comforting starter at any time of the year.

In Nice, we like to prepare this soup with most of the vegetables diced into tiny cubes. In fact, in most marketplaces there are piles of freshly shelled white beans and neatly diced vegetables ready-prepared for the busy cook.

Soupe au Pistou can be prepared two or three days in advance. It can be served hot or at room temperature, and the basil mixture is always added to the warm broth at the table so that the heady potent scent of the herb can be enjoyed by all your guests. Remember that the quantity of basil and garlic depend on the quality and freshness of the ingredients and also on your personal taste, so keep tasting and correcting before stirring the *pistou* into the soup. It is always better to gather the basil leaves a few hours in advance so they lose some of their moisture.

SERVES 4–6

FOR THE SOUP

*225 g (8 oz) fresh, dried or semi-dried shelled white
or red and white haricot beans*

4 onions

1 leek

1 tomato, skinned

4 potatoes

2 carrots

2 turnips

1 celery stick

4 courgettes

225 g (8 oz) green beans

3 tablespoons olive oil

2 bay leaves

a few fresh sage leaves

1.75 litres (3 pints) water

salt and freshly ground black pepper

FOR THE PISTOU

2 handfuls of fresh basil leaves

3 garlic cloves

4 tablespoons grated Gruyère or Parmesan

3 tablespoons olive oil

TO SERVE

grated Gruyère or Parmesan

crisp slices of bread

If you are using dried beans, soak them overnight in cold water. Drain and rinse. Place in a pan, cover with fresh water, bring to the boil and boil vigorously for 10 minutes then reduce the heat and simmer for about 1 hour until soft. Drain well.

Chop all the vegetables into 2.5 cm (1 in) pieces. Heat 2 tablespoons of the oil in a frying pan and fry the onions and leek for 3 minutes. Add the tomatoes, potatoes, carrots, turnips and celery and cook for 10 minutes, stirring occasionally. Transfer to a large pan. Heat the remaining oil in the frying-pan and fry the courgettes, green beans, bay leaves and sage for a few minutes. Meanwhile, bring the water to the boil in a separate pan. Add the courgette mixture and the water to the vegetables with bay leaves and sage. Return to the boil and simmer, uncovered, for 30 minutes. Add the cooked haricot beans.

Meanwhile, prepare the *pistou*. Use a mortar

and pestle to grind and pound the basil leaves, garlic, salt and pepper to a thick paste then add the cheese and oil. Alternatively, you can use a food processor. Pour the soup into a warm tureen and bring it to the table. Stir in the *pistou* then sprinkle a little cheese on top. Pass a bowl of grated cheese and a basket of crisp slices of bread around the table.

NORMANDY AND PARIS

Bisque de Crabes
CRAB BISQUE

Once, bisques were thick stew-like soups prepared with beef, pigeons or game. Today they are only made with crayfish, lobsters, prawns or crabs. They are considered immensely elegant and so complicated and expensive to prepare that few sensible home cooks would venture to try them. Considering the number of utensils needed – mortar, sieve, saucepans – it seems like a true labour of endurance and love. Considering the price of lobster, crayfish and even prawns, it would seem that bisques are out of reach for most of us today. However, this recipe for an unctuous, velvety and spirited Crab Bisque is one that I often prepare and is really worth trying. Crabs are richly flavoured and quite inexpensive, while the help of a friendly food processor makes the whole procedure very straightforward.

In France, the *live* shellfish would be cooked in hot butter. I found this too difficult to face and I cook the crabs separately in boiling water, using the cooking broth later for the soup. Bisques are traditionally thickened with rice, cream of rice, potato flour or arrowroot.

In colloquial French, *bisquer* means to get angry. I suppose this comes from the fact that the dish is the colour of an angry face.

SERVES 4–6

2 x 675 g (1½ lb) crabs
salt
5 bay leaves
2 tablespoons butter
1 tablespoon vegetable oil
1 carrot, diced
1 onion, diced
1 celery stick, diced
1 garlic clove, crushed
1 sprig of fresh thyme
1.2 litres (2 pints) crab cooking liquid or water
300 ml (10 fl oz) dry white wine
a pinch of cayenne pepper
4 egg yolks
5 tablespoons single cream
1 tablespoon arrowroot or cornflour
1 tablespoon brandy
2 tablespoon chopped fresh chervil, parsley or tarragon

TO SERVE
4 slices bread made into Croûtons (see p.233)

If you buy live crabs, bring a large pan of salted water to the boil, add 2 bay leaves and simmer for 5 minutes. Add the live crabs, cover and cook for 30 minutes. Leave to cool in the cooking liquid then strain, reserving the liquid.

Now you can start the soup. Place the cooked, cold crabs, back down, on a wooden board or strong work surface. Twist and break off the legs and claws from the body. Cut along each side of the leg shell with scissors and remove as much meat as possible with a skewer or knitting needle. Crack the claws and remove the meat with a knitting needle. Twist off and discard the tail from the body then crack the central section of the shell under the tail and prise it apart. Remove the meat from the shell and discard the grey, spongy gills, the 'dead men's fingers', the head sac and the coral-coloured roe. Prise out the meat, discarding

any membrane. The left-over pieces and the broken shell will flavour the broth. Dice the crab meat and put it to one side for later use.

With a heavy mallet, pound the shells until they are crushed. Place them in a food processor with a little cooking stock or water and switch on and off for a few minutes until they are finely crushed. It will be very noisy.

Heat I tablespoon of the butter with the oil in a very large pan and sauté the carrot, onion and celery for about 10 minutes until soft. Add the remaining bay leaves, the garlic and thyme then stir in the crushed shells and stir with a wooden spoon over a low heat for 5 minutes. Add the cooking stock or water and the wine, bring to the boil, cover and simmer for 30 minutes. Stir well with a wooden spoon. Cover and simmer for a further 30 minutes. Leave to cool.

Scrape the shell and vegetable mixture into a coarse metal sieve and strain the broth into a pan, mashing the shell mixture with a spoon. Bring the broth to the boil and season with cayenne pepper. Mix the egg yolks, cream and arrowroot or cornflour in a bowl, stir in a little of the hot broth, then stir the mixture into the pan and simmer over a low heat, stirring, for 5–10 minutes until the broth thickens. Do not let the soup boil or the egg will curdle.

Heat the remaining butter in a separate pan and sauté the crab meat for a few minutes. Stir in the brandy then add the mixture to the soup. Pour into a warm tureen and serve sprinkled with fresh herbs with the Croûtons passed separately.

Soupe à l'Oignon
ONION SOUP

There is nothing like a fragrant and invigorating onion soup covered with a golden crust to evoke in an instant a cosy supper after an evening out. But onion soup is not only the privilege of the *noctambules*, the night-owls. Followed by raw oysters or a platter of *charcuterie* and a watercress or chicory tossed salad, it is also the core of many traditional Sunday family meals.

Is onion soup an elaborate Lyonnaise treat, a hearty country dish or a Parisian invention? No one is sure. The purists argue endlessly over exactly how the soup should be prepared. Should the onions be grated, sliced or puréed? Should one use beef, chicken or veal broth or water? Should it be a light or a thick soup? Should one try to add Camembert, Brie or Roquefort cheese instead of Gruyère? Should there be alternate layers of toasted bread and cheese with the hot broth poured on top before the final baking? Should one stir in a drop of vinegar, cognac, port, milk or white wine before serving the soup? I have no definitive answers to these questions so you must decide for yourselves. The most authentic version I ever tasted was prepared by Pierre Sauvet at Paris' 'intellectual' brasserie, the Brasserie Balzar near the Sorbonne. But, here, I have decided to give a more sumptuous recipe that has been my favourite for years.

SERVES 4–6

1.75 litres (3 pints) chicken, beef or veal stock or water
2 teaspoons dried thyme
2 bay leaves
675 g (1½1b) yellow onions
4 tablespoons butter
1 tablespoon groundnut oil

salt
½ teaspoon sugar
2 tablespoons plain flour
300 ml (10 fl oz) dry white wine
freshly ground black pepper
225 g (8 oz) Gruyère
10 slices baguette cut 2.5 cm (1 in) thick or large
slices cut into triangles
2 egg yolks
1–2 tablespoons cognac (optional)
2 tablespoons port, sherry or Madeira

Bring the stock or water, thyme and bay leaves to the boil while you peel and slice the onions under water to avoid tears. Heat 2 tablespoons of the butter with the oil in a large pan and cook the onions on a low heat until soft. Sprinkle with salt, sugar and flour and cook for 5 minutes, uncovered, until the mixture turns brown. Stir the mixture occasionally and add a little stock if it sticks to the pan. Stir in the wine then pour in the hot stock and simmer, uncovered, for 30 minutes. Season with salt and pepper. You can cool, cover and chill the soup at this point if you wish then re-heat and garnish it later.

Meanwhile, grate half the cheese and thinly slice the other half. Toast the bread slices on one side, turn them and sprinkle with grated cheese and then grill for a few seconds until the cheese has softened.

Pre-heat the oven to 180°C, 350°F, Gas 4.

Arrange the slices of cheese at the bottom of a large ovenproof tureen or in individual tureens or soufflé dishes. Pour over the hot soup, top with the bread and cheese and dot with the remaining butter. Bake in the oven for about 20 minutes until the cheese is browned. If it is not, flash it under a hot grill for a minute until browned.

Beat the egg yolks with the cognac, if using, and the port, sherry or Madeira and sprinkle with pepper.

Bring the soup to the table. Lift a bit of the cheese and bread crust with a fork, pour in the egg mixture and blend gently. This blending is called *touiller* and is a ritual needed to ensure a truly perfect Onion Soup. Serve at once.

NOTE

In parts of the south-west, the onion is sautéed in goose fat and Roquefort blue cheese is added to the Gruyère for a spirited version of the dish. Some cooks like to add a pinch of grated raw onion on crisp toast or a few poached eggs to the soup just before serving.

BREAD

These are the most popular breads in France.

Baguette: *Made with flour, salt, water and yeast. A baguette à l'ancienne is made with slightly sour dough.*

Ficelle: *Thin, short baguettes about 4 cm (1½ in) wide.*

Pain de Campagne: *Made with rye or wholewheat flour, they may be hearty or disappointingly bland.*

Pain de Mie: *Dense sandwich bread made with butter, flour, sugar and milk.*

Fougasse: *A large, brown loaf covered with sea salt or herbs and made with flour, salt, yeast and olive oil, and sometimes herbs or cripsy bacon.*

Pain Viennois: *Made with flour, sugar and milk, these are shaped like a plump baguette and dusted with*

CHARENTES AND NORMANDY

Mouclade

CREAMY MUSSEL DISH

Every region along the Mediterranean, Atlantic or Channel coasts has its own recipe for mussel soup. But *Mouclade* comes from Charentes, where mussels have been farmed for the last seven centuries, either flat in parks, hanging on ropes or on wooden posts, *bouchots*, driven into the sea bed. Ships have sailed to La Rochelle from the Orient for hundreds of years, bringing curry powder, cayenne pepper and saffron; while cognac, butter and cream abound in the region.

SERVES 4–6

1.8 kg (4 lb) mussels
600 ml (1 pint) dry white wine
1 bay leaf
2 onions, chopped
3 tablespoons butter
2 shallots, coarsely chopped
2 garlic cloves, finely chopped
½ teaspoon curry powder or ground saffron
juice of 1 lemon
2 egg yolks
200 ml (7 fl oz) double cream
1 tablespoon cognac (optional)
a pinch of cayenne pepper
salt and freshly ground black pepper
2 teaspoons chopped fresh parsley

Soak the mussels in cold water for 30 minutes then drain and rinse. Scrub the shells with a hard brush and cut off the beards. Discard any open ones. Rinse the mussels in several changes of cold water.

Heat the wine, bay leaf and onions in a large pan then add the mussels Cover and cook for about 5 minutes, shaking the pan from time to time, until the mussels have opened. Discard any that remain closed. Remove the mussels from the liquid with a slotted spoon and place them in a bowl. Wearing oven gloves to protect your hands, discard the top shells and half the bottom shells. Cover the mussels with kitchen foil or a thick towel and keep warm in a warm, turned-off oven. Strain the cooking liquor through a muslin-lined sieve.

Heat the butter in a large pan and sauté the shallots for 5 minutes until soft. Add the garlic, curry powder or saffron, lemon juice and the strained cooking liquor. Bring to the boil over a medium heat.

Beat the egg yolks and cream in a bowl, stir in a ladleful of the hot broth then pour into the pan and simmer over a low heat for 5 minutes, stirring. Do not let the mixture boil. Add the cognac, if using, and taste the soup; it should be highly seasoned. Season to taste with cayenne, salt and pepper.

Place the mussels and the remaining shells on a warm, large shallow dish, pour the hot, fragrant, creamy broth over and serve sprinkled with parsley using a ladle or two large spoons. Place spoons, paper towels and finger bowls on the table for each guest.

Potage Crécy

LIGHT CARROT SOUP

Crécy is a town near Paris where the best carrots in France are grown and they use them to prepare this smooth, fragrant, puréed soup. You can make it either with fresh, tender spring carrots or large winter ones. It needs a thickening agent, and you can use rice, potato or wheat flour. I like to garnish *Potage Crécy* with Croûtons or diced potatoes sautéed in butter, added to the soup just as it is brought to the table.

SERVES 4

75 g (3 oz) butter
1.4 kg (3 lb) carrots, sliced
1 onion, sliced
3 potatoes, sliced
1 tablespoon chopped fresh thyme
1.2 litres (2 pints) vegetable, chicken or beef stock or water
1 teaspoon sugar
1 tablespoon chopped fresh chervil
salt and freshly ground black pepper

TO SERVE

4 slices bread made into Croûtons (see p.68) or 1 large diced potato sautéed in butter

Melt a little of the butter in a large pan and cook the carrots and onion over a low heat until soft. Add the potatoes, thyme and stock or water, bring to the boil, cover and simmer for 35 minutes until the vegetables are soft.

Purée the soup in a food processor or rub through a sieve. Stir in the remaining butter with the sugar and chervil. Taste and season with salt and pepper. Pour into a warm tureen and serve sprinkled with Croûtons or diced sautéed potatoes.

Consommé de Viande

BEEF CONSOMMÉ

Consommé is not only for invalids, new mothers or elderly people, it is a truly sophisticated dish. But it must be intensely flavoured and be thoroughly degreased. A Consommé is basically the broth of a *Pot au Feu* made with twice the amount of meat. It used to take eight hours to prepare a Consommé so that all the juices would be extracted and the liquid would be reduced to its essence. Today we add a little uncooked meat to the bone and vegetables in order to flavour the broth.

You can make Consommé with beef and veal, or you may add chicken wings, necks, carcase or giblets. I like to prepare the following recipe because it is richly flavoured and only uses easily available ingredients. If you cannot buy bones at your local supermarket, you will certainly be able to obtain them from the butcher.

Beating egg whites into the cold Consommé then re-heating it causes the cloudy bits to rise to the surface so that they can be easily discarded to give a sparkling clear Consommé.

A little Madeira or sherry can be added just before serving. Each person is usually served about 300 ml (10 fl oz) of Consommé. You may like to add a few bits of shredded, raw carrot as you serve.

SERVES 4

900 g (2lb) beef shank, brisket or shin
1.8 kg (4 lb) beef bones, cracked
2.75 litres (5 pints) water
225 g (8 oz) carrots, quartered
150 g (5 oz) turnips, quartered
100 g (4 oz) leeks, halved
1 stick celery
1 onion studded with 4 cloves
1 head garlic
2 sprigs of fresh thyme
3 bay leaves
2 sprigs of fresh parsley
1 teaspoon salt
8 black peppercorns
2 egg whites

TO SERVE

2 tablespoons Madeira, port, cognac or dry sherry
4 slices bread made into Croûtons (see p.233)

Place the meat, bones and water in a large pan and bring slowly to the boil. Add the vegetables and herbs, salt and peppercorns, return to the boil, partially cover and simmer gently for 3–4 hours, skimming as necessary. Leave the broth to cool then strain and refrigerate.

Skim the fat from the surface with a large spoon. Re-heat the broth until liquid. Taste and correct the seasoning. Whisk the egg whites in a bowl until they hold soft peaks. Add to the broth, whisking until thoroughly mixed. Bring gently to the boil, whisking all the time so that you incorporate all the impurities. Be sure to stop whisking before the broth reaches boiling point. At boiling point the albumen in the egg white coagulates and forms a crust which holds all the impurities. Do not whisk once this has happened. Let the crust rise to the top of the pan then turn off the heat and let it subside. Repeat, allowing the top of the crust to rise to the top of the pan again then let it subside.

Line a colander with 2 layers of muslin and stand it over a large bowl. Gently ladle the crust into the colander and pour in the broth. The clear, sparkling broth will drain into the bowl and the egg whites, meat and bone particles will remain in the colander and can be discarded. Strain again, through the egg white, if necessary.

Re-heat the Consommé and stir in the Madeira, port, cognac or dry sherry just before serving. Serve with a basket of Croûtons.

Starters

LES ENTRÉES
ET LES HORS D'OEUVRE

*I*n France a starter is an *hors d'oeuvre*, which implies it stands 'out of the main part of the meal'. Its mission is to be seductive and entice you to move lightly to the more substantial *plat de résistance* which follows. Starters are meant to amuse your palate, hence their nickname *amuse-gueules*.

A starter is a breathing space at the beginning of a meal, a suspended moment one enjoys before diving into the heart of the matter. 'It is only the principle that counts,' my mother would explain. She never skipped hors d'oeuvre in her life, even when she was in a hurry, in a bad mood or eating by herself. She always found a tasty titbit, a handful of pink radishes, half a tomato topped with a leaf of basil, a hard-boiled egg sprinkled with a drop of olive oil, a few olives and fresh favas, a bit of crisp toast spread with tapenade to start her meal. It was a light pause before serious feeding and it made her feel civilized.

A starter comes in many guises. It can be cold or hot, simple or sophisticated, grand or cheap, but quantity, diversity and appearance are all-important. Each region has its own preferences. Terrines, hams and sausages in Alsace and Lyon; shellfish in Brittany, Normandy and the Atlantic coast; raw or fried, a platter of *Petits Farcis* (see p.85) throughout the south; cured ham, dried pork liver sausages and peppers of all kinds in the Basque country. But egg dishes such *Brouillade* (see p.113), *Oeufs en Meurette* (see p.108) and omelettes of all kinds are traditional starters throughout France and so are stuffed savoury crêpes, foie gras, smoked salmon, shellfish or meat salads and vegetable tarts.

There should always be variety in a menu: *Salade Niçoise* (see p.80) should not start a meal if you plan to serve rabbit in tomato sauce later; no *Gougère* (see p.270) if it is followed with a cheese and chicken gratin; and no soufflé if you have prepared a bowl of *Oeufs à la Neige* (see p.305) for dessert.

A delicate balance is important in a meal, so the starter must always carefully complement the main course. No *Flamiche* (see p.250) or cheese soufflé before a *Blanquette* (see p.179), a *Cassoulet* (see p.204) or an *Aïoli* (see p.76). And if you choose a grand starter like *Jambon Persillé* (see p.222), *Gâteau de Foies* (see p.108) or *Mouclade* (see p.71), make sure the main course is light. It is interesting to see many regional chefs offering miniature version of local dishes as starters – tiny quiches or *flamiches* (they even have a word for it *quichette* and *flamichette*), a few mouthfuls of *Truffade* (see p.255), a small wedge of *croque-monsieur*, one or two sardines in *escabèche* – all delicious, evocative but light enough to allow room and appetite for the main dish to come.

Starters must never be overwhelming. The grand, elaborate hors d'oeuvres of yesterday are no longer fashionable. I love to start a meal with a tossed green salad with fish, meat or cheese titbits, a bowl of shredded carrots and olive oil, *Céleri Rémoulade* (see p.81), chicory and walnuts, marinated herrings on a bed of warm potatoes. I sometimes serve as a first course a large dish of steamed vegetables simply seasoned with a fragrant dressing like *Pistou*, *Gribiche* or *Anchoïade* (see pp.76-78 and p.101).

Restaurants often offer an hors d'oeuvre trolley – a tempting assortment of creamy egg mayonnaise, grated carrots, cooked beetroot, shredded red cabbage, melons, fish and vegetable terrines, squid salad, mackerel in wine, artichokes. They also propose staggering *Plateaux de Charcuterie* (see p.212) and *Assiettes de Fruits de Mer* (see p.137). But the success of such glorious offerings is their wide variety so that each guest may sample a bit of this and a bite of that while 'remaining on his hunger', eager for the next course.

At home, starters can often be made conveniently ahead of time. Pâtés and terrines (see pp.213-17), *Salade de Poivrons Rouges aux Anchois* (see p.228), boiled chick pea or lentil salads (see p.82), *Ratatouille* (see p.237), *Poireaux Vinaigrette* (see p.81), aubergine with tomato purée (see p.238) are prepared and chilled until ready to use. And, of course, many left-overs may be turned into starters. Nobody will recognize the shredded boiled beef with its fresh mustardy mayonnaise, nor the bits of yesterday's fish or chicken when they are tossed in a rice or green salad and seasoned with a lemony mayonnaise.

But whether they are nibbled with aperitifs or eaten more formally at the table, whether they are grand or simple, one must remember that starters should not be treated too seriously. In fact in my house in Provence we start the meal in the most carefree of manners. We just ... nibble the table centrepiece: a basket filled to the brim with raw vegetables, un *Panier de Crudités* (see p.76)!

Crudités

RAW VEGETABLES WITH A SELECTION OF SAUCES

Crudités are a blessing whenever you feel lazy and want to enjoy your own party. A wide assortment of raw vegetables along with a selection of sauces for dipping into, such as *Mayonnaise* (see p.101), *Tapenade*, *Anchoïade* and *Pistou* encourage relaxed conversation. The sauces can be prepared in advance and kept, covered, in a cool place or the fridge, and the vegetables can be arranged on the platter or in the basket, sprinkled with a little cold water, covered with cling film and chilled.

Any left-over vegetables can be seasoned with one of the sauces and mixed with a few tablespoons of *Vinaigrette* to make a salad. Alternatively they can be transformed into vegetable soup. All the sauces serve about 4 people.

Vegetables

Choose a selection from the following list. Quantities are according to the occasion.

radishes with 2.5 cm (1 in) stems
button mushrooms, trimmed, with part of the stem on
chicory leaves, halved lengthways if wide
cauliflower florets
mangetouts
watercress sprigs
spring onions with 5 cm (2 in) of their green stems
carrots cut into sticks or whole spring
carrots with their green leaves
cucumbers, peeled, seeds removed, cut into sticks
broccoli florets
fennel bulbs, cut into sticks
celery sticks about 7.5 cm (3 ins) long
small green asparagus spears, about 10 cm (4 in) long

green, red and yellow peppers, cut into sticks
sprigs of fresh flatleaf parsley
sprigs of fresh basil

Place the vegetables on a platter or in a basket, and garnish with a few sprigs of parsley and basil.

Aïoli

5 garlic cloves
2 small egg yolks
½-1 teaspoon Dijon mustard
150 ml (5 fl oz) groundnut oil
150 ml (5 fl oz) olive oil
salt and freshly ground black pepper

Crush the garlic cloves in a mortar then pound them. Stir in the egg yolks and mustard. When smooth, continue as for making *Rouille* (see p.77).

VINAIGRETTE

1½ tablespoons red wine vinegar

6 tablespoons olive oil, vegetable oil or a mixture

1½ teaspoons Dijon mustard

2 tablespoons finely chopped mixed fresh herbs

1½ tablespoons finely chopped shallots

salt and freshly ground black pepper

Vigorously stir all the ingredients together in a small bowl, or shake them together in a screw-top jar.

Rouille

This fragrant sauce is based on the same principle as Mayonnaise except it is made with a pestle and mortar. If your pestle isn't big enough to take all the oil, transfer the garlic, when crushed, to a larger bowl. Keep all the ingredients at room temperature, place the mortar on a cloth and add the oil gradually.

4 garlic cloves
1 large egg yolk
120 ml (4 fl oz) olive oil
120 ml (4 fl oz) groundnut oil
juice of 1 lemon
½ teaspoon saffron strands, crushed
1 teaspoon cayenne pepper
salt and freshly ground black pepper

Crush the garlic cloves in a mortar, then pound them to a paste. Add the egg yolk, stirring and pounding constantly, then gradually stir in oil as for Mayonnaise (see p.47). When the sauce is firm and all the oil incorporated, stir in the lemon juice, saffron, cayenne pepper, salt and pepper; the sauce should then be smooth and quite firm. After 1 hour in the fridge it will thicken.

Pistou

I use *Pistou* (in Provence it is called a *pommade* or 'creamy mixture' rather than a sauce) to flavour vegetable soup, fill raw tomatoes and flavour fresh noodles. I spread it on browned lamb chops, hamburgers and crisp toast, and I stir it into warm rice. When there is not enough basil, I use fresh mint or flat leaf parsley, just like everyone in the Alps used to do. I cannot grow basil in winter so sometimes I freeze *Pistou* for the cold-weather months.

5 garlic cloves, crushed
1 teaspoon coarse salt
2 handfuls of fresh basil leaves
120 ml (4 fl oz) olive oil
50 g (2 oz) Gruyère, Parmesan or Pecorino Romano, grated
freshly ground black pepper
salt

Crush the garlic and coarse salt in a mortar to make a paste, or use the back of a fork and a small mixing bowl. Pour into food processor with the basil leaves and olive oil and mix on a high speed. Add the grated cheese, pepper and a little salt if needed and mix for an instant.

NOTE

If the *Pistou* is too thick, add a peeled, seeded and sieved tomato and a little oil.

Tapenade

Tapenade is most often made with Nyons olives, or any plump black variety, but plump green olives are occasionally used to make an interesting variation.

The name comes from *tapenado*, Provençal for 'capers' which were used to enhance the olives and cover any faults.

I spread *Tapenade* on baked fish or warm, crisp chicken; I add a spoonful to beef stew; I use it to stuff hard-boiled eggs, tomatoes, cucumbers and celery sticks. I spread it on boiled chicory or celery hearts, and it gives new life to sliced, cold beef or pork. I also add a handful of stoned olives to *Tapenade* then stir it into rice or fresh noodles. *Tapenade* can be frozen.

SERVES 4–6

200 g (7 oz) plump black olives, stoned
6 anchovy fillets, crushed
2 tablespoons capers
2 garlic cloves, crushed
1 teaspoon chopped fresh thyme
1 tablespoon Dijon mustard
juice of 1 lemon
120 ml (4 fl oz) olive oil
freshly ground black pepper
1 tablespoon brandy (optional)

Put all the ingredients in a food processor. Mix at a high speed for 1 second until smooth and soft; if necessary, add a few more drops of oil. Pour into a bowl. Just before serving adjust the seasoning, if necessary.

Anchoïade

Anchoïade is more pungent when made with anchovies that have been kept in brine rather than those packed in oil.

I like to spread *Anchoïade* on grilled red mullet; I toss it with raw fennel salad, and with thickly sliced hot potatoes, I season warm bean, lentil or chick pea salads with it, but I mostly love it on warm slices of bread.

SERVES 4–6

20 anchovy fillets packed in brine or oil
5 tablespoons olive oil
1 tablespoon red wine vinegar
2 garlic cloves, crushed
salt and freshly ground black pepper

If using anchovies that have been packed in brine, rinse very well to remove excess salt, then pat dry. Place all the ingredients in a food processor then mix at a high speed for 1–2 seconds. Season to taste and transfer to a bowl. Stir well before serving.

VARIATION

For *Bagna Cauda*, warm *Anchoïade* with 1 teaspoon of butter and serve as a dip for raw celery, tiny raw purple artichokes and cardoons.

Fromage de Chèvre à l'Huile d'Olive

GOATS' CHEESE MARINATED IN OLIVE OIL

Jenny Fajardo de Livry and her family live practically under the craggy cliffs of Les Baux in Provence. Out of her window are the sounds of gentle bees, the ticking of cicadas and the faint bleating of goats from nearby farms.

Fresh goats' cheese has a lovely mild taste on its own, but Jenny marinades it with a tasty olive oil and pungent flavourings. The longer the cheese is left, the stronger it will taste. If you cannot find small, soft fresh cheeses, cut a round log cheese into slices, each about 4 cm (½ in) wide. If this is not possible try using a dry, crumbly goat's cheese – it will do just as nicely.

SERVES 4
4 small fresh goats' cheeses, or 4 slices of a log cheese
salt and freshly ground black pepper
4 sprigs of fresh summer savory or thyme
4–6 tablespoons virgin olive oil
1–2 tablespoons marc or brandy

Place the cheese on a plate. Season with salt and pepper and scatter the leaves from the herb sprigs evenly over the top of the cheeses. Spoon over the oil and marc or brandy and leave for 30 minutes.

NOTE

If you want the cheeses to have a stronger flavour, leave them in a cool place, but not the fridge, for 2–3 hours, basting the cheeses occasionally with the oil and marc or brandy.

Pissenlit aux Lardons et à la Vinaigrette

WARM DANDELION, SPINACH, OR ENDIVE SALAD
WITH BACON

Tossed with a pungent dressing and garnished with crisp Croûtons flavoured with garlic and olive oil, this salad makes an invigorating first course or a refreshing accompaniment to a rich main course such as Roast Duck with Spinach Stuffing (see p.124).

SERVES 8
2 tablespoons vegetable oil
225 g (8 oz) lean bacon or lean salt pork, cut into 1 cm (½ in) dice
about 8 handfuls crisp dandelion leaves or young spinach leaves or endive
4 tablespoons red wine vinegar
2–3 teaspoons Dijon mustard
salt and freshly ground black pepper
4 slices wholemeal or good firm white bread, made into Small Garlic-flavoured Croûtons (see p.233)

Heat the oil in a heavy-based frying-pan, add the bacon or pork and fry until crisp.

Meanwhile, fill a salad bowl with hot water to warm it. Empty and dry the bowl. Tear the dandelion or spinach leaves, or endive into pieces and put into the bowl. Pour over the bacon or pork and the warm cooking juices.

Stir the vinegar into the frying-pan, bring to the boil, then stir in the mustard. Pour over the salad. Sprinkle with pepper, and a little salt if needed. Add the Croûtons, toss and serve.

PROVENCE

Salade Niçoise

MIXED RAW VEGETABLE SALAD WITH EGGS,
ANCHOVIES, TUNA AND OLIVES

Give us our daily *Salade Niçoise*! Throughout the summer, whether eating in a gazebo covered with jasmine, on a terrace overlooking the sea or under an olive tree on a wooden table, a *Salade Niçoise* is always a part of a meal in Provence. The fresh, crisp vegetables, pungent flavours and light dressing capture perfectly the spirit of the area.

In Provence, most people try to grow their own row of vegetables and almost every household has some basil growing in a pot on the window sill or balcony. In Provence and along the Riviera all the towns and villages have markets offering piles of vegetables, fresh herbs and barrels of olives so that from May to October everybody can easily find the ingredients to prepare *Salade Niçoise*. It can be dressed up or dressed down and although everyone has their own favourite recipe, cooked vegetables such as potatoes, green beans and beetroot do not belong in a true *Salade Niçoise*. Neither does raw fish. The only acceptable fish are tuna packed in olive oil and anchovies kept in brine or olive oil. The tradition is to use either anchovies or tuna, but I use them *both*.

SERVES 4

1 small cucumber
4 firm, fleshy tomatoes, seeded and thickly sliced
150 g (5 oz) very young, fresh broad beans
(optional)
4 small purple artichokes, quartered (optional)
1 fennel bulb, very thinly sliced
2 small green or red peppers, sliced
4 small spring onions, thinly sliced
100 g (4 oz) radishes with short green stems
2 hard-boiled eggs, peeled and halved lengthways or
quartered
6 anchovy fillets, rinsed
1 x 200 g (7 oz) can tuna in oil, drained
100 g (4 oz) small black Nice olives, or larger, oil-
cured black olives, stoned
salad leaves such as rocket, batavia or lettuce

FOR THE DRESSING
8 tablespoons virgin olive oil
salt and freshly ground black pepper
2 garlic cloves, crushed
10 fresh basil or mint leaves, finely chopped

Peel and slice the cucumber, then place on kitchen paper for 10 minutes, to drain.

To make the dressing, mix together the oil, salt, pepper, garlic and basil or mint.

Arrange the salad vegetables, eggs, anchovy fillets, tuna and olives attractively in a wide, shallow dish, then surround with salad leaves. Pour over the dressing and take the dish to the table without stirring it. Toss lightly just before serving.

Céleri Rémoulade

CELERIAC SALAD

Raw, shredded celeriac tossed with a pungent mustard-flavoured mayonnaise is a popular dish in bistros, where it is often served as a first course with a bowl of grated carrots seasoned with lemon juice, a dish of diced boiled beetroot seasoned with parsley, and a bundle of pink radishes. It is also served at buffets and taken on picnics.

Celeriac discolours soon after it has been grated, so add the dressing at once. Cream and Vinaigrette dressing are both good with celeriac.

SERVES 4
1 celeriac bulb

FOR THE DRESSING
1 egg yolk
2 tablespoons Dijon mustard
150 ml (5 fl oz) vegetable oil or a mixture of vegetable and olive oil
about 1 tablespoon red wine vinegar or lemon juice
salt

To make the dressing, beat the egg yolk and mustard together for 1 minute, then beat in about a quarter of the oil, a drop at a time, until all the oil is incorporated into the sauce. When there is about 1 tablespoon of firm sauce, the oil can be added a little more quickly. Add wine vinegar or lemon juice and salt to taste.

Using a heavy, sharp knife, quarter the celeriac, then peel it. Grate the celeriac into a serving bowl, add the dressing and stir to mix. Cover and chill lightly.

VARIATIONS

Cream dressing Mix together the juice of 1 lemon and 2 tablespoons of Dijon mustard, then stir in 300 ml (10 fl oz) of whipping or double cream. Add salt and whisk lightly, if liked.

Vinaigrette dressing Stir 2 tablespoons of finely chopped fresh chives, tarragon or chervil into Vinaigrette (see p. 76).

Poireaux Vinaigrette

WARM LEEK SALAD

Every serious bistro in France boasts a *Poireaux Vinaigrette*. Leeks are sometimes called the poor man's asparagus, and certainly when prepared in this way, they can be classed as a 'Great Simple Dish'. Choose firm leeks and only use the white part.

SERVES 4
8 slim leeks, each about 12.5 cm (5 in) long
2 teaspoons Dijon mustard
salt and freshly ground black pepper
1 tablespoon white or red wine vinegar
2 hard-boiled eggs
120 ml (4 fl oz) virgin olive oil
2 tablespoons coarsely chopped fresh parsley

TO SERVE
warm, toasted wholemeal bread

Slice the leeks in half lengthways and rinse under cold running water. Tie the leeks with string into 4 bundles and cook in boiling salted water for about 10 minutes until just tender.

Meanwhile, in a bowl, stir together the mustard, salt, pepper and vinegar. Cut the eggs into halves lengthways then scoop the yolks into the bowl. Mash them together with a fork then slowly mix in all but 1 tablespoon of the oil until the dressing is smooth.

Drain the leeks well then remove the strings. Lay the leeks on several layers of kitchen paper, cover with more kitchen paper and leave for a few minutes to absorb the excess moisture. Transfer the leeks while still warm to a heated serving dish and pour over the egg yolk dressing. Finely chop the egg whites and sprinkle over the leeks with the parsley and the remaining oil. Serve warm or at room temperature with a basket of warm, toasted wholemeal bread.

LIMOUSIN

Légumes secs en Salade

WARM CHICK PEA, OR HARICOT BEAN, SALAD

One of France's main culinary skills has always been the knack of transforming ordinary ingredients into something special. In Limousin, warm *mojettes*, small, white haricot beans, are served with pungent dressings. I saw an entire family involved in the preparation of the main ingredient of this dish. Each family member had a role: the growing, picking and drying of the beans was done by the son; the separating of the stalks from the pods was undertaken by the grandparents; and finally the game of jumping on the piles of dry, discarded stems was practised with equal fervour by both the family dog and the small children.

A handful of rocket, dandelion leaves or corn salad adds a refreshing texture and flavour to the dish. Warm salads such as this can be served as a first course or as accompaniment to plainly cooked meat.

SERVES 4

350 g (12 oz) chick peas or haricot beans, soaked overnight then drained and rinsed
1 carrot, halved
1 onion, halved, studded with 1 clove
1 bay leaf
1 sprig of fresh thyme

FOR THE DRESSING

1 tablespoon finely chopped fresh parsley
2 spring onions, finely chopped
3 tablespoons olive oil
1 tablespoon red wine vinegar
1 tablespoon Dijon mustard
1 teaspoon finely chopped fresh chives or tarragon
½ teaspoon freshly grated nutmeg
salt and freshly ground black pepper

TO GARNISH

chopped, fresh, flat leaf parsley
chives or tarragon

Place the chick peas or beans in a pan with the carrot, onion, bay leaf and thyme. Cover with plenty of cold water, bring to the boil and boil for 10 minutes. Cover and simmer for 1–1½ hours until tender.

Meanwhile, mix together all the dressing ingredients. Drain the chick peas or beans and discard the vegetables and herbs. Put the warm chick peas or beans in a warm china or earthenware serving bowl and pour over the dressing. Toss gently and sprinkle with parsley, chives or tarragon. Serve warm.

VARIATION

In Provence, chick pea, lentil and white bean salads are dressed whilst warm but served at room temperature; a dressing flavoured with 3 garlic cloves and 3 crushed anchovy fillets is often used.

PROVENCE

Beignets de Courgettes
COURGETTE FRITTERS

I was brought up nibbling crisp fritters and have eaten them as *hors d'oeuvres*, vegetable accompaniments, desserts and snacks. I have had fritters made with flaked salt cod, anchovies, whitebait, aubergines, courgettes, artichokes, acacia and courgette blossom. Piping hot, crunchy outside and soft inside, I still cannot dream of a greater treat.

I enjoyed the following recipe in Grasse. Annick Pellissier and her mother, Yvonne, prepared them almost with their eyes closed. Resembling well-schooled dancers they moved around the kitchen with quick, confident gestures, light feet and skilful hands. Meanwhile, Annick's son laid the table under the lemon and pepper trees, and her husband and I gathered wild salad leaves from the garden.

SERVES 4

7–8 courgettes, coarsely grated
salt
15 fresh mint leaves
vegetable oil for frying

FOR THE BATTER

175 g (6 oz) plain flour
2 large eggs, separated
200 ml (7 fl oz) beer
1 teaspoon olive oil
freshly ground black pepper

For the batter, put the flour into a large bowl, make a well in the centre, add the egg yolks, beer and olive oil, then gradually stir the flour into the liquids to make a smooth batter. Cover and leave in a cool place for 1 hour.

Place the courgettes in a sieve, sprinkle with salt then place a plate on the courgettes and a weight on the plate. Leave for 1 hour. Rinse the courgettes under cold water then dry with kitchen paper. Stir the courgettes and mint leaves into the batter and season with pepper.

Whisk the egg whites until stiff but not dry then, using a tablespoon, gently fold into the batter.

Heat the oil in a frying-pan, then add tablespoonfuls of the courgette mixture. Cook for 3–4 minutes on each side until golden brown. Using a fish slice, transfer the fritters to kitchen paper to drain. Keep warm while frying the remaining mixture. Serve hot.

NORTH-WEST AND THROUGHOUT FRANCE

Harengs Saurs
MARINATED CURED HERRING FILLETS

A true bistro staple that is a particular speciality of Boulogne. Just a look at the big brown or white dishes of *harengs saurs* on the table will tell you whether you are in a serious place or not.

This is one of the easiest dishes to prepare at home, and it will keep covered in the fridge for at least one week. *Harengs saurs* are salted and smoked whole; for convenience and availability, kipper fillets can be substituted for them.

SERVES 4

8 harengs saurs or kipper fillets, each about
13 cm (5 in) long
1 onion, sliced
1 carrot, sliced
2 bay leaves
1 sprig of fresh thyme
1 lemon, sliced
10 black peppercorns
about 300 ml (8–10 fl oz) mixed olive
oil and groundnut oil
fresh flatleaf parsley leaves

TO SERVE

*good country bread and unsalted butter, or warm
sliced potatoes seasoned with oil, vinegar, parsley or
chives and salt*

Place the kipper fillets in the bottom of an
attractive, round or rectangular, white china or
brown earthenware dish. Cover with the
onion, carrot, bay leaves, thyme, lemon and
peppercorns. Pour over sufficient oil to cover
generously. Cover the dish with foil or cling
film and leave in the fridge for at least 2 days,
turning the fillets over twice during that time.
Sprinkle over the parsley and serve at room
temperature with the bread or potatoes.

VARIATION

Add 1 or 2 crushed garlic cloves an hour before
serving.

Petites Courgettes
et Tomates Farcies
STUFFED COURGETTES AND TOMATOES

I was served these delicious, light stuffed vegetables by Annick Pellissier as I sat in the sun
with her family overlooking the fragrant, herb-
covered hills of Grasse. As long courgettes are
more readily available than round Nice ones, I
have made the recipe using them.

SERVES 4–6

*3½ tablespoons fresh breadcrumbs
2 tablespoons milk
4 courgettes
5 tomatoes
3½ tablespoons olive oil
1 onion, finely chopped
225 g (8 oz) lean minced beef
2 small eggs, beaten
4 tablespoons crème fraîche
6 tablespoons chopped fresh basil
salt and freshly ground black pepper
25 g (1 oz) Gruyère, grated*

Pre-heat the oven to 190°C/375°F/Gas 5.
Butter a baking dish.

Leave 1½ tablespoons of the breadcrumbs to
soak in the milk. Cut the courgettes in half
lengthways and then, using a teaspoon, carefully scoop out the seeds and flesh from the centres, and chop finely. Cut a small slice from the
tops of 4 tomatoes and carefully scoop out and
discard the seeds from the tomatoes. Place
them upside down to drain. Skin the remaining
tomato, discard the seeds and chop the flesh.

Heat 1½ tablespoons of oil in a frying-pan,
add the onion and cook over a moderate heat,
stirring occasionally, for about 5 minutes until
softened. Stir in the chopped courgette flesh
and the chopped tomato and cook for a further
2–3 minutes. Remove from the heat and stir in
the beef, eggs, crème fraîche, basil, salt and
pepper. Squeeze the soaked breadcrumbs dry
and stir into the pan. Divide the mixture
between the courgettes and tomatoes.

Place the filled vegetables in the baking dish.
Sprinkle the remaining breadcrumbs, cheese
and olive oil over the vegetables. Bake in the
pre-heated oven for about 25 minutes until the
courgettes are just tender and the topping is
brown. Serve hot, warm or cold.

PROVENCE

Petits Farcis

STUFFED VEGETABLES

In Provence, onions, courgettes, aubergines, tomatoes, peppers and even dainty courgette blossoms are filled with many different ingredients, but usually the stuffing is made from what is at hand or in the garden. There may be basil, thyme, a slice of ham, a piece of chicken, grated cheese, garlic, a bit of this, a pinch of that – all are welcome as long as the stuffing is light and fragrant. The variety and quantity of vegetables served is always generous, and there should be at least four *Petits Farcis* per person. They can be served hot, warm or cold.

SERVES 4–6

4 tablespoons olive oil
2 small aubergines
2 medium-sized tomatoes
2 small green or red peppers, top and stem cut off,
seeds and central stem discarded
2 whole onions
2 medium-sized courgettes
1 onion, chopped
50 g (2 oz) lean streaky bacon
1 tomato, skinned, seeded and chopped
225 g (8 oz) beef, lamb, ham, chicken or lean streaky
bacon, finely chopped
100 g (4 oz) cooked long-grain rice
8 tablespoons finely chopped fresh flatleaf parsley
1 tablespoon chopped fresh thyme
2 garlic cloves, crushed
salt and freshly ground black pepper
2 eggs, lightly beaten
50 g (2 oz) Parmesan or Gruyère, grated
50 g (2 oz) fresh breadcrumbs

Pre-heat the oven to 180°C/350°F/Gas 4. Oil a baking sheet.

Brush the aubergines with ½ tablespoon of olive oil and place on the baking sheet. Bake for about 15 minutes until soft. Leave until cool enough to handle then cut into halves lengthways and scoop the flesh from the aubergines into a large bowl. Leave a 1 cm (½ in) shell and take care not to pierce the skin.

Cut the tomatoes in half lengthways, sprinkle with salt and leave them upside-down on kitchen paper for 10 minutes. Gently squeeze out the excess juice and scoop out the pulp. Place the pulp in the bowl.

Meanwhile, bring a large pan of salted water to the boil, add the peppers and boil for 5 minutes then add the whole onions and boil for about 5–7 minutes. Add the courgettes and continue to boil for a further 5 minutes. Drain all the vegetables and leave until cool enough to handle.

Cut the onions in half crossways, then remove the centres leaving about 2 layers of skin. Put the centres into the bowl with the aubergine flesh and tomato pulp.

Cut the courgettes in half lengthways and, using a teaspoon, scoop the flesh into the bowl. Using kitchen scissors, chop the vegetables which are in the bowl.

Increase the oven temperature to 190°C/375°F/Gas 5. Brush 1 or 2 baking sheets with oil and place all the vegetable shells on them.

Heat 1 tablespoon of olive oil in a frying-pan and add the chopped onion and bacon. Cook gently for 4–5 minutes until tender. Stir in the flesh from the vegetables, the chopped tomato then the meat, rice, parsley, thyme, garlic, salt and pepper. Cook, stirring occasionally, for 3–4 minutes then remove from the heat and stir in the eggs. Divide between the vegetable shells then sprinkle the cheese and breadcrumbs over the tops. Trickle over the remaining olive oil and bake for about 20 minutes. Serve hot, warm or cold.

PROVENCE

Pissaladière

ONION AND ANCHOVY TART

This is Nice's special onion tart. It is sold in markets, bakeries, *traiteurs* and charcuteries. It is eaten in restaurants, on picnics, in the streets, at home, by the seashore. As always in France, every cook has their very own definite way of making the best *Pissaladière*, including me. Some love a thick soft crust, some a light crisp one, some have a thin layer of onions, some cover the base with a thick blanket of onion purée, some add garlic and thyme and some prefer anchovy fillets to the traditional puréed anchovies (called *pissalat*, hence the name of the tart).

SERVES 4

FOR THE DOUGH

225 g (8 oz) strong white plain flour
1 teaspoon salt
2 teaspoons easy-blend yeast
onion liquid (see method)
lukewarm water (see method)
4 teaspoons olive oil

FOR THE FILLING

2 tablespoons olive oil
1.25 kg (2½ lb) medium-sized yellow
onions, thinly sliced
2 garlic cloves, crushed
1 bay leaf
3 sprigs of fresh thyme
salt and freshly ground black pepper

FOR THE GARNISH

1½ tablespoons fresh thyme
15 anchovy fillets, halved lengthways
about 16 whole, small black
Nice olives, or 12 large, oil-cured
black olives, stoned and halved
1 teaspoon olive oil
freshly ground black pepper
fresh basil leaves (optional)

For the filling, heat the oil in a large frying-pan, add the onions, garlic, bay leaf, thyme, salt and pepper (the salt will draw water from the onions, preventing them drying) and cook gently, stirring occasionally, with a wooden spoon, for about 1½ hours until the onions are very soft. Remove from the heat, discard the bay leaf and thyme then squeeze the onions gently to one side of the pan with a slotted spoon, draining off the liquid into a measuring jug. Make up to 150 ml (5 fl oz) with the water.

Sift the flour and salt into a large bowl. Stir in the yeast, form a well in the centre, and slowly pour in the onion liquid and 1 teaspoon of olive oil, stirring constantly to make a smooth dough. Beat well until the dough comes away from the sides of the bowl, then transfer to a lightly floured surface and knead well by stretching the dough away from you using the heel of one hand to push the dough from the centre outwards. Pull it back with the fingers, slap it on the work surface and repeat the process, turning the dough slightly with each movement. Continue for about 15 minutes until the dough is soft, smooth and elastic. Add a little more olive oil if it is not supple enough. Form the dough into a ball, place in an oiled bowl and turn it over. Cover with a damp cloth and leave in a warm place until doubled in volume, about 1¼-1½ hours.

Pre-heat the oven to 220°C/425°F/Gas 7. Oil a 23 x 33 cm (9 x 13 in) Swiss-roll tin or a 25–28 cm (10–11 in) round, flat tin.

Turn the dough on to a lightly floured surface, and punch it down. Roll out the dough using a lightly floured rolling pin, to a rectangle approximately 23 x 33 cm (9 x 13 in) or 25–28 cm (10–11 in) round. Lightly fold one half of the dough back over the rolling pin then carefully transfer to the baking tin. Press the dough into the corners and slightly up the sides.

Taste the onion purée to check that the seasoning is correct and then spoon it evenly over the dough. Sprinkle over the thyme. Arrange the anchovy fillets on top in a lattice pattern or like the spokes of a wheel if using a round tin, and place olives in the spaces. Sprinkle the top with olive oil and freshly ground black pepper.

Bake in the pre-heated oven for 25–35 minutes, depending on the thickness of the base, until the dough has shrunk slightly from the sides of the tin and is golden and crisp. Remove from the oven and serve warm garnished with basil.

If the *Pissaladière* is cooked in advance, sprinkle it with olive oil and re-heat for 15–20 minutes in a pre-heated oven at 150°C/300°F/Gas 2.

NOTE

To use dried yeast, measure 4 tablespoons of the onion/water mixture into a small bowl, and stir in ½ teaspoon of caster sugar. Sprinkle 1½ teaspoons of dried yeast over the surface, stir once and leave until there is a good head of froth, about 10–15 minutes. Pour into the well in the flour with the remaining onion/water mixture.

To use fresh yeast, pour the 150 ml (5 fl oz) of onion/water mixture into a small bowl, crumble over 15 g (½ oz) fresh yeast then blend in using a teaspoon. Add to the flour as in the recipe.

ALSACE

Tarte Flamée

ALSACE PIZZA

This is one of Alsace's most popular dishes. It is baked in special wood ovens at a high temperature for a short time so that the pastry is very crisp but the onions and bacon on top are barely cooked. In a pretty inn, the *Bürestubel* in Pfulgriesheim, just outside Strasbourg, I saw a cook bake 370 *Tartes Flamées* in one evening. They were served piping hot on a long-handled wooden rectangular baker's shovel.

As I tried to reproduce *Tarte Flamée* at home I found that a very hot oven really was important, and that the onions and bacon had to be finely cut and not cooked at all before being put on the dough to be baked. A mixture of soft curd cheese and soured cream makes a good substitute for the fresh cheese used at the *Bürestubel*.

The problem is that once you can make a good *Tarte Flamée* one is never enough, and two, three or four always seem to be needed because it is so easy for everyone to become addicted to them.

FOR 1 *TARTE* SERVING 4 AS A STARTER
275 g (10 oz) strong plain flour
1 teaspoon salt
1½ teaspoons instant dried yeast
120 ml (4 fl oz) warm water
1 egg, beaten
1 teaspoon vegetable oil

FOR THE TOPPING
100 g (4 oz) soft curd cheese
150 ml (5 fl oz) soured cream
salt and freshly ground black pepper
1 tablespoon groundnut oil
100 g (4 oz) streaky bacon, cut into 5 mm (¼ in)
wide strips
1 onion, cut into slivers

Sift the flour and salt into a large bowl and stir in the yeast. Form a well in the centre and pour in the water, egg and oil. Using a wooden spoon, gradually draw the dry ingredients into the liquids then beat well until the dough comes away from the bowl. Turn on to a lightly floured surface and knead for 10–15 minutes until the dough is elastic and smooth. Form into a ball and place in an oiled bowl, cover with a clean, damp cloth, and leave to rise in a warm place for 1 hour.

Pre-heat the oven to 230°C/450°F/Gas 8. Butter a large baking tray.

Turn the dough on to a lightly floured work surface, punch it down then knead briefly before rolling it out as thinly as possible to a rectangle approximately 33 x 23 cm (13 x 9 in). Fold the dough back over the rolling pin and carefully lift it on to the tin. Use your fingers to ease it into shape.

Mix together the cheese, soured cream, salt, pepper and groundnut oil for the topping and spread on the dough. Sprinkle with the bacon and onions. Bake in the oven for 20 minutes until the edges are crisp and slightly charred. Serve hot and eat, rolled or folded, with your fingers.

NOTE

To use dried yeast, measure 2 tablespoons of boiling water into a small bowl, add 2 tablespoons of cold water and stir in ½ teaspoon of caster sugar. Sprinkle 1½ teaspoons of dried yeast over the surface, stir once and leave until there is a good head of froth, about 10–15 minutes. Pour into the well in the flour with the egg yolk and oil and only 50 ml (2 fl oz) more water.

To use fresh yeast, heat the 120 ml (4 fl oz) of water in the recipe until it is lukewarm, pour into a small bowl, crumble over 15 g (½ oz) of fresh yeast, then blend in using a teaspoon. Add to the flour with the egg and oil.

Sauces

LES SAUCES

*I*n classic cuisine, the ruling principle used to be: sauces and more sauces! But with the new appetite for fresh, healthy food and carefully chosen ingredients, we no longer follow the old saying, '*C'est la sauce qui fait passer le poisson*', 'It is the sauce which makes the fish edible'. We now want to taste the fish itself – and the vegetables, the chicken and the lamb – and we don't enjoy cloying sauces. Many of the sauces which we do still enjoy come from regional dishes. Here, the sauces are an integral part of the dish and have absorbed all the juices and seasonings during cooking.

Nouvelle cuisine introduced the idea of coating plates with a sauce then placing a portion of the cooked meat, fish or cake on top so that its appearance and texture, whether crunchy or moist, would not be masked by the sauce. I believe this custom is here to stay.

Sauces should never be used lightly or as a second thought. Whatever the ingredients and cooking method, it does modify both the texture and appearance of a dish. Today, when we choose a sauce we want its flavour to speak loud and clear and we want it to be an integral part of the final dish; neither a mask nor a distraction. A sauce without a sharp, decisive personality which does not relate to its base is like clothes without … an emperor.

THROUGHOUT FRANCE

Sauce Hollandaise

EGG YOLK AND BUTTER SAUCE

Hollandaise Sauce is a grand old lady of French cuisine. Today, few people dare to prepare it at home, and yet once the basic principles are understood this is a simple sauce to master. Since this rich and delicate sauce has no thickening agent, it is very sensitive to heat so if you use the traditional method, a double boiler is a must to heat the egg yolks very gently as the butter is gradually added and absorbed. I will also propose here two simpler ways: the cold butter method and the blender method. Stainless steel pans should be used because aluminium will give an unappetizing grey tone to the sauce.

It is served with steamed fish, vegetables and poached eggs. The sauce can be chilled for up to two days.

MAKES ABOUT (300 ML) 10 FL OZ
2 tablespoons white wine vinegar
1 tablespoon water
1 teaspoon crushed white peppercorns
3 egg yolks
salt and freshly ground white pepper
175 g (6 oz) butter, cut into walnut-sized pieces
1 tablespoon cold water (optional)
juice of 1 small lemon, warmed
a pinch of cayenne pepper (optional)

Place the wine vinegar, water and peppercorns in a heavy-based pan, bring to the boil and boil over a high heat until reduced to 1 tablespoon. Place the egg yolks in a heatproof bowl, stir in the reduced wine with a wooden spoon and season with salt and pepper. Place the bowl over a pan of simmering water over a low heat and whisk until the sauce becomes frothy and thickens. Add the pieces of butter one at a time, whisking constantly as you would to make Mayonnaise (see p.101) and waiting until one piece has melted into the sauce before adding the next. The sauce should be thick enough to coat the back of a spoon. The sauce must not become too hot or it will curdle; you must always be able to touch the bowl with your bare hands. If the sauce becomes too thick, slowly whisk in a teaspoonful of water. When all the butter has been absorbed, remove from the heat, add the lemon juice and season to taste with salt and cayenne pepper. To keep the sauce warm, cover the bowl and stand it over a pan of warm but not boiling water. If the sauce starts to curdle, pour it into a cold bowl, add a little warm water or an egg yolk and stir well before returning the sauce to the double boiler.

Cold Butter Method

This is a much quicker method, but remember that the saucepan and the butter must be chilled.

MAKES ABOUT 300 ML (10 FL OZ)
4 egg yolks
2–3 teaspoons lemon juice
¼ teaspoon salt
⅛ teaspoon white pepper
225 g (8 oz) butter, chilled

Cool a saucepan briefly in the fridge. Whisk the egg yolks, lemon juice, salt and pepper in the saucepan until blended. Cut the cold butter into cubes. Place the saucepan over a low heat and add the butter a piece at a time, whisking continuously until the sauce thickens. Keep in a warm container until ready to serve.

Blender Method

A blender makes this sauce child's play. The proportions are a little different from hand-made Hollandaise as you use less butter.

MAKES ABOUT 300 ML (10 FL OZ)
3 egg yolks
¼ teaspoon salt
½ teaspoon freshly ground white pepper
juice of 1 lemon
100 g (4 oz) butter

Place the egg yolks, salt and pepper in a blender and blend at top speed for a few seconds until well mixed. Warm the lemon juice, pour into the blender and blend again until the mixture thickens slightly. Melt the butter. With the blender running at low speed, gradually pour in the hot butter. The sauce will thicken as you add the butter. Pour into a bowl, cover and place over a pan of lukewarm water until ready to use.

NOTE

To serve the sauce with boiled fish, stir in a teaspoon of well-drained capers. Chopped fresh herbs or a little orange juice and grated orange rind may also be added to the Hollandaise.

I will share a well-kept secret here: if the meal lingers or the guests are late and you must keep this sauce thick and smooth, whip one or two tablespoons of Béchamel Sauce (see p.95) into the pan of Hollandaise and your sauce will remain perfect. Restaurants would never admit to it, but most of them do it!

THROUGHOUT FRANCE

Sauce Mousseline

CREAMY HOLLANDAISE SAUCE

There are two *Sauces Mousseline*: a cold one made with whipped cream or egg whites gently blended into a bowl of Mayonnaise and this warm one made with a Hollandaise Sauce which is lovely with soufflés, steamed asparagus and steamed fish.

MAKES ABOUT 400 ML (14 FL OZ)
300 ml (10 fl oz) Hollandaise Sauce (see p.91)
120 ml (4 fl oz) whipping cream, chilled

Prepare the Hollandaise. Beat the cream in a chilled bowl until stiff. Fold the cream into the warm Hollandaise just before serving, whipping until it is frothy. Keep the sauce warm over a pan of warm water until ready to serve.

Sauce Bordelaise

WINE, HERB AND SHALLOT SAUCE

Sauce Bordelaise used to be prepared with a *fond brun* – a rich stock made from bones, meat and bacon rinds which was simmered for hours – with shallots and white wine. But times have changed even in Bordeaux. *Sauce Bordelaise* is now prepared with a reduction of shallots, herbs and red wine and without a stock base. It is served with grilled meats, but also with poached eggs. In Paris, a variation of this sauce is called *A la Marchand de Vin*, in the style of a wine merchant. This pungent version of the sauce, made with or without bone marrow, is one I use with beef.

MAKES ABOUT 250 ML (8 FL OZ)

300 ml (10 fl oz) Bordeaux red wine
3 shallots, coarsely chopped
3 tablespoons beef stock
1 garlic clove, crushed
½ teaspoon freshly grated nutmeg
2 teaspoons dried thyme
2 bay leaves
a pinch of cayenne pepper
salt and coarsely ground black pepper
100 g (4 oz) beef marrow bones (optional)
1 tablespoon brandy
3 tablespoons butter

Heat the wine then add the shallots, stock, garlic, nutmeg, thyme, bay leaves, cayenne pepper, salt and pepper. Bring to the boil then simmer, uncovered, until reduced to one-third of the original amount.

Meanwhile, wrap the marrow bones, if using, in a piece of muslin and plunge them into a pan of boiling water. Simmer for 15 minutes then drain.

Add the brandy to the sauce and remove it from the heat. Swirl in the butter a little at a time then place the sauce back over a low heat, stirring for a few minutes. Just before serving, slide the marrow out of the bone, finely chop the marrow and stir it into the sauce.

Sauce Raïto

WINE, TOMATO AND HERB SAUCE

This spirited sauce has such fragrance, that spooned over chicken, veal, fried or baked fish, *morue*, pasta, vegetables, fritters or even poached eggs, it transforms them instantly into a Provençal treat. Traditionally, *Sauce Raïto* was made at Christmas time with *vin cuit*, a fortified home-made wine, but a red vermouth, a sweet wine, even a hearty red wine will make an honourable *Sauce Raïto* any time.

MAKES ABOUT 600 ML (1 PINT)

2 tablespoons olive oil
3 medium onions, finely chopped
600 ml (1 pint) sweet red vermouth, sweet Banyuls,
red Muscat or a good hearty red wine
300 ml (10 fl oz) water
2 garlic cloves, crushed
4 plump ripe tomatoes, skinned, seeded and chopped
2 cloves
2 teaspoons dried thyme
2 teaspoons dried savory
2 bay leaves
1 teaspoon fennel seeds or aniseeds (optional)
salt and freshly ground black pepper
2 tablespoons purple or black olives in brine or
plump, black oil-cured olives from Nyons, Italy or
Greece, stoned and coarsely chopped
3 teaspoons capers, chopped
3 teaspoons chopped gherkins (optional)
2 tablespoons chopped fresh flatleaf parsley

Heat the oil and fry the onions for about 15 minutes until soft. Add the wine and water and simmer for a few minutes, uncovered. Add the garlic, tomatoes, cloves, thyme, savory, bay leaves, fennel seeds or aniseeds, if using, salt and pepper and simmer for 1 hour, uncovered, until the sauce is quite thick. Discard the bay leaves. Purée the sauce in a food processor or rub through a sieve. Stir in the olives, capers, gherkins and parsley. Pour over warm meat, fish or vegetables.

NOTE

Sometimes a few pounded walnuts are added to the *Sauce Raïto* at the end of cooking to thicken the sauce.

BURGUNDY

Sauce Meurette
WINE SAUCE

This Burgundian sauce makes the most of Burgundy's favourite ingredients. It is used to coat poached eggs served on garlic toasts, but it is also served with freshwater fish.

There is no need to use a great wine, a good hearty one will do. *Meurette* is made with red wine in Burgundy, but is prepared with white wine elsewhere in France. It is an unctuous, rich sauce. Lately, experimental chefs are serving it as a single reduction of wine and herbs. Their *Meurette* is fresh and light but it lacks the explosive flavours and the velvety texture we like in this sauce. This makes enough for four people.

MAKES ABOUT 900 ML (1½ PINTS)
2 tablespoons butter
75 g (3 oz) streaky bacon, cut into small slivers
1 large onion, chopped
2 carrots, chopped
2 garlic cloves, chopped
1 leek, white part only, chopped
1.2 litres (2 pints) hearty red wine
2 bay leaves
1 sprig of fresh thyme
1 clove
5 peppercorns
1 teaspoon butter kneaded with 1 teaspoon plain flour (Beurre Manié, see p. 101) or 1 teaspoon arrowroot (optional)
1 teaspoon sugar (optional)
salt and freshly ground black pepper
1 tablespoon marc brandy (optional)

FOR THE GARNISH
2 slices bread made into Garlic Croûtons (see p. 233)

Heat the butter in a frying-pan and sauté the bacon for 1 minute. Add the onion and cook for 5 minutes. Add the carrots, garlic and leek and cook over a low heat until soft. Add the wine, herbs, clove and peppercorns, bring to the boil then simmer, uncovered, for about 30 minutes until reduced by half. Rub the sauce through a sieve, pounding the vegetables with a wooden spoon. Return the sauce to a low heat.

If you are using the sauce for *Oeufs en Meurette* (see p. 108), it is ready to serve. If you are using the sauce with meat or fish, whisk in the *Beurre Manié* or arrowroot to thicken the sauce and simmer for 5 minutes. Add a little sugar if the sauce is too acid. Season to taste with salt and pepper then add the brandy. Serve with garlic Croûtons.

THROUGHOUT FRANCE

Sauce Béchamel

WHITE SAUCE

Béchamel Sauce is indeed the most versatile of sauces. It can be prepared in only a few minutes using milk, cream or broth, and is not only used with fish, chicken, veal, eggs and vegetables, but also provides the base for many soups, gratins and soufflés.

Cream, egg yolks and spices can all be used to improve on a basic Béchamel Sauce. Grated cheese, tomato purée, chopped mushrooms, all kinds of spices such as curry or saffron and a great variety of other ingredients can be added to create a range of different sauces.

For a delicate *Sauce Parisienne* or *Sauce Poulette*, prepare a pan of Béchamel. Blend 2 egg yolks and 8 tablespoons of single cream in a bowl then blend in a little of the Béchamel Sauce. Stir for a few minutes then pour the smooth mixture into the rest of the warm Béchamel, stirring until it just reaches boiling point. Remove from the heat immediately, stir in the juice of a lemon and serve at once.

MAKES ABOUT 300 ML (10 FL OZ)
1 tablespoon butter
1½ tablespoons plain flour
300 ml (10 fl oz) milk or beef, chicken or vegetable stock
salt
a pinch of freshly grated nutmeg
a pinch of cayenne pepper

Slowly melt the butter in a heavy-based pan. Stir in the flour and cook on a low heat for 3–4 minutes, stirring with a wooden spoon, until the mixture froths without turning brown. Meanwhile, heat the milk or stock in a separate pan just to boiling point. Remove the butter and flour from the heat and stir for a few seconds until cooled slightly. Add the hot milk or stock and whisk vigorously until smooth. Season to taste with salt, nutmeg and cayenne pepper. Return the sauce to a low heat and bring to the boil. Reduce the heat and simmer for 5–10 minutes, stirring steadily, until smooth and velvety. Check and adjust the seasoning to taste.

You can keep the sauce on a low heat for immediate use or pour it into a bowl, add a little milk or a dot of butter on top to prevent a skin forming then re-heat gently when required.

For a richer sauce, add a tablespoon of butter or a few tablespoons of single cream to the sauce, stirring for a few minutes. If you do find a few lumps, rub the sauce through a metal sieve. You can thin your Béchamel Sauce with either milk or stock.

Sauce Soubise

ONION SAUCE

This is prepared with a Béchamel base flavoured with an onion purée. I use lots of onions for a stronger flavour, but half the quantity would still make a tasty sauce. Serve *Sauce Soubise* with eggs, chicken, lamb or vegetables.

MAKES ABOUT 300 ML (10 FL OZ)
3 tablespoons butter
225 g (8 oz) onions, sliced
1 quantity Béchamel Sauce (see p. 95)
2 tablespoons double cream
a pinch of freshly grated nutmeg
a pinch of sugar
salt and freshly ground black pepper

Heat 2 tablespoons of the butter, add the onions, cover and cook over a medium heat for about 15 minutes, stirring occasionally, until they are soft but not brown. Purée in a food processor or rub through a sieve.

Prepare the Béchamel Sauce. Stir in the onions and whisk vigorously until smooth. When you are ready to serve, stir in the remaining butter and cream and season to taste with nutmeg, sugar, salt and pepper.

NOTE

Sometimes a little white wine or beef broth is added to the onion purée and the mixture is reduced for a few minutes before adding it to the Béchamel Sauce.

Sauce Mornay

CHEESE SAUCE

This delicate sauce made with a Béchamel base is perfect for poached eggs, grilled fish or veal, poached chicken, steamed vegetables and also to coat crêpes and gratins. Don't let it reach boiling point. Only stir in the cheese at the last moment or the sauce will become rubbery.

If the sauce is used with fish, add 2 tablespoons of the fish cooking liquid. If it is served with poultry, add a little of the cooking juices. If you use Mornay Sauce to cover crêpes or gratins, use only 50 g (2 oz) of cheese to prevent it from becoming stringy.

MAKES ABOUT 300 ML (10 FL OZ)
1 quantity Béchamel Sauce (see p. 95)
3 egg yolks
3 tablespoons single cream (or more for a thinner sauce)
50–100 g (2–4 oz) Gruyère or Gruyère and Parmesan, grated
salt
a pinch of cayenne pepper
a pinch of freshly grated nutmeg
1 teaspoon butter

Prepare the Béchamel Sauce. Beat the egg yolks and cream together. Add the hot Béchamel Sauce, stirring vigorously. Pour the mixture into a pan and simmer over a low heat for a few minutes, stirring continuously. Stir in the cheese and let it melt. When the sauce is smooth, season to taste with salt, cayenne pepper and nutmeg and remove it from the heat. Spread a little butter on the top to prevent a skin forming.

Sauce Béarnaise

EGG YOLK AND BUTTER SAUCE FLAVOURED WITH
SHALLOTS, WINE AND HERBS

This wonderful sauce is another grand old lady so intimidating that few ever dare make it at home without qualms. It is a more concentrated cousin of the Hollandaise, using vinegar instead of lemon juice and flavoured with lively tarragon.

It should be prepared in a stainless steel or copper saucepan, not aluminium as this will give a grey colouring to the sauce. It tastes delicious with grilled meat or fish, egg dishes, steamed vegetables and vegetable flans.

If you are nervous of trying this traditional method, experiment with the quicker technique.

MAKES ABOUT 250 ML (8 FL OZ)
175 g (6 oz) butter
2 tablespoons red wine vinegar
2 tablespoons dry white wine
3 tablespoons finely chopped shallots (about 3 small shallots)
1 tablespoon chopped fresh tarragon
½ teaspoon coarsely ground black peppercorns
salt
2 small egg yolks
1 tablespoon water
1 tablespoon chopped fresh chives, parsley or tarragon
a pinch of cayenne pepper

Melt the butter over a low heat or in the top of a double boiler over gently simmering water. Skim and discard the white particles from the top and keep the butter lukewarm.

Heat the wine vinegar, wine, shallots, tarragon, peppercorns and a pinch of salt in a stainless steel pan and let the mixture simmer, uncovered, for about 5 minutes until reduced

to about 1 large tablespoon. Rub the mixture through a sieve and let it cool.

Stir the egg yolks into the shallot-vinegar mixture in a heatproof bowl or the top of a double boiler. Add a pinch of salt, 1 tablespoon of the melted butter and the water and beat vigorously with a whisk. Place the bowl over a pan of hot water over a gentle heat and continue to beat vigorously. When the mixture starts to thicken, add the remaining melted butter a little at a time, stirring continuously until the sauce has the consistency of a custard. Remove from the heat, stir in the herbs and season to taste with salt and cayenne pepper. Keep the sauce covered with a plate on top of the pan of lukewarm water until ready to use. It is served lukewarm, never hot.

Quick Béarnaise Sauce

MAKES ABOUT 250 ML (8 FL OZ)
2 tablespoons red wine vinegar
2 tablespoons dry white wine
3 tablespoons finely chopped shallots
1 tablespoon chopped fresh tarragon
salt and freshly ground black pepper
2 egg yolks
100 g (4 oz) butter

Heat the wine vinegar, wine, shallots, tarragon and seasoning in a stainless steel pan and simmer, uncovered, for about 5 minutes until reduced to about 1 large tablespoon. Rub the mixture through a sieve into a cold bowl, add the egg yolks and whisk until blended.

Melt the butter until liquid and bubbling. Pour the hot butter gradually into the egg yolk mixture while beating on medium speed with an electric hand whisk. The sauce will thicken with the heat of the butter. Pour into a warm sauce boat and serve.

NOTE

To rescue the sauce if it does not blend, add 1 to 2 teaspoons of water and whisk vigorously. Alternatively, pour 2 teaspoons of water into a cold bowl and gradually whisk in the sauce.

SOUTH-WEST

Sauce de Sorges

COOKED EGG SAUCE WITH SHALLOTS AND HERBS

A favourite in the south-west, this sauce is often served with a poached chicken.

MAKES ABOUT 250 ML (8 FL OZ)
2 eggs
135 ml (4½ fl oz) groundnut oil, olive and ground-
nut oil or groundnut and walnut oil
3 tablespoons red wine vinegar
3 tablespoons chopped fresh herbs
1 tablespoon finely chopped shallot
salt and freshly ground black pepper

Place the eggs in a pan of water, bring to the boil and boil for 2 minutes. Remove from the pan and dip in cold water. Peel the eggs and separate them carefully. The yolks should be soft. If the whites are still runny, return them to the boiling water for a further 1 minute. Whisk together the oil, wine vinegar, herbs and shallot and season with salt and pepper. Stir in the soft egg yolks. Chop the egg whites and stir them gently into the sauce.

LANGUEDOC

Sauce Aillade

WALNUT AND GARLIC SAUCE

A speciality of Languedoc, *Sauce Aillade* is often served with *Magrets de Canard* (see p.162). The proportions vary considerably from household to household so experiment and choose what-ever quantities of walnuts and garlic you prefer. Bottles of walnut oil should be refrigerated after opening. This is a thick sauce.

MAKES ABOUT 300 ML (10 FL OZ)
3 garlic cloves, crushed
handful of walnuts, peeled
¼ teaspoon salt
freshly ground black pepper
150 ml (5 fl oz) walnut oil or walnut and groundnut
oil
2 tablespoons red wine vinegar
1 soft-boiled egg yolk
1 tablespoon chopped fresh parsley

Pound the garlic and walnuts to a paste in a mortar. Blend in the salt, pepper, oil and wine vinegar. Add the egg yolk and when it is well blended, add the parsley.

NOTE

In the eastern part of Provence and in Savoie, a similar sauce made with walnuts, garlic and olive oil is used to top hot pasta and tiny cheese ravioli.

Coulis de Tomates

TOMATO SAUCE

In the south-west and Provence, *Coulis* is a cooked sauce prepared with ripe tomatoes and herbs. It is traditionally used either as the base for or the accompaniment to many dishes such as *Potée* (see p.194), *Pot au Feu* (see p.198), pasta, boiled rice, grilled fish, sautéed squid, stuffed lamb and poached or fried eggs. It is also used to deglaze chicken, fish or meat cooking juices in the bottom of their cooking pan. Sprinkled with a handful of chopped fresh herbs, it can turn into a last-minute, fragrant soup.

Today we still love this traditional *Coulis*, but we also prepare another version with raw tomatoes for a fresher flavour. Raw *Coulis* is served lukewarm or cold with poached eggs, stuffed vegetables, grilled peppers, cold beef or poached fish. For a healthy snack, rub a piece of toast with a cut garlic clove then spread a little raw *Coulis* on top.

Store *Coulis* in sterilized screw-top jars for 3 to 4 days in the fridge since tomatoes ferment easily. The oil will float to the top to protect the *Coulis*.

Cooked Coulis

MAKES ABOUT 600 ML (1 PINT)
2 tablespoons olive oil
2 onions, chopped
2 garlic cloves, chopped
900 g (2 lb) ripe tomatoes, skinned, seeded and coarsely chopped
2 bay leaves
2 teaspoons dried thyme
5 cm (2 in) piece of orange peel, dried in a low oven for 15 minutes
1 teaspoon sugar

handful of basil leaves (optional)
3 tablespoons chopped fresh flatleaf parsley
½ teaspoon cayenne pepper
salt

Heat the oil and fry the onions and 1 of the cloves of garlic over a low heat for 10 minutes until soft. Add the tomatoes, bay leaves, thyme, orange peel and sugar, bring to the boil and simmer, uncovered, for 20 minutes on a fairly high heat so that most of the water evaporates. Rub through a sieve for a smooth consistency. Add the remaining garlic, the basil and parsley and season to taste with cayenne pepper and salt. If the sauce is too thin, cook it for a further 10 minutes, uncovered. Add a drop of olive oil; it will rise to the surface and protect the sauce. Leave to cool then chill in tightly-closed sterilized jars or freeze.

Re-heat the sauce on a low heat as needed.

Raw Coulis

MAKES ABOUT 600 ML (1 PINT)
900 g (2 lb) ripe tomatoes
1 tablespoon chopped fresh basil
a pinch of ground coriander
1 tablespoon chopped fresh parsley
2 spring onions or tiny fresh onions, finely chopped
salt and freshly ground black pepper
3 tablespoons olive oil

There are two ways to prepare raw *Coulis*.

The first way is to dip the tomatoes in a pan of hot water then skin them with a sharp knife. Seed and chop them into small dice then mix them with the remaining ingredients.

The second way is to prepare the sauce in a food processor. Prepare the tomatoes as above, then place all the ingredients in the blender and process for about 3 minutes.

Sauce Fleurette à l'Estragon
TARRAGON CREAM SAUCE

A delicate, cold sauce used for green and mixed salads.

MAKES ABOUT 300 ML (10 FL OZ)
½ teaspoon Dijon mustard
1 teaspoon red wine vinegar
300 ml (10 fl oz) single cream
1 teaspoon chopped fresh tarragon leaves
salt and freshly ground black pepper

Stir the mustard into the vinegar then add the cream, tarragon, salt and pepper. When the mixture is well blended, correct the seasoning and serve.

Beurre Manié
KNEADED BUTTER

Sauces can be thickened by slow simmering; by whisking in butter, cream or egg yolks; by adding tomato, onion or carrot purées; or by stirring a little arrowroot or potato flour, diluted in cold water, into the hot sauce. But *Beurre Manié* remains the quickest and safest way to turn a sauce or broth into a velvety mixture. Keep the sauce simmering and do not let it reach boiling point.

FOR 300 ML (10 FL OZ) HOT LIQUID
2 tablespoons butter
2 tablespoons plain flour

Knead the butter and flour with a fork or between your fingers to a paste. Divide it into pea-sized balls for easy cooking. Toss a piece of beurre manié into the pan of hot stock or sauce and shake the pan a few times. Simmer the sauce for a few minutes, whisking gently and adding the beurre manié a little at a time until the sauce reaches the desired consistency.

NOTE

A *roux* is an alternative to *beurre manié* made with equal quantities of butter and flour kneaded and heated together, and is used at the beginning of cooking a sauce. It can be made in advance for later use. Melt the butter in a pan over a low heat, add the flour and stir or whisk constantly for about 2 minutes for a white roux, and up to 10 minutes for a deeper brown colour. Add the liquid, remove the roux from the heat and whisk constantly until all the liquid has been absorbed. Return the sauce to the heat and stir until it reaches boiling point.

Mayonnaise

Mayonnaise is one of the most useful of sauces, and it is one of the easiest to prepare despite what some people believe. All the ingredients should be at room temperature, a tea towel should be placed under the bowl to prevent it from sliding as you beat the sauce with a whisk or fork, and the oil must be added slowly. If the Mayonnaise separates, place a fresh egg yolk in a clean bowl, add a little mustard and start stirring, slowly adding the curdled mixture until the sauce is silky and firm. You can use all groundnut oil if you prefer.

MAKES ABOUT 300 ML (10 FL OZ)
1 large egg yolk
1 teaspoon Dijon mustard
120 ml (4 fl oz) olive oil
120 ml (4 fl oz) groundnut oil
1½ teaspoons wine vinegar or the juice of a lemon
salt and freshly ground black pepper

Beat the egg yolk and mustard with a hand whisk for 1 minute, then beat in about a quarter of the oil, a drop at a time, until it is incorporated into the sauce. When there is a tablespoon or so of firm Mayonnaise you can proceed a little more quickly but always with an attentive eye and a steady hand. When all the oil has been absorbed, add the wine vinegar or lemon juice to taste and season with salt and pepper.

VARIATIONS

Lemon Mayonnaise Omit the wine vinegar and add about 1½ teaspoons of lemon juice.

Herb Mayonnaise Stir 2 tablespoons of chopped mixed fresh herbs into the mayonnaise.

Curry Mayonnaise Stir 2 teaspoons of curry powder into the mayonnaise.

Sauce Gribiche

PIQUANT HARD-BOILED EGGS 'MAYONNAISE'

This spirited sauce, made with hard-boiled eggs, is used with cold fish, shellfish, cuts of meat and chicken.

MAKES ABOUT 300 ML (10 FL OZ)
2 hard-boiled eggs with crumbly yolks, separated
2 teaspoons Dijon mustard
salt and freshly ground black pepper
10 fl oz (300 ml) olive oil or groundnut oil
1 tablespoon red wine vinegar
2 teaspoons finely chopped gherkins
2 teaspoons capers, chopped
2 teaspoons chopped fresh parsley or chervil

Press the egg yolks through a sieve into a bowl then stir in the mustard and season with salt and pepper. Blend the ingredients to a paste; only when it is very silky and smooth will it absorb the oil. Slowly pour in the oil and whisk with a wire whisk as you would for Mayonnaise (see p.92) until the mixture thickens. Slowly add the wine vinegar. Place the chopped gherkins with the capers in a little piece of muslin and squeeze to extract the excess moisture then stir them into the sauce with the parsley or chervil. Press the egg whites through a sieve and stir them into the sauce. Check and correct the seasoning with oil, wine vinegar, salt or pepper.

NOTE

Sauce Ravigote is a cousin of *Sauce Gribiche* and *Sauce Tartare*. It is prepared in the same way but without the eggs and with the addition of a minced onion.

Sauce Verte

GREEN MAYONNAISE

There are two equally interesting versions of *Sauce Verte.*

Sauce Verte 1

This is served with cold fish, meat or poultry, shellfish, or grilled fish. It is a Mayonnaise sauce enriched with herbs. It is sometimes called *Sauce Vincent* after a famous eighteenth-century cook Vincent Lachapelle.

MAKES ABOUT 300 ML (10 FL OZ)

300 ml (10 fl oz) Mayonnaise (see p. 101)
2 tablespoons chopped fresh chives, chervil, tarragon,
sorrel or parsley (or a mixture of 2 or 3 herbs)
1 tablespoon chopped fresh spinach or watercress
salt and fresly ground black or white pepper

Prepare the Mayonnaise. Plunge the herbs and spinach or watercress into a pan of boiling water and leave to stand for 3 minutes. Drain, rinse under cold water and drain again. Purée in a food processor or crush in a mortar. Whisk this green purée into the Mayonnaise then season to taste with salt and pepper. Cover and chill until ready to serve.

NOTE

I sometimes use blanched spinach and fresh uncooked herbs for a more pungent version of Sauce Verte.

Sauce Verte 2

MAKES ABOUT 300 ML (10 FL OZ)

100 g (4 oz) frozen leaf spinach, thawed and
drained thoroughly
1 hard-boiled egg, peeled
5 anchovy fillets
1 slice white bread, crusts removed and moistened
150 ml (5 fl oz) olive oil
2 tablespoons red wine vinegar
3 teaspoons chopped gherkins
1 teaspoon chopped capers
salt and freshly ground black pepper

Place the spinach, egg, anchovies, bread, oil and wine vinegar in a food processor and blend until smooth. Pour into a bowl, stir in the gherkins and capers and season to taste.

Sauce Rémoulade

MAYONNAISE FLAVOURED WITH ANCHOVIES,
SHALLOTS AND HERBS

This lively, cold sauce based on Mayonnaise is easy to make and instantly transforms a bowl of steamed shellfish or left-over poultry, fish or vegetables into an interesting starter.

MAKES ABOUT 350 ML (12 FL OZ)

300 ml (10 fl oz) Mayonnaise (see p. 101)
1 tablespoon chopped gherkins
2 teaspoons Dijon mustard
2 shallots, finely chopped
1 tablespoon capers (optional)
1 tablespoon chopped fresh, preferably flatleaf, parsley
1 tablespoon chopped fresh tarragon or chervil
2 anchovy fillets, chopped (optional)

Prepare the Mayonnaise. Stir all the ingredients gently into the Mayonnaise. The sauce will keep for a few days in a screw-top jar in the fridge.

Eggs

LES OEUFS

Eggs are the symbols of life; the richest and the simplest of foods. When I was a child, this was taken literally, and whenever we felt tired or listless at school we had to swallow the yolk of a raw egg beaten with orange water and sugar; or worse, to suck the pierced shell of a raw egg for instant energy. Now, the thought of an uncooked egg gives me the shivers. But we do have an enormous repertoire of recipes for frying, stuffing and baking eggs, and for transforming them into a rich variety of omelettes, sauces, and soufflés. The possibilities of egg preparation in French cooking are a measure of one's imagination – limitless.

There are a few points to remember: freshness is all-important. Eggs must be free-range, dated, and kept chilled. A fresh egg should have a plump yolk covered with some of the white, the rest of the white is more liquid. There should be no microbes within an egg, so always rinse the shell of an egg before using it. Always add a drop of vinegar to the boiling water when you cook eggs and remember they must be at room temperature before you boil them so the shell will not crack.

Red wine and eggs don't get along at the table, so serve water or at best a dry white wine or a light rosé.

Oeufs Pochés
POACHED EGGS

Break the eggs into a bowl so that you can check that the yolks are firm and the eggs are very fresh. Add ½ a teaspoon of vinegar for each egg but no salt as it will prevent the whites from coagulating. Bring a wide pan of water to a rolling boil. Carefully slide the eggs into the boiling water so that the bubbles shape the whites neatly. Don't cook too many eggs at once or they will reduce the temperature of the water. Simmer for about 4 minutes so that the yolks remain soft when lightly pressed. Remove the eggs from the pan with a slotted spoon and trim the whites with scissors before serving.

You can keep the eggs warm in a pan of warm salted water. If you wish to re-heat a poached egg, place it in a bowl and carefully pour over some boiling water. Leave it to stand for 2 minutes. Snip off the loose bits of egg white with scissors.

You can serve poached eggs on toast, on a bed of warm ratatouille or a layer of warm watercress purée. You can place each egg in a hollow scooped out of a baked jacket potato or of a cooked, trimmed artichoke and spoon some sauce over the top. A variety of sauces can be served: Béarnaise (see p.97), Hollandaise (see p. 91) to make Eggs Benedict, Mornay (see p. 96), Mousseline (see p.92), Meurette (see p. 94), Béchamel (see p.95) or *Coulis de Tomates* (see p.99).

Oeufs Mollets
EGGS MOLLETS

These are soft-boiled eggs cooked in their shells until the white is firm but the yolk soft. Bring a pan of water to the boil then gently lower the eggs into the water and simmer for 5–6 minutes. Remove the eggs from the pan with a slotted spoon and plunge them into a bowl of cold water for a minute. Tap them lightly with the back of a knife to make them easier to shell, then rinse under cold water.

Re-heat in a pan of hot water for 3–5 minutes before using. They can be arranged on a bed of cooked spinach, covered with Béchamel Sauce (see p. 95) and then baked.

Oeufs Frits
FRIED EGGS

Fried eggs are usually cooked gently in a lightly greased frying-pan until the whites are firm and lightly browned underneath. Alternatively, pre-heat the oven to 180°C/350°F/Gas 4 and separate the eggs. For each person, add ½ teaspoon butter and ½ teaspoon water (to prevent the whites from browning) to a small round cast iron or enamel dish and sprinkle with a little salt. Heat over a medium heat then add the egg whites and place in the oven for about 2 minutes; the top should remain soft. Sprinkle with a few drops of red wine vinegar then slide in the egg yolks on top. Return to the oven for a further 2 minutes. Season to taste.

Oeufs Miroir
SHIRRED EGGS

Also known as *Oeufs au Plat* and *Oeufs sur le Plat*, shirred eggs are broken into a buttered flameproof dish then basted with either plain butter or browned cooked butter, herbs, cream or cheese, or they can be broken on to a bed of softly cooked vegetables. Cook them under a hot grill for about 3½ minutes until the white is just softly set and the yolk still liquid.

NOTE

A more sophisticated version is prepared when you separate yolks and white. Pour a little butter and a drop of oil into a flameproof dish, sprinkle with salt and heat on top of the stove for a minute. Add the egg whites then bake in a medium oven for 1½ minutes. Sprinkle with salt and wine vinegar then add the egg yolks and bake for 2 minutes. Serve with *Mouillettes* of bread sprinkled with chopped herbs (see p. 69). It is complicated, but you are sure that the egg white is firm and that the egg yolk is moist but warm.

Oeufs Brouillés
SCRAMBLED EGGS

Scrambled eggs are made by beating whole eggs with salt and pepper and just enough water to blend. Pour most of the mixture into a lightly buttered pan and cook over a low heat for about 5 minutes, stirring slowly and continuously with a wooden spoon. When the eggs begin to scramble and thicken, pour in the reserved egg with your chosen seasonings: cream, butter, chopped fresh herbs, chopped ham, grated cheese or chopped mushrooms and heat through gently. Remove from the heat and keep stirring until the mixture is slightly thinner than you prefer, as the eggs will continue to cook off the heat. Scrambled eggs can be prepared 15–20 minutes in advance, covered and kept in a warm place. They should be highly seasoned and remain creamy.

The regional version is called *Brouillade* (see p. 113).

Piperade

This is *the* Basque omelette. The word *piperade* comes from the dialect word for red pepper, *piper*. Generally it is a flat pepper and tomato omelette, but sometimes *Piperade* is a soft scrambled egg mixture which is served with warm cured ham. I have also seen it prepared like a moist rolled omelette stuffed with cooked peppers and tomatoes. The following creamy egg and vegetable purée is supposed to be the authentic recipe.

SERVES 4

4 tablespoons olive and groundnut oil or half goose fat and half oil
900 g (2 lb) large tomatoes, skinned, seeded and chopped
1 large red pepper, seeded and chopped
1 green pepper, seeded and chopped
a pinch of cayenne pepper or 1 tiny chilli pepper, seeded and chopped
2 onions, chopped
2 garlic cloves crushed
1 sprig of fresh thyme or 2 teaspoons dried thyme
2 bay leaves
1 tablespoon chopped fresh parsley
salt and freshly ground black pepper
7 eggs, beaten
1 tablespoon butter
2 tablespoons goose fat or 3 tablespoons olive oil
4 thin slices cured Bayonne or prosciutto ham, cut into thin slivers.

Heat 3 tablespoons of the oil in a frying-pan and sauté the tomatoes, peppers, cayenne pepper or chilli pepper, onions, garlic and herbs. Simmer gently for about 45 minutes to 1 hour until most of the liquid has evaporated and the mixture becomes thick and unctuous. Season with salt and a little cayenne pepper to taste. Purée in a food processor or rub through a sieve. Return the mixture to the pan and simmer gently, uncovered, until reduced to about 750 ml (1¼ pints). Leave to cool.

Heat the remaining oil in a frying-pan. Pour in the vegetable mixture and bring to the boil over a medium heat, stirring. Add the eggs and stir the mixture in a circular motion with a wooden spoon, working from the edges of the pan to the centre until the eggs are creamy but firm. Taste and season to taste with salt and pepper and stir in the butter.

Meanwhile, heat the goose fat or oil and fry the ham.

Arrange the creamy *Piperade* in a shallow, warm serving platter and place the ham on top.

NOTE

Stoned black olives are sometimes added at the last minute. The ham can also be served on a separate plate, sliced or cut into slivers and sautéed.

BURGUNDY

Oeufs en Meurette

EGGS IN WINE SAUCE

A potent Burgundian dish, this makes a spirited lunch if you serve it with an endive or dandelion tossed salad. It also makes a lovely starter for dinner. The sauce improves if it is prepared in advance and re-heated.

SERVES 4

FOR THE SAUCE
1 quantity Sauce Meurette (see p.94)
1 teaspoon sugar
salt and freshly ground black pepper

FOR THE EGGS
1 tablespoon red wine vinegar
4 eggs

FOR THE CROUTONS
2 tablespoons butter
1 tablespoon oil
3 slices bread, cut into triangles
2 garlic cloves, halved

TO SERVE
3 tablespoons chopped fresh flatleaf parsley

Prepare the Sauce Meurette. Season to taste with sugar, salt and pepper.

Bring a wide pan of water to the boil and add the vinegar. Do not add salt as this will prevent the whites from coagulating. When the water is boiling vigorously, break each egg into a ladle and slide it into the hot water in one quick movement so that the white coagulates at once around the yolk. When all the eggs are in the water, lower the heat and simmer for 3 minutes.

Meanwhile, prepare the Croûtons. Heat the butter and oil in a frying-pan and sauté the bread on both sides until crisp. Remove from the pan and rub on both sides with the garlic.

Remove the poached eggs from the pan with a slotted spoon and trim any extra bits of egg white with scissors. Place the eggs on a warmed serving dish, spoon over the hot sauce and garnish with the Croûtons. Serve sprinkled with the parsley. Or else place the eggs on top of the Croûtons and spoon the sauce over.

LYONNAIS

Gâteau de Foies de Volailles

CHICKEN LIVER CUSTARD

One of the great traditions of Lyon is that of the *mères*: those formidable women who helped create the city's reputation for gastronomy. In the late nineteenth and early twentieth century, women used to take in paying guests. Little by little, these *mères* started restaurants which served the same hearty home cooking but with a definite touch of refinement. The names of the women are still reflected in the names of Lyonnais restaurants – *Mère Guy*, *Mère Fillioux*, *Chez Lea*, *Chez Paulette* and, one of the last great *mère* restaurants which still has a woman at the helm, *Mère Brazier*. Jacquotte Brazier keeps up the traditional dishes – *poularde demi-deuil*, *fonds d'artichauts au fois gras* and *gâteau de foies de volailles*. In Lyon, these custards are often cooked in individual ramekins and turned out on a small plate with the tomato sauce poured round.

SERVES 6–8

500 g (1lb 2 oz) chicken livers
5 eggs
500 ml (17 fl oz) single cream
a pinch of freshly grated nutmeg
a few sprigs of fresh parsley, finely chopped
salt and freshly ground black pepper
1 quantity Coulis de Tomates (see p.89)

Pre-heat the oven to 180°C/350°F/Gas 4. Butter a 1.5 litre (2½ pint) soufflé dish.

Put all the ingredients, except the *Coulis de Tomates*, in a food processor, seasoning generously, and process until smooth. If you do not have a food processor, mince or chop the livers as finely as possible. Beat the eggs, add the cream then add the livers and the remaining ingredients. Pour the mixture into the prepared soufflé dish and stand the dish in a baking tray filled with 2.5 cm (1 in) of water. Cook in the oven for about 50 minutes until the custard is firm and a skewer inserted in the centre comes out clean. Serve it warm but not piping hot, with a bowl of *Coulis de Tomates*.

THROUGHOUT FRANCE

Oeufs en Cocotte

BAKED EGGS

For the simplest of starters, you can break one or two eggs per person into a little buttered *cocotte* – an individual pottery or china ramekin – and cover the top with cream before baking until the yolks are lukewarm and creamy and the whites lightly set. You may also like to spread cooked shallots, mushrooms or thinly sliced Gruyère in the bottom before you add the egg and sprinkle the tops with minced fresh herbs, or a little cream, or any of the following sauces before baking: *Soubise* (see p.96), *Coulis de Tomates* (see p.99), *Béchamel* (see p.95) or *Mornay* (see p.96).

SERVES 4

2 tablespoons butter
4 tablespoons single cream
4 eggs
salt and freshly ground black pepper
a pinch of freshly grated nutmeg
2 tablespoons minced fresh chives

Pre-heat the oven to 190°C/375°F/Gas 5. Use a little of the butter to grease 4 ramekin dishes. Place them in a deep ovenproof dish and add enough water to come half-way up the dishes. Bake in the oven for 5 minutes.

Warm the cream. Pour it into the ramekins and break the eggs carefully on top. Sprinkle with salt, pepper, nutmeg and chives and dot with the remaining butter. Bake in the oven for about 15 minutes until the egg whites are milky-coloured.

Omelettes

ROLLED OMELETTES

There are many types of omelettes: the flat, thick vegetable omelettes which are served in the country; soufflé omelettes which are generally only eaten for dessert stuffed with jam, fruits, ice-cream or custard; and the creamy, *baveuse*, or 'rolled' omelette which is a dish served mainly in restaurants and by the Parisians.

A rolled omelette is a quick dish to prepare. The eggs must not be beaten for too long; just enough for the yolks and whites to be lightly blended. The frying-pan must be smooth with round edges so it is easy to roll the omelette on to the plate. It must be light so you can handle it easily and it should not be sticky, so it is better not washed but rubbed clean with kitchen paper and rough salt. If you must wash it, it should be dried carefully then lightly oiled.

SERVES 2

1 tablespoon butter

2 teaspoons oil

4 eggs

2 tablespoons cream, milk or water

salt and freshly ground black pepper

This soft, creamy rolled omelette is easy to prepare once you have done two or three. The size is important. The best rolled omelettes are made with a 23 cm (7 in) frying-pan with 3 to 4 eggs or a 25 cm (10 in) frying-pan with 6 to 8 eggs. It is always better to make several rolled omelettes rather than one large one, since cooking an omelette takes only a few minutes. The trick is to cook the omelette over a high heat and to use a frying-pan made of stainless steel, enamel, treated aluminium or the old 5 mm (⅛ in) thick French type of black plain iron. In a good pan, the omelette will slide easily without sticking to the bottom.

Heat the butter and the oil over a high heat and tilt the pan so that the bottom and sides of the pan are well coated. Break the eggs into a bowl, whisk in the cream, milk or water and season with salt and pepper. When the butter begins to foam, pour the eggs into the pan. They should seize immediately and make few bubbles. Stir with the flat of a fork for about 10 seconds until the egg begins to set. Pull the set edges to the centre, tipping the uncooked egg to the sides for about 30 seconds until lightly set. Hold the handle of the pan in one hand, flip over the side of the omelette closest to you with a fork, and tip the pan away from you. Place the lip of the pan on the serving plate, tilt both the pan and plate then turn the frying-pan upside down so that the omelette rolls on to the plate with the seam underneath. Serve at once. The rolled omelette is never prepared for more than 2 or 3 persons.

NOTE

Omelettes may be stuffed with anchovies; asparagus tips; cubes of stale bread sautéed in butter; left-over rice; grated cheese; thick cream; diced, cooked or cured raw ham; sautéed and sliced goose or chicken livers; mushrooms; steamed mussels; cooked onions; diced, sautéed potatoes and herbs; prawns; poached scallops; cooked sorrel; truffles; chopped tomatoes; chopped walnuts and herbs.

Omelette aux Fines Herbes
HERB OMELETTE

The most popular of rolled omelettes

SERVE 1
2 eggs
a pinch of salt
freshly ground black pepper
1 tablespoon butter
1 tablespoon groundnut oil
2 teaspoons fresh chervil, parsley, tarragon and
chives, cut finely with scissors

Mix the eggs, salt and pepper and beat together for a few seconds. Melt the butter and oil over a high heat and tilt the pan so that the bottom and sides of the pan are well coated. When the butter begins to foam, pour the eggs into the pan. They should seize immediately and make few bubbles. Stir with the flat of a fork for about 10 seconds until the egg begins to set. Add half the minced herbs and cook until the omelette is lightly browned on the base and lightly set and creamy on the inside. Hold the handle of the pan in one hand, flip over the side of the omelette closest to you with a fork, and tip the pan away from you. Place the lip of the pan on the serving plate, tilt both the pan and plate then turn the frying-pan upside down so that the omelette rolls on to the plate with the seam underneath. Sprinkle with the remaining herbs and serve at once.

THROUGHOUT FRANCE
Omelettes de Campagne
FLAT OMELETTES

Flat, open-faced omelettes look like plump pancakes. Prepared in the morning, they used to be given to school children and farm workers for their lunch. I find flat omelettes fresher and lighter – not least because they use half the number of eggs – than the classical rolled omelettes and they are wonderful when a great number of guests are expected. They can be made very large, and can be served warm or cold.

They are prepared with grated courgettes; chopped leeks; slivered peppers; drained tomatoes; sliced onions; chopped olives; capers and anchovies; sliced artichoke hearts; peas; chopped spinach; sorrel; or Swiss chard. And for a more substantial dish, use grated potatoes or potatoes mixed with onions and diced bacon. *Omelettes de Campagne* are a must for picnics and buffets in the summer.

Spinach Omelette

I usually use frozen leaf spinach for this omelette. It's a great saving of time and I find both the texture and taste very good.

SERVES 4
2 tablespoons oil
1 tablespoon butter
1 small onion, grated
3 eggs
275 g (10 oz) defrosted leaf spinach, squeezed
2 tablespoons chopped fresh parsley
50 g (2 oz) Gruyère or Parmesan, grated
a pinch of freshly grated nutmeg
salt and freshly ground black pepper

TO SERVE
olive oil or softened butter

Heat the oil and butter and fry the onion for 1 minute. Pour the eggs, spinach, parsley, cheese, nutmeg, salt and pepper into a bowl and beat lightly. Pour the mixture on top of the onion in the hot frying-pan. Cook for about 5 minutes over a medium heat, stirring lightly from the sides to the centre until the base is set and golden. Place a plate on top of the pan and, holding it firmly against the pan, invert it so that the omelette falls upside-down on to the plate. Add a little more oil to the pan, if needed. Slide the raw side of the omelette into the frying-pan and cook for 1–2 minutes. Sprinkle with a drop of olive oil or a dot of softened butter to serve.

NOTE

You may like to fry 50 g (2 oz) diced streaky bacon or cured ham until crisp, drain it then add it to the egg and spinach mixture.

Courgette Omelette
You need to use firm courgettes for this recipe.

SERVES 4

2 tablespoons oil
1 tablespoon butter
5 courgettes, unpeeled, coarsely grated
1 garlic clove, chopped
5 eggs
salt and freshly ground black pepper

TO SERVE
1 tablespoon chopped fresh parsley or mint (optional)
softened butter or olive oil (optional)

Heat 1 tablespoon of the oil and the butter and cook the courgettes and garlic for about 10 minutes until soft, stirring with a wooden spoon. Drain them carefully. Put the eggs, salt and pepper together in a bowl and beat lightly then add the cooked courgette mixture. Heat the remaining tablespoon of oil, pour in the egg and courgette mixture and cook over a low heat for 4 minutes. Place a plate on top of the pan and, holding it firmly against the pan, invert it so that the omelette falls upside-down on to the plate. Add a little more oil to the pan,

if needed. Slide the raw side of the omelette into the frying-pan and cook for a further 2 minutes. Alternatively, cook the first side of the omelette then place the omelette under a grill to cook the top before sliding on to a plate to serve. Sprinkle with the chopped parsley or mint and a dot of softened butter or olive oil, if liked.

Tomato Omelette
I never skin tomatoes because I like the crunchy skin, but you may prefer to do so.

SERVES 4
1 tablespoon groundnut oil
1 onion, grated
1 garlic clove, sliced
3 ripe tomatoes, seeded and diced
1 teaspoon plain flour
1 teaspoon dried or 2 teaspoons chopped fresh thyme
salt and freshly ground black pepper
5 eggs, beaten
1 tablespoon olive oil

TO SERVE
1 tablespoon chopped fresh parsley or basil
a few drops of olive oil

Heat the groundnut oil in a frying-pan. Add the onion, garlic and tomatoes, and sprinkle with the flour, thyme, salt and pepper. Cook over a medium heat for 10 minutes. Beat the eggs in a bowl then add the hot mixture to the eggs. Then proceed as for the previous recipe.

NOTE

With firm, fleshy tomatoes, there is no need to cook them. You can add raw, seeded and thinly sliced tomatoes to finely grated raw onion and eggs and proceed as above.

Onion Omelette

Follow the recipe above, replacing the tomatoes with 3 sliced onions and 2 cloves cooked until soft. Discard the cloves and add the onions to the beaten eggs with a little salt and pepper.

Potato Omelette

Diced potatoes, diced pieces of streaky bacon and grated onion should be sautéed until crisp then flavoured with 2 tablespoons of chopped fresh chives or parsley and added to the beaten eggs for a plump, hearty flat omelette.

SOUTH

Brouillade aux Cèpes
CREAMY MUSHROOM SCRAMBLED EGGS

A *Brouillade* is a southern version of scrambled eggs. It should be creamy yet thick enough to be eaten with a fork. I like to prepare *Brouillade* with chopped olives or *Tapenade*, or finely chopped anchovy fillets. In Poudenas, Gascony, Marie-Claude Gracia prepared a luscious *Brouillade* with *cèpes*, using the finely chopped stems to make the *Brouillade* and the sliced caps to decorate it. I have added garlic and parsley to her recipe, since we usually have to use plain button or creamy field musrooms which are more readily available and less expensive than *cèpes*.

SERVES 4

8 eggs
2 tablespoons single cream
salt and freshly ground black or white pepper
2 tablespoons butter
1 tablespoon groundnut oil
8 mushrooms, diced
2 mushrooms, sliced
1 small garlic clove, crushed
2 teaspoons chopped fresh parsley

TO SERVE

thin slices of toast

Break the eggs into a bowl and beat them with a fork for 1 minute. Add the cream, season and beat for a further 1 minute.

Melt ½ tablespoon of the butter and the oil and fry the diced mushrooms for 1 minute then transfer them into a side dish and reserve. Sauté the sliced mushrooms then transfer them into a side dish and reserve.

Heat the remaining butter in a frying-pan and pour in the beaten eggs. Whisk them in a steady movement from the edges of the pan to the centre over a medium heat for a few minutes until the mixture is smooth and creamy but still fairly liquid. Remove from the heat. Stir in the diced mushrooms, garlic and parsley and return to a high heat for a few seconds, stirring until the mixture has the consistency of a thick custard. Pour into a warm shallow dish or individual dishes, arrange the sliced mushrooms on top in a star pattern and serve at once with thinly sliced toast.

Quiche Lorraine

Once served on the first of May to celebrate the coming of spring, *Quiche Lorraine* is delicious, simple enough to make and it can be prepared in advance. This savoury open tart is served as a starter or a main course for a light lunch, with a freshly tossed green salad and a crisp white wine. It comes from the region of Lorraine, more specifically from the city of Nancy, and is traditionally prepared with streaky bacon, eggs and cream. Sometimes a sliced browned onion and a little grated Gruyère are added to the egg mixture.

An immensely popular dish in the rest of France, it is now also often prepared with ham, onions, tomatoes, crab, mushrooms, courgettes, spinach, mussels and a variety of cheeses: soft, blue, hard or fromage frais. *Quiche Lorraine* is cooked in a 25 cm (10 in) tin or a loose-bottomed quiche tin in which the outer rim is easily slipped off.

SERVES 4–6

250 g (9 oz) plain flour
3 tablespoons groundnut oil
150 g (5 oz) unsalted butter, softened
a pinch of salt
4–5 tablespoons cold water
125 g (4½ oz) bacon, cut into 1 x 2.5 cm
(½ x 1 in) pieces
2 eggs
300 ml (10 fl oz) single cream
freshly ground black pepper
a pinch of freshly grated nutmeg
1 tablespoon finely chopped fresh herbs

Pour the flour on to a work surface and make a well in the centre. Place 2 tablespoons of oil and the butter in the well then lightly rub the mixture together until it turns into flakes. Add the salt and water and mix lightly with the fingertips until quite smooth, gathering the pastry into a ball. Add a little water if it is too crumbly. Wrap in greaseproof paper or a plastic bag and chill for a few hours to firm the dough.

Grease a 25 cm (10 in) flan tin, preferably loose-bottomed. Remove from the fridge a few minutes before starting, then roll out the pastry about 3 mm (⅛ in) thick, sprinkling with flour if necessary. Roll the pastry over the rolling pin and unroll over the prepared tin, pressing into the bottom and sides of the tin. Prick the surface lightly with a fork and chill for a further 1 hour.

Pre-heat the oven to 190°C/375°F/Gas 5. Bake the pastry case in the oven for 25 minutes until it shrinks a little from the sides. Leave to cool on a wire rack.

Heat the remaining oil and fry the bacon until crisp. Remove it with a slotted spoon. You can prepare to this point in advance.

When you are ready to bake the quiche, beat the eggs vigorously then add the cream, salt, pepper, nutmeg and herbs. Place the pastry shell on a baking sheet and scatter the bacon over the surface, pressing gently so it will remain at the bottom as you pour in the egg mixture. It should not be more than three-quarters full as it will puff as it cooks. Bake in the lower part of the oven for 30–35 minutes until the top is golden and a knife plunged into the centre comes out clean.

If you have a quiche tin with a loose base, place the dish on a jar and discard the rim. Slide a spatula under the quiche to make sure it will be removed easily, slide it on to a warm platter and serve hot or lukewarm.

Crêpes and Galettes

Ignited with a flourish by waiters in restaurants or bathed with orange butter, *crêpes* have now become a great culinary spectacle, but they used to be a simple, staple food of Breton farmers and fishermen, and were eaten in the same way as bread. Originally they were made with buckwheat and called *galettes*, but, after wheat was introduced to the area, wheat flour was used for *galettes* for the sick and rich people as it makes the mixture lighter. Nowadays, these are generally called *crêpes* and will have a sweet filling whereas buckwheat *galettes*, being heavier, are usually savoury. But beware, the definitions can vary from one part of Brittany to another, and outside the region the word crêpe is often used for both sweet and savoury pancakes. They are served at Candlemas, for dessert or as a base for left-overs.

In Pont l'Abbé, I spent a morning at the *Hôtel Bretagne* with Madame Josette Cossec, who makes about 1,600 *galettes* and *crêpes* a day. I watched her beat the batter, spread it over the galettière, special griddle, with a deft movement of the special wooden spatula, flip it over then top it with beaten egg. As she worked she told me how she used to spend her Fridays with Granny, each child preparing a pile of *galettes*, and explained how the first is always for the dog (too thick and too pasty), the second always offered to the farm-hands (out of courtesy), how *crêpes* and *galettes* wrapped in fine fabric were added to a soldier's pack, or taken on religious processions as a snack, how some were kept to be dried on a string stretched across the room as they were made, how buckwheat makes a soft galette and wheat a more crisp one, and how buckwheat *galettes* can be made with just plenty of beating and no eggs if you are skilful enough. As I was too busy tasting I didn't have any questions to ask nor response to make except a satisfied purring.

Galettes

SERVES 4–6

150 g (5 oz) wheat flour
100 g (4 oz) buckwheat flour
1 teaspoon salt
2 eggs
475 ml (16 fl oz) water
butter for frying

Stir the flours and salt together in a bowl, and make a well in the centre. Pour the eggs into the well then, stirring with a wooden spoon, slowly pour in the water until the mixture feels like a creamy custard. Beat for about 10 minutes to incorporate air bubbles that will allow the batter to absorb butter as it cooks, moistening it and making it tastier.

Melt a small knob of butter in a frying-pan. Swirl it around to cover the bottom of the pan then pour it out. Add 2 or 3 tablespoons of the batter to the pan, swirl it around to cover the base in a thin layer then cook over a fairly high heat until set and light brown underneath. Turn over and brown on the other side. Add a little more butter to the pan and continue making more *galettes* until all the batter has been used.

For the Fillings

Galettes were originally spread with lightly salted butter and folded in four but nowadays the range of fillings is staggering.

- Coarsely chopped onions sautéed in butter.
- Chopped and sautéed slivers of ham or bacon.
- Finely chopped fresh parsley, chervil, chives, shallot and garlic stirred into softened butter with a little pepper.
- An egg broken into the centre of the galette,

sprinkled with salt, pepper and dotted with butter.

- Chopped fried sausages mixed with diced cooked apples.
- Chopped tomatoes and onions cooked with a little thyme, then chives or parsley sprinkled over the folded *galette*.
- Finely chopped bacon, tomatoes, onions and parsley cooked slowly in butter, then a little cider added.
- 'Johnny' – sautéed chopped onions, mixed with a little dry white wine, salt and pepper, then topped with a knob of butter after placing on the *galette*. (These are named after the men who went to England to sell onions which they hung round their necks and from their bicycles.)
- Grated or sliced cheese with a little butter or herb butter on the top.
- Skinned sardine fillets, with a knob of butter placed on the folded galette. Wait for a second before serving.
- Skinned smoked trout fillets with a little butter and herbs.
- Seafood such as mussels, cockles, prawns and scallops, plus their cooking liquid and a drop of brandy spooned over.
- Fish topped with sautéed shallots, parsley and nutmeg, covered with light tomato sauce and a little white wine and baked.

You can also try, scrambled eggs, sausages and smoked salmon.

Crêpes

MAKES ABOUT 12 CRÊPES
100 g (4 oz) wheat flour
2 small eggs, beaten
1 tablespoon sugar (optional)
300 ml (10 fl oz) light-flavoured beer, milk or water
1 tablespoon melted butter or vegetable oil
2 tablespoons orange flower water, or brandy (optional)
1 teaspoon salt

FOR THE FILLINGS
jam
honey and lemon juice
cooked sliced pears, spread on butter
grated plain chocolate or cocoa powder
sliced apples marinated in lemon juice and sugar, then baked. You can also sprinkle calvados or Benedictine over just before serving piping hot

Put the flour into a bowl. Make a well in the centre, add the eggs, and sugar, if using, and beat well. Add the beer, milk or water then the butter or oil, the orange flower water or brandy, if using, and salt. Allow the mixture to rest.

After 1 hour stir again: there should be no lumps and the batter will be perfectly smooth.

Add a small knob of butter to a hot frying-pan. Pour about 3 tablespoons of batter into the pan then tilt in all directions so that the batter runs in a thin film over the surface. Pour off any excess batter into a bowl. After a minute or so, the sides of the *crêpe* will separate from the sides of the pan. Shake the pan. Lift the edge of the *crêpe* with a spatula and turn, or toss it in the air. Brown the other side for a few seconds then slide the *crêpe* on to a plate placed over hot water. Add a little oil or butter to the pan and continue to make more *crêpes* until all the batter has been used.

NOTE

If you don't have friends and children around you in the kitchen eagerly waiting to take each *crêpe* as it comes from the pan, you can keep the *crêpes* warm by stacking them on a plate placed over a saucepan of simmering water.

Fish & Shellfish

LES POISSONS ET
LES CRUSTACES

*I*n France the choice of fish and shell-fish is staggering. Stand on the quays of Guilvinec, La Rochelle, Trouville or Dieppe and watch the boats unloading their bounty; attend a fish auction at Concarneau, walk through the stalls of a market and you will be stunned by the variety and quantity of fish displayed. There are bushels of shrimps, piles of crabs, baskets of scallops, mussels, oysters, clams, and everyday all is sold out and gone by noon.

France has so many rivers, ponds and lakes that Burgundy, Alsace, Savoy and Auvergne's markets' offering not only of carp, perch, trout, pike, salmon and trout but also frogs, snails and eels remain abundant all year long.

Fish has always been a familiar item on French tables. *Pauchouse* (see p.120), *Bouillabaisse* (see p.125), *Marmite Dieppoise* (see p.123) are the core of a convivial meal. We love a platter of shellfish to start a family lunch or to end an evening on the town. The mad infatuation for salmon in all its forms: raw, thinly sliced and tossed with fresh herbs and olive oil, cooked on one side only, steamed, served with a beurre blanc or prepared with a red wine sauce still prevails and gone forever are the days where farm workers would complain because salmon had been served to them three times a week.

Lately the concern with health and the trend for non-fattening food have made fish even more popular. Whether it is a delicate salad of warm scallops (see p.146), a bass cooked in red wine (see p.135) or a spirited *Lotte à l'Armoricaine* (see p.138), the traditional way of serving fish after the first course and before the meat is seldom followed today. Fish is either a starter or the main course on most menus.

Fish is healthy, not fattening and invigorating, but choosing, trimming and cooking fish is sometimes foreboding to home cooks. Fishbones, fish skin and fish heads intimidate some, the strong taste or texture of anchovies, squid, tuna or eels may repel others. Of course, industrial frozen food caters abundantly to all those who 'don't like a fishy taste' and want fish to taste like bland chicken nuggets, and I do fear the day when all children will think fish are born rectangular and evenly breaded out of a brightly coloured box. Although some frozen fish is firm and tasty, I still tend to prefer a plain, fresh whiting to a frozen lobster. Fish filets are easily available and are safe for the non-adventurous, there is no waste and no trimming. But it is well worth buying a fish whole. Bones and fish heads make for the best fish soups, the most fragrant *fumets*, and left-overs can become fish croquettes, soups, stuffed *crêpes*, fish terrines or gratins.

Time to choose one's fish is more important than preparing and cooking it. It must have bright, clear eyes, red gills, firm flesh and shiny scales adhering to the skin. Go to your local wholesale market to know what types of fish are available in your region then ask your fishmonger or your supermarket fish attendant to sell it. Filleting is not hard, but a friendly fishmonger will save your time and he will keep heads and bones for you.

A fish must not be undercooked, or it will turn sticky and gooey, nor overcooked, or it will be dry. Remember to leave on the skin when you grill a fish as it will protect it, and to remove it for a fish when it is steamed. Fish may be eaten raw, grilled, poached in stock or wine, cooked in butter or olive oil, steamed, simmered in a vinegar or wine-flavoured broth, cooked *au bleu* or fried. It may be marinated. It may be wrapped in foil or vine leaves before it is grilled or baked on a bed of sliced potatoes, lemons, tomatoes and wild fennel. Chicory, sorrel or leeks will add a light, pungent flavour and an interesting texture to a bland fish, but lemon, tarragon, thyme, bay leaves, capers, parsley, garlic or shallots remain the most faithful companions.

We love fish to taste like fish and the sauce must not hide its flavour, so a delicate *Beurre Blanc* (see p.127-8), or *Beurre Rouge* (made with red wine), a fresh tomato sauce, a drop of virgin olive oil with the juice of a lemon will only enhance it perfectly. Today they seem to be everyone's favourites.

La Pauchouse

BURGUNDIAN FISH STEW

The best *Pauchouse* I ever ate was prepared in Verdun-sur-le-Doubs. The occasion was not quite in the same league as the banquet which Philippe the Good, Duke of Burgundy, served there in 1454 to a few chosen friends including an emperor and a pope, in order to seal their friendship. In comparison, our gathering was more like Renoir's *Fête Champêtre*, but it had the typical lusty, generous sparkling Burgundy atmosphere.

All around us there were fields of yellow rape, creamy Charolais cattle, tall walnut trees, rivers and canals, and barges. I had joined Monsieur and Madame Bonnot, their daughter, Claude Siegnist, their grand-children and their friends for a memorable day during which Claude, a Beaune wine négociant, and I were introduced into the *Confrérie de la Pauchouse*. This is a select group of gourmets dedicated to promoting this wonderful Burgundian fish stew. Among much laughter we pledged allegiance to *La Pauchouse* and the formal ceremony was completed by drinking from the traditional silver goblet proffered by our 'brothers', resplendent in their red and yellow robes.

Pauchouse is a medieval dish. The name, which can also be spelt *pouchouse*, *pôchouse* and *pochouse*, is derived from *poche*, the bag in which a fisherman puts his catch. The freshwater fish, such as carp, eel, perch, pike, tench and trout that are abundant in the region, and the local dry white wine are the essence of this dish, but each restaurant and each family has its own tricks to personalize its *Pauchouse*. Most will follow the tradition, though, of using two white fish, such as perch and pike, and two richer ones, such as trout and eel.

SERVES 8

2 tablespoons groundnut oil
70 g (2½oz) butter
5 garlic cloves, crushed
2 onions, sliced
2 bay leaves
1 sprig of fresh thyme
10 black peppercorns
2 kg (4½lb) mixed freshwater fish, cut into 5 cm (2 in) pieces
salt
600 ml (1 pint) dry white wine, preferably Burgundy
1.2 litres (2 pints) fish stock
2 tablespoons plain flour
1 tablespoon brandy (optional)
50 ml (2 fl oz) double cream
4–6 slices good, firm bread, made into small Garlic Croûtons (see p.233)

Heat the oil and 25 g (1 oz) of butter in a heavy-based-pan, add the garlic, onions, bay leaves, thyme and peppercorns and cook for about 4 minutes, stirring occasionally. Add the fish, sprinkle with salt and stir gently. Pour in the wine and stock, bring just to the boil then lower the heat and cook gently for 5 minutes, stirring from time to time. Using a slotted spoon transfer the fish to a warm bowl, cover and keep warm.

Blend the flour with the remaining butter to make a *beurre manié*, then gradually whisk into the broth and boil until very lightly thickened. Add the brandy, if using, and boil for a further 2–3 minutes. Stir in the cream, taste and add salt if necessary.

Place the Croûtons in a warm, shallow serving dish, place the fish on top and strain over the broth.

VARIATION

Red wine may be used instead of white wine, and diced streaky bacon, button onions and mushrooms added.

PROVENCE AND LANGUEDOC

Bourride

WHITE FISH SOUP ENRICHED WITH AÏOLI

This rich, creamy fish soup is prepared with a variety of white fish, such as monkfish, John Dory, bass, whiting and bream. The ritual is spectacular and the dish glorious.

Some people line a shallow serving dish with thick slices of bread, then pile the pieces of cooked fish on them and finally pour the rest of the soup over. Sometimes the *Aïoli*-thickened-broth is served with crisp, garlicky croûtons as a first course, the fish is coated with the rest of the *Aïoli* and served with steamed potatoes as a second course. Many chefs add a few spoonfuls of double cream to the hot broth to make it truly unctuous. I find this much too rich, but it is definitely worth trying.

In Languedoc, carrots, leeks, celery, Swiss chard and tomatoes are chopped and slowly cooked with pieces of monkfish, then *Aïoli*, diluted with the cooking juices, is poured in to make a dish that is more like a stew than a soup.

SERVES 8

900 g (2 lb) monkfish
900 g (2 lb) sea bass
900 g (2 lb) bream or whiting
double quantity Aïoli *(see p. 76)*
16 slices baguette, prepared as Garlic Croûtons (see p. 233)

FOR THE BROTH

1.75 litres (3 pints) water
300 ml (10 fl oz) dry white wine
1 leek, white part only, sliced
1 carrot, sliced
1 onion, sliced
thinly pared rind 1 orange
3 sprigs of fresh thyme or 2 teaspoons dried thyme

2 teaspoons fennel seeds or aniseeds
3 bay leaves
salt and freshly ground black pepper
3 egg yolks

Fillet all the fish and remove the skins; be sure to also remove the fine membrane that covers the monkfish. Reserve the fish bones, heads and skins. Cut the fillets into 2.5 cm (1 in) pieces.

For the broth, pour the water and wine into a large pan, add the fish bones, heads and skin, the leek, carrot, onion, orange rind, thyme, fennel seeds or aniseeds, bay leaves, salt and pepper, bring to the boil, remove the scum that rises to the surface, then simmer for 20 minutes.

Add the pieces of fish to the hot broth, lower the heat and simmer gently for 10 minutes. Using a slotted spoon, remove the fish to a warm, shallow dish. Cover and keep warm.

Pour the broth through a sieve into a pan, pushing the bones, vegetables and herbs with a spoon against the sieve. Discard the contents of the sieve. Boil the broth hard for about 3 minutes then keep it warm over a low heat.

Stir the egg yolks into about two-thirds of the *Aïoli*. Gradually stir a ladleful of hot broth into the *Aïoli*, making sure each addition is incorporated before adding the next. Heat the broth to just below simmering point, then slowly pour in the *Aïoli* mixture, stirring constantly. Heat gently, stirring until lightly thickened. Do not allow to boil. Check and correct the seasoning. Pour over the fish and serve with the Garlic Croûtons and the remaining *Aïoli*.

NOTE

The egg whites that are left can be used to make *Oeufs à la Neige* (see p.305) or *Tuiles* (see p.329).

NORMANDY

Marmite Dieppoise

CREAMY MIXED FISH AND SEAFOOD FLAVOURED

WITH CURRY

This hearty soup of fish, shellfish and vegetables flavoured with curry powder represents the very soul of Normandy. The spices that were first taken to the region by merchant ships returning from the Orient centuries ago beautifully enhance the flavours of local ingredients.

Marmite Dieppoise is a sumptuous dish and it is both easy to make and to serve; the broth can be prepared ahead of time and kept in the fridge for even greater convenience. I prefer to serve the guests myself so I can make sure everyone has all the different types of fish.

With *Crudités* (see p.233) as a starter, and a bowl of Fruit Compote (see p.281) for dessert you will have a memorable meal.

SERVES 8

1 litre (1¾ pints)/750 g–1 kg (1¾ lb) mussels
100 g (4 oz) butter
8 leeks, washed, trimmed, split and sliced
5 celery sticks, sliced
2 onions, chopped
750 ml (1¼ pints) dry white wine
salt and freshly ground black pepper
1 carrot, sliced
2 sprigs of fresh parsley
2 bay leaves
8 black peppercorns
750 g (1½ lb) fish bones and fish heads
1 litre (1¾ pints) water
8–10 x 10 cm (4 in) pieces cod and either halibut or haddock
8–10 small fillets of sole or plaice
8–10 Dublin Bay prawns
8–10 scallops, shelled (see p. 104)
juice of 1 lemon
300 ml (10 fl oz) double cream

1–2 teaspoons curry powder
½–1 teaspoon cayenne pepper

TO SERVE

2 tablespoons finely chopped fresh chervil or parsley
4 slices good, firm bread, made into
Small Croûtons (see p. 233)

Leave the mussels to soak for 2–3 hours in a sink or bucket of cold salty water to remove any sand or grit.

Heat 50 g (2 oz) butter in a heavy-based frying-pan. Add the leeks, celery and 1 onion. Cook over a low heat for 4–5 minutes, stirring occasionally, until softened. Purée in a food processor. Transfer to a bowl and reserve.

Drain the mussels and scrub the shells with a hard brush. Cut off the beards. Place the mussels in a large pan, add half the wine, and half the remaining onion, salt and pepper. Cover and cook over a high heat for 5 minutes, tossing occasionally, until the mussels open; discard any that remain closed. Drain. Pass the liquid through a sieve lined with muslin and then reserve. Remove the mussels from their shells. Place 8–10 shells and all the mussels in a bowl. Discard the other shells.

Heat the remaining butter in a pan. Add the remaining onion, the carrot, parsley, bay leaves and peppercorns and cook for 5 minutes. Add the fish bones and fish heads. Pour in the remaining wine and the water, bring to the boil, skim the froth from the surface then simmer for 20 minutes. Pour through a sieve into a large pan, pressing down hard on the fish bones and vegetables, forcing the vegetables through the sieve with a wooden spoon. Add the strained mussel liquid and simmer for a few minutes.

Sprinkle the cod and either halibut or haddock with salt and add to the hot broth. Simmer gently for about 4 minutes, then add the sole or plaice fillets and Dublin Bay prawns, and cook for 3 minutes. Add the scallops and cook for a

further 2 minutes. Using a slotted spoon transfer the fish, prawns and scallops to a warm tureen. Add the mussels and mussel shells, sprinkle over the lemon juice, cover and keep warm.

Stir the puréed leeks and celery into the fish broth and boil until reduced to about 1.6 litres (2½ pints). Stir in the cream and add curry powder, cayenne pepper and salt and pepper to taste; the broth should be highly flavoured.

Pour the very hot broth into the tureen and take to the table with warm plates, a bowl of chopped herbs and the Croûtons.

Place a piece of fish, a fish fillet, a Dublin Bay prawn, a scallop, some mussels and a mussel shell on each plate. Spoon a ladleful of soup on top, sprinkle with a little chopped chervil or parsley and add a few Croûtons.

PROVENCE

Soupe de Pêcheurs
PROVENCE-STYLE FISH SOUP

In Provence most fishermen's wives sell their husband's catch every morning in Cannes' market, Forville, Marseille's harbour or under the arcades of St Tropez. They are used to selling the best fish.

The fish which cannot be sold is given to their imaginative talents to turn into family treats. But the 'make something with nothing' principle has always been at the core of French regional home cookery and it is well known that fish soup is generally prepared from almost nothing. Of course if a crab is added, so much the better.

A *Soupe de Pêcheurs* can be one of the most inexpensive of fish soups and may not contain any actual pieces of fish at all. But the rich broth, the fiery *Rouille* (see p.77) sauce and the crisp Croûtons (see p.233) can be enough to make a delicious soup. It helps if you have a fishmonger who saves you fish heads and bones.

SERVES 8

2.25 kg (5 lb) mixed white fish such as halibut, cod and monkfish
2 tablespoons olive oil
1½ tablespoons chopped fresh thyme
salt
2 teaspoons saffron strands
2 tablespoons fennel seeds

FOR THE BROTH

2½ tablespoons olive oil
2 tablespoons groundnut oil
4 large onions, chopped
2 large leeks, white part only, chopped
6 tomatoes, chopped
6 garlic cloves, crushed
A few sprigs of fresh parsley
1 kg (2 lb) fish heads and bones, if available
bouquet garni of 1 sprig of fresh parsley, 1 sprig of fresh thyme and 1 bay leaf
a few sprigs of fresh fennel or about 2 teaspoons fennel seeds
5 cm (2 inch) piece orange rind, dried in a low oven for 15 minutes
8 sprigs of fresh thyme
salt and freshly ground black pepper
1.5 litres (2½ pints) water
450 ml (15 fl oz) dry white wine
1 tablespoon Pernod (optional)

TO SERVE

Rouille (see p.77)
16 slices baguette, prepared as Garlic Croûtons (see p.233)
grated Gruyère or Parmesan

Clean and fillet the fish and cut into 5 x 5 cm (2 x 2 in) pieces. Reserve the heads, trimmings and bones. Place the pieces of fish in a large bowl, add the olive oil, thyme, salt, saffron and fennel. Toss, cover and leave in a cool place or the fridge, for a few hours.

Meanwhile, make the broth. Heat 1½ tablespoons of olive oil and a little groundnut oil in a large frying-pan. Add the onions and sauté for about 8 minutes until golden. Add the leeks then the tomatoes, garlic and parsley and cook for 2–3 minutes. Pour into a large pan.

Add a little more groundnut oil to the frying-pan and sauté the fish bones, heads and trimmings for a few minutes on all sides. Add the bouquet garni, fennel sprigs or seeds, the orange rind, thyme and salt. Cook for 5 minutes then pour into the pan and add the water and wine. Bring to the boil, skim the froth from the surface then cover and simmer for 30–60 minutes.

Add a little fish broth to the *Rouille* and pour into a bowl. Pour the remaining fish broth through a sieve, pressing down on the fish bones and vegetables with a wooden spoon. Discard the contents of the sieve. Taste and add salt and pepper, if necessary.

Heat the broth until it comes to the boil, add the pieces of fish, lower the heat so the liquid barely simmers and cook for 10 minutes. Add the remaining oil and the Pernod, if using. Pour into a large, warm, soup tureen and take to the table with the Croûtons and the cheese.

Pour a ladle or two of soup into each warm soup plate or bowl. Top some of the Croûtons with *Rouille* and cheese and float on the surface of the soup. The Croûtons should remain partially crisp as the soup is started. Leave the remaining *Rouille* and bread on the table.

VARIATION – BOUILLABAISSE

Bouillabaisse is the most glorious *Soupe de Pêcheurs*. It is made from a variety of different types of white and red fish, such as red mullet, red gurnard, John Dory, monkfish, bream and conger eel. But the most important fish, according to many people, is *rascasse*, scorpion fish. This is rarely available away from the Mediterranean, which is why it is often said that it is impossible to make a genuine *Bouillabaisse* anywhere except along the southern French coast.

Bouillabaisse is really a fisherman's dish, so the fish should either be left whole or cut into pieces, not skinned and filleted as in the *Soupe de Pêcheurs* recipe. However, I think an adequate *Bouillabaisse* can be made without the *rascasse* by adding sliced potatoes to a *Soupe de Pêcheurs* and simmering them in the sieved broth for 15–20 minutes before cooking the fish.

THROUGHOUT FRANCE

Poisson au Court-Bouillon

POACHED FISH

A court-bouillon is the aromatic liquid that is traditionally used for poaching whole, large fish, although it can be used for most fish and even cuts of both fresh and frozen fish such as steaks, cutlets and fillets. There are three kinds of court-bouillon, each of which is ideal for a specific purpose (see recipes).

Poaching keeps the fish flesh moist and helps retain the flavour, nutrients and texture. The heads and tails of a whole fish are left on, and as the skin is normally removed before the fish is served, there is no need to remove the scales. Instead of gutting the fish in the usual way by slitting the belly, pull the entrails through one of the gills. Hold the fish's mouth under a cold running tap until the water flowing from the rear vent runs clear. Dry the fish carefully then place on a rack that will fit inside a fish kettle or large, deep roasting tin or similar baking dish. If you do not have a suitable rack, wrap the fish in a piece of muslin or cheesecloth that is large enough for its ends to hang over the sides of the cooking pan. Lower the fish into the fish kettle, tin or dish and cover with the appropriate court-bouillon, but do not drown it; large fish should be covered in cold court-bouillon, but for small pieces the court-bouillon should be warm. Heat to about 70°C (160°F), just below simmering point, and cook for 8–10 minutes for every 2.5 cm (1 in) of thickness, starting from when the liquid reaches the correct temperature. Using the rack or cloth, remove the fish from the court-bouillon. Carefully remove the skin and scrape out the bones lying along the back of the fish. Using two long spatulas, or fish slices, transfer the fish to a large plate.

Whether served warm or cold, the fish can be simply seasoned with lemon juice and a drizzle of good olive oil. For a more luxurious cold dish, serve with plain, Herb or Curry Mayonnaise (see p.101), *Aïoli*, *Tapenade*, or *Rouille* (see pp.76-78). If the fish is to be eaten warm, serve with *Beurre Blanc* (see pp.127-28), or warm *Anchoïade* (see p.78).

Steamed or boiled new potatoes, cauliflower, artichoke hearts or asparagus, a vegetable *timbale* such as Spinach (see p.260) or a vegetable purée (see p.239-41), can accompany warm poached fish whereas cherry tomatoes, lemon wedges, sprigs of parsley, capers, olives, watercress and halved hard-boiled egg go well with it when it is cold.

Court-Bouillon with White Wine

Use for whole large fish such as salmon, halibut, tuna and cod. Follow the recipe and method for Court-Bouillon with Vinegar using white wine instead of the vinegar.

Court-Bouillon with Vinegar

Use for fresh-water fish such as pike, trout and carp.

MAKES 1 LITRE (1¾ PINTS)
175 ml (6 fl oz) red wine vinegar
900 ml (1½ pints) water
1 carrot, chopped
1 small onion, chopped
4 sprigs of fresh parsley
1 sprig of fresh thyme
½ bay leaf
salt
4 black peppercorns

Place all the ingredients, except the peppercorns, in a large pan, bring to the boil, then simmer for about 20 minutes. Add the peppercorns, cover the pan and remove from the heat. Leave to cool, then pour through a sieve lined with muslin or cheesecloth in to a large bowl.

Court-Bouillon with Milk

This should be used to poach very delicate fish, such as sole as its lightness enables the fine flavour of the fish to stand out.

MAKES 1.2 LITRES (2 PINTS)
300 ml (10 fl oz) milk
900 ml (1½ pints) water
1 carrot, chopped
1 onion, chopped
4 sprigs of fresh parsley
1 sprig of fresh thyme
½ bay leaf
salt
4 black peppercorns

Follow the method for Court-Bouillon with Vinegar.

Truite au Bleu

POACHED TROUT

Those who are lucky enough to have access to a trout stream or live near a trout farm can enjoy this recipe as really fresh fish, preferably those that are live, are essential. But why *au bleu*? Why 'blue trout?' Because if it is handled delicately and neither washed nor dried, the natural coating of slime remains on the fish's skin and the trout develops a bluish tinge when it is cooked. It will also curve whereas a not-so-fresh trout will remain stiff.

SERVES 4

4 whole trout, each weighing 225 g (8 oz)
200 ml (7 fl oz) white wine vinegar
2.25 litres (4 pints) water
1 carrot, chopped
1 onion, sliced
salt and freshly ground black pepper

TO GARNISH

sprigs of fresh parsley

TO SERVE

warm melted butter
lemon juice
finely chopped fresh parsley

If the fish are alive, give a sharp blow to their heads. Carefully pull out the intestines through the gills. Run cold water through the fish from the mouth, taking care not to disturb the slime on the skin, if it is still present. Sprinkle a little vinegar over the fish.

Select a large pan, deep frying-pan, or large flameproof dish or baking dish in which you can place the whole trout without bending them. Add the water, remaining vinegar, carrot, onion and salt and pepper, and bring to the boil.

Lower the heat so the liquid is just on simmering point, add the fish and poach for 5–7 minutes until the flesh feels slightly springy to the touch. Remove the fish from the broth and place on kitchen paper to drain. Transfer to a warm serving plate and garnish with parsley sprigs. Serve with warm melted butter, flavoured with lemon juice and chopped parsley.

VARIATION

Truite au Bleu is also delicious when eaten cold with Lemon Mayonnaise (see p. 101).

Saumon au Beurre Blanc

POACHED SALMON WITH WHITE BUTTER SAUCE

Beurre Blanc remains one of the most celebrated sauces in France at a time when many French sauces have fallen out of fashion. According to the local legend it was invented, albeit by accident, by a Madame Clémence in the 1890s just south of the Loire estuary. *Beurre Blanc* became a speciality of guinguettes, the lively little restaurants along the Loire where good, inexpensive food, local Muscadet wine and energetic dancing were all to be found. Farmers, wine-makers and families who worked all week in the busy city of Nantes and who needed fresh air, would meet in the *guinguettes* to enjoy piles of frogs' legs, eels, snails and the exquisite sauce which complemented delicate river fish such as pike and *zander* (pike-perch). Nowadays *Beurre Blanc* is served with a great variety of dishes: poached or grilled seafish and shellfish as well as freshwater fish, poached eggs, asparagus, beans and almost any other steamed or boiled vegetable.

Beurre Blanc is a simple emulsion of hot, reduced, shallot-flavoured, white wine vinegar or the local wines Muscadet and Gros Plant which have high acidities, and cold butter. It is not a difficult sauce to master providing the liquid is hot and the cold butter is added gradually and then thoroughly whisked. Most people add a spoonful of whipping cream at the last moment to help prevent the sauce turning oily and enable it to be kept a little longer before being served.

SERVES 4

4 pieces of fillet of salmon, each weighing
150 g (5 oz)
about 450 ml (15 fl oz) Court Bouillon with
Vinegar (see p. 126)

FOR THE BEURRE BLANC
3 tablespoons white wine vinegar
3 tablespoons Muscadet, Gros Plant or other dry
white wine
8 tablespoons finely chopped shallot
225 g (8 oz) lightly salted butter, diced
salt and freshly ground black pepper
1 tablespoon whipping cream or Court
Bouillon with Vinegar (see p. 126), (optional)

Lay the salmon in a single layer in a frying-pan, pour over sufficient *Court-Bouillon* to cover and bring just to simmering point. Cover with a piece of buttered greaseproof paper, butter-side down, and poach gently for 5–6 minutes. Using a fish slice, transfer the salmon to a warm plate, cover and keep warm.

Meanwhile, make the *Beurre Blanc*. Bring the vinegar and wine to the boil in a small, heavy-based, stainless steel pan. Add the shallot and simmer very gently, uncovered, until soft and the liquid reduced to 1 tablespoon. Add one piece of butter at a time, whisking vigorously after each addition. Do not allow the mixture to boil. The sauce will thicken and become white and frothy. Off the heat, add salt and pepper to taste, and the cream if liked. Pour into a warm sauceboat and serve with the salmon.

VARIATION

Monsieur Jean-François Hatet, chef at the *Auberge Nantais*, St-Julien-de-Concelles, sautéed the salmon in butter for 3–4 minutes each side.

NOTE

The sauce can be kept warm over hot water or over the pilot light of a gas stove for about 30 minutes. If it does separate, pour a little sauce into a very cold bowl, beat firmly until it is smooth again, then gradually add the rest of the sauce.

NORMANDY AND THROUGHOUT FRANCE

Sole Meunière

SOLE FRIED IN BUTTER WITH LEMON AND PARSLEY

Sole Meunière is a staple in French cookery, yet when a fresh, tender sole is carefully browned, coated with fresh parsley, lemon and good butter, its perfection still pleases. After all, it is the most sympathetic way of cooking this light fish. *Sole Meunière* is served all over France but in Normandy where fresh sole and good butter abound, it is at its very best.

Why *meunière*, miller's style? Probably because of the flour that is used to protect the delicate skin of the sole as it cooks, and to make it crisp as it browns. The coating of flour should only be light, though, and the butter for frying needs to be hot. It is for this reason that the butter is clarified, so removing the fine particles that burn at high temperatures and which spoil the appearance and flavour of this dish.

Diced, peeled cucumber sautéed in butter, or grapes are fitting accompaniments.

SERVES 4

175 g (6 oz) unsalted butter, diced
3 tablespoons plain flour
salt and freshly ground black pepper
4 sole, about 350 g (12 oz) each, heads and dark
skin removed and filleted
juice of 2 lemons
2 tablespoons finely chopped fresh
flatleaf parsley

FOR GARNISH
parsley sprigs
lemon wedges

TO SERVE
steamed tiny new potatoes

First, you must clarify 100 g (4 oz) butter. To do this, heat it gently in a small pan until it foams. Carefully skim the foam from the surface and pour the clear butter slowly through muslin wrung out in very hot water into a small bowl, leaving the milky sediment behind.

Season the flour with salt and pepper and place on a plate. Dip the fish in the seasoned flour to coat lightly and evenly.

Heat the clarified butter in a large frying-pan until it sizzles. Add 1 or 2 fish – it is vital that they are not crowded – and cook over a moderate heat for about 4–5 minutes on each side until crisp but not brown. Shake the pan from time to time and turn the fish with a fish slice.

Using the fish slice, transfer the fish to a warm plate. Keep warm. Fry the remaining fish in the same way.

Pour the cooking juices from the pan and wipe the pan with kitchen paper. Add the butter that has not been clarified to the pan and heat until it foams and turns light golden brown. Add the lemon juice and parsley then pour immediately over the fish. Garnish with parsley sprigs, add lemon wedges, and serve with steamed potatoes.

VARIATION

The same method is suitable for small whole fish such as trout, flounder, small whiting and small bass, or for fish fillets (if the fish are large the outside would become dry before the inside was cooked).

PROVENCE

Rougets Grillés aux Feuilles de Vigne

BARBECUED RED MULLET

On Lulu Peyraud's estate near Bandol we witnessed the old saying 'the family who cooks together enjoys life together' at work as we followed the cheerful group from the vineyard, to the kitchen, to the long table under the tall shady trees for a long and chatty meal.

Lulu owns the beautiful *Domaine Tempier*, where she has a lovely, informal herb garden by her kitchen door. Her husband and sons make their olive oil and wines which fill a large, cool cellar nearby.

If the fish are fresh, the fire very hot and the herbs fragrant, Barbecued Red Mullet is one of the simplest and most delicious of dishes. The fish quickly cooks to become crisp outside, moist inside and fragrant all over.

Red mullet should not be gutted or scaled as emptying the fish removes part of the flavour, and the scales protect the flesh against becoming dry during the cooking.

Serve with rice flavoured with bay leaves and olive oil, and sliced courgettes or fennel sautéed in olive oil.

The fish can also be cooked on a grill rack beneath a hot grill.

SERVES 4

4 whole red mullet, with heads and tails on, each weighing 450 g (1 lb)
4 sprigs of fresh fennel, or 3–4 tablespoons fennel seeds
juice of 1 lemon
salt and freshly ground black pepper
4 teaspoons chopped fresh savory, if available
2 tablespoons olive oil
8 vine leaves, or thick lettuce leaves
a large pinch of dried herbs

FOR THE GARNISH

sprigs of fresh flatleaf parsley or watercress
lemon slices

Pre-heat the barbecue.

Rub the outside of the fish lightly with a kitchen paper. Place a sprig of fennel or some fennel seeds on each fish and sprinkle lemon juice, salt and pepper, savory, if available, and a little olive oil over the skin then wrap each fish in a vine leaf or thick lettuce leaf to help keep the fish moist; as the fish cooks the leaves crumble away. Place the fish in a double-sided barbecue fish grill.

When the barbecue is almost white-hot, sprinkle a large pinch of dried herbs over the wood or charcoal and place the fish grill over it. Cook the fish for about 8 minutes on one side, turn them over and cook the other side for about 10–15 minutes, depending on the thickness of the fish, until the flesh flakes easily and becomes opaque. Brush away the dry vine or lettuce leaves and then either place the fish on a warm serving plate and garnish with watercress or parsley, and sliced lemons or mash a small knob of softened butter with 1 anchovy fillet and a little fresh pepper and place on top of each fish as it is about to be served.

AUVERGNE

Saumon aux Lentilles

SALMON WITH LENTILS

The lovely Art Deco *Hôtel Radio* perches on a hill in Chamalières overlooking the sombre city of Clermont-Ferrand. The chef-patron, Michel Mioche's much-emulated recipe is the marriage of two Auvergnat ingredients: salmon from the Allier river and the famous tiny green Le Puy lentils. Pink peppercorns add piquancy.

If you can't find Le Puy lentils at speciality delicatessens, the larger, flat, dull greenish-brown variety are a good substitute.

SERVES 6

400 g (14 oz) tiny green Puy lentils, or brown lentils
1 onion, halved
2 cloves garlic
1 bay leaf
1 sprig of fresh thyme
3 shallots, finely chopped
20 g (¾ oz) butter
4 tablespoons double cream
salt and freshly ground black pepper
2 tablespoons olive oil
6 pieces salmon fillet, each weighing about 150 g (5 oz)
1 tablespoon chopped fresh chervil or dill
1 teaspoon pink peppercorns

Rinse the lentils in cold water then place in a pan with the onion, garlic, bay leaf and thyme. Cover with cold water, cover the pan with a lid or foil and bring to the boil. Simmer for 25 minutes to 1 hour, depending on the quality and freshness of the lentils, until they are tender but not too soft. Drain well and discard the onion, garlic and herbs.

Sauté the shallots in the butter for 3–4 minutes. Add the lentils and cream. Season with salt and pepper to taste, then cover and keep

warm over a very low heat, shaking the pan occasionally.

Heat the oil in a frying-pan. Season the salmon with salt and pepper and cook for about 5 minutes, depending on thickness, so the underside is lightly cooked and the top barely warm. Serve the salmon on the lentils and sprinkle over fresh herbs and pink peppercorns.

VARIATION

Michel Mioche cuts each piece of fish into strips, then curves the strips round each other to make a flower shape.

Saint Pierre à l'Oseille

JOHN DORY WITH SORREL

According to the legend, the two black spots which are on the sides of a John Dory are the prints of Saint Peter's fingers, hence the fish's French name – St Pierre. It is a delicate sea fish which closely resembles sole in both texture and flavour.

In France, sorrel is eaten both in omelettes and soups as well as being used to enhance white meats and fish. In this recipe sorrel is mixed with flour and cream to soften its acidity and make it a good complement to the delicate flavour and texture of John Dory.

LA MORUE

Dried salt cod

Dried salt cod is available in many different ways today. Throughout France, it is sold in grocers and super-markets sometimes as a whole fish, fins and tail included and as hard as wood, sometimes as fillets. It is sometimes packed in a little wooden box, and sometimes wrapped in plastic and frozen. In Nice, dried salt cod is often sold soaking in a pan of running water so that it is ready to be cooked at once.

For centuries, dried salt cod has been served on Fridays, during Lent and on Christmas days because the Papacy decreed these to be meatless days. Dried salt cod is therefore often referred to as "the lean days' beef", although recently it has also become fashionable and is served on any day of the week.

Dried salt cod is mainly eaten along the Mediter-ranean, but in other areas such as Brittany, Lyon Auvergne and Burgundy, it can be found in a variety of local dishes.

Dried salt cod must be soaked for about 24 hours in several changes of water before being cooked. Place the

soaked fish on a heatproof plate or an upturned small, heatproof dish in the pan so the fish does not touch the bottom of the pan, and to allow the salt to drop easily. Cover with cold water and bring to the boil. Lower the heat, poach gently for 3–5 minutes depending on size, then remove the pan from the heat and leave the fish to cool in the water.

Dried salt cod can become a true ally in the kitchen because it can be used to make a great many different light and pungent dishes. It may be either served in 5 x 5 cm (2 x 2 in) pieces, shredded or puréed. It may be flavoured with cream, garlic, oil and lemon, red or white wine, melted butter, Vinaigrette (see p. 76) or béchamel sauce. It can be added to potatoes, onions, tomatoes, spinach, leeks, anchovies or peppers, or it may be included in a spinach gratin or Bouillabaisse de morue or turned into fritters, croquettes or a salad.

Always choose thick fillets, preferably those that have come from the centre of the fish, and allow about 100 g (4 oz) dry weight, per person.

SERVES 4

40 g (1½ oz) unsalted butter
225 g (8 oz) sorrel, about 4 handfuls, stems
removed, shredded with scissors
1 teaspoon plain flour
1 tablespoon double cream
2 egg yolks
salt and freshly ground black pepper
1.25 kg (2¾ lb) John Dory, filleted

Pre-heat the oven to 190°C / 375°F / Gas 5. Butter a shallow ovenproof dish.

Heat half the butter in a pan. Add the sorrel and stir with a wooden spoon over a moderately high heat until the leaves have wilted and any liquid evaporated. In a small bowl, stir together the flour, cream and egg yolks. Stir into the sorrel. Cook gently, stirring, for about 3 minutes until lightly thickened; do not allow to boil. Add salt and pepper to taste.

Place half of the sorrel mixture in the dish then lay the fish fillets on top. Sprinkle with salt and pepper and pour over the remaining sorrel mixture. Dot with the remaining butter and bake in the oven for 20 minutes until the fish flakes easily when tested with the point of a knife.

PROVENCE

Daurade au Four

BAKED BREAM WITH FENNEL, LEMON AND HERBS

An uncomplicated dish, but the ingredients must be fresh.

SERVES 4

4 tablespoons olive oil
3 onions, thinly sliced
1 fennel bulb, trimmed, thinly sliced into rounds
about 10 sprigs of fresh parsley
2 bay leaves

salt and freshly ground black pepper
1.25 kg (2¾ lb) bream, halibut or bass, filleted
4 tomatoes, seeded and sliced
4 teaspoons fennel seeds or aniseeds
1 lemon, sliced
5 tablespoons dry white wine
3 or 4 large iceberg coarse lettuce leaves
juice of 1 lemon

Pre-heat the oven to 180°C / 350°F / Gas 4.

Heat 2 tablespoons of olive oil in a frying-pan, add the onions and fennel and cook over a moderate heat, stirring occasionally, for about 5 minutes until beginning to soften.

Place half of the onions and fennel, the parsley and 1 bay leaf in a baking dish. Sprinkle with a little salt and pepper. Lay half of the fish on top, skin-side down, sprinkle with salt, pepper and olive oil. Place the remaining fish on top, skin-side up. Cover with the tomatoes, remaining onions, fennel and bay leaf, the fennel seeds or aniseeds and the lemon slices. Pour over the wine and a little olive oil.

Lay a few lettuce leaves loosely on top and bake in the oven for about 25 minutes until the flesh is milky when tested with the tip of a knife. Discard the lettuce leaves. Using 2 fish slices, carefully transfer the fish to a warm serving dish. Sprinkle with the lemon juice and a little pepper, then trickle over the remaining olive oil and serve immediately.

BURGUNDY

Bar au Vin Rouge

SEA BASS WITH RED WINE SAUCE

Burgundy boasts an abundance of good wine, good fish, good poultry, serious home-cooks and ambitious chefs. But although the half-timbered houses, ivory coloured mansions and varnished roofs speak of permanence and evoke continuity, cookery in Burgundy is a living art and as such is constantly evolving. In fact, during the last few years it has done many, perhaps *too* many, acrobatic performances. Fortunately, although the French tend to be thrilled by innovation and love to be surprised and fashionable, they also know that home cooking based on local products remains the true barometer of a good chef. So even Michelin three-star chefs in very sophisticated restaurants appreciate the value of the regional cuisine.

The following recipe resulted from a delicious meal we enjoyed in Saulieu at the restaurant *Côte d'Or*. Monsieur Bernard Loiseau, who for over ten years has been both inventive and controversial and praised and criticized, uses the best Burgundian ingredients, works with local farmers, fishermen and cheese makers and blends traditional methods with modern techniques. His *Bar au Vin Rouge* is an inspired combination of tastes and textures and gains much of its character from the skilful partnership of a red wine with a fish. The fish is cooked on one side only so that it remains crisp and is not overcooked, the sauce is thickened with a carrot purée to balance the wine reduction and the shallots provide a complementary flavour.

SERVES 4

120 g (4½ oz) unsalted butter
350 g (12 oz) shallots, thinly sliced
salt and freshly ground black pepper
2 tablespoons sugar
225 g (8 oz) carrots, sliced
900 ml (1½ pints) soft, fruity red wine, such as Gamay
1 tablespoon groundnut oil
4 fillets sea bass
2 teaspoons plain flour

Heat 40 g (1½ oz) butter in the frying-pan, add the shallots, sprinkle with salt and cook over a low heat for about 25 minutes, stirring occasionally. Off the heat, tilt the frying-pan to one side then, using a slotted spoon draw the shallots to the other side of the pan so the liquid drains away then transfer the shallots to a saucepan. Sprinkle over the sugar, cover and cook over a low heat for a further 25–30 minutes until the mixture turns into a purée.

Meanwhile, cook the carrots in boiling, salted water until tender. Drain well, then purée. Boil the wine until reduced to 150 ml (5 fl oz). Stir in the carrot purée then lower the heat and gradually whisk in 50 g (2 oz) of the butter. Remove from the heat, season with salt and pepper, cover and keep warm over a very low heat.

Heat the remaining butter and the oil in a wide frying-pan over a high heat. Season the fish, sprinkle flour lightly over the skin then place in the pan, skin-side down, and cook for about 4–5 minutes. Do not turn the fish, but put a lid on the pan, and cook over a very low heat about 2 minutes. Remove the pan from the heat.

Pour a quarter of the wine sauce on each plate, add a quarter of the shallots then place a piece of fish, skin-side up, in the centre of each plate.

Brandade

SALT COD AND POTATO PURÉE

Dried salt cod has been a staple of French Mediterranean cookery for centuries. It was taken to Provence and Languedoc by Norwegian and other traders from northern waters. It is still very popular and is prepared in innumerable ways.

The process which transforms a hard, dry, grey piece of fish into *Brandade*, an ivory, fluffy mousse, is not a complicated one. It used to require endurance and a steady hand as the ingredients were pounded in a mortar and then stirred over a low heat but today, with the help of a blender or a food processor, *Brandade* is child's play. And whereas traditional *Brandade* required a great amount of olive oil, the recipe I use now contains less oil but more milk and potatoes so is lighter and less rich. When it is served as a white pyramid, sprinkled with black olives and surrounded by crisp Croûtons it makes a splendid, fragrant dish. Any *Brandade* that is left over makes a delicious filling for an omelette, formed into croquettes, or used as a base for poached eggs.

A large bowl of crisp salad seasoned with *Vinaigrette* (see p.76) is a good accompaniment.

Brandade can be prepared in advance. Warm through gently and beat in 2 tablespoons of warm milk or cream.

SERVES 6

750 g (1½ lb) dried salt cod
2 bay leaves
1 onion, studded with 1 clove
450 g (1 lb) potatoes, unpeeled
300 ml (10 fl oz) milk
250 ml (8 fl oz) olive oil
3 garlic cloves, crushed
2 teaspoons freshly grated nutmeg
juice of 1 lemon or 1 orange
freshly ground white pepper
2 tablespoons Niçoise or black Greek olives, halved if large, stoned
3 slices good, firm bread prepared as Triangular Croûtons (see p.233), or 6 slices baguette, prepared as Croûtons (see p.233)
1 tablespoon chopped fresh parsley

Place the dried salt cod in a large pan or basin and cover with cold water. Soak for at least 24 hours, changing the water 5 or 6 times.

Drain the dried salt cod then place on an upturned heatproof plate or small dish in an enamelled or stainless steel saucepan and cover with cold water. Add the bay leaves and onion and bring slowly to the boil. Lower the heat, poach for 3 minutes, then turn off the heat and leave the cod to cool in the water. Drain well, remove the skin and any bones and flake the flesh with a fork.

Cook the potatoes in boiling water until soft. Drain well, leave to cool then peel and press through a sieve.

Warm the milk and all except 1½ table-spoons of the oil in separate pans. Place a few pieces of cod in a food processor and mix briefly. Add the garlic and more flaked cod, and continue processing, alternately pouring in milk and oil, and adding cod until you have a smooth ivory purée. Transfer to a bowl and gradually beat in the potato. Add nutmeg, lemon or orange juice and pepper.

Transfer to a warm shallow dish. Sprinkle over the remaining olive oil, stir and mound into a dome. Arrange the olives in the centre of the dome. Dip a tip of Triangular Croûtons, or edge of large ones into the *Brandade*, then into chopped parsley and place round the dish.

THROUGHOUT FRANCE

Assiette de Fruits de Mer

SEAFOOD PLATTER

A sumptuous platter piled high with many different types of cooked and live seafood and perched on top of a wire stand is a wonderful sight whether it is served as a starter, a main dish at home or a refreshing snack in a brasserie after the theatre.

I remember a glorious Sunday lunch in Roscoff where I sat with three generations of sea- and shellfish-loving people sharing a staggering display. Everyone was as dainty and swift with their tools as medieval craftsmen. Tiny fingers catching winkles briskly, big fingers cracking claws vivaciously. With perseverance and anticipation they attacked everything from the tiniest grey shrimps to the fiercest looking crabs, extracting delicate pieces, chewing, biting, sucking and cracking enthusiastically. As they enjoyed the messy, fragrant, traditional Sunday ritual, sharing tools, memories and jokes, there was plenty of time to see how the meal made them close to each other.

Whether the seafood is cooked or live, make sure it is all really fresh; if it is cooked it should, of course, still be in its shell. Ideally, there should be a choice of different types of oysters and clams, but away from the coast this is not always possible. The time of year will also affect and influence the selection of fish in an *Assiette*.

Don't forget to put the paraphernalia of crab pickers, nutcrackers, tiny forks and pins as well as finger bowls and paper napkins on the table.

SERVES 4

12–16 clams
12–16 mussels
12 Dublin Bay prawns
450–750g (1–1½ lb) prawns
about 350 g (12 oz) brown shrimps
about 450 g (1 lb) cockles and winkles
8–12 oysters
1 cooked crab, shell cracked (see p.144)

FOR THE BROTH

1.75 litres (3 pints) water
salt
300 ml (10 fl oz) dry white wine
1 small onion studded with 1 clove
2 bay leaves
2 sprigs of fresh thyme
6 black peppercorns

TO SERVE

fresh seaweed or cracked ice
thinly sliced rye and country bread
unsalted butter
Mayonnaise (see p.101) or
Aïoli (see p.76)
lemon quarters

Leave the clams and mussels for 2–3 hours in a large basin or bucket of heavily salted cold water, stirring occasionally with a wooden spoon to get rid of the sand.

Put all the ingredients for the broth into a large pan, bring to the boil then boil gently for 10 minutes. Add the Dublin Bay prawns and simmer for 2½ minutes. Add the prawns, cook for 2 minutes, add the shrimps and cook for a further 2 minutes. Remove all the prawns and shrimps using a sieve or slotted spoon, and leave to drain. Add the cockles and winkles to the pan and poach for 4 minutes. Remove and drain. Reserve the pan of broth.

Scrub the clams and mussels with a hard brush under cold running water. Discard any that are not tightly closed, or have damaged shells. Remove and discard the 'beards' from the mussels. Remove the onion from the broth then pour off all but 150 ml (5 fl oz). Bring the broth remaining in the pan to the boil, add the mussels, and clams that are to be eaten cooked, cover and cook over a high heat, shaking the pan occasionally, for about 5 minutes until the shells have opened. Drain, discard any shells that have remained closed, then leave to cool.

Open the clams that are to be eaten raw, and the oysters (see p.229) just before serving. Line a large plate with seaweed or cracked ice and arrange all the seafood on it.

Place thinly sliced rye and country bread, unsalted butter, a bowl of Mayonnaise or *Aïoli* and plenty of lemon quarters on the table.

BRITTANY

Lotte à l'Armoricaine

MONKFISH WITH TOMATO, HERB, GARLIC AND
WINE SAUCE

The following recipe is adapted from a sumptuous meal I ate in Audierne, on the very tip of Brittany. In this most mystical of places contrasts exist side by side – granite and fig trees, mimosa and a grey ocean. The inhabitants are used to challenges being the descendants of valiant fishermen and bold pirates. Monsieur Adolf Bosser, the chef-patron of the *Le Goyen* restaurant, is the living embodiment of those virtues and so is his cuisine.

Lobster is the traditional main ingredient but it is so expensive that monkfish (the so-called poor man's lobster) is considered a perfect substitute. Other firm-fleshed fish such as cod will also be enhanced by the spirited sauce.

I suggest serving buttered rice or tiny boiled potatoes, and steamed vegetables with *Lotte à l'Armoricaine*.

SERVES 6

*2 skinned monkfish tails, each weighting about
750 g (1½ lb)
salt and freshly ground black pepper
3 tablespoons olive oil
40 g (1½ oz) butter
1 small leek, chopped
1 onion, chopped
2 small shallots
1 garlic clove, crushed
5 tomatoes, chopped
1–2 tablespoons tomato purée
2 sprigs of fresh thyme
1 sprig of fresh tarragon
½ bay leaf
450 ml (15 fl oz) dry white wine
2 tablespoons brandy
cayenne pepper
1 teaspoon sugar (optional)*

TO GARNISH
chopped fresh parsley and tarragon

Remove and discard the fine membrane covering the monkfish tails, fillet each tail then slice into approximately 5 cm (2 in) pieces on the diagonal. Season lightly.

Heat the oil and 15 g (½ oz) of butter in a deep, heavy-based frying-pan and sauté the fish for a few minutes, turning occasionally, until brown. Transfer to a warm plate. Cover with foil.

Add the leek, onion, shallots and garlic to the pan and cook slowly for 5 minutes until soft. Stir in the tomatoes, tomato purée, thyme, tarragon, bay leaf, wine and brandy. Bring to the boil then simmer the sauce for 20 minutes.

Strain the sauce through a sieve then pour back into the pan. Add the fish and cook gently for 8–10 minutes. Add a little cayenne pepper and check the seasoning. Add a little sugar, if necessary, to balance the acidity of the tomatoes. Away from the heat, stir in the remaining butter. Garnish with parsley and tarragon.

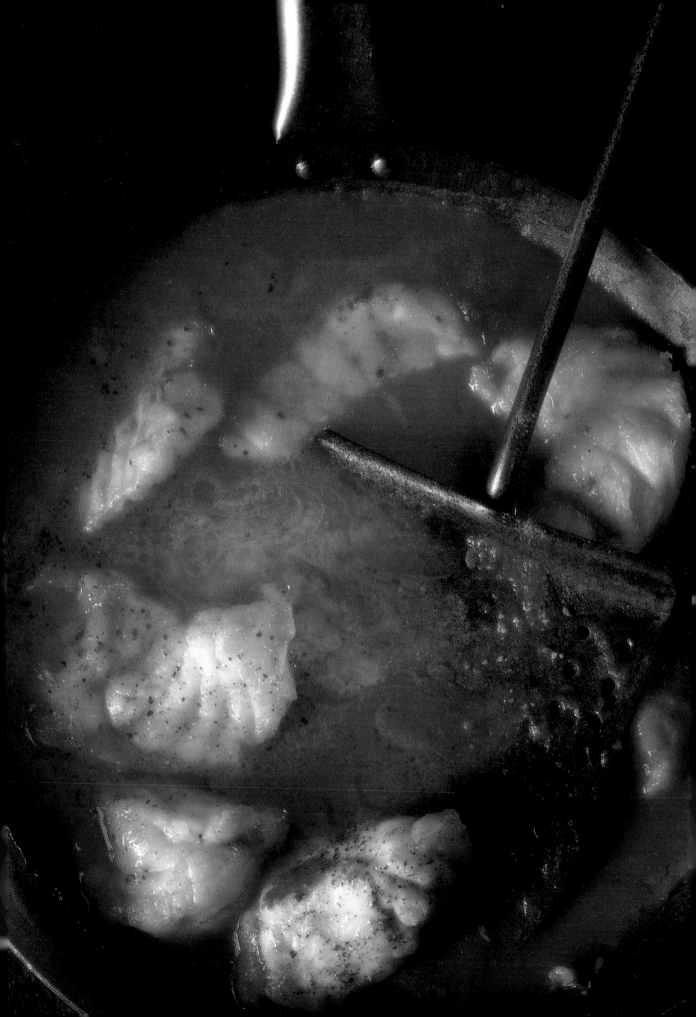

Suppions Farcis

STUFFED SQUID

Squid are lean, and reasonable in price so I serve them in many guises, but on very hot summer days the following recipe is light and refreshing. I use spinach for the stuffing as it is widely available but a sorrel and Swiss chard mixture (use the green part of the Swiss chard and keep the stalks for another dish) can be used in place of the spinach. As a variation two chopped, hard-boiled eggs and 2 teaspoons of fresh breadcrumbs can be added with the spinach.

SERVES 4

900 g (2 lb) small whole squid
2 tablespoons olive oil
75 g (3oz) spring onions, white part only, finely chopped
3 garlic cloves, crushed
175–200 g (6–7 oz) cooked, drained spinach or Swiss chard
salt and freshly ground black pepper
2 tablespoons chopped fresh flatleaf parsley or basil

Pre-heat the oven to 180°C/350°F/Gas 4.

Rinse the squid then, holding the head just below the eyes, gently pull it away from the body pouch. Discard the soft innards that come away with it. Pull out and discard the fine, flexible, transparent quill that is attached to the inside of the pouch. Cut the head from the tentacles just below the eyes, and discard. The tentacles will be joined together – in the centre is a beak-like mouth, which can be removed by squeezing it out. Slip the fingers under the skin covering the body pouch and peel it off. Cut the fins away from either side of the pouch. Rinse the pouch and dry thoroughly. Finely chop the tentacles.

Heat 1 tablespoon oil in a frying-pan, add the spring onions and garlic and cook, stirring occasionally, for 2–3 minutes. Add the chopped tentacles and cook for a further 2–3 minutes.

Transfer the mixture to a food processor, add the spinach and mix for about 1½ minutes. Season then divide the stuffing between the squid body pouches. Close the openings with wooden cocktail sticks then place the squid close together in a baking dish. Sprinkle with the remaining oil and bake in the oven for about 20 minutes. Remove the cocktail sticks and sprinkle the squid with chopped parsley or basil.

Moules et Palourdes Farcies

STUFFED MUSSELS AND CARPETSHELL CLAMS

Palourdes, which grow to 7.5 cm (3 in), are the largest of the European clams that are considered worth eating. They can be eaten raw, like oysters, or cooked in the same way as mussels. Also, like mussels, they are grown off the coasts of Brittany and the Vendée and there are a number of different recipes for stuffing them. Serve the stuffed mussels or clams piping hot with thin slices of crusty bread to mop up the juices.

SERVES 4

2kg (4 lb)/2.25 litres (4 pints) mussels or clams
salt
300 ml (10 fl oz) water
3 sprigs of fresh thyme

FOR THE CREAM AND CHEESE STUFFING
50 g (2 oz) butter
1 large shallot, finely chopped
120 ml (4 fl oz) double cream
100 g (4 oz) Gruyère, grated
about 25 g (1 oz) fresh breadcrumbs
3 tablespoons finely chopped fresh, flatleaf parsley

Discard any mussels or clams that are not tightly closed or are damaged. Scrub the mussels or clams under cold running water, using a hard brush. Place in a sink or bowl of salty water, discard any that float, then leave the others for 2–3 hours to remove all the sand. Drain the mussels or clams and rinse again. Remove the stringy 'beards' from the mussels.

Bring the water to the boil in a large pan. Add the thyme and mussels or clams, cover tightly and cook over a high heat, shaking the pan from time to time, for about 5 minutes until the shells open. Strain off the liquid. Discard the top shell of each clam or mussel, and any that remain closed.

For the cream and cheese stuffing, pre-heat the grill. Line 4 shallow heatproof dishes with crumpled foil.

Heat half the butter in a frying-pan, add the shallot and cook gently for about 3 minutes. Stir in the cream and bring to the boil. Remove from the heat and stir in the cheese, about three-quarters of the breadcrumbs and the parsley. Using a teaspoon place a little of the mixture around each clam or mussel, sprinkle with the remaining breadcrumbs, and dot with the remaining butter. Arrange in the dishes and place under the grill for 2–3 minutes until brown.

VARIATIONS

Bacon, Tomato and Herb Stuffing

1 tablespoon olive oil
1 onion, finely chopped
175 g (6 oz) lean streaky bacon
50 g (2 oz) cooked or raw ham such as Bayonne, diced
2 garlic cloves, finely minced
1 large tomato, skinned seeded and chopped
3 tablespoons white wine
1½ tablespoons finely chopped mixed fresh herbs such as parsley, chervil, basil and mint
salt and freshly ground black pepper
1 egg, lightly beaten
juice of 1 lemon

Pre-heat the oven to 220°C/425°F/Gas 7. Line 4 shallow baking dishes with crumpled aluminium foil.

Heat the oil in a frying-pan, add the onion and cook, stirring occasionally, for 3–4 minutes. Stir in the bacon, ham, garlic and tomato and cook for about 5 minutes. Stir in the wine, herbs, salt and pepper and simmer for 4–5 minutes.

Remove the pan from the heat, and stir in the egg. Fill each mussel or clam shell, arrange in the foil, and bake in the oven for about 8 minutes. Drizzle a few drops of fresh lemon juice over and serve.

Butter, Shallot and Herb Stuffing

4 shallots, chopped
1 garlic clove, chopped
2½ tablespoons chopped fresh parsley
1 teaspoon chopped fresh chervil
175 g (6 oz) butter, softened
1½ tablespoons white wine
salt and freshly ground black pepper

Pre-heat the oven to 230°C/450°F/Gas 8. Line 4 shallow baking dishes with crumpled foil.

Place the shallots, garlic and herbs in a food processor and mix briefly. Place the butter in a bowl, add the shallot mixture, wine and seasonings, and beat together. Spoon a little of the butter around each clam or each mussel in its half shell, place in the dishes and bake in the oven for 3–4 minutes.

VENDEE

Sardines en Brochettes
SARDINE AND PEPPER BROCHETTES

I discovered this simple dish on the charming island of Noirmoutier, in the Atlantic ocean just off the Vendée coast. Noirmoutier is a holiday resort which resembles a Greek island, with its stark windmills and whitewashed, blue-shuttered cottages. The sardines were prepared using the local fragrant sea salt, newly harvested and smelling faintly of violets. They were served with the renowned Noirmoutier Charlotte potatoes.

From Brittany to Provence there are endless ways of using sardines – raw with lemon and oil, marinated in lemon juice, grilled, stuffed and fried. In this dish they are treated very simply. Dipping them in sea salt adds flavour and makes them easier to fold onto the skewers.

SERVES 1

4 sardines, each weighing about 100 g (4 oz)
about 75 g (3 oz) coarse sea salt
½ teaspoon dried thyme
½ red pepper, cut into 4 cm (1½ in) pieces
½ green pepper, cut into 4 cm
(1½ in) pieces
¼ onion, separated into layers, cut into 4 cm
(1½ in) pieces
1½ tablespoons olive oil
freshly ground black pepper

Pre-heat the grill.

Working from tail to head and using a knife, scrape the scales from the sardines. Slit along the underside of each fish then remove the intestines. Cut off the heads. Open out each fish and place, skin-side up, on a board. With a thumb, press lightly along the centre of the back of one fish, then turn the fish over and lift away the backbone. Leave the boned fish in coarse sea salt for 30 seconds. Remove from the salt and carefully brush off all the excess. Sprinkle over a little thyme and pepper.

Brush the peppers and onion with olive oil and sprinkle with sea salt and pepper. Skewer sardines, red pepper and green pepper and onion alternately along a skewer until all the ingredients have been used. Grill for 5–8 minutes, turning a few times.

ALONG THE FRENCH COASTS

Moules Marinières
MUSSELS COOKED IN WHITE WINE AND HERBS

The best mussels are *bouchots*, so called because they attach themselves to, and grow on, wooden posts, *bouchots*, erected by fishermen in the water along many stretches of the French coastline. There are many different recipes for cooking them but this light, fresh-tasting mussel dish

is popular everywhere. Mussels should be tightly closed before they are cooked and they must be eaten the same day they are bought. Cooked mussels which are not open should be discarded.

SERVES 4 AS A FIRST COURSE

2 kg (4 lb) / 2.25 litres (4 pints) mussels
50 g (2 oz) butter
2 tablespoons oil
1 garlic clove, crushed
3 shallots or ½ onion, finely chopped
300 ml (½ pint) dry white wine
1 bay leaf
1 sprig of fresh thyme
parsley stems
salt and freshly ground black pepper
3 tablespoons chopped fresh flatleaf parsley

TO SERVE

rye or wholemeal bread and butter

Scrub the mussels with a hard brush, under running cold water, then place in a sink filled with cold salted water and discard those which float or are not tightly closed. Leave for 2–3 hours. With a knife or with your fingers pull out the 'beards' which come out of each shell then rinse well under cold running water until the water is free of sand and the shells are clean.

. Heat the butter and oil in a very wide frying-pan or pan. Add the garlic and shallots or onion and cook gently for 3–4 minutes until soft. Pour in the wine and bring to the boil. Add the herbs, salt and mussels, cover and cook for about 5 minutes, shaking the pan, and tossing it with an up-and-down motion twice so that the mussels cook evenly. The shells should all be open; discard any that remain closed. Scoop out the mussels with a wide, flat, draining spoon, and place them in a warm, deep dish. Discard the empty top half of each shell using oven gloves. Cover the dish and keep the mussels warm.

Strain the cooking liquid through a sieve lined with a double thickness of muslin. Rinse the pan, return the liquid to it, bring to the boil then boil for 5 minutes. Pour over the mussels and sprinkle with pepper and chopped parsley. Serve at once in warm soup plates, with rye or wholemeal bread and butter.

VARIATIONS

- For a richer dish, the cooking liquid can be reduced over a high heat for 10 minutes then 5 or 6 tablespoons of double cream and lemon juice to taste stirred in before pouring on to the cooked mussels.
- Cider may be used instead of wine if you want to make *Moules Marinières* following a Brittany or Normandy recipe.
- Diane and Alexandre Faidy, aged four and six, who made *Moules Marinières* for me in Roscoff, did not use garlic, bay leaf and thyme.

BRITTANY

Crabes à la Mayonnaise
CRAB MAYONNAISE

One of the most enjoyable ways of spending an early morning or late afternoon is to visit the harbour at Guilvinec or Concarneau when the fishing boats return with their catches. Crates and baskets filled with scallops, conger eels, rock salmon (dog fish), lobster and crabs are carried to the other side of the quay where, at the *marché à la criée*, wholesale fish market, the auctioneer calls for bids on the lots and the customers respond in all kinds of peculiar ways: wriggling their nose, rubbing their ears, shaking their thumbs or raising their eyebrows. A little later the local fish market opens in the square for the villagers. Although the amount and variety of fish and shellfish every day is staggering, crabs, particularly *tourteaux*, common crabs, are the most abundant and the most reasonable in price. Other crabs may be *araignées*, spider crabs, which, as their name suggests, have long, thin legs, and small *étrilles*, fiddler or velvet crabs.

Crabs are available all year round but are at their best during the summer. Choose crabs that smell fresh and feel heavy for their size. If buying a cooked crab, which many people prefer to do, keep it cool and eat it on the same day.

In Brittany, and elsewhere, crab is often preferred to lobster, and there is no better way of enjoying it than this simple recipe. Don't forget to have on the table all the necessary paraphernalia – nutcrackers, crab pickers, pins stuck on corks, and last but not least, finger bowls with lemon slices floating in them.

SERVES 4

4 freshly-boiled crab, each weighing about
450 g (1 lb)
2 tablespoons whipping cream
Lemon Mayonnaise (see p.101)
1 tablespoon finely chopped fresh chives, parsley and
chervil
a pinch of cayenne pepper
Vinaigrette (see p.76)

TO SERVE

fresh seaweed, cracked ice or crisp salad leaves
thinly sliced country bread
slightly salted butter

Place one crab on its back. Twist the claws backwards and break them from the body. Remove the legs in the same way, snapping them loose at the lowest joint, as close as possible to the shell. Crack the claws into large pieces with a blow with the back of a heavy knife, but take care not to crush the meat inside. Lift the pointed apron flap, or tail,

break it away from the body and discard it. With the point of a sharp knife, prise up the central part of the shell, then pull it free. Discard the spongy gills (dead men's fingers) from the sides of the main body section. Also discard the small bag-like stomach sack and the attached threads, situated near the crab's mouth. Crack the central section in half, if liked. Repeat with the remaining crabs.

Place all the pieces of crab on a bed of seaweed, ice or crisp salad leaves. Lightly whip the cream, then lightly fold into the Mayonnaise. Gently stir in the herbs and add cayenne pepper, to taste. Serve this sauce, the Vinaigrette, thinly sliced country bread and slightly salted butter with the crab.

VENDÉE

Huîtres Chaudes

WARM OYSTERS WITH CREAM AND CHIVES

Traditionally, oysters are eaten raw with buttered bread and a squeeze of lemon juice, or a drop of vinegar as we do in Paris, but today warm oysters bathed in either a light or a rich sauce are becoming fashionable.

The easiest way to prepare warm oysters is to nestle them on their half shells in a 1 cm (½ in) layer of coarse sea salt, rock salt or sand so they will not slip, then place them in an oven preheated to 180°C/350°F/Gas 4 for 3 minutes and serve with a bowl of whipped cream or soured cream and a large peppermill. But my favourite way is this very special recipe from Valentin Brun, chef of *La Marée*, one of La Rochelle's most popular seafood restaurants.

Choose oysters that are very fresh, very full, heavy and tightly closed. Unopened oysters can be kept deep-shell down and wrapped in a damp cloth, so they stay moist, in the fridge or in a cool place for four to five days; do not put them in water. Once opened, oysters must be eaten as soon as possible.

Six to twelve oysters per person is usually adequate but for the following recipe, four should be enough as the topping is luxurious.

SERVES 4

16 plump oysters
25 g (1 oz) butter
1 shallot, very finely chopped
175 ml (6 fl oz) crème fraîche
2 tablespoons lemon juice
2 tablespoons finely snipped fresh chives
salt and freshly ground white pepper

FOR THE LEEKS

25 g (1 oz) butter
1 small, slim leek, white part only, finely chopped
1 tablespoon snipped fresh chives

Pre-heat the oven to 180°C/350°F/Gas 4. Line a shallow baking dish with crumpled foil.

Rinse the oyster shells. Cover one hand with a thick cloth, then place the oyster, rounded-side down, in your palm. Insert a strong knife with a short, pointed blade where the growth rings start in the shell, alongside the hinge. Holding the two halves of the oyster together, give the knife a quick upward turn, cutting through the muscle at the hinge. Slide the knife under the oyster to cut it free from the shell. Discard the top shells and the liquor. Place the oysters in the dish and keep warm for about 3 minutes.

For the leeks, melt the butter in a small pan, add the leeks and cook gently until softened. Stir in the chives. Remove from the heat and keep warm.

Melt the butter in a small frying-pan, add the shallot and cook over a moderate heat, stirring occasionally, for about 4 minutes until soft-ened. Stir in the crème fraîche and boil for 2–3 minutes until slightly thickened. Add the liquor

from the oysters, the lemon juice, chives, salt and pepper, and simmer for 1–2 minutes. Spoon a bed of leeks and chives into each oyster shell and place the oysters on top. Spoon the shallot mixture over each oyster then place in the oven for a few minutes.

Using oven gloves, place the oysters in their shells on a plate lined with a napkin or coarse salt so they will not slide.

THROUGHOUT FRANCE

Salade de Coquilles St Jacques
SCALLOP SALAD

I have loved this recipe for a long time and use it often as the ingredients are neither overly rare nor expensive. From October until May, when fresh scallops are available, this is one of the quickest and easiest recipes to prepare. I serve the scallops either on a bed of crisp lettuce leaves, such as batavia (escarole) or a bed of chicory, lightly cooked in butter for 15 minutes.

SERVES 4

1 head batavia (escarole)
16 scallops on the half-shell
(50 g) 2 oz butter
1 teaspoon vegetable oil
salt and freshly ground black pepper
juice of 1 lemon
1 large avocado pear
2 tablespoons chopped fresh chervil, thyme or flatleaf parsely

FOR THE DRESSING

5 tablespoons mixed olive oil and vegetable oil
2 tablespoons white wine vinegar
1 tablespoon double cream
salt and freshly ground black pepper

Stir the dressing ingredients together in a bowl, or shake them together in a screw-top jar. Wash and trim the batavia (escarole) and separate the leaves. Place on a large flat plate.

Use a sharp knife to sever the scallops from their shells and separate the corals from the white bodies. Discard the membrane surrounding the corals and bodies, and the dark organs and crescent-shaped muscles from the bodies. Rinse and pat dry.

Heat the butter and oil in a wide frying-pan, add the scallops and corals and cook for 1½ minutes on each side. Using a fish slice, remove from the pan, sprinkle with salt, pepper and lemon juice, then using a sharp knife, thinly slice each body; leave the corals whole. Scatter the scallop slices and corals over the batavia (escarole).

Quickly peel the avocado, cut in half, discard the stone and slice the flesh. Arrange the slices around the plate. Shake or stir the dressing then pour over the salad. Scatter the chervil, thyme or parsley on top. Take to the table and toss just before serving.

BURGUNDY

Escargots à la Bourguignonne

SNAILS WITH PARSLEY AND GARLIC BUTTER

There are two main types of snails eaten in France, the little grey ones, *petits gris*; and the large, brownish *escargots de Bourgogne*, which are generally considered to be the best variety.

The Romans loved snails and centuries later, during the Middle Ages, monasteries and convents had snail parks, but it was not until the end of the nineteenth century that snails really became a popular food in France. Today it is estimated that an average French person eats 20–30 dozens of snails a year. However, a large majority of these snails are imported, mainly from eastern European countries, because the native snail population is declining. When imported snails have been cooked according to any traditional French recipe they become, if not quite the brothers of French snails, at least their well-meaning cousins.

SERVES 4–6

24 large, or 36 small canned snails, drained and rinsed

FOR THE FILLING
225 g (8 oz) butter
3 garlic cloves, finely chopped
1 shallot, finely chopped
3 tablespoons finely chopped fresh parsley
salt and freshly ground black pepper
juice of 1 lemon
4 tablespoons dry white wine

TO SERVE
thin slices of bread

Pre-heat the oven to 220°C/425°F/Gas 7. Line 4 individual baking dishes with crumpled foil, unless you have a special snail plate.

Mix together the butter, garlic, shallot, parsley, salt, pepper and lemon juice. Using a small teaspoon or the tip of a knife, place a little butter mixture in each snail shell. Place the snails back in the shells and place a little more of the butter mixture on top. Put the snails on their snail cooking plate or in the dishes. Spoon a little wine over each snail and bake in the oven for about 5 minutes. Serve hot with thin slices of bread.

Poultry

LES VOLAILLES

What was once but a dream – a chicken in every pot every Sunday – has become today one of the most reasonably priced items on a menu. But, of course, there is chicken and there is chicken. A plump, silky, white-fleshed Bresse chicken fattened on maize and milk and running free has truly nothing in common with a mass-produced chicken which will melt away in a pool of water as it cooks. So the first rule – if you don't have a friendly farmer nearby – is to trust your local butcher or find a dependable supermarket where you can buy free- (or semi-free as is often the case) range chicken. In France, labels of quality are help-ful, mentioning both origin and breeding. If you buy a wrapped chicken, always check the date on the package, make sure the skin is dry and the smell is light and delicate. The differ-ence between yellow skin and white-skinned chicken is only in the appearance but it does make any dish more appetizing. Always store poultry in the coldest part of the refrigerator and for no more than two days.

Brillat-Savarin claimed that poultry was to a cook what canvas was to a painter, and indeed, dishes improvized around a chicken are inumerable. They range from a simple roast chicken, with just a pinch of salt, two garlic cloves and a knob of butter in the cavity, served with its juices rendered and nothing else to a stuffed hen (*Poule au Pot Farcie* p.152), a pungent sautéed chicken flavoured with wine vinegar (*Poulet au Vinaigre* p.151), or a fresh salad of walnuts, sautéed mushrooms and strips of lukewarm chicken on a bed of crisp greens seasoned with a warm vinaigrette and fresh herbs.

Whether it is in portions or whole, chicken may be seasoned with peeled or unpeeled garlic (even as many as 40 cloves, as cooked garlic is mild and has a nutty flavour), shallots, olives, peppers, tomatoes, artichokes, courgettes, potatoes, herbs or *Tapenade* (see p.78). Its cooking juices may be deglazed with single cream, calvados, cognac, wine or broth, and it may be simmered in a hearty red wine (*Coq au Vin* p.154), a dry white wine or a mellow dessert wine.

There is no waste in poultry. Gizzard, neck and bones simmered with an onion and a carrot will make a good broth (*Consommé* p.72) to be used later for a soup, a sauce, to deglaze a roast or to cook fragrant rice or pasta. The left-overs will turn into omelettes, croquettes, savoury, pancakes, gratins, soups, stuffed vegetables, pâtés and terrines. And cold chicken served with a bowl of *Rouille (see p.77)* or *Rémoulade* (see p.102) will make a glorious lunch.

To test when a chicken is cooked, prick the thigh with a fork: the juices should be yellow and clear not pink. Stuffed birds should always cook for fifteen minutes longer than those without stuffing.

The most commonly found types of duck in France are *nantais*, *rouennais* and *barbarie*. They are all quite small and quite lean. If you cannot find these types easily, use whatever is available, but first get rid of as much fat as possible, by pulling all the loose fat from the cavity and around the neck and pricking the skin on the thighs and chest with a fork so the fat will escape as it cooks. (You can then cook and render this fat with a little water so that you can keep it in a jar for sautéeing potatoes or seasoning a dish.)

Ducks and geese may be accompanied with turnips, sauerkraut or olives, all pungent enough to enhance their flavour. But they are also superb with oranges – sweet or the bitter seville variety – peaches, bitter cherries, apples (with perhaps an extra touch of calvados), prunes and chestnuts.

Chicken, geese, turkey and rabbit are white-fleshed and must always be well cooked. Duck, guinea fowl, pheasant, pigeons and quails are dark-fleshed and don't need full cooking. They are drier than chicken and need more butter or oil as they cook. Pheasant is best with fresh white grapes and fresh walnuts in its cooking juices.

What do we serve most often with chicken or poultry dishes? Often it is simply a tossed green watercress or dandelion salad seasoned with vinaigrette, a bowl of steamed new potatoes sprinkled with minced fresh herbs, or a bowl of fresh pasta or rice to absorb the juices. If we are hungrier we may try a *Gratin de courgettes* (see p.243), buttered chicory, a fragrant *Ratatouille* (see p.237), a *Pain d'Endives* (see p.245), a crisp *Galette de Pommes de Terre* (see p.257) or a steaming hot platter of sautéed mushrooms. And when the chicken is brought to the table in such good company, all the guests feel that yes, no matter what the day, it does feel like Sunday.

Poulet à la Crème et aux Morilles

CHICKEN WITH CREAM AND MOREL MUSHROOMS

Arguably the best chickens in the world come from the Bresse area of Burgundy. These very special birds can be identified in the shops by the Government-regulated *label rouge* on them. This guarantees that the white-feathered, blue-grey legged Bresse breed of chicken have been raised according to strict controls that specify the area of open space they must be given in which to roam, define a diet containing plenty of corn and milk, and state the minimum age at which the birds can be killed. Real devotees of Bresse chicken only eat them roasted to fully savour their pure flavour, but the following dish is also very popular, especially on the menus of *ferme-auberges*, farms in France which serve their own products, in this case, chickens. I tasted one version on the Perrin family's *ferme-auberge*, *Les Plattières*. The elder Madame Perrin was responsible for looking after the chickens, protecting them from foxes and buzzards, checking the quality of the grass, feeding them corn and monitoring them in the cooking pot.

For my luxurious version, do try to use the best quality free-range chicken you can find. Morel mushrooms are very expensive and rarely available fresh so are more often used in their dry form. These are sold in packets of about 20 g (¾ oz) and although these may also seem expensive, they are highly-flavoured and a few go a long way. I add fresh mushrooms for extra texture.

SERVES 4

20 g (¾ oz) dried morels
2 tablespoons vegetable oil
15 g (½ oz) butter
1.5 kg (3 lb) free-range chicken, cut into 8 pieces
225 g (8 oz) fresh mushrooms
about 450 ml (15 fl oz) chicken stock (see method)
2 tablespoons brandy
120 ml (4 fl oz) double cream
juice of 1 lemon
salt and freshly ground black pepper

TO GARNISH
chopped fresh parsley

Put the morels into a small bowl. Just cover with boiling water and leave to soak for 30 minutes.

Meanwhile, heat the oil and butter in a heavy casserole, add the chicken in batches and cook over a moderate heat for about 10–15 minutes until evenly browned. When the chicken is brown, transfer to a warm plate, cover and keep warm. Add the fresh mushrooms to the casserole and fry for 4–5 minutes, stirring occasionally. Remove using a slotted spoon. Discard any fat left in the casserole then return the chicken and fresh mushrooms to it.

Remove the morel mushrooms from the soaking liquid. Pour the liquid through a sieve into a measuring jug and add enough chicken stock to bring the liquid up to 600 ml (1 pint) and pour over the chicken. Wash the morels again to get rid of any remaining sand. Add the mushrooms to the chicken, cover and simmer gently for about 40 minutes or until the chicken is completely cooked.

Remove the chicken from the casserole, cover and keep warm. Add the brandy to the casserole, bring to the boil quickly and continue to boil for 2–3 minutes. Add the cream and lemon juice, and boil until the liquid is thickened and rich-tasting. Season then return the chicken pieces to the casserole and heat through for about 5 minutes. Serve sprinkled with chopped parsley.

THROUGHOUT FRANCE

Poulet au Vinaigre

CHICKEN WITH CUCUMBER IN VINEGAR AND CREAM SAUCE

Poulet au Vinaigre is a delicious dish which is popular throughout France, but this is my favourite version: a free-range chicken, good red wine vinegar and a fiery Dijon mustard will ensure this *Poulet au Vinaigre* is a sumptuous treat. Serve with rice or noodles and braised fennel, buttered broad beans or sautéed, grated courgettes.

SERVES 4

2 tablespoons vegetable oil
25 g (1 oz) butter
1.5–1.75 kg (3½-4 lb) free-range chicken,
cut into 8 pieces
2 extra chicken breast portions (optional)
salt and freshly ground black pepper
2 garlic cloves, finely chopped
2 shallots, finely chopped
1 onion, finely chopped
4 tablespoons red wine vinegar
1 tablespoon brandy
250 ml (8 fl oz) dry white wine
1 cucumber, peeled, halved lengthways, seeded and
cut into 1 cm (½ in) dice
3 tablespoons Dijon mustard
3 tablespoons double cream
1½ tablespoons chopped mixed fresh herbs such as
chives, dill or parsley

Pre-heat the oven to 200°C/400°F/Gas 6.

Heat the oil and butter in a large, heavy-based frying-pan. Season the chicken then add the legs to the pan and cook for about 15 minutes, turning occasionally with tongs, until they are golden on all sides. Transfer to a shallow, ovenproof dish, cover with foil and place in the oven. Cook the chicken breasts in the pan for about 10 minutes until evenly browned then add to the legs. Cover the dish again and leave in the oven with the heat switched off.

Discard half of the fat from the pan, add the garlic, shallots and onion and cook for 4–5 minutes until soft. Pour the wine vinegar, brandy and wine into the pan and bring to the boil, scraping up the coagulated juices from the bottom with a wooden spoon. Add the cucumber and simmer for 10 minutes. Stir in the mustard, lower the heat then stir in the cream. Add the chicken pieces, turn in the sauce to coat them then cook gently for 10–15 minutes. Check the seasoning then sprinkle with the herbs. Serve from the casserole or transfer to a warm, shallow dish.

BURGUNDY

Poulet au Fromage

CHICKEN WITH CHEESE, WINE AND VEGETABLES

This recipe was inspired by a former mayor of Dijon, Monsieur Gaston Gérard. He deglazed the juices of a sautéed chicken with white wine, then covered the bird with a rich sauce of cream and mustard, before baking it until crisp. I have made it many times, each time experimenting with different vegetables and spices. Now, with an interesting combination of leeks, celeriac and ginger, this is my favourite chicken recipe. It is rich and delectable.

I serve *Poulet au Fromage* for a buffet as it keeps warm in its baking dish, for an elegant dinner because it is easy to serve and needs only a little tossed salad for an accompaniment, and for an informal lunch.

SERVES 4

3 tablespoons groundnut oil
25 g (1 oz) unsalted butter
1 large free-range chicken, cut into 8 pieces
2 extra chicken breasts (optional)
salt and freshly ground black pepper
1 small celeriac bulb
2 leeks, white part only, sliced
2 celery sticks cut into 2.5 cm (1 in) pieces
300 ml (10 fl oz) dry white wine
200 ml (7 fl oz) whipping cream
2 tablespoons Dijon mustard
1½ tablespoons finely chopped fresh ginger
a pinch of freshly grated nutmeg
a pinch of cayenne pepper
175 g (6 oz) Gruyère, grated
3 tablespoons fresh breadcrumbs

Pre-heat the oven to 90°C/375°F/Gas 5.

Heat 2 tablespoons of oil and half the butter in a wide frying-pan and cook the chicken pieces, in batches, skin-side down first, for about 10 minutes or until brown. Turn them over and cook the other side for another 10 minutes. Transfer the chicken pieces when they are browned to a heavy casserole. Sprinkle with salt and pepper.

Meanwhile, peel the celeriac and cut into 2.5 cm (1 in) cubes and cook in boiling salted water for about 8 minutes. Heat the remaining oil and butter in a frying-pan and cook the leeks and celery, stirring occasionally, for 4–5 minutes. Add to the casserole with the drained celeriac.

Spoon off excess fat from the frying-pan, then pour in the wine and scrape up the coagulated juices at the bottom with a wooden spoon. Bring to the boil and boil for 2–3 minutes. Remove from the heat, cool slightly then stir in the cream, mustard, ginger, nutmeg, cayenne pepper and two-thirds of the cheese. Pour over the chicken and vegetables. Sprinkle over the breadcrumbs and the remaining cheese. Cover with foil and bake in the oven for 20 minutes. Remove the foil and cook for another 20–25 minutes until the top is brown.

THROUGHOUT FRANCE

Poule au Pot Farcie

POACHED STUFFED CHICKEN

Henri IV was a liberal king and open-minded about many things. He changed his religion from protestant to catholic in order to keep France united, and although he married quite young, he retained an active interest in the opposite sex all his life. One point on which he was to remain utterly inflexible, though, was his wish that each family in his kingdom should have a poached chicken every Sunday. This was a good way of cooking older hens that had stopped laying eggs so were no longer useful, as the long, slow, gentle cooking tenderized their flesh. Every region has its own recipe for the stuffing, but whether the chicken is filled with country ham and spinach, as in the following recipe, with pork and chopped cabbage, a spicy sausage, onion and parsley mixture, or with a mixture containing plenty of vegetables, it is always welcome at family meals. The ritual of serving and eating the dish has varied little over the years: first, the broth is served on Croûtons (see p. 233) sprinkled with fresh herbs, then the carved chicken and the stuffing are served with the vegetables and a bowl of well-flavoured Vinaigrette (see p. 76).

I like to cook the vegetables separately as I think their crisper textures and fresher flavours are more appealing than vegetables cooked in the pan with the chicken. I spoon a little hot broth over the steamed vegetables before serving the dish. The combination of fragrant chicken, tasty stuffing and fresh vegetables is truly a winning one.

SERVES 6–8

FOR THE STUFFING

1 ½ tablespoons vegetable oil
2 medium onions, chopped
100 g (4 oz) chicken livers, chopped
225 g (8 oz) frozen chopped spinach, thawed, drained and squeezed dry
450 g (1 lb) lean streaky bacon or raw ham, coarsely chopped
4 garlic cloves, chopped
10 sprigs flatleaf parsley, chopped
4 shallots, chopped
1 tablespoon chopped fresh thyme
a pinch of freshly grated nutmeg
2 eggs, lightly beaten
salt and freshly ground black pepper

FOR THE CHICKEN

2 kg (4½ lb) free-range chicken
15 g (½ oz) butter
2 tablespoons groundnut oil
1 bay leaf

2 sprigs of fresh thyme
1 onion, halved, each half studded with 1 clove
salt
5 black peppercorns
2 additional large chicken legs (optional)
2 tablespoons finely chopped fresh chives or flatleaf parsley

FOR THE VEGETABLES

Choose as large a selection as you like
8 carrots, halved lengthways and cut into 5 cm (2 in) pieces
4–8 small purple turnips, depending on size, halved or quartered
8 leeks, white part only, split lengthways, cut into 10 cm (4 in) pieces, and tied into a bundle with a piece of string
4 onions, halved
4 bulbs fennel, cut in half lengthways
8 celery sticks, cut into 5 cm (2 in) lengths

TO SERVE

double quantity Vinaigrette (see p. 76)

To make the stuffing, heat the oil in a frying-pan and sauté the onions for 3–4 minutes. Add the chicken livers, stir with a wooden spoon for 1 minute then remove from the heat. Stir in the spinach, bacon or ham, garlic, parsley, shallots, thyme, nutmeg, eggs and salt and pepper. Spoon into the cavity of the chicken, making sure it is not tightly packed. Sew up the opening, and truss the bird so that it will not lose its shape during cooking.

Heat the butter and 1 tablespoon of oil in a large frying-pan over a fairly high heat, add the chicken and brown lightly all over. Remove from the heat and place in a large pan. Add the bay leaf, thyme, onion halves, salt and peppercorns, cover with water, cover the pan and bring slowly to the boil. Immediately lower the heat so the liquid barely simmers and cook gently for 1¼ hours.

Add a little more oil to the frying-pan and fry the chicken legs, if using, until lightly browned. Add to the saucepan. If cooking the vegetables with the chicken, add them as well. Cook for a further 45 minutes.

If you prefer to steam the vegetables, about 30 minutes before the chicken is cooked bring a pan of water to the boil. Put the vegetables in a steaming basket, cover and place over the saucepan. Cook for 15–20 minutes until tender – if necessary, they can continue to cook while you carve the chicken.

Carefully remove the chicken and the legs, if using, from the pan. Discard the chicken skin, if liked, then remove the stuffing and place on a warm plate. Carve the chicken and add to the plate. Spoon over a few tablespoons of hot broth, and sprinkle with chives or parsley. Place the vegetables on another warm plate; spoon a little hot broth over the steamed vegetables and season with salt and pepper. Pour some of the remaining broth into a hot sauceboat or jug and serve with the bowl of Vinaigrette, the chicken and the vegetables.

VARIATION

Add 2 chopped hard-boiled eggs to the Vinaigrette.

Coq au Vin

CHICKEN COOKED IN RED WINE

Coq au Vin is one of the most enduring of the great traditional dishes. It is served in many different settings – country inns, small bistros, grand restaurants, family homes – yet no one ever tires of it.

It is an old dish. It may be as old as our Gallo-Roman civilization. According to the legend, when the cheeky, prosperous Gauls were besieged by the Romans they sent them an insolent *bon appétit!* message hung around the neck of one of their thinnest and most scrawny chickens. Julius Caesar, an astute man, decided that if the making of fine roads and good laws had not yet convinced the Gauls of the Romans' abilities he would try another route. He invited them to join him for dinner and served the rooster metamorphosed into a succulent, tasty dish by long simmering in Roman wine and herbs. The Gauls took one bite, then another, and concluded that the Romans were at long last displaying some sign of civilization. Hence the beginning of a long lasting relationship.

To be truly authentic, a cockerel should, of course, be used, but though it is difficult for most of us to find a mature cockerel today we can compensate by marinating a free-range chicken overnight in red wine and cooking it in a very flavourful wine-based sauce. I usually cut the chicken into pieces and add extra breasts to make sure there are plenty of meaty portions as they absorb the juices so much better.

Opinions vary about what wine to use: some people say it should be a good one, others advise that it should be a simple, hearty wine. I have tried both and my vote lies with the latter.

The chicken can be cooked in the wine and broth or stock up to a day or so in advance, cooled and kept in the refrigerator. Re-heat it over a low heat for about 40 minutes and then proceed with the recipe, thickening the liquid and adding the vegetables and bacon.

With *Coq au Vin* I like to serve a Vegetable Purée such as Celeriac or Fennel (see p. 160–61), tiny steamed potatoes, rice or noodles to absorb the sauce, and a bowl of salad.

SERVES 6

2 kg (4½) free-range chicken (with giblets), cut into 6 joints
2 extra chicken breasts (optional)
salt and freshly ground black pepper
2 tablespoons chopped fresh thyme
15–25 g (½-1 oz) butter
2–3 tablespoons vegetable oil
100 g (4 oz) thick-cut lean streaky bacon, diced
350 g (12 oz) button onions or shallots, peeled
2 carrots, thickly sliced
2 celery sticks, cut into 1 cm (½ in) cubes
225 g (8 oz) button mushrooms
2 bay leaves
2 sprigs of fresh parsley
1 sprig of fresh thyme
1 large onion, sliced
1 tablespoon plain flour beaten with 15 g (½ oz) unsalted butter
1–2 tablespoons brandy
the chicken's liver, finely chopped
3 garlic cloves, crushed
2 tablespoons double cream
a pinch of freshly grated nutmeg
juice of 1 lemon

FOR THE MARINADE

600 ml (1 pint) red wine
1 onion, sliced
1 carrot, sliced
2 bay leaves
2 garlic cloves, crushed
2 sprigs of fresh thyme
10 black peppercorns
2 tablespoons olive oil

FOR THE BROTH

300 ml (½ pint) chicken stock
or
chicken neck, bones and giblets, except the liver
1 onion, stuck with 1 clove
1 bay leaf
salt
1 sprig of fresh thyme
4 black peppercorns
600 ml (1 pint) water

TO SERVE

2 slices bread, made into Triangular Garlic Croûtons (see p.233)
2 tablespoons finely chopped fresh parsley

Combine all the ingredients of the marinade in a pan. Bring to the boil, lower the heat and simmer for 10 minutes. Cool.

Place the pieces of chicken in a single layer in a large, flat, non-metallic dish. Pour over the cold marinade, cover and leave in the refrigerator overnight, turning the chicken 2 or 3 times.

If you do not have a good chicken stock available, put the other ingredients for the broth into a large pan and simmer, uncovered, for 30 minutes, skimming the scum from the surface occasionally.

Correct the seasoning, then pour the stock through a sieve. Measure out 300 ml (½ pint) and reserve. Discard the contents of the sieve.

Lift the pieces of chicken from the marinade and pat dry with paper towels. Reserve the marinade liquid, vegetables and herbs. Sprinkle each piece of chicken with salt, pepper and thyme.

Heat 15 g (½ oz) of butter and 2 tablespoons of oil in a large, heavy-based frying-pan. Add the chicken legs and thighs, skin-side down, and cook over a high heat until crisp and golden, turn over and brown the other side. Transfer to a heavy flameproof casserole. Add the breasts to the pan, skin-side down, and cook for 2 minutes, turning them over half-way through, and adding a little more butter if necessary. Transfer to the casserole.

Add the streaky bacon to the frying-pan, adding more oil if necessary, and cook until crisp and brown. Remove and set aside. Add the button onions or shallots, carrots and celery to the pan and cook for 4–5 minutes, turning them with a wooden spoon. Remove the vegetables and set aside. Add the mushrooms to the pan for a few minutes. Sprinkle them with salt, remove from the pan and set aside.

Remove as much fat as you can from the surface of the liquid left in the frying-pan and pour any remaining cooking juices into the casserole. Pour in the reserved marinade liquid, vegetables and herbs, and the chicken stock or broth. Bring just to simmering point, lower the heat and add the herbs and sliced onion. Cover and simmer gently for about 45 minutes until the chicken is tender and the juices of the chicken run clear when you prick the thickest parts with a fork.

Transfer the pieces of chicken to a warmed serving dish. If you dislike skin, discard it. Cover the chicken and keep warm. With a spoon remove and discard the fat from the surface of the cooking liquid. Gradually whisk in the flour and butter mixture then boil until lightly thickened. Add the carrots and celery. Lower the heat and simmer for 10 minutes. Return the pieces of chicken to the casserole, cover and cook gently for 10 minutes. Dip one corner of each Croûton into the sauce, then into the chopped parsley.

Discard the bay leaves, parsley and thyme sprigs from the casserole. Stir in the brandy, chicken liver, bacon, mushrooms, button onions or shallots, garlic and cream. Add nutmeg, lemon juice, salt and pepper to taste, cover the casserole and cook for 2 minutes. It is ready. Transfer to the serving dish and place the Croûtons around the edge.

THROUGHOUT FRANCE

Pintade au Porto, Pommes et Poires

GUINEA FOWL BRAISED IN PORT, WITH APPLES
AND PEARS

The flesh of guinea fowl is dark red and lean. When cooked in port with apples, pears and onions, it makes an elegant dish with a hint of the wild. I like to serve this dish with either Celeriac Purée (see p.240), Cabbage Purée (see p.241), sautéed chestnuts, sautéed mangetouts, cabbage simmered in butter, or steamed rice. Alternatively, it can be accompanied by a simple, tossed chicory or watercress salad.

SERVES 4

2 teaspoons chopped fresh thyme
salt and freshly ground black pepper
1.5 kg (3 lb) guinea fowl
40 g (1½ oz) unsalted butter
2 tablespoons groundnut oil
2 thin slices streaky bacon
2 apples, peeled, cored and
thickly sliced
1 pear, peeled, cored and thickly sliced
4 tablespoons port
12 pearl onions
3 tablespoons double cream

Place a pinch of salt, the thyme and 15 g (½ oz) of butter in the cavity of the bird. Rub the breast, back and legs with 15 g (½ oz) of butter and 1 tablespoon of oil and season the skin with salt and pepper. Truss the bird with string so that it keeps its shape while cooking and lay the streaky bacon over the breast.

Heat the remaining butter and oil in a heavy casserole, add the bird and brown on all sides for a few minutes, then cover and cook, basting occasionally with the cooking juices, for 25 minutes. Add the apples, pear and port and cook over a low heat for about 25 minutes.

Meanwhile, simmer the onions in lightly salted water for about 10–15 minutes until tender. Drain well and add to the casserole with the cream. Cover and cook for a further 5 minutes.

Transfer the guinea fowl to a warm plate. Cut and discard the strings holding the bacon in place. Cover the bird and leave in a warm place to 'relax' for 5–10 minutes. Cut the pieces of bacon in 2.5 cm (1 in) pieces. Check and correct the seasoning of the apples and pear.

Carve the guinea fowl and arrange the slices on a warm plate. Spoon over the bacon, apples, pear and onions and half of the cooking juices. Serve the remaining juices in a warm bowl.

PROVENCE

Pigeonneaux aux Olives
PIGEON WITH OLIVES

Beware if a man calls you his 'little pigeon', the word 'little' may be misleading: it's time to lose weight!

I usually use tender, plump farm-bred pigeon. A three to four month old bird, sometimes called 'squab', weighs 450 g (1 lb) and is generally enough for two people but you may prefer to serve one pigeon per person. Pigeons need fat to protect them as they cook. You can coat them with butter, but I prefer to wrap them in larding fat or bacon. This dish is lovely with sautéed mushrooms, peas cooked with lettuce leaves and diced bacon, or any potato dish.

SERVES 2 OR 4
2 young pigeons, each weighing about
450 g (1 lb)
salt and freshly ground black pepper
1 tablespoon chopped fresh thyme
2 bay leaves

4 slices streaky bacon
1 tablespoon vegetable oil
25 g (1 oz) butter
75 ml (3 fl oz) sweet white wine
2 shallots, finely chopped
8–16 large green olives, stoned
1 large tomato, skinned, seeded and
diced
3 tablespoons water
½–1 lemon, thinly sliced
2 tablespoons finely chopped
fresh parsley

Season the outside of the birds with salt, pepper and thyme. Place a little salt, pepper and 1 bay leaf in the cavity of each bird. Truss them then wrap individually in 2 bacon slices. Tie the bacon in place with string.

Heat the oil and butter in a heavy casserole over a moderate heat. Add the pigeons and cook for about 10 minutes until evenly browned.

Pour in the wine and scrape up the coagulated cooking juices with a wooden spoon as best you can. Cover and cook for 30 minutes over a low heat, turning the birds a few times using tongs.

Cut the strings holding the bacon in place and remove both the strings and the bacon. Add the shallots to the casserole, cook for 2 minutes, add the olives and tomato and cook for 10 minutes. Transfer the pigeons to a warm dish, cover and keep warm. Remove and discard the fat on top of the cooking juices with a spoon. Stir the water into the casserole, scraping up the coagulated juices. Bring to the boil, simmer for 2–3 minutes then add the lemon slices and parsley. Cover the casserole and keep warm.

Cut each pigeon in half lengthways, pour over the cooking juices and surround the pigeons with olives and lemon slices.

Caneton Rôti et sa Farce

ROAST DUCK WITH SPINACH STUFFING

In France many types of duck are sold, such as Muscovy with their generous amounts of firm breast meat, large Barbary and the smaller, more tender and delicately-flavoured Nantais or Challans. Now, these are becoming more widely available in Britain, and there are also two special breeds of British duck that have a higher than average proportion of flesh to fat, Lunesdale and the larger Gressingham.

A stuffed duck can be delicious, but it can also be unpleasantly greasy. To be sure of a successful dish, roast the bird for quite a long time, prick it frequently to get rid of most of the fat, and cook the stuffing separately. Also, of course, use the best duck you can.

Sautéed diced turnips or a simple, crisp, green salad make a good accompaniment.

SERVES 3

2–2.5 kg (4½-5 lb) duck, preferably fresh, thawed if frozen
1½ tablespoons chopped fresh thyme
juice of 1 lemon
salt and freshly ground black pepper
2 garlic cloves, halved
2 bay leaves
5 tablespoons dry white wine
1 tablespoon brandy
3–4 spring onions, with 2.5 cm (1 in) green, cut in half lengthways
15–24 large green olives, stoned
2 teaspoons finely grated lemon rind

FOR THE STUFFING

1 tablespoon groundnut oil
1 garlic clove, chopped
duck's liver, if available, chopped
200 g (7 oz) frozen spinach, thawed, well-drained and chopped
4 tablespoons cooked rice
1 large egg, lightly beaten
3 tablespoons chopped fresh flatlef parsley
2 teaspoons chopped fresh thyme
a pinch of grated nutmeg
salt and freshly ground black pepper

Pre-heat the oven to gas mark 230°C/450°F/Gas 8. Butter a 12 cm (4½ in) round, or 5 x 9 cm (2 x 3½ in) china or earthenware dish.

Remove as much fat and excess skin from the neck and tail end of the duck as possible. Sprinkle thyme, lemon juice and salt and pepper on the skin and put the garlic cloves and bay leaves in the cavity. Season inside the bird with salt, then truss it and prick the breasts and legs several times with a fork. Put on a rack placed in a roasting tin. Roast in the oven for 20 minutes, then pour as much fat as you can from the tin. Lower the oven temperature to 180°C/350°F/Gas 4 and cook for a further 1¼-1½ hours until the juices between the legs and breasts run pale yellow.

Meanwhile, prepare the stuffing. Heat the oil in a frying-pan, add the garlic, and liver, if available, and sauté for 2–3 minutes. Stir in the spinach and cook for 2–3 minutes, then stir in the rice, egg, parsley, thyme and nutmeg and season with salt and pepper. Spoon into the dish, cover tightly with foil and place on the shelf below the duck when the temperature is at the lower setting. Cook for 40–45 minutes.

Transfer the rack with the duck on it to a plate and leave to 'rest' in the oven with the heat turned off and the door slightly ajar. Spoon or pour off surplus fat from the roasting tin

then stir the wine, brandy, spring onions and olives into the tin, scraping up the coagulated juices with a wooden spoon. Simmer on the hub for a few minutes. Stir in the grated lemon rind, salt and pepper.

Carve the duck and arrange on a warmed serving plate. Unmould the stuffing, cut into slices and arranges with the duck. Spoon the sauce over the duck and stuffing

THROUGHOUT FRANCE

Cailles au Genièvre et au Cognac

QUAILS WITH THYME, JUNIPER BERRIES AND BRANDY

Lucky quail: to be plump has always been considered a virtue for this bird. But the quails of yesterday are not the quails of today. While once upon a time a quail wrapped in bay leaves or in a fresh vine leaf and plainly roasted exploded with flavours, the little farmed quails we find today are bland. Amusing, crisp, pretty perhaps, but they do need a little help from the cook to improve their charms. After trying the usual ploys – cherries, quinces, grapes, mushrooms and even a few small pieces of truffle – my solution is now quite definite: I add a pungent twist to quails by cooking them with thyme, juniper berries, shallots and brandy. For interest, I sometimes substitute gin for the cognac or brandy. Serve the sauce in a separate bowl so both the toasted bread and the birds will remain crisp. One quail per person should be just enough if the accompaniment is quite generous. I serve either sliced fennel sautéed in butter, Fennel Purée (see p.240), or *Gratin de Pommes de Terre* (see p.249).

SERVES 4

12 juniper berries
12 black peppercorns
salt and freshly ground black pepper
4 quails
25 g (1 oz) butter, softened
3 tablespoons chopped fresh thyme
8 thin slices streaky bacon
4 slices firm bread, buttered, crusts removed
2–4 shallots, very finely chopped
2 tablespoons brandy
1 tablespoon finely chopped fresh parsley

TO SERVE
1 lemon, thinly sliced
watercress

Pre-heat the oven to 230°C/450°F/Gas 8.

Place 3 juniper berries, 3 peppercorns and a pinch of salt in the cavity of each quail. Spread butter over each bird then sprinkle with pepper and thyme and wrap in two slices of bacon. Tie these in place with string.

Place each bird on a slice of bread and place in a small roasting tin. Bake in the oven for 15 minutes.

Transfer the quails on their pieces of bread to a warm serving plate, discard the strings holding the bacon in place, cover and keep warm.

Stir 4 tablespoons water into the cooking juices then add the shallots and simmer for about 2 minutes. Stir in the brandy and parsley, bring to the boil, then simmer again for about 1½-2 minutes. Check the seasoning, and pour into a warm bowl. Garnish the serving plate with lemon slices and watercress.

Dindonneau aux Marrons

ROAST TURKEY WITH MUSHROOM, CHESTNUT AND OLIVE STUFFING

Dodu dindon (plump turkey), or *jesuit*, because it was imported from North America by the Jesuits in the seventeenth century, roast turkey is the traditional family dish for Christmas and New Year's Eve throughout France. In the following recipe the roast, stuffed bird is served with sautéed chestnuts and crisp sausages. To accompany the bird I serve a bowl of watercress tossed with an olive oil and lemon juice dressing. If you are using a frozen turkey, leave it in its plastic wrapping in the refrigerator for 2 days to thaw.

SERVES 6–8

3 kg (7 lb) turkey, with giblets
salt and freshly ground black pepper
3 tablespoons groundnut oil
450 g (1 lb) mushrooms, quartered
75 g (3 oz) butter
3 shallots, finely chopped
450 g (1 lb) streaky bacon, finely diced
100 g (4 oz) green olives, stoned and halved
or quartered
2 tablespoons brandy (optional)
10 walnut halves, roughly chopped (optional)
2 tablespoons finely chopped fresh parsley
1 tablespoon chopped fresh thyme
1 egg, beaten
225 g (8 oz) peeled, cooked chestnuts (see p.239), or
whole chestnuts canned in brine or water, drained
350 ml (12 fl oz) dry white wine

FOR THE GARNISH
1 tablespoon vegetable oil
2 long, thin, tasty sausages
175 g (6 oz) peeled and cooked chestnuts
(see p.239), or whole chestnuts canned in
brine or water, drained
40 g (1½ oz) unsalted butter
2 tablespoons finely chopped fresh chervil

Pre-heat the oven to 240°C/475°F/Gas 9.

Remove the giblets from the turkey. Rinse and thinly slice the heart, rinse and dice the liver. Wash the bird inside and out and dry carefully. Sprinkle salt and pepper over the skin and in the cavity.

Heat 2 tablespoons of oil in a frying-pan, add the mushrooms and sauté for 3–4 minutes. Using a slotted spoon, transfer to a bowl. Add half the butter and the remaining oil to the pan and sauté the shallots for 1½ minutes, stirring with a wooden spoon. Add to the bowl. Add the bacon to the pan and cook for 3–4 minutes. Add the heart, sauté for 1 minute then add the liver. Toss everything with a wooden spoon, remove from the heat and stir. Add to the bowl with the olives, brandy and walnuts if using, the parsley, thyme, egg and salt and pepper. Stir well. Halve or quarter the chestnuts, if liked, then stir into the bowl.

Spoon loosely into the turkey's neck cavity as the stuffing will swell as it cooks. Fold the neck skin over the stuffing and sew or secure it with skewer. Spoon the remaining stuffing into a small baking dish and cover with foil.

Truss the bird and spread the remaining butter over the surface of the breast, back and legs. Place the turkey on a rack, breast-side up, in a large roasting tin, cover the bird with a piece of buttered or oiled foil, or, better still, a large piece of muslin dipped in vegetable oil, to keep it moist while it cooks. Place in the oven, lower the oven temperature to 230°C/450°F/Gas 8 and roast for 30 minutes. Lower the temperature to gas mark 200°C/400°F/Gas 6 and pour 600 ml (1 pint) of water into the roasting tin to prevent the juices burning and smoking. Cook for another 1–1¼ hours. Put the dish of stuffing in the oven. Remove the foil or the muslin from the turkey and cook for a further 30 minutes until the juices run pale yellow when you test the thickest part of the leg with a fine skewer.

Transfer the cooked turkey to a warm plate and discard the trussing string or skewers. Cover the bird loosely and leave in a warm place for 20–30 minutes.

For the garnish, heat the oil in a frying-pan, add the sausages and fry, turning occasionally, for about 5 minutes, until crisp and brown. Meanwhile, toss the chestnuts in butter over a moderate heat for about 5 minutes then sprinkle with the chervil.

To serve, remove the stuffing from the turkey with a tablespoon and place it in the centre of a warm serving plate. Remove the legs and the wings then cut each leg into 2 joints. Slice the breasts and arrange around the stuffing. Cut the sausages into 5 cm (2 in) lengths and place on the plate with the chestnuts.

Carefully spoon or pour the fat from the roasting tin, then stir the wine into the pan, scraping up the sediment with a wooden spoon. Boil for 1–2 minutes on the hob, season lightly, spoon some over the stuffing and turkey and pour the remainder into a sauceboat.

GASCONY

Magrets de Canard
DUCK BREASTS

The fattening of geese and ducks – one of the main activities in Gascony – is mainly done to produce the celebrated, silky foie gras. The drumsticks and thighs are cooked and preserved in duck or goose fat for *Confit* and used in winter in a variety of dishes, or they may be roasted. Bones, gizzard and neck are added to soups. Any left-over bits are turned into terrines and *Rillettes*.

But for decades this left many unused parts of the birds, and it took a brave musketeer, a modern d'Artagnan, André Daguin, the owner and chef of Auch's *Hôtel de France*, to solve this particular problem.

Magret, in the southern dialect, means 'lean'. In a duck, the only lean part is the breast, the *magret*. It was always neglected because no one knew quite what to do with it. Some forty years ago, however, Monsieur Daguin discovered that barely-cooked duck breasts could compete with beef in a region where ducks were numerous and beef cattle almost non-existent. He proceeded to serve large, sautéed or grilled duck magrets, quite rare and skinless, to his clients without whispering a word about where they came from.

Over the years *Magrets de Canard* have become the rage everywhere in France. They are prepared almost rare, sliced on the diagonal, but may also be grilled, poached or sautéed. They may be marinated in a mixture of salt, shallots, herbs and garlic overnight and served pink. They may be browned, deglazed with vinegar and honey then cooked with apple quarters and mushrooms or seasoned with lime juice and grated lemon rind. They may be served with potato chips or with white grapes, yellow peaches or wild, bitter cherries and their juices deglazed with a sweet dessert wine or a hearty red wine.

When Daguin cooked *Magrets de Canard* for us, he wrapped them in a huge spectacular shell of sea salt. The meat was served with a rich Béarnaise Sauce (see p.97) prepared with duck fat instead of butter, and accompanied with a celeriac purée and grilled aubergine. I have prepared this superb dish at home several times, although I do not use duck fat for the sauce

since I find it overwhelmingly rich. Curiously, all the duck flavours are sealed within the salt shell and so no excess salt is left on the meat.

It is now possible to buy duck breasts in the supermarket. However, if you buy whole duck, remove the legs and thighs, which you can keep for another recipe or freeze for later, then cut down the breast along the breastbone on the side of the ridge. You will then be able to lift it in one solid piece away from the ribcage.

SERVES 4

2 x 450 g (1 lb) duck breasts, boned and halved, skin on
coarsely ground black pepper
1.8 kg (4 lb) coarse sea salt or kosher salt
100 g (4 oz) plain flour
5 egg whites
3 tablespoons dried thyme
1 quantity Sauce Aillade (see p.98)

Trim any excess fat off the duck breasts and pat dry with kitchen paper. Using a sharp knife, score the skin at 2.5 cm (1 in) intervals without piercing the flesh. Place the duck pieces in a heavy-based frying-pan and fry without any oil over a medium heat for several minutes until the skin is crisp and brown. Sprinkle the top with pepper. Pour off and discard the fat. Remove the duck from the pan and tie the breasts together with string, skin side out.

Pre-heat the oven to 230°C/450°F/Gas 8.

Mix together the salt, flour, egg whites, thyme and pepper in a large bowl and stir vigorously for 5 minutes. It is heavy work. Spread a piece of oiled kitchen foil in an ovenproof dish and pour in a thick layer of the salt mixture. Place the duck on the salt and cover with the remaining salt mixture. Press hard with both hands to shape a shell. Roast the duck in the centre of the oven for 17 minutes then remove it from the oven and stand it on a rack for 10 minutes.

Bring the dish to the table. Crack the white, hardened shell with a small hammer or a big heavy knife. The shell will open. Remove the duck breasts, cut and discard the string and brush off any bits of shell. Discard the skin and slice the meat diagonally into thin slices. Arrange them on a warm serving platter, sprinkle with pepper and serve with *Sauce Aillade* and a bowl of tossed green salad or a *Gratin Dauphinois* (see p.269).

PERIGORD

Canard aux Pruneaux et a l'Armagnac:
DUCK WITH PRUNES AND ARMAGNAC

Armagnac, prunes and duck make for an irresistibly festive dish. One of the best versions of *Canard aux Pruneaux* I ever tasted was prepared with the local Pousse-rapière, an armagnac and orange liqueur. In this recipe I have reproduced this flavour with orange rind and armagnac.

For a variety of texture, use a whole bird; for a more meaty dish, only use the breast. Cut up pieces of duck are easier to cook than a whole bird, most of the fat can be removed and used to prepare *Pommes de terre à la Sardalaise* (see p.249) or *Garbure* (see p.62) and the pieces of duck simmered in a fragrant sauce absorb all the flavours more thoroughly. This dish can be prepared ahead and improves as it is re-heated. You can serve the dish with *Pommes de terre à la Sardalaise* (see p.249), *Pain d'endives* (see p.245) Celeriac or Fennel Purée (see p.240).

This dish is sometimes prepared with a sweet white wine instead of a hearty red wine which makes an equally interesting dish.

SERVES 4–6

1.75 kg (4 lb) duck, cut into 8 pieces, separate the legs at the joint
salt and freshly ground black pepper
2 tablespoons dried thyme or savory
4 tablespoons duck fat or 4 tablespoons unsalted butter and 1 tablespoon groundnut oil
6 shallots, peeled or 1 large onion, sliced
100 g (4 oz) lean streaky bacon, chopped
3 garlic cloves, crushed
1.2 litres (2 pints) hearty red wine
a pinch of dried savory or thyme
2 bay leaves
10 peppercorns
juice of 3 oranges
grated rind of 1 orange
20 large plump prunes
4 tablespoons armagnac

Trim the duck of its excess fat and keep it for later use. Rub salt, pepper and thyme or savory all over the surface of the duck, a few hours ahead of time if possible, then chill. Take the duck out of the fridge an hour before cooking it. Prick the surface with a fork.

Heat the fat or butter and oil in a heavy-based pan over medium heat and brown all the pieces of duck on all sides for 10 minutes until golden, skin side-down to render the fat. (If you use breast, only brown on the skin side as it is very delicate.) Cook in batches, if necessary. Transfer the duck to a side dish.

Add the shallots or sliced onions and bacon to the pan and cook for 5 minutes, then add the garlic and cook for a further 5 minutes. Transfer to a side dish.

Reserve all the fat in the pan for later use. Add the red wine, scraping up the coagulated juices on the base of the pan. Add the dry herbs and peppercorns and simmer, uncovered, for 15 minutes. Add the pieces of duck, the orange juice and the grated orange rind. Reduce the heat, partially cover with a lid and simmer for

50 minutes. The sauce must not boil. The recipe can be prepared in advance to this point.

Pour the sauce through a sieve, pressing with a spoon to extract all the juices. Chill. Discard any extra fat on the top then re-heat over a low flame heat for 30 minutes before you want to serve it. Correct the seasoning and add the cooked onions, bacon, garlic, prunes and armagnac 5 minutes before it is ready.

ALSACE

Oie aux Pommes et aux Pruneaux

ROAST GOOSE WITH APPLE AND PRUNE STUFFING

Prunes, apples and goose do go wonderfully together. In Alsace, the home of this recipe, beer is sometimes massaged into the skin of the goose before cooking for extra flavour. Keep the goose fat to use for frying vegetables.

Serve the goose with chestnuts or potatoes sautéed in goose fat, or a selection of Vegetable Purées (see p.239).

SERVES 6–8

20 no-need-to-soak prunes
4 kg (9 lb) goose, with giblets
25 g (1 oz) butter
1 tablespoon vegetable oil
6 cm (2½ in) thick slices lean streaky bacon, diced
3 onions or 4 shallots, finely chopped
5 apples, such as Granny Smith, peeled, cored and quartered
2 tablespoons brandy (optional)
grated rind of 1 lemon
2 teaspoons dried thyme
1 egg, lightly beaten
salt and freshly ground black pepper
freshly grated nutmeg
400 ml (14 fl oz) Alsace Riesling

Pre-heat the oven to 220°C/425°F/Gas 7. Place a wire rack in a roasting tin.

Place the prunes in a bowl, cover with hot water and leave for about 30 minutes, then drain, carefully remove the stones and cut the prunes into quarters.

Meanwhile, pull out as much fat as you can from inside the goose. Reserve the fat (see Note, below). Remove the giblets from the bird's cavity and reserve the liver for the stuffing.

Melt 15 g (½ oz), butter and the oil in a frying-pan, add the bacon and sauté, stirring occasionally, for 5 minutes. Using a slotted spoon transfer to a bowl. Add the goose liver to the pan and cook, stirring, for about 2 minutes. Using a slotted spoon remove the liver, chop it and add to the bowl. Add the onions or shallots to the pan, sauté for 3 minutes, then add to the bowl.

Add the remaining butter to the pan. When hot add the apples and cook for 2–3 minutes, stirring. Add the brandy, if using, and set alight with a lighted taper. When the flames have died down, tip into the bowl with the lemon rind, thyme, prunes, egg, salt and pepper. Grate over a little nutmeg and stir to mix.

Prick the thighs, back and lower breast of the goose with a sharp fork. Season the cavity with salt and pepper then spoon in the apple and prune mixture. Sew up the opening carefully and truss the goose. Sprinkle salt and pepper on the outside of the bird then place, breast uppermost, on the rack in the roasting tin. Roast for 30 minutes then turn the bird on its side. Reduce the oven temperature to 180°/350°F/Gas 4, and place a baking tin of hot water in the bottom of the oven as the steam will keep the bird moist during cooking. Cook the goose for 30 minutes, baste with a little boiling water and turn the goose onto its other side. Remove the melted fat from the roasting tin using a spoon or bulb-baster and put into a dish. Roast the bird for a further 30 minutes, baste again and turn the bird on its breast. Once more, remove surplus fat from the roasting tin and cook the bird for another hour until the juices run pale yellow when you test the thickest part of the leg with a fine skewer. Remove excess fat from the roasting tin during the hour, if necessary. Switch off the oven, leave the oven door open and allow the goose to 'relax' for 20–30 minutes.

Discard the trussing strings from the goose. Spoon the stuffing into the centre of a warm serving plate. Cut off the legs and separate the drumsticks from the second joints. Slice the breast, and the second joints. Arrange the pieces of goose around the stuffing.

Carefully pour or spoon all the fat from the roasting tin, leaving the juices and sediment behind, then place the tin on the hob. Stir the wine into the coagulated juices, scraping up the sediment with a wooden spoon, then boil for 2–3 minutes. Season with salt and pepper and spoon some of the sauce over the goose and stuffing; serve the remaining sauce separately.

NOTE

Chop the fat from the goose then place it in a small saucepan with a little water. Cover and simmer gently for a few minutes. Remove the lid from the pan and continue to cook until the water has evaporated. Carefully pour the fat through a sieve into a jar or bowl leaving any sediment in the pan. Leave to cool then cover the jar or bowl. Keep in the refrigerator.

Meat

LES VIANDES

*I*n France, butchers are educators. Their shop walls display the 'labels of quality', the various grades of meats, the medals and prizes won by Charollais, Salers and Limousin cattle, and by Sisteron, Paulliac or pré-salé lamb. There are large coloured charts showing the various cuts of meat. What's more, butchers take time to explain why meat must be 'parsleyed' or 'marbled' – when the ivory fat and cherry red lean meat intermingle for a full flavour and a rich texture – and why lamb and beef need to be aged in a cold place to become *bien rassis*, to improve the taste and tenderness. They will explain why 'a good rest' after cooking is

essential for a roast before carving so that all the juices will spread evenly. They emphasize how coarse sea salt (preferably from Brittany) and freshly crushed pepper (preferably coarse) must be sprinkled lightly before cooking and more generously after cooking. Appropriate recipes are offered, and ingenious advice given on what to do with leftovers. They may also offer very special gifts to improve a dish: a large veal bone for the *Sauté de Veau*, a piece of beef cheek for the stew, a few sprigs of parsley for the boiled beef. Chatty and dependable, butchers are pillars of society. And this is why, although we eat vast amounts of fresh vegetables, we remain a nation of meat-lovers. Meat in small quantities – a paper-thin slice of beef, a tiny lamb chop, a chicken wing – remain part of our daily diet.

Visitors are frequently baffled by the most popular dish in France, *le steak frites*: a pan-grilled steak served with potato chips. They are equally puzzled when they observe that rare meat remains a regular dish in the form of *Boeuf Tartare* or *Carpaccio*, and when they notice that Tournedos and fillet steaks are served simply pan-fried (so that none of the pan juices are lost), flavoured with a little parsley butter or a spoonful of a shallot-white wine (*Bercy*) or red wine (*Bordelaise*) sauce and sit happily alongside *Plats Mijotés*, the traditional long-simmered dishes.

For centuries, meat was rare and expensive and only the very rich could afford the prime cuts. Imagination and patience came to the rescue of the home cook: a pinch of herbs, a drop of wine, a teaspoon of brandy, a shallot or two, a leek, a carrot, a few soft prunes, a handful of unpeeled garlic cloves would help this tough little piece of meat taste good and go a long way. And since cheap cuts were also the most flavoursome, miracles appeared in the form of pungent *daubes*, plump *paupiettes*, hearty *potées* and herb-stuffed lamb shoulder. Every last cut of the meat was treated with respect. While *foie gras* and puff pastry-covered *filet mignon* or truffle-studded leg of lamb were reserved for the most opulent

tables, the rest of the nation was busy braising, stewing, stuffing, boiling and enjoying cheaper cuts of meat.

In France, domestic rabbits (except those which have run wild in the *garrigue* feeding on thyme and savoury) are quite large. I always cut them up into pieces before cooking so they will absorb the flavours better and improve with each re-heating. I dust the pieces lightly before sautéing them because their flesh is lean and delicate. I like to cook them with spirited ingredients such as unpitted olives, garlic cloves, tomatoes, herbs, mustard, wine or a little wine vinegar.

Today, when robust flavours and serious food are back in fashion, every bistro boasts about its *morceaux du boucher* – the cheaper but tastier pieces butchers often keep for themselves: *onglet, poire, araignée, bavette*. These thin steaks are simply pan-fried with a few shallots and deglazed with a drop of wine to make an inexpensive but delicious treat. Starred restaurant chefs and home cooks both go back to traditional recipes, interpreted with a new choice of vegetables, of fresh herbs, home-made pasta or tiny Ratte or Charlotte potatoes. Luscious *blanquettes*, fresh *navarins*, sumptuous *parmentiers* remain popular but are now lighter and more pungent than in the past.

The following pages include a selection of my favourite meat dishes. I hope you will enjoy them and they will become yours.

Agneau à l'Ail

ROAST LAMB WITH CREAMY GARLIC AND WINE
SAUCE

The region of Languedoc is a link between the eastern and western parts of southern France. I spent a day with Geneviève Cano, a Languedocienne. She talked about her household where five generations lived under the same roof. Every day the younger members of the family awoke to the chopping sound of the heavy cleaver against the thick board as parsley, garlic and *ventrèche* were pounded to make the *persillade* which would be used during the day to season meats, vegetables, soups and stews.

With *Agneau à l'Ail*, Geneviève served sliced potatoes sautéed to a crisp in goose fat and sprinkled with the beloved *persillade*, homemade *pain d'épice*, tiny goat cheeses drizzled with honey and almonds, and a basket of figs and dark red peaches, *pêches de vigne*, which her uncle had gathered in his vineyard. It was a truly glorious meal.

Goose fat is available in tins in many shops, but oil or butter can replace it as long as you use a good, firm garlic. The overwhelming quantity of garlic makes for a surprisingly gentle, nutty flavour; the garlic looses its force when cooked and its taste changes completely. Geneviève's young son explained to me all the ailments that garlic would cure, but I did not need any medicinal justifications to enjoy the sumptuous sauce.

SERVES 6–8

2.25 kg (5 lb) leg of lamb, trimmed
14 garlic cloves, halved
salt and freshly ground black pepper
1 tablespoon goose fat, butter or olive oil
1 tablespoon dried thyme
30 garlic cloves, unpeeled
4 tablespoons cold water
600 ml (1 pint) dry white wine, still or sparkling

Pre-heat the oven to 190°C/375°F/Gas 5.

Stab the lamb all over with a very sharp knife and insert the garlic halves into the meat. Sprinkle it with salt and pepper and rub it in with your hands. Spread the goose fat, butter or oil over the lamb then place the meat in a deep roasting tin and roast it fat-side down for 30 minutes. Turn the lamb over, sprinkle the thyme over the top and arrange the unpeeled cloves of garlic around the meat. Cook for 10 minutes. Stir the garlic cloves so that they do not stick to the pan, pour in the water and cook for a further 30 minutes or until the lamb is cooked to your liking.

Transfer the lamb to a warm serving platter and keep it warm in the turned-off oven. Transfer the garlic cloves to a bowl, peel them then mash them with a fork. Drain the fat from the pan. Add the wine and stir, scraping the bottom of the pan to mix in all the lamb juices. If you use a sparkling wine, as Geneviève did, it will sizzle and make a frothy sauce. Stir in the garlic purée and cook for 1 minute. Season to taste with salt and pepper.

Slice the lamb and arrange it on a warm serving platter. Spoon a little of the garlic sauce over the top and serve the rest separately.

Agneau aux Herbes

LAMB WITH HERBS AND GARLIC

Fontvieille is a pretty village near Arles. Nearby are fragrant fields of rosemary and thyme, Daudet's windmill, sheep and goats roaming on terraced pastures, Roman arenas and olive groves. The village houses have long, narrow, wooden shutters and rust-coloured tiles; the little village square, with its green iron tables and chairs, is sheltered by huge plane trees. It is inland Provence at its best and everybody seems to follow the lizard's advice engraved on fountains and sundials all around 'I sip life as I sip the sun, by small gulps. Time passes too fast, perhaps it will rain tomorrow'. Taking the time to enjoy life is a priority.

In the centre of the village is a pretty restaurant situated in a disused oil mill and built around a lovely Provençal garden. It is called *La Regalido*, the Provençaux word for the log of wood which is added to the fire as a welcome when guests arrive.

Hospitality, warmth and pleasure in all the good things of the land were all present as we entered the kitchen of *La Regalido* that morning. There was a big bundle of freshly gathered thyme sprinkled with blue blossoms, piles of fresh vegetables, a stack of flat vegetable omelettes ready to be made into an omelette cake. Monsieur Jean-Pierre Michel was stuffing a chicken with a handful of thyme and 40 garlic cloves, his son was making a thyme sorbet while Madame Michel was making bouquets of flowers. Busy lizards but true lizards. Monsieur Michel made me taste a crisp vegetable *gratin* ('in Paris they would add cream to it, here we only want the concentrated flavours of the garden'), a bite of a tiny purple artichoke that had been cooked briefly in herbs and wine, a morsel of peppery sheep's milk cheese, and an explosive paste of anchovies, oil and garlic as he talked to me about olives and described how local bakers used to crack the stones and place them in the bottom of their ovens to flavour their breads. When the *Agneau aux Herbes* arrived I truly felt like a pampered lizard. As you will see yourself it is very easy to prepare, but the meat must be chosen carefully. It can be served with a *Gratin de Pommes de Terre* (see p.254), *Gratin de Courgettes* (see p.243) or *Ratatouille* (see p.237). Glorious every time. *Allez zou*, let's go, as they would urge in Fontvieille.

SERVES 4

4 thick lamb leg steaks or cutlets
1 teaspoon finely chopped
fresh rosemary
1 tablespoon chopped fresh thyme
3½ tablespoons olive oil
16 garlic cloves
40 g (1½ oz) unsalted butter
salt and freshly ground black pepper

Place the lamb in a dish. Sprinkle over half of the thyme and rosemary and 1 tablespoon of olive oil. Turn the lamb over and sprinkle with the remaining herbs and another tablespoon of olive oil. Cover and leave to marinate for about 2 hours.

Thread the garlic cloves on to 4 wooden cocktail sticks. Heat 1½ tablespoons of olive oil and half the butter in a heavy-based frying-pan. When it is very hot, add the lamb and cook quickly for about 3 minutes, turning frequently with tongs until evenly browned on all sides. Lower the heat to moderate. Sprinkle the lamb with salt and pepper, and add the remaining butter to the pan. When it begins to sizzle add the garlic cloves and cook until tender and evenly browned.

Transfer the lamb and garlic to 1 large, or 4 individual, warm plates and pour over the cooking juices.

NORMANDY

Gigot Rôti aux Haricots Blancs

ROAST LEG OF LAMB WITH HARICOT BEANS,
TOMATOES AND SHALLOTS

Lamb is very popular throughout France. In Provence, they graze on scant grasses but many fragrant herbs and are cooked with thyme, rosemary, olive oil and a handful of unpeeled garlic cloves. In the south-west, they feed on richer grass, and may be stuffed with prunes, anchovies or fruits.

But it is in Normandy that I have tasted the most interesting lamb dishes. Near Mont-Saint-Michel I saw the famous pré-salé lambs grazing on pastures which are swept by the tides, the sea winds and spindrifts. Gulls soared overhead, while the golden steeple of Saint Michel glimmered in the distance. Pré-salé lambs, which means lambs raised on salted pastures, are bold and determined. They leave their barn unaccompanied at eight o'clock each morning, walk some 4 or 5 kilometres to graze on verdant grasses cleared of weeds by the tides and frequent showers, then return at six o'clock every night. Only the high tides in early autumn or spring may force them to stay indoors for a few days in the year. Because they eat fragrant, slightly salty grass, walk a lot and spend their time mostly outdoors, they have a distinctive flavour and texture. The best lambs are those raised in the summer, for a lamb feeding on dune grasses will not taste the same as a lamb raised on lush summer grass. The taste, however, is always delicate, with a slightly gamey flavour. The flesh is red with a firm texture. It is never fat nor bland, and in Normandy they insist that it needs neither herbs nor garlic. In fact, I noticed that they do not even use salt or pepper for fear of smothering the subtle fragrance of the meat. The lambs have naturally long legs (to prevent their bellies dragging in the water), and *gigots* of pré-salé are compared to a ballerina's leg: pink, firm, lean flesh under a thin net of white fat, *la glinette*. Although it sells for twice the price of ordinary lamb, the production of pré-salé cannot fill local demand.

We tasted pré-salé lamb in the lovely home of Daniel Gaslin, looking out over pastures enclosed by the sea. Most of the meals in his house are shared by three generations and, although Normans are known to be cautious and not prone to enthusiasm, all the guests were sipping their cider with anticipation, for they knew we had a treat in store; a pré-salé never disappoints.

Daniel was in charge of the fire but everyone volunteered their advice. He was cooking the lamb on a grill 25 cm (10 in) above the embers to 'seize it', then he wrapped it in foil so that none of the juices would escape. He used no herbs, no mustard, not even a pinch of salt or pepper.

When the meal was served, the part near the shank called 'the muse', which is considered the tastiest part, was given to the eldest cousin. The children shared the centre and all the adults begged for the crisp, tasty bits near the bone at both ends. It was served with a plain dish of lightly buttered green beans.

Since pré-salé is not available to most people, I have created this recipe which will transform a good leg of lamb into a sumptuous dish. If you cook the vegetables while the lamb is in the oven, they should be ready at about the same time. A few tablespoons of fresh cream are often added to the vegetables just before serving.

SERVES 8

FOR THE VEGETABLES

450 g (1 lb) dried white haricot beans
1 large onion studded with 2 cloves
1 bouquet garni
salt and freshly ground black pepper
3 tablespoons butter
1 teaspoon groundnut oil
1 carrot, chopped
2 onions, chopped
3 shallots, coarsely chopped
4 garlic cloves, chopped
3 tomatoes, skinned and chopped
1 tablespoon chopped fresh thyme
3 tablespoons finely chopped fresh parsley

FOR THE MEAT

1.8 kg (4 lb) leg of lamb with bone, trimmed
4 garlic cloves cut into slivers
50 g (2 oz) butter
1 tablespoon dried thyme or 2 teaspoons dried rosemary
120 ml (4 fl oz) dry cider or dry white wine
3 tablespoons single cream (optional)

Soak the beans overnight in cold water according to the instructions on the packet.

Drain the beans, place them in a pan and cover with boiling water. Cover and leave to stand for 1 hour. Drain the beans and return to the pan. Cover with cold water and bring to the boil. Lower the heat and add the clove-studded onion and bouquet garni. Cover and simmer for 1 hour or until the beans are soft, skimming the foam from time to time. The cooking time will depend on the quality and freshness of the beans. Season with salt and pepper and drain.

Meanwhile, pre-heat the oven to 230°C/450°F/Gas 8.

Prepare the meat. Make a few incisions in the lamb with the point of a sharp knife and insert the slivers of garlic. Rub the lamb with the butter, sprinkle with thyme or rosemary and press the herbs over the surface. I never add salt to lamb before cooking since it makes the cooking juices run freely. Place the lamb in a roasting tin, add a little water so the juices do not burn and bake in the oven for 10 minutes. Reduce the oven temperature to 200°C/400°F/Gas 6 and cook for about 1¼ hours for medium or 2 hours for well-cooked meat, basting occasionally.

Half an hour before the lamb is ready, start to cook the vegetables. Heat the butter and oil in a large frying-pan and add the carrot, onions, shallots, garlic and tomatoes. Cook for about 15 minutes until most of the moisture has evaporated then crush the vegetables coarsely with a fork and add them to the cooked beans. Sprinkle with thyme and parsley, cover and keep warm.

Transfer the lamb to warm platter, cover with kitchen foil and keep in a warm place. Add the cider or wine to the roasting tin and bring to the boil, scraping the bottom vigorously to mix in all the cooking juices. Simmer for 5 minutes. Skim as much fat as you can from the top then stir in the cream, if using, and season with salt and pepper.

Carve the lamb and arrange it on a warm serving platter. Sprinkle with salt and pepper and spoon a little of the warm sauce over each slice. The rest of the sauce can be served separately. The beans and vegetables can be arranged around the meat or served in a separate dish.

Épaule d'Agneau Farcie aux Légumes et aux Fruits

CATALAN STUFFED LAMB SHOULDER

With its bustling squares, elegant palm trees and *Belle Époque* buildings, the lovely, lively city of Perpignan is the French capital of Roussillon. It is also very much a part of Catalonia, the ancient region which spreads from Valencia in Spain through Barcelona to Perpignan.

For the last seven centuries, the Arabic influence has transmitted a variety of surprising habits and tastes to the cooking of the region. Catalan foods are light and highly flavoured. Their fragrant *charcuterie* is prepared with dried, uncooked pork and seasoned with a variety of strong spices and herbs, marjoram being a particular favourite. There is a mingling of meats and fruits: goose or lamb with pears, chicken with garlic and lemon, rabbit with prunes and greengages. In pastries, there are accents of aniseed, lemon, almonds and honey. Beef is not cooked in the region, but pork is served in all kinds of ways, mainly with unripe fruits. Sauces are not thickened with egg yolks, butter, cream or flour, as they are elsewhere in France, but with honey and crushed almonds. In one day I was blessed by an instant education – visually, gastronomically and historically – on Catalan food by Eliane Thibaut-Comelade and a few of her friends. Her garden in the very centre of Perpignan grows the essentials: almond, lemon, orange, palm, fig trees and lots and lots of aromatic herbs. She prepared this lamb dish for us because it embodied all the characteristics and delights of Catalan cooking.

SERVES 6

1 large shoulder of lamb, boned and flattened to a rectangular shape
a few thin slices pork fat or streaky bacon
4 tablespoons olive oil
300 ml (10 fl oz) chicken stock or water

FOR THE STUFFING

1 tablespoon olive oil
1 thick slice stale bread
225 g (8 oz) meat from the centre of the lamb, chopped
225 g (8 oz) streaky bacon, chopped
75 g (3 oz) pigs' liver or chicken livers, chopped (optional)
25 g (1 oz) almonds, crushed
1 tablespoon snipped fresh chives
1 tablespoon chopped fresh marjoram or savory
2 tablespoons chopped fresh rosemary
1 tablespoon fennel seeds
1 clove star anise
6 garlic cloves, crushed
1 tablespoon rosemary honey
salt and freshly ground black pepper
1 tablespoon grated lemon rind

TO GARNISH

4 small purple globe artichokes, trimmed
12 tiny new potatoes
1 tablespoon olive oil
100 g (4 oz) wild or button mushrooms
6 small fleshy peaches, peeled and stoned
6 fresh figs, pricked with a needle (optional)
6 small dessert apples, peeled and cored
6 small pears, peeled and cored

Heat the oil and fry the bread until golden. Drain and place in a bowl. Add the remaining stuffing ingredients and mix together by hand or in a food processor. The mixture should not be too smooth. Spread the stuffing across the narrow part of the lamb about 5 cm (2 in) from the edges and roll it tightly so the stuffing is

enclosed. Sew it all along into a neat cylinder. Wrap the fat or bacon round the meat and tie with string if necessary. Heat the oil in a heavy-based pan and fry the lamb until browned on both sides. Lower the heat, cover and cook for 20 minutes.

Cook the artichokes and potatoes in boiling salted water for 5 minutes. Drain well, then arrange around the lamb, cover and cook on a medium heat for 25 minutes, shaking the pan from time to time so that the vegetables brown on all sides. Heat the oil and fry the mushrooms for a few minutes, season with salt and pepper, then add to the lamb with the peaches and figs and cook for a further 5 minutes. Add the apples and pears to the pan and simmer for a further 10 minutes. When everything is golden on all sides, add a little stock and heat through.

Remove the meat from the pan and discard the string. Cut the meat into thin slices and arrange on a warm serving platter. Arrange the fruits and vegetables around it.

Stir the cooking juices in the pan well then spoon them delicately over the meat and vegetables and serve at once.

MOROCCO AND THROUGHOUT FRANCE

Tagine d'Agneau aux Oignons

LAMB AND ONION STEW

One of the legacies of France's colonial history has been the development of North African — Maghreb — communities in French cities. Moroccans, Tunisians and Algerians have all imported their highly flavoured cuisine, which has enlivened native French palates. Couscous and *tagines* are among the most popular dishes for the French to cook at home.

Fatma Maziani came to Paris from Casablanca in 1983. An office cleaner by day, after work she's in great demand as an informal caterer. Fatma makes delicious stews, salads and couscous for people to serve at home. This *tagine* is typically Moroccan: meat and vegetables in a salty-sweet sauce. It is best made with Moroccan saffron powder, if you can find it, and served with rice or plain couscous.

SERVES 6

900 g (2 lb) lean lamb
2 tablespoons olive oil
2 tablespoons peanut oil
4 teaspoons cinnamon
1 teaspoon ground ginger
3½ tablespoons sugar
1 small bunch of fresh parsley, chopped
1 small bunch of fresh coriander, chopped
a pinch of saffron powder
salt and freshly ground black pepper
1 garlic clove, finely chopped
1 tomato, skinned, seeded and chopped
1 onion, chopped
3 teaspoons ground cumin
75 g (3 oz) raisins, soaked in warm water and then drained

Cut the lamb into 5 cm (2 in) squares. Heat half the olive and peanut oils in a deep, heavy-based flameproof casserole dish. Add the meat. Add 1 teaspoon of cinnamon, the ginger, 2 tablespoons of sugar, parsley, coriander, a pinch of saffron and salt and pepper. Fry over a fairly high heat until brown. Turn the heat to low. Add water to cover the meat, then add the garlic and tomato. Cover and simmer gently for about 1 hour. Check, stirring occasionally, and add a little water if the meat starts to stick.

Meanwhile, heat the remaining oil in a separate pan and add the onions and the remaining cinnamon, sugar and cumin. Cook for about 15 minutes, stirring, until the onion is light golden. After the meat has cooked for 1 hour, spoon the onions on top of the lamb, without stirring them in. Cover and simmer for a further 20 minutes.

Stir in the raisins just before serving.

SALT

Where there is salt, there is life. Salt is essential to mankind; it is sacred, a symbol of purity and wisdom. For centuries it was also a means of trading. Roman soldiers were paid with salt, hence the word 'salary'. In France, la gabelle, a tax on salt imposed in the Middle Ages which continued until the Revolution, gradually crept back into the tax system in other guises and was not finally dismissed until after 1945. Even today, one cannot take a litre of salty sea water without the permission of the Ministry of Finance.

Salt is gathered both from mines, sel gemme, *which is of lesser quality, and from the sea,* sel de mer, *along the Mediterranean and the Atlantic. Since the fourteenth century, the salt marshes along the Atlantic coast have provided the best salt, receiving no chemical purification treatment. It is rich in magnesium, potassium and calcium.*

The coarse bluish-grey salt, le sel gris, *coloured by the clay in the soil, and the coarse sea salt,* le gros sel, *are used for cooking; they awake and enhance all the natural flavours. The fine, delicate* fine fleur *or* fleur de l'eau *salt that is gathered on the surface of the water is kept for seasoning at the table.*

Salt has been used as a preservative for centuries. It turns plain cod fish into the fragrant morue. *In charcuterie, hams, sausages and* petit salé *are rubbed by hand with rough sea salt to preserve them and impart flavour and colour. The splendid* jambon de Bayonne *from the south-west is cured with two salts, one from Salies de Bearn and one from Bayonne.*

Cooks love sea salt. They bake a whole fish, a chicken or some duck breasts under a thick layer of sea salt with thyme to seal in all the flavour (see p.162). Potées (see p.158), Pot au Feu *(see p.198), fresh radishes, spring onions and raw, tender butter beans are always served with a tiny pot of* gros sel *as a condiment.*

In cooking, it is impossible to give precise quantities of salt. Some salts are more pungent than others, some palates require more salt than others, people are accustomed to a different levels of saltiness in the cuisine of their particular region. That elusive dose is called le grain de sel. *It is that pinch of magic which enhances all the flavours of the dish.*

Navarin d'Agneau

LAMB AND VEGETABLE STEW

The best Navarins are prepared in spring when young, tender carrots and turnips are available. The variety of lamb is important: shoulder or leg because they are lean and meaty, breast, ribs and neck because they give flavour and texture. Navarin must be prepared in advance. The pieces of meat are sautéed then simmered and refrigerated. An hour before the meal, the fat can be lifted off the top of the pan and the bones discarded. The vegetables are steamed separately so that they remain crisp and provide a fresh counterpoint. Frozen peas or green beans can be added at the last minute, otherwise fresh vegetables are essential.

SERVES 6

FOR THE MEATS

1.5 kg (3 lb) lamb (shoulder, leg, neck, ribs)
3 tablespoons groundnut oil
1 tablespoon sugar
salt and coarsely ground black pepper
1 tablespoon plain flour
1 large onion, chopped
3 garlic cloves, whole
900 ml (1½ pints) beef stock or water
3 bay leaves
1 sprig of fresh thyme
4 tomatoes, skinned and chopped

FOR THE VEGETABLES

Choose a selection from the following vegetables:
6 small carrots with 1 inch (2.5 cm)
green stem or carrots cut into sticks
6 small turnips
100 g (4 oz) green beans
12 tiny spring onions with 2.5 cm (1 in) green stem
1 fennel bulb, cut into 2.5 cm (1 in) pieces
175 g (6 oz) fresh peas or small frozen peas

50 g (2 oz) mangetouts
900 g (2 lb) potatoes, cut into
5 cm (2 in) pieces

TO GARNISH

a pinch of ground coriander
2 tablespoons chopped fresh thyme, chives, chervil or
flatleaf parsley
1 tablespoon fresh parsley, cut up with scissors

Trim the meats, remove the bone from the shoulder and reserve. Cut the meat into 5 cm (2 in) cubes and pat dry on kitchen paper. Choose a large, heavy-based frying-pan and cook the meat in batches so it has room to brown easily. Heat a little oil over a medium heat and sauté the pieces of meat for about 10 minutes until golden brown on all sides. Sprinkle with a little sugar; it will caramelize in a minute. Sprinkle with salt and pepper and stir until crisp and brown. Sprinkle with a little flour, lower the heat and stir so the flour turns golden and the meat is coated. Transfer the meat and bones to a large flameproof casserole dish and keep them warm while you sauté the remaining batches of meat.

Add a little more oil to the pan and fry the onion and garlic for 2 minutes. Pour in a little broth or water and stir well to scrape up the meat juices. Pour over the meat and add enough stock or water to cover the meat. Bring to the boil, stirring occasionally, then lower the heat, cover and simmer for 30 minutes. Add the bay leaves, thyme and tomatoes and cook for a further 1 hour, uncovered, until the meat is very tender. Leave to cool then cover and chill overnight.

An hour before the meal, remove the fat congealed on the top of the pan and lift the meat out of the broth. Trim away any gristle or fat and discard the bones and herbs. Heat the broth over a high heat for a few minutes to reduce it a little. Add the pieces of meat to the broth and simmer for about 30 minutes. Taste and season with salt and pepper.

Meanwhile, cook your chosen vegetables in a steamer or a large pan of salted water for about 30 minutes, adding them one type at a time so that they all complete cooking together. They should remain quite firm and almost crunchy. Place the carrots and turnips in first, then add green beans, spring onions and fennel and finally the peas and mangetouts. The potatoes can be cooked separately in boiling salted water until tender.

Arrange half the steamed vegetables on a warm serving platter and spoon the meat on top. Add the rest of the vegetables and spoon over most of the meat cooking juices. Sprinkle with the coriander and herbs. Arrange the potatoes in a separate dish and sprinkle with salt and parsley.

THROUGHOUT FRANCE

Blanquette de Veau

VEAL CASSEROLE WITH MUSHROOMS, PEARL
ONIONS AND CREAM

There are a great many ways of making a *blanquette*. In Paris, and in fashionable restaurants, it is a very white and delicate dish, in Brittany it is enhanced by cider and served with artichokes, and in some country kitchens it is prepared the way I saw when I visited Madame Léa Lajudie on her family's cattle farm outside Limoges – the veal was sautéed in oil then some vegetables and herbs added, but no cream or egg yolks were included.

I have used the following recipe for *Blanquette de Veau* for a long time. It is pungent and light, yet also unctuous and exquisite.

Selecting the correct meat is important. The veal must be whitish-pink in colour with enough bones and cartilage left in the neck or breast to provide flavour and to thicken the sauce. You may need to order the veal specially from your butcher. A *blanquette* is usually served with plain rice or tiny new potatoes. It is also good with steamed asparagus, braised chicory, sliced artichoke hearts, tiny broad beans or mangetouts.

SERVES 4–6

900 g (2 lb) breast or neck of veal, cut into 5 cm (2 in) lean pieces
450 g (1 lb) boned shoulder of veal, cut into 5 cm (2 in) pieces
1 cracked veal bone (optional)
salt and freshly ground black pepper
300 ml (10 fl oz) dry white wine
1 large onion, studded with 4 cloves
1 large garlic clove, peeled
12 oz (350 g) button mushrooms, divided into stems and caps
2 sprigs of fresh parsley
2 bay leaves
3 sprigs of fresh thyme
1 long strip lemon rind
50 g (2 oz) butter
2 tablespoons plain flour
3 carrots, sliced
12 pearl onions, fresh or frozen, or spring onions with about 2.5 cm (1 in) green stem
1 tablespoon vegetable oil
juice of 2 lemons
2 egg yolks
150 ml (5 fl oz) double cream
1 teaspoon freshly grated nutmeg
1 teaspoon grated lemon rind
2 tablespoons chopped fresh chervil or flatleaf parsley

Place all the veal and bones in a large pan. Sprinkle with salt, cover with cold water and bring slowly to the boil, skimming off the scum as it rises to the surface. Continue to boil gently for 30 minutes, removing the scum as it appears. Add the wine, onion, garlic, mushroom stalks, parsley, bay leaves, thyme and strip of lemon rind to the pan, cover and simmer very gently for 1 hour. Uncover and cook for a further 30 minutes. Lift out the meat and bones using a slotted spoon. Pour the liquid through a sieve placed over a deep bowl. Discard the lemon rind and herbs from the sieve and press the vegetables through the sieve into the liquid. Return the liquid and sieved vegetables to the pan and bring to the boil. Continue to boil until 550 ml (18 fl oz) is left.

Melt 25 g (1 oz) of butter in a small pan, stir in the flour and cook, stirring, for about 2 minutes. Remove from the heat and gradually stir in about half of the hot broth. Return to the heat, bring to the boil, stirring, then simmer for about 5 minutes. Stir into the pan of broth and cook for another 5 minutes. Add the veal, carrots and pearl or spring onions, cover and simmer gently, stirring from time to time, for about 15 minutes, until the carrots and onions are tender.

Meanwhile, heat the remaining butter and the oil in a frying-pan and fry the mushroom caps on all sides for 3–4 minutes. Sprinkle with salt and pepper, then add the juice of 1 lemon and cook for about 2 minutes more.

Stir the egg yolks and cream together then stir in a little of the hot broth. Stir this mixture into the pan of veal, vegetables and broth over a very low heat. Add the nutmeg, grated lemon peel, remaining lemon juice and salt to taste. The sauce should be silky and highly flavoured. Sprinkle with fresh chervil or flatleaf parsley.

VARIATION

In Provence, lamb is used for a *blanquette*.

THROUGHOUT FRANCE

Poche de Veau Farcie
STUFFED VEAL BREAST

This is a lovely dish, quite inexpensive and easy to prepare. If you find veal breast hard to come by, you can use lamb's breast instead. Ask your butcher to remove all the bones and reserve them for the broth. The meat will look like a large pocket waiting to be stuffed. The filling can include fresh or frozen peas or tiny butter beans, Swiss chard or cabbage. Make sure there is plenty of flatleaf parsley and garlic in your filling so that it is highly flavoured.

Poche de Veau looks like a plump cushion and is served either warm or cold. Serve with steamed vegetables, sautéed, diced potatoes, glazed carrots, plain rice, buttered noodles or a gratin of tomatoes and aubergines.

SERVES 4–6
1 veal or lamb breast, about 900 g (2 lb), boned

FOR THE STUFFING
2 tablespoons groundnut oil
2 spring onions or 1 onion, chopped
225 g (8 oz) lean streaky bacon, chopped
15 g (½ oz) frozen leaf spinach, chopped
7 tablespoons chopped fresh flatleaf parsley
3 garlic cloves, chopped
1 egg
a pinch of freshly grated nutmeg
4 tablespoons cold cooked rice
2 tablespoons grated Gruyère or Parmesan (optional)
10 black, green or purple olives, stoned
2–3 tablespoons brandy

FOR THE COLD SAUCE
2 tablespoons chopped fresh parsley or basil
1 teaspoon ground coriander
6 tablespoons olive oil
1 large tomato, skinned, seeded and chopped

FOR THE BROTH
a few veal bones
3 bay leaves
1 clove
green part of 1 spring onion or leek

FOR THE VEGETABLES
1 tablespoon groundnut oil
1 tablespoon butter
3 onions, sliced
5 carrots, sliced
3 spring onions
1 large fennel bulb, quartered
2 leeks, white part only, sliced
1 garlic clove, crushed

TO FINISH
1 tablespoon groundnut oil
1 tablespoon butter
120 ml (4 fl oz) dry white wine
salt and freshly ground black pepper

TO SERVE
chopped fresh parsley, basil or tarragon

First, make the stuffing. Heat the oil and sauté the spring onions or onion and bacon for a few minutes until soft. Stir in the remaining stuffing ingredients. Fill, but do not overstuff, the veal or lamb breast, fold over and sew up the opening with a large needle and cook's string. Prick the surface with a fork. Bring a large pan of salted water to the boil with the veal bones, bay leaves, clove and green part of a spring onion or leek. Cover and simmer for 30 minutes. Add the veal, return to the boil, lower the heat, cover and simmer for 1½ hours. Leave to cool in the broth.

Heat the oil and butter and sauté the onions until soft. Add the carrots, spring onions, fennel and leeks and sauté for 5 minutes. Stir in the garlic. Remove from the heat and reserve.

Half an hour before the meal, remove the veal from the broth, drain it and pat dry on kitchen paper. Heat the oil and butter and brown the veal on all sides. Add the wine and scrape the coagulated juices in the pan. Add the cooked vegetables, cover and heat through for about 20 minutes.

To prepare the sauce, mix the parsley or basil and coriander in a bowl then whisk in the olive oil. Add the tomato and season.

Transfer the meat to a chopping board and discard the string. Using a sharp knife and holding a plate against the stuffing to hold it together, cut the meat into thick slices and arrange them on a warm serving plate. Sprinkle with salt and pepper. Surround the meat with the vegetables and spoon a little broth over the top. Skim the fat off the pan juices and strain over the meat. Sprinkle with parsley, basil or tarragon. Pass the sauce separately.

NOTE

If you serve this cold, it will be much easier to slice. If using lamb add a few prunes or raisins and a tablespoon of marc brandy to the filling. Serve it with potatoes sautéed in olive oil.

Escalopes Vallée d'Auge

VEAL ESCALOPES WITH MUSHROOMS, WINE AND
CREAM

The cooking of Normandy is based on cattle, cider or calvados, and rich cream, all of which are used in this typical regional recipe. Serve with Fennel Purée (see p.240), potatoes, Vegetable Timbales (see p.241-42), buttered, steamed rice or a simple watercress salad.

SERVES 4

4 veal escalopes, each weighing about 100 g (4 oz)
salt and freshly ground black pepper
40 g (1½ oz) butter
1 tablespoon groundnut oil
175 g (6 oz) mushrooms, sliced
1 tablespoon calvados
800 ml (10 fl oz) dry white wine
175 g (6 fl oz) whipping or double cream

TO GARNISH
sprigs flatleaf parsley

Place the veal between two sheets of grease-proof paper or cling film and pound with a mallet or a rolling pin until they are about ¼–½ in (5 mm–1 cm) thick. Discard the paper or cling film. Season the veal on both sides with salt and pepper.

Heat 15 g (½ oz) of butter and the oil in a large frying-pan over a moderately high heat. Add 2 escalopes to the pan, cook briskly for 2 minutes, turn over and cook for a further 2 minutes. Transfer to a warm plate, cover and keep warm. Cook the remaining 2 escalopes in the same way and transfer to the plate.

Add the remaining butter to the pan and sauté the mushrooms for 5 minutes, stirring occasionally with a wooden spoon. Add to the veal on the plate.

Stir the calvados and wine into the pan, scraping up the sediment with a wooden spoon. Bring to the boil then simmer for 4–5 minutes. Stir in the cream and simmer for another 4–5 minutes. Slide the veal and mushrooms back into the pan, cover and cook gently for 2–3 minutes. Season to taste.

Lift the veal on to a warm serving plate and spoon over the mushrooms and sauce. Garnish with parsley sprigs.

VARIATIONS

• The veal escalopes can be replaced by veal chops or chicken breasts, but the cooking time should be 20–25 minutes over a moderate heat.
• You can also add 2 finely chopped shallots with the calvados.

Foie de Veau à la Moutarde

CALVES' LIVER WITH MUSTARD AND WINE SAUCE

In Auvergne I ate venison liver enriched with cream and mustard, I ate slices of delicate goose liver on cooked apples in Alsace, and in Provence, pork liver with onions, but calves' liver as I tasted it in Limousin remains, for me, the most flavourful of them all.

Liver must be carefully trimmed so there are no nerves or membranes, and cooked within a day of buying it. The slices can be very thin or very thick; I like them to be at least 1 cm (½ in) thick. Serve this recipe with Celeriac Purée (see p.240), Vegetable Timbales (see p.241-42), *Pommes Frites* (see p.252) or with a crisp, tossed salad.

SERVES 4

450 g (1 lb) calves' liver, sliced
salt and freshly ground black pepper
2 tablespoons plain flour
50 g (2 oz) butter
2 tablespoons vegetable oil
2 shallots, sliced, or 4 spring onions sliced
lengthways
4 tablespoons dry white wine
2–3 teaspoons Dijon mustard
1 tablespoon finely chopped fresh flatleaf parsley

Sprinkle both sides of the slices of liver with salt and pepper and dust lightly with flour.

Heat 40 g (1½ oz) butter and 1 tablespoon oil in a frying-pan. When it is very hot, sauté the liver for about 1 minute on each side, depending on the thickness. Remove to a warm plate, cover and keep warm.

Add the remaining butter and oil to the pan and sauté the shallots or spring onions for 2–3 minutes. Stir the wine then the mustard into the pan, then add salt and pepper and the parsley. The sauce will thicken a little. Pour over the liver and serve at once.

BORDEAUX

Entrecôte Bordelaise
STEAK WITH MARROW, SHALLOTS AND WINE

Bordeaux is an elegant city and an important port. The wines are clearly all-important, but I also tasted piles of fragrant cèpes, crisp *ventrèche* – and dainty caramelised *canelés* cakes.

The most famous speciality, however, remains *Entrecôte Bordelaise*. The dish started with steak cooked on a fire of old wine barrels or grape vine cuttings, then garnished with shallots and wine. Simply prepared with wine and shallots, it is called *Marchand de Vin*; with marrow it becomes *Bordelais*. Some add a tablespoon of

beurre manié and some redcurrant jelly to thicken the wine sauce. In the *Brasserie de Noailles*, Martial Dehaut was thickening his sauce with a piece of bitter chocolate and said that a great Bordeaux wine was not essential to the dish; what was needed was a good, natural wine with a high alcohol content. Since it is barely cooked, the meat must be of the best quality and the sauce short, pungent and powerful. I never prepare this dish for more than five or six guests and tend to use less butter than in classic recipes since I find the addition of marrow rich enough for the sauce. The shallot-herb-wine sauce can be prepared in advance and spooned over the steaks just before serving.

SERVES 4

4 lean steaks, each weighing 225 g (8 oz), trimmed
3 tablespoons groundnut oil
salt and freshly ground black pepper

FOR THE SAUCE

75 g (3 oz) shallots, finely chopped
4 garlic cloves, chopped
600 ml (1 pint) full-bodied, hearty red wine
1 tablespoon cognac (optional)
1 bay leaf
1 sprig of fresh thyme
a pinch of freshly grated nutmeg
2 tablespoons red wine vinegar
150 ml (5 fl oz) beef stock or water
2 teaspoons coarsely ground black pepper
a pinch of cayenne pepper
1 tablespoon cold butter

FOR THE MARROW

2–3 veal or beef marrow bones (optional)
coarse salt
5 teaspoons red wine vinegar

TO GARNISH

4 tablespoons fresh parsley or parsley and chives cut
up with scissors

Rub the surface of the steaks with a little oil and season lightly with salt and pepper. Place on a plate, cover with cling film and chill for a few hours.

Remove the steaks from the fridge an hour before you cook. Pat them dry with kitchen paper. Mix together the shallots, garlic, wine, cognac if using, bay leaf, thyme and nutmeg in a saucepan. Bring to the boil and boil, uncovered, for about 15 minutes until reduced by two-thirds. Strain, reserving both the shallot mixture and the liquid. Discard the herbs.

If you are using marrow bones, dip the ends of the bones into rough salt, wrap them in a piece of muslin and place in a pan of cold water with the wine vinegar. Bring to the boil then simmer for 10 minutes. Drain well and remove the muslin. Slide the blade of a knife inside the marrow bones and the marrow will slip out. Dice or slice the marrow.

Heat 1 tablespoon of the oil in a heavy-based frying-pan until very hot then add the steaks and cook for 2 minutes on one side. Season with salt and pepper then turn on the other side and cook for a further 5 minutes. They should still be rare inside. Remove the steaks from the pan, spread half the shallot mixture over the steaks and cover with a lid.

Pour the wine vinegar into the hot pan, bring to the boil and boil for 2 minutes, scraping up the juices in the pan. Add the stock or water, return to the boil and simmer for a few minutes. Add the remaining shallot mixture and the cooking liquid, the pepper and cayenne, stir well and boil until reduced to about 300 ml (10 fl oz). Stir in the butter.

Heat the remaining oil in a separate pan and cook the steaks for about 3 minutes on each side. Sprinkle the diced marrow on top of the steaks and grill under a hot grill for 1 minute. Arrange the steaks on a warm serving platter, spoon over the sauce and serve at once, sprinkled with the parsley or parsley and chives.

Paupiettes de Boeuf

BEEF SLICES STUFFED WITH VEGETABLES AND

HERBS

These stuffed beef rolls are often called *Alouettes sans Têtes* or 'headless larks' because of their plump shape. Each slice of beef is flattened, wrapped around a very fragrant filling and cooked in wine, herbs and vegetables. In the south-west, a few pine nuts, a pinch of saffron and cinnamon is added to give a Catalan touch.

Paupiettes are usually cooked in advance and kept in the fridge. The fat rises to the top and can easily be lifted off and discarded. Then you can remove the string and slowly re-heat them for about 20 minutes so they are easy to serve. They can be served with rice, noodles, sautéed mushrooms or glazed carrots.

SERVES 4

10 x 4 in (10 cm) square thin slices lean chuck steak,
eye of silverside or top round

FOR THE FILLING

2 tablespoons groundnut oil, groundnut and olive oil
or goose fat
1 small onion, chopped
50 g (2 oz) lean streaky bacon or cured ham,
chopped
50 g (2 oz) mushrooms, chopped
2 garlic cloves, crushed
1 teaspoon dried thyme
1 size 3 egg yolk
½ teaspoon ground bay leaves
a pinch of ground coriander
2 tablespoons finely chopped fresh parsley
1 teaspoon dried savory
50 g (2 oz) Gruyère, grated
50 g (2 oz) frozen leaf spinach, thawed, chopped and
drained thoroughly
salt and freshly ground black pepper
2 tablespoons groundnut oil
1 tablespoon unsalted butter
2 tablespoons plain flour
250 ml (8 fl oz) dry white wine
300 ml (10 fl oz) beef stock
a few coriander seeds, ground
a pinch of dried thyme
1 x 5 cm (2 in) strip orange rind
1 tomato, skinned and chopped
1 clove star anise
1 bouquet garni
5 carrots, sliced
2 onions, sliced
1 tablespoon Dijon mustard

TO SERVE

2 tablespoons chopped fresh parsley or basil

Place each slice of meat between 2 sheets of waxed paper and flatten it to about 3 mm (⅛ in) with a wooden mallet or rolling pin.

Heat the oil or fat and fry the onion over a moderate heat until softened. Add the bacon or ham and mushrooms and fry gently for a few minutes. Remove from the heat and stir in the garlic, thyme, egg yolk, ground bay leaves, coriander, parsley, savory, cheese and spinach and season with salt and pepper. Chop the mixture with a heavy knife or process in a food processor.

Season the beef slices with salt and pepper. Spread a small spoonful of the filling on each slice, roll them up into neat cylinders about 4 cm (1½ in) wide and tie with string.

Heat the oil and butter until hot then add the *paupiettes*, a few at a time if necessary, and fry for about 2 minutes until browned on all sides. Remove from the pan. Lower the heat, sprinkle with the flour and mix together. Pour in the wine and stock and stir until blended. Sprinkle with coriander and thyme, add the orange rind, tomato, star anise and bouquet garni. The liquid should just cover the meat. Bring to a simmer, cover and simmer for 1 hour.

Add the carrots and onions, cover and simmer for a further 30 minutes until the meat is tender. Discard the orange rind and bouquet garni, remove the string from the *paupiettes* and stir in the mustard. Sprinkle with the chopped parsley or basil to serve.

VARIATION

Paupiettes may also be filled with a mixture of chopped ham, gherkins, tarragon, anchovies and diced pork cooked in goose fat with shallots, carrots and wine and sprinkled with fresh basil.

Boeuf à la Ficelle

POACHED BEEF

Chez Camille is a pretty restaurant in Arnay-le-Duc, a small town in the centre of a region where they know how to enjoy *le bien vivre*, the good life. I remember the rich polished wood counter, the faded green wicker chairs, the metre high display of white lilacs, the dazzling selection of perfect dry and fresh goats' cheeses, the platter of walnuts and grapes, the sparkling sky-light above the dining room, the inspired chef-patron, Armand Poinsot, and, behind it all, in time-honoured fashion, his vivacious, cheerful, pretty, efficient wife, Monique. Somehow she managed to keep an eye on the flowers, an eye on the immaculate tables, an eye on their three-year old daughter, and an eye on the splendid Charollais cattle, poultry and vegetable garden she and her husband keep so they have at hand top quality ingredients (and because they give such pleasure), yet still greet customers as if they were her one and only concern in life.

Monique took me for a walk in the fields nearby and we saw her memorable Charollais bull, which weighed about 1200 kg (540 lb), her beautiful creamy cows and her snowy white Bresse chickens. After a day of such physical delights the *Boeuf à la Ficelle* Armand cooked for dinner was as I expected – delicious. With the beef Armand served little crisp croquettes flavoured with plenty of mustard.

Boeuf à la Ficelle is a simple recipe requiring no more than adding tender, well-flavoured beef to a mustard-enhanced broth and cooking it briefly so it remains almost rare inside.

SERVES 4

450 g (1 lb) sirloin of beef, cut across into 4 slices
2 carrots, halved lengthways, cut into 5 cm (2 in) lengths
1 celery stick, halved lengthways, cut into 5 cm (2 in) lengths

FOR THE MUSTARD CROQUETTES

50 g (2 oz) good, firm bread without crusts, crumbled or crumbed
5 tablespoons milk
2 potatoes cut into large chunks
½ cabbage, separated into leaves
1 tomato
1.75 litres (3 pints) water
2 bay leaves
2 sprigs of fresh thyme
2 tablespoons Dijon mustard
6 black peppercorns
salt
2–3 teaspoons Dijon mustard
salt
1 egg white
vegetable oil for frying

With the point of a sharp knife, make a hole through each piece of beef, near one edge. Pass a long piece of string through each hole. Tie the ends of the strings to a carving fork so the meat can be suspended in a pan without touching the bottom. Keep the beef to one side.

Place the herbs, peppercorns, carrots, celery, potatoes and cabbage in a pan of boiling water, place the tomato on top and boil for 10 minutes. Strain off the cooking fluid, make up to 1.75 litres (3 pints) with water and put into another pan with the mustard and salt. Keep the vegetables warm. Bring the mustard liquid to the boil, add the beef tied to the fork and simmer gently for 5–7 minutes.

Meanwhile, put the bread for the croquettes in a small bowl, sprinkle over the milk and leave for 10–15 minutes.

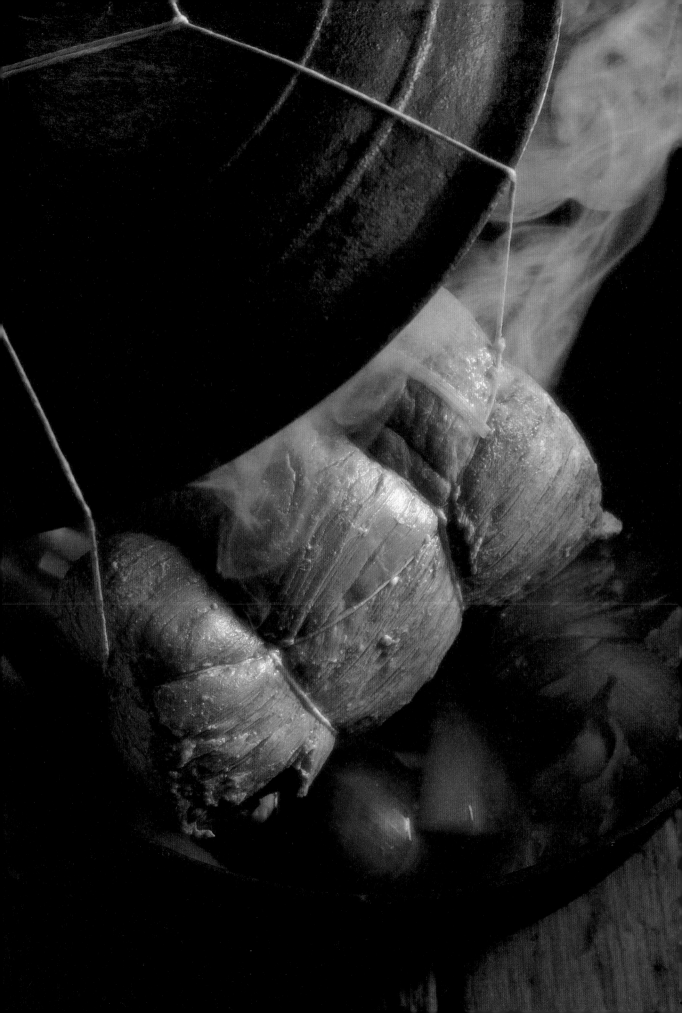

Drain the vegetables. Place the beef and vegetables on a warm plate, cover and keep warm.

Stir the mustard and salt into the soaked breadcrumbs. Whisk the egg white until stiff but not dry then lightly fold into the breadcrumb mixture. Lightly oil a non-stick frying-pan and place over a medium heat. Drop small spoonfuls of the mustard mixture into the pan, taking care not to crowd them. Cook for 1½-2 minutes, until set and golden underneath then turn over and cook on the other side for a further 1½ minutes. Transfer to a plate and keep warm while frying the remaining mixture. Serve hot with the beef and vegetables.

VARIATIONS

- Leave the beef in one and cook for 15–20 minutes.
- The potatoes, cabbage and tomato can be replaced by 1 onion studded with 2 cloves, a diced, small celeriac bulb and 2 sliced leeks.

PROVENCE

Daube aux Olives

BEEF STEW WITH OLIVES

This is one of the oldest Provençal dishes and most local cooks have their own distinctive ways of achieving perfection. For example, the meat may be sautéed before being cooked in the wine or it may be put directly into the cold wine, pork rind, salt pork, a calf's foot or cap mushrooms may be added. The only golden rule they all share is that the *Daube* must cook very slowly for a long time so that the meat is tender and the flavours mingle perfectly. Traditionally plump, earthenware *daubières* were used. These are now difficult to find but a *doufeu* makes an excellent substitute.

A *doufeu*, a sturdy, enamelled cast-iron casserole with a shallow lid that is filled with cold water so the aromatic steam rising from the casserole is quickly condensed and drips on to the meat and vegetables to keep them moist, is wonderful for this type of stew.

The following recipe is my favourite, but the *Daube* prepared near Nyons by Madame Hélène Charrasse-Moinier was superb, especially as not only were her daughter and grand-daughter helping, but her husband made the best *Tapenade* (see p.78) in Provence to be added as a final touch to the piping hot stew.

Serve the *Daube* with buttered macaroni, noodles, new potatoes or ravioli (in Nice, *Daube* is used with Swiss chard to stuff the ravioli as well), or with a tossed green salad.

SERVES 6–8

225 g (8 oz) lean salt pork or streaky bacon, diced
1 onion, chopped
2 tablespoons olive or groundnut oil
1.25 kg (2½ lb) chuck steak, cut into (5 cm) 2 inch cubes
salt and freshly ground black pepper

600 ml (1 pint) hearty red wine
6 medium tomatoes, coarsely chopped
3 carrots, sliced
3 garlic cloves
2 bay leaves
3 sprigs of fresh thyme or marjoram
1 clove
5 cm (2 in) wide strip orange rind dried in an oven
or the open air
2 tablespoons Tapenade (see p. 49)
2 tablespoons chopped fresh flat leaf parsley

Sauté the pork or bacon and the onion in the oil in a heavy-based frying-pan for 5 minutes, stirring once or twice. Add some of the beef to the frying-pan and sauté on all sides for about 8 minutes until lightly browned. Sprinkle with salt and pepper then transfer the beef, onions and pork or bacon to a large, heavy casserole. Add the wine to the casserole, cover and start to cook over a low heat.

Meanwhile, sauté the rest of the beef in several batches, adding the pieces to the casserole as they are cooked. Sprinkle a little salt and pepper on top, add the tomatoes, carrots, garlic, bay leaves, thyme or marjoram, clove, orange rind, and enough water to cover the meat. Cover tightly and simmer very gently for 3½ hours. Stir in the *Tapenade*. Correct the seasoning, remove and discard the bay leaves, thyme or marjoram and the orange rind, then sprinkle finely chopped parsley evenly over the *Daube*.

NOTE

The *Daube* may also be cooked in an oven pre-heated to 140–150°C/275–300°F/Gas 1–2.

The flavour of the *Daube* will improve if it is cooked a day in advance and re-heated. Follow the recipe as far as the addition of the carrots, but instead of adding them, leave the *Daube* to cool and keep in a cold place overnight. About 45 minutes before the meal, heat to simmering point, stirring frequently, add the carrots and continue with the recipe.

A teaspoon of red wine vinegar may be added to the wine to help tenderize the meat.

VARIATION

To make *Daube en Gelée*, Jellied Beef Stew, add a split pig's trotter or a large piece of pork rind to the *Daube*. After it has been cooked, arrange some of the remaining carrots, and enough olives and bay leaves to cover the bottom of a bowl and carefully spoon over the rest of the *Daube*. Cover and leave in a cool place to set. To unmould, wrap a warm towel around the bowl for a few minutes, then invert the bowl on to a cold plate.

THROUGHOUT FRANCE

Hachis Parmentier

BEEF, PARSLEY AND GARLIC POTATO GRATIN

André Parmentier brought the potato plant from America in the eighteenth century and was a zealous promoter of the potato in French cuisine. *Hachis Parmentier* is usually made with the left-overs from *Pot au Feu* coarsely chopped, moistened with cooked onions, tomatoes, white wine and chopped parsley, covered with a light potato purée. *Hachis Parmentier* is an irresistible family dish: inexpensive and easy to prepare in advance. It is placed in the oven half an hour before sitting down to the meal and is welcomed by everyone from seven months to seventy-seven years.

I prepare *Hachis Parmentier* often and never wait for left-overs to appear. Ironically, I make it in vast quantities so it might itself make interesting left-overs to add to omelettes, to stuff courgettes or aubergines or to make into crisp croquettes.

In my version of the dish my secret weapon is an inordinate amount of parsley. Whether the top is covered with breadcrumbs, dotted with butter or olive oil, grated cheese or a beaten egg, there must be plenty of fragrant crust for everyone, so use one or two wide dishes for the *Hachis*. Serve with an endive, dandelion, watercress or chicory tossed salad.

SERVES 4

FOR THE TOPPING
900 g (2 lb) potatoes
1 tablespoon butter
600 ml (1 pint) milk
salt and freshly ground black pepper
a pinch of freshly grated nutmeg

FOR THE FILLING
2 teaspoons groundnut oil

100 g (4 oz) lean streaky bacon, chopped
2 onions, chopped
2 bay leaves
2 teaspoons dried thyme
1 large bunch fresh flatleaf parsley, basil or chives, chopped
2 garlic cloves, crushed
675 g (1½ lb) lean beef or left-over beef, chopped

TO FINISH
100 g (4 oz) Gruyère or Parmesan, grated
2 tablespoons breadcrumbs
2 tablespoons butter

Wash the unpeeled potatoes, place them in a pan and cover with salted water. Bring to the boil and simmer for about 25 minutes until tender. Using a thick tea towel or oven gloves, peel the warm potatoes. Mash or purée them with the butter, gradually adding enough milk to make the mixture moist but not sticky. Season to taste with salt, pepper and nutmeg.

Pre-heat the oven to 180°C/350°F/Gas 4. Butter one or two shallow ovenproof dishes.

Heat half the oil in a large frying-pan and sauté the bacon for a few minutes until crisp. Add the onions, bay leaves and thyme and stir over a low heat for a few minutes. Add the parsley and garlic, stir well, then remove from the pan, discard the bay leaves and set aside.

Heat the remaining oil and sauté the beef for a few minutes, stirring it evenly so that it breaks up as it cooks. Stir in the bacon and onion mixture.

Spoon a thin layer of the potato purée into the prepared dish then add the meat and vegetable mixture. Spoon the rest of the potatoes on top and spread evenly with a fork. Sprinkle with grated cheese and breadcrumbs, dot with butter and bake in the oven for 30 minutes. If the top begins to brown too much, lower the oven temperature. Serve in the cooking dish wrapped in a tea towel and accompanied by a tossed green salad.

BURGUNDY

Boeuf Bourguignon

BURGUNDY BEEF CASSEROLE WITH BUTTON
ONIONS AND MUSHROOMS

Each region has its own definite interpretation of beef stew. Burgundy's version, with bacon, button onions and mushrooms is probably the most famous of them all. It is better if this dish is prepared ahead of time so you have time to skim off the excess fat and to allow all the flavours to develop. It can be served just with a salad of chicory or endive and watercress, or rocket and batavia (escarole), with *Vinaigrette* (see p.76), and good bread; or with tiny new potatoes boiled in their jackets or noodles, and Celeriac Purée (see p.240) and sautéed carrots.

SERVES 6

1.1 kg (2¼ lb) chuck steak, cut into 4 cm (1½ in) cubes
3 tablespoons vegetable oil
2 garlic cloves, crushed
1½ tablespoons plain flour
1 tablespoon brandy
salt and freshly ground black pepper
225 g (8 oz) piece lean streaky bacon, cut into 1 cm (½ in) dice
350 g (12 oz) button onions or shallots
100 g (4 oz) button mushrooms
2 tablespoons chopped fresh flatleaf parsley

FOR THE MARINADE

1 onion, sliced
1 carrot, sliced
1 celery stick, chopped
salt and freshly ground black pepper
600 ml (1 pint) hearty red wine, preferably Burgundy
2 garlic cloves, crushed
1 bay leaf
3 sprigs of fresh thyme

Place the pieces of beef in a large bowl, add all the ingredients for the marinade, stir then cover and keep in the fridge overnight or for a whole day.

Remove the pieces of meat from the marinade and dry with kitchen paper. Strain the marinade and reserve the liquid, carrot and onion. Heat 2 tablespoons oil in a heavy casserole and sauté the meat, a few pieces at a time, for about 10 minutes, until brown on all sides. Turn the pieces carefully using tongs or a wooden spoon. As the beef is cooked, transfer to a bowl using a slotted spoon.

When all the meat is browned, add the reserved onion and carrot, and the garlic to the casserole and cook, stirring occasionally, until browned. Return the meat, and any juices that have collected in the bowl, to the casserole. Sprinkle over the flour, then stir in the brandy and reserved marinade liquid. Add the salt and pepper and bring to just below simmering point. Cover tightly and cook very gently for 2 hours.

Heat the remaining oil in a frying-pan, add the bacon and button onions or shallots and cook, stirring occasionally, until lightly browned. Using a slotted spoon, transfer to the casserole. Add the mushrooms to the pan and cook, stirring a few times, for 2–3 minutes. Add to the casserole, cover and cook for a further hour. Remove any fat from the surface and sprinkle over the chopped parsley.

NOTE

Boeuf Bourguignon can also be cooked in an oven pre-heated to 140°C/275°F/Gas 1, for the same length of time.

The stew can also be cooked as far as the preparation of the bacon, shallots and mushrooms a day ahead. Cool it quickly and keep it in a cool place. Remove fat from the surface before continuing with the recipe.

Carbonade de Boeuf

BEEF AND ONION STEW COOKED IN BEER

This traditional stew is a favourite throughout Picardy and the northern provinces because of its pungent mixture of beer, vinegar and brown sugar. In spite of its name, 'charcoal cooked', *Carbonade* is not grilled but simply browned to a crisp before it simmers with the onions. It can be prepared in advance and re-heated half an hour before you want to serve it with an accompaniment of boiled potatoes, *Pain d'Endives* (see p.245), sliced cabbage and potatoes simmered in butter, turnip gratin, *Carottes Vichy* (see p.238) or a fresh tossed green salad. Beer is a must with *Carbonade*.

SERVES 4

*2 tablespoons pork fat or 2 tablespoons butter and
1 tablespoon groundnut oil
550 g (1¼ lb) flank steak or lean steak, sliced about
1 cm (½ in) thick
4 onions, thinly sliced
salt and freshly ground black pepper
1 tablespoon chopped fresh thyme or 2 teaspoons
dried thyme
10 juniper berries
3 bay leaves
1 large sliced country bread, crusts removed
2 tablespoons Dijon mustard
600 ml (1 pint) light beer
1 tablespoon brown sugar
2 tablespoons red wine vinegar
1 tablespoon chopped fresh parsley*

Pat the meat dry with kitchen paper. Heat the fat in a frying-pan and brown the beef on all sides until crisp. Transfer to a side dish. Add the onions to the pan and fry for a few minutes until lightly browned. Spoon half the onions into a flameproof pan and sprinkle with salt and pepper. Top with the beef then sprinkle with salt, pepper, thyme and juniper berries and add the bay leaves. Spread the bread with the mustard and place it on top then sprinkle over the remaining onions and season again with salt and pepper.

Pour the beer into the frying-pan and deglaze, scraping the coagulated cooking juices with a spatula. Add the brown sugar then pour over the onions and beef. Bring to the boil, cover then simmer for about 1½ hours. Move the lid so that the pan is half-covered and simmer for a further 30 minutes until the meat is tender and the cooking juices have reduced.

If you plan to cook in advance, leave to cool then chill, then remove the layer of fat on the top when you are ready to reheat it. Otherwise, simply skim off the fat from the top with a large spoon and correct the seasoning.

A few minutes before the end of cooking, sprinkle with the wine vinegar. Sprinkle with parsley and bring to the table. You may like to serve the *Carbonade* in its cooking pan wrapped with a thick tea towel, or in a shallow china dish.

NOTE

Sometimes the mustard-covered rounds of bread are placed on top of the *Carbonade* and grilled briefly before the dish is brought to the table.

Rôti de Porc aux Pommes

ROAST PORK WITH APPLES, WINE AND SPICES

Once upon a time, when pigs roamed freely and fed on acorns and chestnuts, their meat needed little seasoning. Today fresh pork can be rather dull, so potent regional flavours are welcomed. I serve *Rôti de Porc* with a celeriac purée flavoured with some fresh apples. But you may like to serve it with sliced leeks or shredded cabbage simmered in butter, unpeeled boiled or sautéed potatoes, unpeeled cloves of garlic or plain boiled rice.

If it is possible, marinate the flat piece of pork overnight then roll and tie it into a roast. Pork meat is fat enough, so it should not be basted with its own juices but with milk, water, wine or cider.

SERVES 4–6

FOR THE MARINADE

1 teaspoon sea salt
2 teaspoons dried thyme
5 peppercorns
2 teaspoons ground coriander
300 ml (10 fl oz) dry cider or dry white wine
1 tablespoon calvados

FOR THE MEAT

900 g (2 lb) boneless loin or shoulder of pork
salt and freshly ground black pepper
2 tablespoons groundnut oil
1 tablespoon butter
a few juniper berries, crushed (optional)
1 teaspoon ground coriander (optional)
1 teaspoon coarsely ground black pepper
3 tablespoons double cream

TO GARNISH

6 large cooking apples, 3 large quinces or 3 apples
and 3 pears
juice of 1 lemon
2 small onions, very finely chopped
2 tablespoons butter
2 tablespoons sugar
½ teaspoon salt

Grind the salt, thyme, peppercorns and coriander in a mortar or in a blender then rub over the surface of the pork. Place in a bowl, pour over the cider or wine and calvados, cover and chill overnight.

Lift the meat from the marinade and pat dry on kitchen paper. Sprinkle with salt and pepper on both sides then roll it up and tie it into a neat cylinder shape.

Pre-heat the oven to 180°C/350°F/Gas 4.

Heat the oil and butter in a heavy-based pan and fry the meat for a few minutes until golden on all sides. Place in a flameproof roasting tin about 7.5 cm (3 in) wider than the meat and cook it in the oven for about 30 minutes, turning twice. Pour the marinade into the dish and cook for a further 1–1½ hours, basting the meat and adding a little more wine if it becomes too dry. The meat will caramelize and most of the juices will evaporate.

Meanwhile, peel, core and quarter the apples, quinces or apples and pears and sprinkle with lemon juice. Place them in a saucepan with the onions, dot with the butter and sprinkle with the sugar and salt. Cover and simmer over a low heat for 10–15 minutes until soft but not mushy.

Remove the meat from the oven and transfer the glazed golden roast to a warm serving platter. Cover and keep warm in the turned-off oven. If there is too little liquid in the roasting tin, add a little more wine. Cook the sauce over a high heat, scraping the coagulated juices. If you like a spirited sauce, add the juniper berries, coriander and pepper. Stir in the cream and simmer for a few minutes. Taste and correct the seasoning with salt and pepper.

Cut and discard the string from the meat. Slice it and arrange the pork in overlapping slices on a warm serving platter. Spoon the warm cream sauce over the meat so that each slice is coated and arrange the cooked apples round the edge of the platter. Extra sauce can be served in a sauce boat. If the apples have overcooked and become mushy, serve them separately in a shallow dish.

NOTE

I once tasted an interesting version made by Martine O'Jeanson in Tours. She stuffed each peeled and cored apple with a plump local Damas prune for a flavourful accompaniment.

AUVERGNE AND THROUGHOUT FRANCE

Potée

PORK AND BEAN STEW

Most regions in France have a version of this dish. A chicken, half a pig's head, a breast of lamb, a piece of smoked streaky bacon, a *jambonneau*, pork spare ribs and most vegetables may be added to the smoked pork and the sausages.

Potée should be made in large quantities. It will keep refrigerated for a few days.

SERVES 6–8

FOR THE VEGETABLES

750 g (1½ lb) dried white haricot beans
1 green cabbage, shredded
1 tablespoon butter
2 tablespoons oil
5 carrots, cut into 5 cm (2 in) chunks
2 large onions, quartered
4 small white or pink turnips, quartered
8 garlic cloves
4 leeks, white parts only tied together with string
salt and freshly ground black pepper

FOR THE MEAT

green part of the leeks
3 bay leaves
1 tablespoon dried thyme
2 onions studded with 2 cloves
10 peppercorns
10 juniper berries
900 g (2 lb) lean streaky bacon
900 g (2 lb) piece pork spare rib
900 g (2 lb) shoulder of pork, boned and rolled
piece country ham (optional)
1 ham bone (optional)
a few Toulouse or boiling pork sausages

FOR THE VINAIGRETTE
1½ tablespoons white wine vinegar
6 tablespoons olive oil
1½ teaspoons Dijon mustard
2 tablespoons finely chopped fresh chives or coriander and chives
1 tablespoon chopped fresh flatleaf parsley
1½ tablespoons finely chopped shallots
salt and freshly ground black pepper

TO SERVE
1 tablespoon chopped fresh parsley
1 tablespoon snipped fresh chives
2–3 different kinds of mustard
small bowl of sea salt
bowl of gherkins

Soak the haricot beans in cold water for 1 hour, or as directed on the packet. Drain, then place in a pan, cover with water and bring to the boil for 10 minutes. Lower the heat, cover and simmer for 1 hour. Drain and cool.

While the beans are cooking, bring a large pan of water (about 5 litres/9 pints) to the boil. Add the green parts of the leeks, the bay leaves, thyme, clove-studded onions, peppercorns and juniper berries. Boil for 10 minutes. Add all the meats except the sausages, return to the boil, lower the heat, cover and simmer for 1 hour.

Meanwhile, bring a saucepan of salted water to the boil, add the cabbage and return to the boil. Lower the heat then simmer for 10 minutes. Drain and rinse under cold water.

Heat the butter and oil and cook the carrots, onions and turnips for 10 minutes. Add the garlic and leeks and cook for a further 5 minutes until lightly browned.

Add the cabbage and browned vegetables to the meat and simmer for a further 10 minutes. Add the cooked beans, stir with a long-handled spoon and simmer for 10 minutes. Prick the sausages with a fork to prevent them from split-

ting and add them to the pot. Simmer for a further 20 minutes.

Place all the ingredients for the vinaigrette in a bowl and stir with a fork until well blended.

When ready to serve, remove and slice the meats and arrange them on a warm serving platter. Spoon a little of the broth over them, season with salt and pepper and sprinkle with a little parsley. Keep them warm. Arrange the beans and vegetables attractively on a warm serving dish, discarding the string round the leeks, and spoon a little of the broth over them. Sprinkle with salt, pepper and chives. Serve the platters of meat and vegetables with a tray containing the vinaigrette, mustards, salt and gherkins and a basket of crusty bread.

NOTE

A few crisp, spicy or garlic-flavoured Italian sausages can be sautéed in oil and arranged around the vegetables at the last moment. Left-over vegetables can be turned into soup or gratin, and left-over meats sliced and served cold with a well-seasoned vinaigrette or used to stuff chicken or a *Poche de Veau Farcie* (see p.180).

Porc aux Herbes et aux Légumes

PORK ROAST SEASONED WITH HERBS
AND VEGETABLES

Monsieur Joel Robuchon is France's finest palate, the most absolute reference for anyone interested in cooking, and the most rigorous and attentive of chefs. I saw him prepare the following recipe as he explained each of the important turning points of what was originally a simple home dish. There were no exotic or expensive ingredients – pork has always been enhanced by sage and juniper berries and is generally deglazed with wine. The technique was minimal but perfectly confident. But it is the sum of decisive gestures – marinating the meat with herbs and salt (so it would be permeated with flavours), browning it to crisp before final cooking (so the meat retains all its piquancy), salting it only after the surface is crisp and brown, adding a fine tuning of bitter and acid elements (vinegar, juniper berries, the green parts of the leeks), the coarse cutting of the onions and leeks (to give texture), the bones added to the meat as it simmers (to add taste), the rubbing instead of mincing of sage leaves (to enhance flavour) – which made Monsieur Robuchon's version unique. There is nothing dogmatic about vegetables or herbs – if there are no leeks, then fennel bulb thinly cut would do, savory could replace thyme – the only concern for him was to fix all the flavours, to preserve the texture of the vegetables and not to dilute the cooking juices, so the dish will explode with fresh flavours. I have prepared the following version inspired by Monsieur Robuchon very often and always with the same delight.

SERVES 4

*900 g–1.4 kg (2–3 lb) pork roasting joint, trimmed
and boned*
4 garlic cloves, cut into slivers
2 teaspoons chopped fresh thyme
salt
2 tablespoons groundnut oil
a few beef bones (optional)
5 spring onions or 5 shallots, halved
3 tomatoes, skinned and coarsely chopped
*4 leeks, white and 5 cm (2 in) of green, trimmed and
halved*
2 teaspoons sugar
300 ml (10 fl oz) dry white wine
1 tablespoon red wine vinegar
5 juniper berries
freshly ground black pepper
2 teaspoons dried thyme
10 fresh sage leaves
2 tablespoons butter

Sprinkle the meat with the garlic, fresh thyme and salt, roll it and tie it into a neat cylinder. Wrap it in cling film and chill overnight. If the roast is already rolled, sprinkle the salt and thyme on the surface and stud slivers of garlic into the meat.

When you are ready to cook, pat the meat dry carefully. Heat the oil in a heavy-based pan, add the bones and the meat and brown on all sides, uncovered, until slightly caramelized. Add the spring onions, tomatoes and leeks, sprinkle with sugar and cook, uncovered, for about 10 minutes. Add the wine and wine vinegar and stir the coagulated juices with a wooden spoon. Sprinkle in the juniper berries and add a little salt to the vegetables (not much on the meat as it already had salt in the marinade). Sprinkle the roast generously with pepper; this is a highly tasty dish. Sprinkle in the thyme then rub and crush the sage leaves between your palms and add them to the pan. Stir well, cover and simmer for about 1½ hours, stirring from time to time.

Remove from the heat and discard the bones. Stir in the butter, cover and leave to rest for a few minutes before you slice so that the juices flow evenly through the meat. There should be a small quantity of fragrant sauce. Arrange the sliced meat on a warmed serving plate, pour over the sauce and arrange the vegetables around.

ALSACE

Choucroute Garnie
ALSACE SAUERKRAUT AND PORK

Cabbages grow very easily on the Alsace plain and they are used in many local dishes. However, outside the region the most well-known Alsace way of serving cabbage is *choucroute*, pickled cabbage, called *sauerkraut* in Germany. For generations, preparing *choucroute* has been an important autumnal task. Wooden barrels or stoneware pots are lined with thick cabbage leaves, then the barrel or pot is filled with alternate layers of shredded leaves, coarse rock salt, juniper berries and bay leaves. A cloth is spread over the top, followed by a heavy lid that is slightly smaller than the mouth of the barrel or pot, then finally a rock or other weight is placed on top. At the end of month it is ready for turning into one of Alsace's most celebrated dishes *Choucroute Garnie*. Traditionally this is a hearty dish in which the pickled cabbage is cooked slowly for hours with a wide variety of fresh and cured pork, hams and sausages, but recently I ate the lightest, freshest, most crunchy *Choucroute Garnie* I have ever had. It had been prepared by Madame Colette Faller, at the *Domaine des Capucins*, near Colmar. She cooks the *choucroute* separately from the meats, just bringing them together at the last moment so all the ingredients speak loud and clear. The other keys to a good *Choucroute Garnie* are good, uncooked, canned or bottled *choucroute*, not using too much wine and cooking it very slowly. Some people in Alsace like to cook it for as long as, twelve hours, some only two or three. Everyone has their own idea of which and how many spices to add. I like to include some carrots for colour as *choucroute* tends to be grey and I leave the juniper berries, coriander seeds and bay leaves to roam freely during the cooking and when I serve the dish. I do not use goose fat but you may like to add with the oil.

A *Choucroute Garnie* for a small supper or dinner party does not use the same cuts and number of different meats as one for a large family meal, just a selection of bacons, ham hock, pork knuckle or shoulder, frankfurters and smoked sausages can be used.

SERVES 6

1.5 kg (3 lb) choucroute, or canned or bottled sauerkraut
3 tablespoons vegetable oil
1 large onion, sliced
freshly ground black pepper
2 cloves
5 juniper berries, ground
5 coriander seeds, crushed
2 garlic cloves
450 ml (15 fl oz) Alsace Riesling
1 bay leaf
2 carrots, thinly sliced
225 g (8 oz) piece smoked streaky bacon
225 g (8 oz) piece green streaky bacon
450 g (1 lb) piece smoked pork shoulder
1 pork knuckle
3 large smoked sausages, preferably Montbéliard (which are caraway-flavoured); or 3 kielbasa or 3 kabanos
6 frankfurters
1 blutwurst (blood sausage), (optional)
2–3 bratwurst

TO SERVE

Dijon mustard

Rinse the *choucroute* under cold, running water. Drain well, squeeze out excess moisture, then spread on a dish.

Heat 2 tablespoons of oil in a pan, add the onion and cook over a fairly high heat for 3–4 minutes until soft. Stir in the *choucroute* or *sauerkraut* using a wooden spoon and continue to stir for 5 minutes. Add the pepper, all the spices, the garlic and wine and enough water to cover. Cover and cook over a low heat for about 1½ hours, stirring with a fork from time to time. Add the bay leaf and carrots and simmer for 10 minutes.

Meanwhile, place the bacon, smoked pork and pork knuckle in a pan, cover with hot water and simmer, allowing 30 minutes per 450 g (1 lb) from when the water reaches simmering point.

Poach the smoked sausages or *kielbasa* for 25 minutes or so then add the frankfurters and poach for a further 10 minutes. Fry the blood sausage, if using, and *bratwurst* in the remaining oil in a frying-pan for about 5 minutes, turning occasionally.

When everything is cooked, place the *choucroute* or *sauerkraut* on a large, warm plate. Slice the meats and sausages and pile on top of the *choucroute* or *sauerkraut*. Serve with mustard.

NOTE

Of late, a light version of *choucroute* with fish is being served in some fashionable restaurants, but this is not a new marriage – in the Middle Ages, salmon and even herrings were partnered with *choucroute*. I prefer the union of *choucroute* with pheasant and apples. Two chopped apples can also be added to the *Choucroute Garnie* recipe.

THROUGHOUT FRANCE

Pot au Feu

BOILED MEATS WITH MARROW BONES
AND VEGETABLES

Pot au Feu is a glorious cousin of *Poule au Pot Farcie* (see p. 152), and although described as a dish of boiled meats, bones and vegetables cooked together, the secret of its success lies in the details.

Today every region boasts about its version of *Pot au Feu*. In Provence, lamb, garlic and chick peas are used, in Auvergne there is pork and cabbage, in Burgundy sausages and stuffed chicken while in Alsace there are *quenelles* (light dumplings) made from the marrow from the beef bones. Other possible additions to *Pot au Feu* can be turkey, partridge, shin of beef, veal knuckle, oxtail, ham, stuffed breast of veal, rabbit or duck portions plus a variety of spices and vegetables. But whether it is an extravagant display or a plain one, *Pot au Feu* remains a most reassuring dish. There is nothing like a steaming *Pot au Feu* to create a feeling of warmth and happiness around a table. It is easy to prepare, is not expensive and does not require much attention. The meat will shrink a great deal and like all stews, it is at its best if made a day in advance so the fat can be easily removed from the surface, and the flavours allowed to mellow and mature.

Pot au Feu is served in two parts, the broth first with Croûtons (see p.233) and grated cheese, then comes a large plate of boiled vegetables and one of neat, overlapping slices of meats, and a small plate with the marrow bones, more Croûtons, and small spoons for extracting the marrow from the bones.

I prefer to cook the vegetables either in a tiered steamer or in a large pan of boiling water. Celeriac, turnips or parsnips, carrots and potatoes will require 10 minutes longer than the leeks.

Accompaniments could simply be coarse sea salt, gherkins, cherries in vinegar, a pot of mustard or a bowl of horseradish. Or there could be a variety of sauces such as Mayonnaise (see p.101), Aïoli (see p.76) or Vinaigrette (see p.76), according to the occasion and the time available to prepare the meal.

SERVES 8

450 g (1 lb) bones, such as beef ribs or veal knuckle
750 g (1½ lb) piece blade portion of chuck or top rump tied with a string like a package
750 g (1½ lb) piece brisket, tied with a string
750 g (1½ lb) short ribs, trimmed

FOR THE BROTH

3 cloves garlic
2 onions, each studded with 2 cloves
1 large leek, chopped
1 carrot, chopped
4 sprigs of fresh thyme
2 bay leaves
4 sprigs of fresh parsley
10 black peppercorns
salt and freshly ground black pepper
8 pieces marrow bone

FOR THE VEGETABLES

1 bulb celeriac, quartered
4 carrots, cut in half lengthways, then in half crossways
4 parsnips or turnips, halved lengthways
4 leeks, white part only, cut in half lengthways and tied in a bundle with a string
4 potatoes, halved

TO SERVE

16 round Croûtons (see p.233)
grated Gruyère or Parmesan

FOR THE ACCOMPANIMENTS

Choose two or more from:
coarse sea salt
Dijon mustard
gherkins
Vinaigrette (see p.76) flavoured with capers, parsley, chopped shallots and mustard
Herb Mayonnaise (see p.101)
Aïoli (see p.76)

Place the bones, except the marrow bones, in a large pan and pile all the meats on top. Cover with cold water and heat to just on simmering point. After a few minutes, remove the beige scum that rises to the surface, using a slotted spoon. Keep doing this until the scum becomes white and frothy, adding a few tablespoons of cold water twice as you skim the surface. Add the vegetables, herbs, peppercorns and salt for the broth. Bring just to the boil then immediately lower the heat, cover and simmer gently for 2½ hours.

Scoop the meat and vegetables from the broth and put them on a plate. Remove and discard the bones. Taste the broth and add salt and pepper if necessary. Re-heat and boil, uncovered, for 5–10 minutes. Pour into a bowl and leave to cool. Cover the meat and vegetables and the broth and chill overnight.

One hour before serving the meal, discard the fat from the top of the broth. Pour the broth into a large saucepan and bring to the boil. If necessary, boil to concentrate the flavours. Add the meat and the vegetables, if liked, and cook over a moderate heat so the liquid just moves, for about 40 minutes.

Meanwhile, pat some salt into the ends of the marrow bones. Wrap them in muslin and tie with a string. Place the marrow bones in cold water, bring to the boil and simmer for 20 minutes. Keep in the water until ready to serve.

Reserve a bowl of hot broth and serve the rest with 8 Croûtons and the cheese. Serve the reserved broth with the meat and vegetables for the second course, along with bowls of the chosen accompaniments.

Jambon à la Crème

HAM SLICES BAKED IN A FRAGRANT SAUCE WITH
MUSHROOMS AND SHALLOTS

Each region cooks ham in its own way, with cider, wine, broth or cream. A lovely, fragrant dish from Burgundy, this is easy to make and can be prepared in advance and re-heated for twenty minutes before the meal. *Jambon à la Crème* can be served with a crisp *Gratin Dauphinois* (see p.269), braised or steamed spinach, buttered pasta, steamed or sautéed new potatoes.

It is worth repeating the obvious here: although the ham will absorb the flavour of mushrooms, coriander and wine, a good quality ham is all-important. Bring the meal to the table in its cooking dish wrapped in a tea towel to avoid burnt fingers.

SERVES 4

2 tablespoons groundnut oil
75 g (3 oz) butter
275 g (10 oz) mushrooms, thickly sliced
salt and freshly ground black pepper
5 x 5 mm (¼ in) thick slices uncooked ham, whole or cut into 2.5 cm (1 in) slivers
1 teaspoon ground coriander
1 teaspoon freshly ground black pepper
120 ml (4 fl oz) dry white wine
3 tablespoons coarsely chopped shallots or spring onions
450 ml (15 fl oz) double cream
1 tablespoon Dijon mustard
2 medium-sized tomatoes, skinned and diced
½ teaspoon freshly grated nutmeg
50 g (2 oz) Gruyère, grated

Heat 1 tablespoon of the oil and 1 tablespoon of the butter in a frying-pan and sauté the mushrooms for about 5 minutes over a high heat, tossing them from time to time with a wooden spoon. Sprinkle them lightly with salt and pepper then transfer them to a side dish.

Trim the ham and dry the slices or slivers on kitchen paper. Heat the remaining oil with 2 tablespoons of the butter and fry the ham until lightly browned on both sides. Sprinkle the top with the coriander and pepper, transfer to a covered dish and keep aside.

Pour the wine into the frying-pan, scraping up all the coagulated juices. Add the shallots or spring onions and cook for 5 minutes over a high heat. Add the cream and season with salt and pepper. Lower the heat and simmer gently for a further 5 minutes. Add the mustard then taste and correct the seasoning. Add the tomatoes, cover and remove from the heat.

Arrange two slices of ham (or half the slivered ham) on the bottom of a buttered flame-proof dish. Add the mushrooms and their juices and top with the remaining ham. Pour over the cream and shallot sauce, sprinkle with the nutmeg and cheese and dot with the remaining butter. Grill under a warm grill for a few minutes without letting the sauce boil. Serve warm.

NOTE

If you want a thicker sauce, knead together 1 tablespoon of butter with 1 tablespoon of plain flour to make a *beurre manié*, stir it into the warm wine and cream sauce and simmer very gently for 2 minutes.

ALSAGE

Baeckeoffe

MIXED MEAT AND VEGETABLE CASSEROLE

Traditionally *Baeckeoffe* is made with pork and just a small amount of beef, a generous quantity of potatoes and local fruity, dry white wine in a colourful, glazed earthenware dish decorated with flowers. In the days when women in Alsace did all their washing on Mondays they would prepare a *Baeckeoffe* early in the morning, take it to the baker's oven as they walked to the public wash-house, and leave it to be cooked as they did their piles of washing. On their way home they would collect their tasty casserole.

It is important to cook *Baeckeoffe* very slowly in a tightly-covered casserole for a long time. A luting paste is often used to seal the lid to the casserole to make sure that the fragrant steam is trapped inside.

Baeckeoffe is even better if cooked a day in advance. About 1 hour before the meal, pre-heat the oven to 190°C/375°F/Gas 5. Remove the fat from the *Baeckeoffe* then cover and put in the oven for about 30 minutes. Uncover the dish and cook for a further 15–20 minutes.

SERVES 8

450 g (1 lb) boneless shoulder of lamb, cut into 5 x 5 cm (2 x 2) pieces
350 g (12 oz) shoulder of pork, cut into 5 x 5 cm (2 x 2 in) pieces
350 g (12 oz) shoulder or brisket of beef, cut into 5 x 5 cm (2 x 2 in) pieces
1 pig's trotter, split (optional)
2 onions, each studded with 2 cloves
4 leeks, white part only, thickly sliced
4 carrots, thickly sliced
2 celery sticks, cut into 5 cm (2 in) lengths
5 tablespoons chopped fresh parsley
900 g (2 lb) potatoes, cut into 1 cm (½) thick slices
salt and freshly grounds black pepper

FOR THE MARINADE

1 carrot, sliced
1 onion, sliced
3 garlic cloves, crushed
4 sprigs of fresh thyme
2 bay leaves
salt and freshly ground black pepper
600 ml (1 pint) white wine, preferably Alsace Riesling

FOR THE LUTING PASTE

4 tablespoons water
100 g (4 oz) plain flour

Place all the meat in a large bowl with all the marinade ingredients. Cover, and leave overnight in a cool place.

Pre-heat the oven to 170°C/325°F/Gas 3.

Drain the liquid from the marinade and reserve. Discard the bay leaves. Starting with meat, layer all the marinated ingredients and the fresh ingredients in a large, heavy casserole. Sprinkle salt and pepper on each layer as you go and finish with a layer of potatoes. Pour over the marinade liquid and add water to cover if necessary. Cover with the lid.

To make the luting paste, slowly pour the water into the flour, stirring constantly to make a smooth soft paste; do not beat it. Use to seal the lid to the casserole then cook in the oven for 3 hours.

Break and discard the luting paste. Remove any fat visible on top of the potatoes. Serve from the dish.

LANGUEDOC

Cassoulet

A RICH BEAN, PORK, LAMB, DUCK, ONION,
TOMATO AND HERB STEW
BAKED UNDER A BREADCRUMB CRUST

The word *Cassoulet* comes from casserole, the earthenware pot in which *Cassoulet* is baked, and it is a *plat mijoté* – a simmered dish – *par excellence*. It should be cooked at least one day in advance so that all the flavours successfully mingle. It is prepared with many different ingredients and takes a little time but is not difficult and is relatively inexpensive.

Cassoulet is often served at political banquets, family meals and village festivals. Prepared in advance, baked and served in its cooking dish, it needs little attention. Monsieur André Bonnaure remembers a *Cassoulet* served to 400 guests on a national road which went through the centre of his village where local gendarmes had to divert the traffic for hours so that the beloved *Cassoulet* could be enjoyed peacefully outdoors by the whole community.

This glorious stew may have been invented by the Arabs and originally prepared with butter beans and dried goose, but it has been part of southern French repertoire for about ten centuries. With its golden crust and its aromatic, creamy juices, *Cassoulet* is a superb sight. However, I must confess I often find it too heavy, too greasy and also too bland. I remember days of lots of mineral water, vegetable broth and sage teas in my grandparents' house the day after 'a genuine' *Cassoulet* was served.

The three most celebrated versions of *Cassoulet* today are those of Carcassonne, Toulouse and Castelnaudary – the Mecca of *Cassoulet*. In medieval Carcassonne, lamb, and even an occasional partridge, may be included. In Toulouse, the city of *Aérospatiale* where Concorde and the European Airbus are assem-

bled, pieces of preserved duck or goose and local pork sausages enrich the bean stew. In Castelnaudary, preserved duck, onions, garlic, bacon and pork rind are added to the beans.

I have cooked a great many versions of *Cassoulet* over the years and have finally settled on this recipe as the one I prefer. The melting beans are redolent with rich flavours but it is – and I know the choice of word may seem strange – light. Lightness in a *Cassoulet* may sound like a hopeless challenge but this is how it goes. I use this year's crop of beans if possible, blanch the beans to make them more digestible then cook them with streaky bacon, ham and tomatoes in a very fragrant broth made with wine, herbs, meats and vegetables. The lamb is always cooked separately, with more vegetables. Since preserved duck, *Confit*, is hard to find outside France. I roast pieces of fresh duck and use it crisp, keeping some of the cooking fat and juices for later use. Once the beans and meat are cooked, I chill them overnight so most of the fat is easy to discard and all the bones and gristle can be removed. Finally, I mingle all the elements and bake them together in a pot. Tomatoes, with their acid quality, seem to me essential. A *hachis* made with chopped garlic and lard can be added to the stew just before baking. If I need to thicken the sauce, I prefer to use crushed beans than the traditional goose, duck or pork fat. The crust on top is important as it seals in all the aromas. It is traditionally supposed to be delicately broken seven times, but three or four times seems enough, just so that bits of crisp crust are buried with the fragrant mixture.

Left-over *Cassoulet* freezes well and improves as it is re-heated. Since it requires quite a number of ingredients and takes time to prepare, I never make it for fewer than eight people.

As for dishes to accompany this splendid recipe, in Languedoc, asparagus and melon are served before a *Cassoulet*, and it is usually followed by a tossed salad. A lemon, raspberry or armagnac sorbet or a fresh fruit salad are the only desserts one can possibly contemplate after a *Cassoulet*.

SERVES 10

FOR THE DUCK

4 pieces preserved duck, Confit *(see p. 218)
or 5 pieces fresh duck
handful of rough sea salt or kosher salt
3 teaspoons dried thyme
1 tablespoon dry white wine
salt and freshly ground black pepper*

FOR THE BEANS

*900 g (2 lb) dried white haricot beans
675g (1½ lb) unsmoked bacon shoulder joint
piece of rind from bacon, cut into 2.5 cm (1 in)
pieces
2 large onions, chopped
4 tomatoes, skinned and chopped
4 tomatoes, skinned and quartered
6 carrots, sliced
1 leek, thickly sliced
4 teaspoons dried thyme
3 bay leaves
2 cloves
4 garlic cloves, crushed
4 fresh Toulouse sausages (or Cotechino, Salsietta or a
good quality Hungarian sausage)
225 g (8 oz) cured ham (optional)*

FOR THE LAMB

*1 tablespoon groundnut oil
1.4 kg (3 lb) lean stewing lamb, shank or boned
shoulder, trimmed and cut into 5 cm (2 in) cubes
3 onions, chopped
1 celery stick, chopped
5 fresh or canned tomatoes, skinned
6 garlic cloves, crushed
3 bay leaves
900 ml (1½ pints) dry white wine
600 ml (1 pint) water*

TO FINISH

*1 garlic clove
5 teaspoons dried thyme
4 tablespoons dry white wine
4–5 tablespoons chopped fresh flatleaf parsley
100 g (4 oz) fresh breadcrumbs (preferably home-
made)
1 tablespoon groundnut, olive or walnut oil or butter
2 garlic cloves, finely chopped (optional)*

If you have *Confit*, preserved duck, you do not need to season or cook it before adding it to the casserole. If you use fresh duck, rub the pieces with salt and thyme, cover and refrigerate overnight.

Soak the beans overnight in cold water. Drain and rinse then place in a pan, cover with fresh water, bring to the boil and boil for about 10 minutes, as directed on the packet. Leave to cool, then drain.

Place the beans in a large pan with the bacon, rind, vegetables, herbs, cloves and garlic. Just cover with water, bring to the boil, then lower the heat, cover the pot and simmer gently for about I hour. Add the sausages, cover again and continue to simmer for a further 30 minutes until the beans are soft but not creamy. Add the cured ham, if using, for the last few minutes of cooking. Remove from the heat and drain, reserving the stock for later use. Refrigerate the beans and meat and the broth.

Meanwhile, heat the oil in a frying pan. Pat the lamb cubes dry with kitchen paper, add to the oil and brown on all sides. Discard the fat, add a drop more oil and fry the onions and celery for 5 minutes. Add the tomatoes, garlic, bay leaves, wine and water and season with salt. Bring to the boil then simmer for 1 hour, uncovered. Remove the meat from the broth. Strain the broth through a sieve, pushing with a wooden spoon to squeeze out all the juices. Place the lamb back in the broth, cool then chill.

Pre-heat the oven to 190°C/375°F/Gas 5.

Pat the pieces of fresh duck dry with kitchen paper and roast in the oven for 1½ hours. Add the tablespoon of wine to the pan over a low heat and scrape the coagulated juices with a fork. Sprinkle with salt and pepper and reserve both the juices and the duck for later use.

Remove the lamb from the fridge and discard all the fat which will have congealed on the top. Remove the beans and meat from the refrigerator, slice the sausages, cut the bacon into 5 cm (2 in) pieces and cut the cured ham into about 6 pieces.

Rub a large 4.5 litre (8 pint) earthenware or porcelain ovenproof casserole dish with a clove of garlic. Place half the beans in the bottom and sprinkle with a little thyme, wine and pepper. Add the pieces of lamb and the sliced sausages then add more beans. Add the pieces of cooked duck or *Confit* and cured ham and finally the remaining beans. Sprinkle a little salt and pepper on top then add the deglazed juices from the duck. Add enough of the cooking broth to cover the top of the ingredients and keep the rest at hand since you will add a little more later on as the juices evaporate, and the beans must remain moist as they cook. Sprinkle with the parsley then the breadcrumbs and sprinkle with oil. You may like to prepare everything up to this pint then refrigerate until 2 hours before you are ready to serve.

Pre-heat the oven to 190°C/375°F/Gas 5.

Place the *Cassoulet* dish in the top third of the oven and cook for 20 minutes. Pierce the golden crust on top three or four times with the back of a spoon but don't stir, and add a little broth on the edges of the dish so the beans remain moist. Reduce the oven temperature to 150°C/300°F/Gas 2 and continue to cook for a further 1½ hours.

Just as you are ready to serve, you might sprinkle a little finely chopped parsley and garlic on top. Wrap the dish in a thick towel, bring it straight to the table and serve from the baking dish.

NOTES

Today, local chefs in search of interesting variations prepare *Cassoulet* with lentils – tiny green lentils or brown ones – and also fresh and dried lima beans. I once tasted a *Cassoulet* made with salt cod, beans, anchovies and seasoned with saffron. Some cooks like to add a handful of chopped fresh mint leaves just before the final baking. A simpler *Cassoulet* can be made by omitting the lamb stew.

AUVERGNE AND THROUGHOUT FRANCE

Chevreuil en Ragoût

VENISON CASSEROLE

Every autumn in France some men feel the call of the wild, and from September to the New Year they gather on Sundays to walk, eat, drink, talk and sometimes they even bring home a hare, a partridge or two, or a wild duck. I am told some actually bring back wild boar and venison.

Wild venison should be hung for a few days to allow the flavour to develop and make the flesh tender. Nouvelle Cuisine chefs made it fashionable to eat venison without marinating but I think a day or two in a pungent marinade makes a more memorably flavoured dish.

In Auvergne, where *Cantal*, *Bleu d'Auvergne* and *St Nectaire* cheeses mature in caves, green valleys are populated by beautiful chestnut Salers cattle and rambling streams are rich with fish, this glorious venison stew was served to me on a bleak, rainy Sunday by the Cantal Federation of Hunters. With it we ate *Truffade* (see p.253). With my version of the dish you can also serve Chestnut and Potato Purée (see p.239) or Celeriac Purée (see p.240), green lentils, noodles or potatoes and prunes cooked in red wine.

SERVES 6

1.25 kg (2¼ lb) boneless loin or shoulder of venison,
cut into 5 cm (2 in) cubes
2 tablespoons groundnut oil
1 tablespoon plain flour
2½ tablespoons red wine vinegar
4 shallots, chopped
3 garlic cloves, chopped
3 sprigs thyme
1 bay leaf
salt and freshly ground black pepper
50 g (2 oz) unsalted butter
150 g (5 oz) smoked or unsmoked lean streaky bacon,
diced
175 g (6 oz) whole button mushrooms
1 tablespoon chopped fresh flatleaf parsley

FOR THE MARINADE

1 tablespoon vegetable oil
1 carrot, sliced
1 onion, studded with 1 clove, quartered
2 garlic cloves
3 shallots, halved
salt and freshly ground black pepper
600 ml (1 pint) red wine
1 teaspoon crushed coriander seeds
2 sprigs of fresh thyme
1 tablespoon juniper berries, crushed
1–2 tablespoons redcurrant jelly

For the marinade, heat the oil in a pan or large frying-pan, add all the vegetables, sprinkle with salt, cover and cook, shaking the pan occasionally, for about 8 minutes. Add the wine, bring to the boil then lower the heat, add the coriander seeds, thyme and juniper berries, cover and simmer for 15 minutes.

Leave to cool completely.

Put the venison in a large bowl, pour over the marinade, add pepper, stir to mix all the ingredients then cover and leave overnight in a cool place.

Using a slotted spoon lift the venison from the marinade and dry with kitchen paper. Strain the marinade and reserve everything.

Heat the oil in a large frying-pan, add the venison in batches and cook over a fairly high heat, stirring occasionally, for about 10 minutes, until evenly browned. Using a slotted spoon, transfer the venison as it is done to a heavy casserole. If necessary, add a little more oil to the frying-pan. Stir the flour into the pan and cook, stirring, until browned. Slowly pour the reserved marinade liquid and the vinegar into the frying-pan, stirring constantly, and bring to the boil. Continue to boil for 1 minute. Pour into the casserole and stir in the reserved marinade vegetables and flavourings, the fresh shallots, garlic, thyme, bay leaf, salt and pepper. Cover tightly and cook gently for 1½-2 hours until the meat is tender. Skim and discard any fat there is on the top.

Meanwhile, heat the butter in a small frying-pan, add the bacon and sauté for 3–4 minutes. Transfer to a dish and reserve. Add the mushrooms to the pan and sauté for about 4 minutes.

Stir the mushrooms and bacon into the casserole. Stir in redcurrant jelly and salt and pepper to taste, and simmer gently for 15 minutes. Sprinkle with parsley to serve.

Lapin en Civet

JUGGED RABBIT SIMMERED IN HERBS AND RED
WINE

Anne Majourel lives in Languedoc, in an old country-house hotel surrounded by green oaks, juniper and bay trees. There is a store room full of local produce, a well-stocked wine cellar (Anne's father is a *vigneron*), two bread ovens and a vegetable garden.

While I stayed at their hotel, *Les Demeures du Ranquet*, Jean-Luc was busy gathering mushrooms from dawn until midday while Anne was sprinkling garlic and minced parsley on top of a stew, adding crushed fresh anchovies to a bowl of greens, filling halved tomatoes with a purée of potatoes and salt cod, *Brandade*.

She simmered a stew of wild boar flavoured with candied fruit, and cooked a platter of little grey snails *à la cévenole* with walnuts and anchovies. She served a duck liver perfectly cooked to brown outside and pink inside with her own home-made fig jam. She spread a thick layer of ratatouille on a pumpkin gratin, and made ravioli stuffed with chestnuts and anchovies and coated with a fragrant onion sauce. Late afternoon, with the light around us turning into a pale mingling of delicate lilac and blues, we spoke of many things: woman's place in the world, man's place in the kitchen, Protestant and Catholic culinary habits, Europe as friend or foe. We nibbled dried, rolled pigs' liver and thinly sliced purple artichokes as we sipped her father's wine. As the sun was setting, we both agreed that Montaigne must have been thinking of *Les Demeurs du Ranquet* when he said our masterwork was to live well.

The following recipe is inspired by Anne. A basis of southern cooking, *civet* comes from the Latin word *cive*, onion. Traditionally, the blood of the animal or some crushed walnuts are used to thicken the sauce but she used bitter chocolate. I, for one, like to marinate the rabbit in red wine, orange rind and herbs overnight as I cannot easily find wild, herb-fed rabbit like Anne! I always cut the rabbit into small pieces so each piece is enriched with the cooking juices and I can add extra leg pieces if I wish. I serve it with polenta, noodles, tiny steamed potatoes or *millas*, a cornflour and milk dish fried in oil. To accompany, I choose shredded cabbage or sautéed carrot sticks.

SERVES 4

1 x 1.8 kg (4 lb) fresh rabbit or back legs and saddle if frozen

FOR THE MARINADE
1 onion, chopped
1 strip of orange rind
4 cloves
1 sprig of fresh thyme
1 sprig of fresh parsley
600 ml (1 pint) hearty red wine

2 tablespoons groundnut or grapeseed oil
225 g (8 oz) streaky bacon, diced
225 g (8 oz) mushrooms, halved and quartered
1 large onion, sliced
salt and freshly ground black pepper
2 tomatoes, skinned, seeded and chopped or 1 teaspoon tomato purée
2 tablespoons plain flour
1 garlic clove, crushed
1 tablespoon chopped fresh or dried thyme
300 ml (10 fl oz) water or stock
1 tablespoon cognac
1 tablespoon red wine vinegar
1 tablespoon butter
1 square plain chocolate
1 tablespoon chopped fresh flatleaf parsley
4 slices bread made into triangular Croûtons (see p.68)

Cut the rabbit into 8 pieces. Mix the marinade ingredients, pour over the rabbit and marinate overnight.

Heat a little of the oil and sauté the bacon then transfer to a bowl. Add a little more of the oil to the pan and sauté the mushrooms then add them to the bacon. Heat a little of the oil and sauté the onion until soft then transfer to a separate bowl. Drain the rabbit and pat dry on kitchen paper. Strain and reserve the marinade. Heat the remaining oil and sauté the rabbit on all sides; the pieces should be crunchy and almost caramelized. Season with salt and pepper. Stir in the tomatoes or tomato purée, sprinkle with the flour and stir well. Add the sautéed onions, the garlic, thyme, wine marinade and water. Bring to the boil, cover and simmer for 20 minutes until the rabbit is tender, stirring occasionally.

Transfer the rabbit to a plate. Boil the cooking juices for 5 minutes then rub them through a sieve and return to the pan. Add the bacon and mushrooms, the cognac, wine vinegar, butter and chocolate and stir until blended. Return the rabbit to the sauce and stir gently until heated through. Spoon on to a warm serving dish, sprinkle with the parsley and serve garnished with the Croûtons.

THROUGHOUT FRANCE

Lapin à la Moutarde

SAUTÉED RABBIT SEASONED WITH MUSTARD, WINE AND HERBS

Lapin à la Moutarde belongs to traditional home-cooking. It is a fragrant, light dish, easy to prepare, and is a staple on the menus of many country inns or city bistros. Serve it with sautéed vegetables, boiled potatoes, carrots, rice or fresh buttered pasta.

SERVES 4

1 x 900 g–1.4 kg (2–3 lb) fresh rabbit or 2–3 back legs and 2 saddle pieces if the rabbit is frozen
salt and freshly ground black pepper
3 tablespoons groundnut oil
2 shallots or 1 onion, coarsely chopped
100 g (4 oz) streaky bacon, chopped
2 garlic cloves, chopped
2 carrots, sliced
2 leeks, white part only, sliced
1 tablespoon plain flour
300 ml (10 fl oz) dry white wine
2 bay leaves
3 teaspoons dried thyme
1 sprig of fresh rosemary
2 tablespoons strong Dijon mustard
2 tablespoons chopped fresh flatleaf parsley

Cut the rabbit into 8 pieces and pat dry on kitchen paper. Reserve the liver, if you are using fresh rabbit, and chop it coarsely. Sprinkle the rabbit with salt and pepper. Heat the oil in a heavy-based frying-pan and sauté the pieces over a medium heat for about 10 minutes until golden on all sides. Remove to a side dish. Add a little more oil, if necessary, and sauté the shallots or onion, bacon, garlic, carrots and leeks for a few minutes, stirring well. Return the rabbit to the pan, sprinkle with flour and cook for 1 minute. Stir in the wine and herbs, bring to the boil, cover and simmer for 1 hour, stirring once or twice. Stir in the mustard and liver, if you have it, and season with salt and pepper. Simmer for a few minutes, check and adjust the seasoning and serve sprinkled with the parsley.

NOTE

In Provence, a handful of unstoned, firm, green olives and 2 chopped tomatoes are added for the last 30 minutes of cooking.

Charcuterie

PORK SPECIALITIES

French regional cooking is mostly founded on the pig. And whether pork is cooked as a fresh meat or turned into prepared, dried, salted, smoked or cooked *charcuterie*, every bit of it is good; '*Dans un cochon, tout est bon*'. Often referred to as *ministre* or *monsieur* – a secretary of state or gentleman – and fed on acorns, chestnuts, apples or potatoes, the pig has always been the most important animal on the farm. Today it remains an essential part of our gastronomy.

The word *charcuterie* comes from *chair cuite*, or cooked meat. It refers both to the art of making pork products, and to the shop in which they are sold. A pork butcher's shop offers different products. Some – like *pâté de campagne* (a coarse country pâté), saucissons and *jambon à l'os*, ham on the bone – are ready to be eaten; some – like *boudins, cervelas* and certain sausages – have to be cooked or at least heated. There are also fresh pork cuts for sale, like *poitrine fumée*, smoked cured streaky bacon, spare ribs, shoulder, pig's trotters and kidneys, and these form the heart of many traditional dishes. Finally, most *charcuteries* offer couscous, salads, stews, French fries, grilled chicken, *choucroute*, gratins and onion pies – all ready to eat. Such freshly prepared dishes cater not only for busy or single parents, or elderly people, but also for the local restaurants and brasseries which offer these *charcuterie*-made dishes on their menus.

Charcuterie products are immensely diverse but are always based on traditional recipes, whether they are prepared at home, in a shop or factory. Every province has its own *spécialités de la région*. Auvergne, Lyonnais, Pyrénées, Provence, Alsace and Brittany produce a variety of terrines and cooked, dry cured or smoked hams and sausages, all made to local recipes.

Sausages are traditionally prepared with coarsely or finely ground neck and shoulder of pork, although occasionally they are made with beef or lamb, as with *merguez*. They are seasoned with spices, pepper and herbs, and the recipe may include onions, garlic, chestnuts, pistachios or truffles according to the region. The finest sausages are always prepared by craftsmen, although some industrially produced products are of fairly high quality. Today the best pork products bear the *label rouge* which is an indication of the highest quality.

Lyon's famous sausages are *rosette* and *Jésus; saucisson de Lyon*, which is boiled and served with potatoes or wrapped in brioche dough; *cervelas* with its fine meat mixture; and the most celebrated in all France, *saucisson à l'ail*. Toulouse sausages are essential for Cassoulet; in the Jura they make flat *gendarme* sausages, *morteau* and *baudet* which are boiled in wine. There are fragrant, dry pigs' liver sausages in Roussillon and Corsica; delicate *roulade* which tastes a little like Mortadella; Auvergne's *saucisse sèche*; Alsace's smoked frankfurters; spicy *merguez* (delicious with couscous); and *andouilles* and *andouillettes* made from tripe. There are also *boudins blancs*, white sausages made with pork or chicken, eggs and cream; and in contrast *boudins noirs*, blood pudding prepared with rice, apples, onions, garlic and chestnuts.

In each region, sausages are fried, poached or grilled according to local taste and served with apples, chestnuts, potato purées, white haricot beans, lentils, braised cabbage or simply a pile of soft, golden onions.

Charcuterie is sometimes used in intriguing ways. On the Atlantic coast, a platter of raw oysters is served with crisp hot sausages, or *Crépinettes*, and white wine or Pineau. In Brittany, a fish is often stuffed with pork pâté, and some gourmands claim that crisp sliced bread spread with *Rillettes* and served with *café au lait* is the best of mid-morning snacks.

Plateau de Charcuterie

A *Plateau de Charcuterie* may be an extravagant display of *charcuteries* punctuated by a few salad leaves or by diced jelly. It may be amusingly formal: neat rows of sliced sausages and ham in semi-circles around a grand goose-shaped mould of *Rillettes*, or it may be simply an assortment of whole sausages piled on a wooden board with a heavy knife.

The offering will vary according to the occasion – a starter, a buffet or the best part of a meal – but whether it is a *Plateau* or a single *Assiette de Charcuterie* it will generally include sliced sausages and at least two kinds of thinly sliced ham: a dry cured ham from Bayonne, Savoie, Corsica or Auvergne, perhaps a smoked ham from Alsace or Brittany, or a few slices of excellent boiled ham, either *jambon à l'os* or *Jambon au Torchon*. The *Plateau* may also include a *galantine*, a boned duck or chicken stuffed with a rich forcemeat and simmered in a fragrant broth, and a *roulade*, a pistachio-flavoured cooked sausage, with perhaps a plump garlic sausage. There will probably be a variety of *Rillettes* (see p.219), country pâtés and chicken liver mousses in their porcelain terrines, and finally a separate tray of mustards, gherkins, unsalted butter and a basket of bread. You will often see the cheeky term *Les Cochonnailles* appear on a menu instead of *Charcuterie*.

Grillons

Grillons start with the principle that everything – but everything – is good in a pig, goose or duck. Crackling in French has evocative names: *grattons, gratterons, frittons, chichons, griaudes, beursaudes, grillons*. They are the little crunchy bits left when preparing rendered pork fat while cooking belly pork, or the left-over meat and bones left from making *Confit* of duck (see p.218). These crisp, brown titbits of wing tips and neck or bits attached to the carcass are scooped out from the bottom of the cooling pan, drained and seasoned with salt and coarsely ground black pepper. If they are very uneven, they can be processed for a second in a food processor or blender, but they are a rustic treat and should remain coarse and crunchy. They can be spread on crisp toast rubbed with garlic and eaten with drinks. Sprinkled with red wine vinegar, parsley and garlic, they can be served hot with sliced apples or potatoes. Blended with a few eggs and fresh herbs they will fill a cooked pastry shell and make a savoury tart. Seasoned with thyme and freshly grated nutmeg, they can enliven an omelette. And stirred into plain dough, they will create a richly seasoned bread.

These crisp, tiny morsels of pork, duck or goose may also be covered with a layer of fat and stored in stoneware or glass jars like their soft cousins *Rillettes*.

Terrine de Campagne

CRUSTLESS MEAT AND HERB PIE

Pâtés and terrines were first made in medieval times and were served in exuberant displays. Today, bistros, brasseries and country inns offer guests a trolley packed with a variety of porcelain terrines with a jar of gherkins to accompany them. Starred restaurants serve as a starter slices of different terrines on the same plate, attractively garnished with watercress or salad leaves.

Both pâtés and terrines are easy to make at home and are consistently better than those that are available in the shops. A pâté is a mixture of pieces of veal, pork, poultry, fish, game or vegetables seasoned with herbs, spices, wine or brandy and baked in a pastry dough crust ('pâté' actually means crust). A terrine is a crustless pâté. It is basically made with the same ingredients and baked, and often served, in an earthenware or porcelain baking dish. Nowadays the names tend to be used interchangeably.

Whether it is a fancy terrine made with goose or duck liver, partridge or hare seasoned with truffles, marrow or pistachios, or a simpler version, the key element in this dish is the fine mingling of flavours and textures. Fragrant slices of chicken, ham, veal, pork, rabbit or duck – often marinated in brandy or wine – spread between layers of ground or chopped, highly seasoned meat, flavoured with a variety of herbs and spices, create the perfect combination for an interesting terrine. Eggs, bread or pork fat are added to bind the mixture together.

You can use a loaf tin to make this terrine, but if you enjoy home-made terrines, it is worth investing in a good quality glazed earthenware or porcelain terrine with a lid.

Pâtés and terrines are best chopped by hand if there is time so the juices do not escape, otherwise a food processor will do. They must be kept chilled for between two and seven days before they are served for all the flavours to develop fully. A terrine will keep for two weeks in the fridge. Serve them with country or wholemeal bread, a pot of butter, gherkins, pickled pearl onions and a tossed salad.

SERVES 6

225 g (8 oz) pig or chicken livers
225 g (8 oz) stewing veal
225 g (8 oz) piece streaky bacon or shoulder steak
100 g (4 oz) pork shoulder, diced
225g (8 oz) chicken breasts, skinned
1½ teaspoons salt
¼ teaspoon black, green or red peppercorns
2 teaspoons dried thyme
1 teaspoon dried sage
a pinch of freshly grated nutmeg
10 juniper berries, coarsely ground
4 garlic cloves, chopped
½ teaspoon ground bay leaves
2 tablespoons brandy
2 teaspoons groundnut oil
2 onions, chopped
6 shallots, coarsely chopped
2 eggs
5 tablespoons dry white wine
20 thin slices streaky bacon or pork fat to line the
terrine and cover the top
a pinch of dried thyme
3 juniper berries, ground
3 bay leaves

Trim the meats, discarding any skin, gristle or extra fat. Slice the chicken breasts in half horizontally and set aside. Coarsely chop the livers and all the meats then mix with the salt, peppercorns, thyme, sage, nutmeg, juniper berries, garlic and ground bay leaves and stir the ingredients together. Sprinkle with the brandy and stir with your hands so that everything is coated with seasoning. Cover and leave to marinate overnight in a cool place.

Pre-heat the oven to 180°C/350°F/Gas 4.

Heat the oil and fry the onions and shallots until soft. Stir into the marinated meat mixture. Place half the mixture in a bowl or a food processor and chop until fairly smooth then add the remainder and chop for a few seconds to obtain a coarser texture. Stir in the eggs and wine and mix together thoroughly.

Remove the rind from the bacon and stretch the rashers with the back of a knife blade. Line the bottom and sides of a 1.2 litre (2 pint) rectangular or oval terrine or mould with the strips of bacon or pork fat. Leave a little overhanging the sides. Spoon half the meat mixture into the terrine, arrange the chicken breasts on top then add the remaining meat mixture and smooth the top with the back of a spoon. Sprinkle with thyme and the juniper berries and arrange the bay leaves on top. Fold the bacon over the terrine and add some more slices of bacon or fat to cover the top, if necessary. Place a piece of oiled foil on top and seal tightly. Put on the terrine lid if you have one. Place the terrine in a deep roasting tin and add enough hot water to come half-way up the sides of the terrine. Bake in the oven for 1½–2 hours.

Remove from the oven, discard the foil lid and leave the terrine to cool for 1 hour. The juices will be clear and yellow and will circulate through the pâté as it cools, making the pâté mellow and fragrant. Cover the top with a piece of cardboard wrapped in foil or a piece of wood the size of your terrine top. Place a few tins on top to weigh the pâté down and make the texture firm and easier to slice. Leave to stand for 2 hours. Remove the tins, cover tightly and chill for 2–3 days for the flavours to develop.

Remove from the fridge about 20 minutes before serving. Dip the bottom of the terrine in hot water, or dip a tea towel in hot water, squeeze it out then wrap the hot towel round the bottom and sides of the dish for a few minutes. Run a knife around the edge of the pâté and unmould on to a serving plate. Alternatively you can cut the pâté into 1 cm (½ in) slices and garnish with green salad, or serve directly from the terrine. Serve the terrine with gherkins and crusty bread and butter.

SAVOIE

Pâté Chaud Familial

VEAL PATE IN A CRUST

Madame Monique Lansard of Chambéry is the acknowledged expert on the food of Savoie. She regaled me with tales of the grand aristocratic dinners of the House of Savoie, when the duchy included much of northern Italy as well as Sardinia. In fact, Savoie voted to join the French republic as late as 1861. This dish reflects the richness of the gastronomic legacy with the use of candied lemon rind. The original recipe uses *cédrat*, citron, a large lemon-like citrus fruit which made its way up to the Alps from southern Italy. Another aspect of Savoyard cuisine is the love of salty/sweet combinations with bitter notes. It's a far cry from the well-known clichés of cheese and potatoes.

SERVES 6

800 g (1¾ lb) veal fillet, diced
120 ml (4 fl oz) white wine vinegar
120 ml (4 fl oz) water
100 g (4 oz) pork fat, finely chopped
150 g (5 oz) pork chop, boned and finely chopped
1 onion, finely chopped
a few sprigs of fresh parsley, finely chopped
75 g (3 oz) candied lemon rind or citron, coarsely chopped
salt and freshly ground black pepper

FOR THE PASTRY

500 g (1 lb 2 oz) plain flour
a pinch of salt
175 g (6 oz) butter
75 g (3 oz) lard
5 egg yolks

FOR THE SAUCE

50 g (2 oz) butter
2 tablespoons plain flour
600 ml (1 pint) beef stock
1 tablespoon red wine vinegar
2 tablespoons Madeira (optional)

Marinate the veal in the vinegar and water overnight.

To make the pastry, place the flour and salt in a bowl and make a well in the centre. Add the butter and lard and work them into the flour until the mixture resembles breadcrumbs. Add 4 of the egg yolks and mix with your hands until the mixture comes away from the sides of the bowl, adding a little water if necessary. Wrap in cling film and chill until required.

Pre-heat the oven to 220°C/425°F/Gas 7. Grease a baking tray.

Drain and dry the veal thoroughly. In a food processor, blend the fat, pork and the onion. Add to this paste the parsley, lemon rind, salt and pepper. Roll out the pastry on a floured board in a rectangular shape. Put one-third of the pork mixture in the middle and flatten it down, leaving a border of 4 cm (1½ in) all round. Then place half the cubed veal over the mixture and follow with another third of the pork mixture. Spread the other half of the veal on top of that and finish with a final layer of the remaining pork. Bring all the pastry edges up over the filling to cover it and seal the edges. Decorate with any left-over pastry cut into shapes. Brush with the remaining egg yolk and bake in the oven for 10 minutes. Cut a small hole in the top to release the steam. Reduce the

oven temperature to 180°C/350°F/Gas 4 and cook for a further 1 hour.

Meanwhile, make the sauce. Melt the butter, add the flour and stir until the mixture is golden. Gradually pour in the stock, stirring all the time to prevent any lumps forming. When the mixture comes to the boil, add the wine vinegar then turn down the heat and simmer for 20 minutes, stirring occasionally. Just before serving, season with salt and pepper and add the Madeira, if using. Serve the pie hot or warm accompanied by the hot sauce.

THROUGHOUT FRANCE

Terrine de Foies de Volaille

CHICKEN LIVER TERRINE

Terrines and pâtés are pillars of *cuisine de ménage*, home cooking, because they are easy to prepare, keep for days in the refrigerator, and taste far better than anything one can buy.

Pâté and terrine-making is a widefield. There are delicate terrines made with sweetbreads, calf liver, fish, goose liver or vegetables. There are exotic pâtés made with chopped lamb, kidney fat, brown sugar, raisins, rum, lemon and pepper wrapped in a light pastry shell. There are potent terrines made with wild boar, partridge or hare. A more conventional *Terrine de Foies* can be prepared using the same quantity of chicken livers as streaky bacon, 2 eggs, spices and a little brandy, all coarsely chopped and baked for 2 hours in a covered terrine.

Pâtés and terrines can be prepared with inexpensive ingredients and often need little preparation. This delightfully light terrine does not even need baking.

SERVES 4

275 g (10 oz) chicken livers,
trimmed
salt and coarsely ground black pepper
a pinch of ground coriander
1 teaspoon dried thyme
1 bay leaf, crushed
1 teaspoon juniper berries, crushed
1 tablespoon butter
1 tablespoon groundnut oil
2 shallots, coarsely chopped
2 tablespoons cognac or port
100 g (4 oz) butter, cut into pieces
3 egg whites
225 g (8 oz) slices pork back fat
3 large bay leaves

Wash the chicken livers under cold water then pat dry on kitchen paper. Sprinkle them with salt, pepper, the coriander, thyme, crushed bay leaf and juniper berries. Heat the butter and oil in a frying-pan and sauté the chicken livers for 2–3 minutes. Add the shallots and cook for a further 2 minutes. Remove 3 livers and cut them in half. Sprinkle them with salt, pepper and the cognac or port, cover and leave to stand for 1 hour.

Place the sautéed liver and shallots in a food processor or blender, add the butter and blend thoroughly. Taste and adjust the seasoning with salt and pepper if necessary. Whisk the egg whites until stiff. Gently fold them into the liver mixture.

Line the base and sides of a terrine with some thin slices of pork back fat reserving some for the top of the terrine. Spoon half the puréed mixture into the terrine, arrange the halved livers on top, then cover with the remaining mixture. Place the 3 bay leaves on top and cover with more fat. Cover with foil and the lid of the terrine if you have one. Chill for 24 hours.

Remove the slices of fat from the top and serve directly from the terrine with a spoon dipped in hot water. Serve it in its terrine, wrapped in a fresh, white tea towel and presented with a basket of lightly toasted brioche or fresh country bread and a pot of unsalted butter.

THROUGHOUT FRANCE

Terrine de Canard

DUCK, HAM AND LIVER TERRINE FLAVOURED WITH
HERBS, GARLIC, SHALLOTS AND COGNAC

A duck terrine may be cooked and served in an oval or rectangular baking dish. It must be made at least two days in advance, but it will keep covered for two or three weeks in the fridge.

Discard any nerves, gristle and any extra fat. If you cannot find duck liver, chicken livers can be used. Garnished with a few sprigs of watercress and served with a pot of fresh butter and a basket of country bread, it can make the centrepiece of a picnic, a buffet, a light summer lunch or a starter.

SERVES 6

FOR THE DUCK

450g (1 lb duck) (either magret, breasts, or boned
thighs)
25g (1 oz salt)
4 teaspoons dried thyme
2 bay leaves, crumbled
8 juniper berries
10 peppercorns
2 tablespoons cognac
120 ml (4 fl oz) Madeira, port or white wine
a pinch of freshly grated nutmeg
4 garlic cloves, crushed
1 tablespoon grated orange rind
2 eggs
salt

FOR THE LIVER MIXTURE
1 tablespoon oil
100 g (4 oz) piece streaky bacon
1 duck liver or 3 chicken livers
3 thick slices boiled ham
3 tablespoons chopped fresh parsley
5 shallots, coarsely chopped
pistachios or hazelnuts, shelled

TO ASSEMBLE
1 tablespoon duck fat
a few thick lettuce leaves
225 g (8 oz) thin strips of pork fat or slices of streaky bacon
3 bay leaves

TO GARNISH
a few sprigs of flatleaf parsley or watercress

Bone the duck, cut it into 1 cm (½ in) pieces and place it in a bowl. Add the salt, thyme, the crumbled bay leaves, the juniper berries, peppercorns, cognac and Madeira, port or wine. Leave to marinate for 1 hour, stirring once or twice. Stir in the nutmeg, garlic and orange rind. Blend in the eggs and season with salt.

Pre-heat the oven to 180°C/350°F/Gas 4 and butter a terrine.

Heat the oil and sauté the bacon for a few minutes. Add the livers and sauté until sealed on both sides so they will have more flavour and will not shrink during the cooking of the terrine. Add the ham, parsley and shallots and stir for a few minutes then add the pistachios or hazelnuts.

In a separate pan, heat the duck fat and sauté the lettuce leaves for 1 minute.

Line the terrine with the thin strips of pork fat or slices of bacon. Spoon alternate layers of the duck mixture and the liver mixture into the terrine until all the ingredients have been used up. Hold the terrine with both hands and shake it so that the meats settle and the marinade penetrates throughout the dish. Arrange the bay leaves on the top then cover with the sautéed lettuce leaves. Cover with a piece of kitchen foil. Stand the terrine in a pan filled with water to come about 5 cm (2 in) up the sides of the terrine. Cook in the oven for 1½ hours.

Turn off the oven, open the oven door and leave the terrine to cool in the oven for 30 minutes. Remove from the oven. Cover a piece of wood or cardboard the size of the top of the terrine with kitchen foil and place it on the terrine then place a couple of tins on top to weigh the mixture down. The cooking juices may overflow, so you can stand the terrine in a shallow dish so that you can collect the jellied juices and dice them to garnish the terrine. Refrigerate for at least 2 days to develop the flavours.

To unmould the terrine, dip the dish in hot water for a second or run a tea towel under hot water, wring it out and wrap it round the dish. Place a plate on top and turn over in one decisive gesture. Discard the bacon or fat and slice the terrine with a warm, sharp knife. Arrange a little of the diced jellied cooking juices around the terrine and garnish with the parsley or watercress.

NOTE

If you serve it straight from the cooking terrine, clean the top and sides with a damp cloth then use a spatula and a sharp knife.

THROUGHOUT FRANCE

Confit de Canard

PRESERVED DUCK

Before refrigeration, different methods of preserving food were vital, and many ways were developed to preserve food while also enhancing the flavours of the products. Fruits, vegetables, meat and fish, for example, were dried for weeks or months. And in the process, plums turned into luscious *pruneaux*, dry cod became the spirited *morue*, dried mushrooms preserved within their brittle, delicate morsels the intoxicating essence of the forest. Salting was another common traditional method of preserving and improving. Preserving pork, turkey, rabbit, duck, goose or sausages in fat, however, is a method which has only ever been used in the south-west. *Confit* – meat preserved in fat – occupies a very special place in local gastronomy as the poultry fattened for *foie gras* acquires a superb texture and a fragrant taste in the process.

So although today duck can be frozen, vacuum-packed or tinned and the necessity to preserve it in this way has vanished, *Confit* remains more popular than ever. Duck *Confit* is more popular than goose because, as I was told by everyone in the south-west, duck is tasty, easier to handle and quicker to cook than goose. The duck starts to improve after one or two weeks as it matures and acquires its full flavour.

Pork *Confit*, but more often duck or goose, is used to enrich soups like *Garbure* (see p. 62) or stews like *Cassoulet* (see p. 204) and *Potée* (see p. 194) to give a rich flavour. It can also be simply grilled, sprinkled with chopped fresh parsley and garlic and accompanied with sautéed potatoes, sautéed mushrooms, chestnut purée, braised cabbage, lentils or haricot beans. Slivered *Confit* is often served cold over a tossed green salad, seasoned with a walnut or olive oil dressing.

When you prepare *Confit*, you can buy separate duck legs and wings and a tin of fat (available in delicatessens), or buy a whole duck, cook and preserve the legs and wings and render the fat from the bird to prepare the *Confit*.

There are two schools of thought about cooking *Confit*. Most people simmer the meat for about 2 hours, while others cook it on a brisk heat for less than an hour and let it cool in the hot fat. Curiously, the latter duck seems to keep longer and better.

SERVES 4

4 duck legs and 4 duck wings or 2 ducks
5 tablespoons coarse sea salt or kosher salt
1 tablespoon coarsely ground black pepper
2 teaspoons dried thyme
1 teaspoon dried rosemary
3 bay leaves, crumbled
6 garlic cloves, studded with 6 cloves
1.4 kg (3 lb) tinned duck or goose fat

If you prepare your own duck fat, remove as much fat as possible from the birds and cook it slowly on a medium heat until liquid. Pour it through a sieve into a jar and store for later use.

To prepare the duck, cut off the wing tips and separate the thighs and drumsticks. Mix together the salt, pepper, thyme, rosemary and bay leaves and rub all over the duck, patting with the palms of your hands. Place the duck pieces in a bowl with the clove-studded garlic cloves, cover and refrigerate for 24–48 hours.

Heat the prepared or tinned duck or goose fat in a large, heavy-based saucepan. Shake the pieces of duck and wipe off the excess salt. Pat the pieces dry on kitchen paper. Place the pieces of duck one at a time into the hot fat; they should be completely covered in fat. Cook for 45 minutes on a medium to high heat until the juices run mother-of-pearl pink when the flesh is pricked with a fork. Remove from the heat and leave to cool in the hot fat for 1 hour.

Remove the duck from the fat with a slotted spoon and pack the pieces in a wide glass, stoneware or porcelain storage jar. Cover with about 5 cm (2 in) of melted fat then seal with a piece of muslin, a layer of coarse salt and finally a piece of thick kitchen foil. Store in a cellar or cool place or in the fridge for up to a year.

After 3 months, you may like to cook the duck again and store it in fat in the same way; its flavour will improve.

When ready to use a piece of *Confit*, remove it from the storage pot and shake off the excess fat. Place it in a dry frying-pan skin-side down, and cook for 10 minutes on each side.

LOIRE

Rillettes

A FRAGRANT SPREAD MADE WITH SHREDDED MEAT SEASONED WITH HERBS

Rillettes can be made with goose, duck, rabbit, pork, or a mixture of all four. The meat is simmered with herbs and spices then shredded and potted under a layer of fat. There are many regional variations of *Rillettes*, but they are a Loire speciality.

Rillettes have a rough, silky quality, and it is the fat which supplies both the flavour and the texture. They are usually served cool, like terrines and pâtés, spread on crisp toast or sliced baguette. But they are also eaten with oysters on their shells, turned into a savoury tart or beaten into an omelette.

Rillons are about 10 cm (4 in) cubes of pork neck, bacon, ham or goose cooked with spices and covered with melted dripping. They are sold in most *charcuteries* and served cold as a starter or warm with apples or potatoes.

Rillettes de Canard

DUCK RILLETTES

In the south-west, duck or goose – including the bones and skin – are cooked in duck fat with pork belly, shredded and seasoned to become unctuous *Rillettes*.

SERVES 4–6

675g (1½ lb) belly of pork, cut into chunks
900 g (2 lb) duck, including bones and skin, cut into chunks
600 ml (1 pint) water
3 bay leaves
2 teaspoons dried thyme
salt and freshly ground black pepper

Follow the recipe for *Rillettes de Porc* (see below) browning the pork then adding the remaining ingredients and simmering for at least 4–5 hours. Strain, discard the bones, shred the meats and season generously with salt, pepper and thyme. Store covered in a layer of fat.

Rillettes de Porc

PORK RILLETTES

Pork *Rillettes* remain the most economical and the most frequently made. They are prepared from whatever pieces of pork are left over from making sausages, and may include some diced goose breast or rabbit. The proportions of fat and lean meat vary from equal quantities to half as much fat as lean, depending on the cook.

1.4 kg (3 lb) pork neck, loin or belly
450 g (1 lb) pork back fat
1–2 pork bones (optional)
1 garlic clove, crushed
2 bay leaves
1 tablespoon chopped fresh thyme
a pinch of freshly grated nutmeg
1 clove
300 ml (10 fl oz) dry white wine
300 ml (10 fl oz) water
salt and coarsely ground black pepper

Cut the meat and fat into 5 cm (2 in) chunks and place them in a large pan with all the remaining ingredients and enough water and wine to cover. Bring slowly to the boil, stirring occasionally, then cover and simmer for about 4 hours, removing any scum on top from time to time. Most of the liquid will evaporate, but check the pan occasionally so that the meat does not stick and add a little water if necessary. Leave to cool.

Strain the mixture, reserving the fat. Taking a spoonful of meats at a time into a clean bowl, shred the meats with a fork in each hand and discard any bones or herbs. Season generously with salt, pepper and a little more thyme; *Rillettes* should be highly seasoned.

As the fat cools, stir as much of it as you want into the meat mixture and stir occasionally until cool. The texture should be rough, not too smooth or puréed. Spoon into glass jars or stoneware pots, cover with waxed paper or kitchen foil and lid if you have one. Keep in a cool place for 2 to 3 days before serving. If you pour about 2.5 cm (1 in) of melted lard on top, the *Rillettes* will keep for 2 to 3 weeks. Serve with olives and gherkins.

Rillettes de Lapin
RABBIT RILLETTES

If you can find wild rabbit this dish will taste superb. However, it is still delicious made with ordinary rabbit. It will keep for a few weeks.

1.4 kg (3 lb) rabbit
450 g (1 lb) belly of pork
225 g (8 oz) pork fat
1 teaspoon dried thyme
2 bay leaves, crumbled
salt
6 tablespoons groundnut oil
900 g (2 lb) onions, sliced
450 g (1 lb) carrots, sliced
1 garlic clove
1.2 litres (2 pints) dry white wine
300 ml (10 fl oz) white vermouth
coarsely ground black pepper
1 tablespoon ground coriander
1 tablespoon chopped fresh chervil
1 teaspoon chopped fresh tarragon
enough rendered pork fat or lard to cover in a 2.5 cm (1 in) layer

Remove the bones and gristle from the rabbit, pat it dry on kitchen paper and cut it into large cubes. Cut the pork and pork fat into large cubes. Place all the meats in a bowl and sprinkle with the thyme, bay leaves and salt. Heat the oil and cook the onions, carrots and garlic for a few minutes until beginning to soften. Add the meat and cook for about 10 minutes until everything is golden brown. Pour in the wine and vermouth, sprinkle with pepper and the coriander and bring to the boil. Cover and simmer gently over a low heat for 3–4 hours until the meat falls apart. Leave to cool.

Strain the mixture, place the meats in a bowl and return the liquid to the pan. With one fork in each hand, shred the meats; the texture should be rough, not puréed. Bring the cooking juices to the boil and add the chervil and tarragon. Simmer, uncovered, for a few minutes to reduce the quantity slightly then pour over the meats and stir well. Transfer the mixture to glass jars or stoneware pots. Heat the pork fat or lard and pour a 2.5 cm (1 in) layer over the dish. Cover with kitchen foil and leave to cool then chill for a few days. Serve with fresh walnuts sprinkled with red wine vinegar.

PROVENCE

Caillettes

CRISP MEAT AND VEGETABLE SAUSAGES

Whether they are called *gayettes*, *crépinettes*, *boulettes* or *caillettes*, each region makes its own version of what is basically a sausage without a casing.

They are prepared with a mixture made from a selection of pig livers, chicken livers, rabbit, ham, bacon, kidneys, pigs' lungs, sweetbreads, pigs' head or pork. They may be enriched with chestnuts, diced celery, Swiss chard, sorrel, cabbage, spinach, olives, pistachios, garlic, dandelion leaves, parsley, basil or thyme. Some are shaped like a ball, others like an oval, flat sausage, and they are wrapped in a piece of caul or with thin slices of pork fat before being baked. They are stored in a jar covered with fat. When required, they can be served cold, or sliced, rolled in egg and breadcrumbs and fried or grilled.

Caillettes, which means 'little quails', is the version favoured in Provence. They are moulded into little balls, although you can also bake the mixture in a terrine. They are served warm with a bowl of bitter green curly endive, dandelion leaves or watercress seasoned with a sharp vinaigrette, or cold as a starter with toast, butter and a bowl of olives.

SERVES 4

450 g (1 lb) fresh spinach leaves, frozen leaf spinach, or spinach and Swiss chard
2 tablespoons oil
2 tablespoons butter (optional)
1 onion, chopped
100 g (4 oz) streaky bacon, chopped
225 g (8 oz) chicken livers or pig liver, trimmed
1 tablespoon plain flour
225 g (8 oz) lean pork, chopped
4 teaspoons dried thyme
2 bay leaves, crumbled
4 garlic cloves, chopped
handful of sorrel leaves, coarsely chopped (optional)
or juice of 1 lemon
5 tablespoons chopped, preferably flatleaf, parsley
1 egg
salt and coarsely ground black pepper
16 sage leaves
450 g (1 lb) thin slices bacon or a piece of caul large enough to wrap the Caillettes

Pre-heat the oven to 190°C/375°F/Gas 5.

If you are using fresh spinach, wash and dry it. Heat 1 tablespoon of the oil and the butter, if using, in a pan, add the greens, cover and cook for a few minutes until soft, stirring occasionally. Drain. If you are using frozen leaf spinach, thaw it and drain it throughly.

Heat the remaining oil and fry the onion over a low heat until soft. Add the bacon and sauté for a few minutes then transfer the mixture to a bowl. Sprinkle the liver with the flour and fry until crisp on all sides then add to the onion mixture. Sauté the pork for 15 minutes, sprinkle with the thyme and bay leaves and cook for a further 10 minutes. Stir in the garlic. Mix together the spinach, the onion mixture, the pork mixture and add the sorrel or lemon juice. Divide the mixture in half and add the parsley to one half. Place this half in a food processor and process for a second so that it is coarsely ground. Remove from the processor and blend the second half so that it is a little smoother. Stir the two mixtures back together, add the egg and season with salt and pepper. If you wish, fry a teaspoonful of the mixture in a little oil or drop it in boiling water so that you can taste it and adjust the seasoning if necessary.

Shape the mixture into little balls about 7.5 cm (3 in) wide and place 1 or 2 sage leaves on top. Criss-cross 2 or 3 slices of bacon around each ball so that they will remain moist during baking and arrange them in a shallow ovenproof dish. Stand the dish in a roasting tin filled with a little water. Flatten the *Caillettes* slightly on the top with your hand and bake them in the oven for 45–50 minutes.

BURGUNDY

Jambon Persillé

HAM IN PARSLEY, GARLIC AND VINEGAR ASPIC

A must in Burgundy on Easter Sunday, *Jambon Persillé* is glorious as a buffet display, as a starter or as the centrepiece of a family summer meal accompanied with a tossed salad and a potato gratin.

I generally present *Jambon Persillé* in its bowl, this way I do not have to add gelatine, and I think this gives a more interesting texture. If you do add the gelatine, it makes the shimmering dome easier to unmould and you can serve slices with a flat spatula and a spoon. The flavour will improve if it is chilled for at least a day, and it will keep, covered, for over a week.

SERVES 8

FOR THE MEAT AND BROTH

1.4 kg (3 lb) uncooked, unsmoked ham or gammon or bacon shoulder joint
450 g (1 lb) veal bones or veal knuckle (optional)
2 onions
4 cloves
3 carrots
3 garlic cloves
1 celery stick
5 black peppercorns
2 sprigs of fresh tarragon
2 sprigs of fresh thyme
600 ml (1 pint) dry white wine
5 tablespoons snipped freshed flatleaf parsley
3 garlic cloves, crushed
3 shallots, coarsely chopped
3 tablespoons red wine vinegar
25 g (1 oz) gelatine (optional)
1 egg white, lightly beaten
salt and freshly ground black pepper

TO SERVE

2 teaspoons red wine vinegar

Remove the rind and most of the fat from the ham or bacon. Soak in cold water to remove the salt, if necessary. Place the ham and bones, if using, in a large pan, preferably not aluminium. Stud the onions with the cloves and add them to the pan with the carrots, garlic, celery, peppercorns, tarragon, thyme and wine. Add just enough cold water to cover the ham (about 1.5 litres (2½ pints)).

Bring to the boil, cover and simmer for 2½ hours until the ham is soft enough to be pierced easily with a fork, skimming the top a few times during cooking. Remove from the heat and leave to cool in the fragrant broth for 1 hour.

Remove the ham from the stock, place it on a board and shred half the meat with one fork in each hand, and chop the remaining half into

large chunks, discarding all the fat. Place it in a bowl and add the parsley, garlic, shallots and red wine vinegar and stir gently. Discard the bones and herbs from the stock. Remove the vegetables, chop or crush them with a fork and add them to the meat mixture. Spoon the mixture into a 1.5 litre (2½ pint) bowl or porcelain terrine.

Strain the stock into a saucepan, return it to a high heat and boil rapidly until reduced to 900 ml (1½ pints). Soak the gelatine, if using, in cold water for 2 minutes until softened. Whisk the egg white into the stock and gently bring to the boil, whisking all the time to incorporate all the impurities. Be sure to stop whisking before it reaches boiling point so that you do not break the crust. (See *Consommé*, p.72.) Leave to settle for 5 minutes. Line a sieve with muslin and strain the stock carefully then return it to the heat. If you have not used bones, you will need to add some gelatine.

Whisk the gelatine into the hot broth until it dissolves. Taste and correct the seasoning with salt and pepper. Spoon the mixture over the meat. Press the mixture down with the back of a spoon, then add a little more stock, if necessary. Cover with a plate, place a few tins on top to weigh it down and chill for about 24 hours. Pour any remaining stock into a bowl and chill to use as a garnish.

Serve the *Jambon Persillé* from the dish, using two large spoons to serve. If you want to unmould it, dip the dish in hot water for a few seconds, or dip a tea towel in hot water, squeeze it out then wrap it around the bottom and sides of the dish for a minute. Run the tip of a knife around the bowl, place a large plate on top and unmould in one decisive movement. Spoon the reserved jelly, chopped, around the edge to decorate and sprinkle with the red wine vinegar. Dip a large knife or spatula into warm water and cut the dome into slices or wedges.

Salads

LES SALADES

Whether they are wildly inventive or sensibly down to earth and prepared with whatever ingredients are to hand, mixed salads, *salades composées*, are reliable friends that can be served as starters or as a meal in themselves.

In the best restaurants and at elegant dinner parties, you will find elaborate affairs enriched with preserved goose or duck livers, lobster, scallops, raw or smoked salmon or truffles. For a more simple dish, you may find they include country sausages, smoked herrings, haddock, ham or cheese. Warm or cold slivers of meat, fish or shellfish, all trimmed to perfection, make tasty additions, and there is no end to the range of vegetables or pulses you can include: potatoes, leeks, green beans, raw spinach, beetroot, courgettes, mushrooms, peppers, shredded cabbage, raw purple artichokes or cooked globe artichokes, crisp spring onions, sliced red onions, fennel roots, celery stalks, lentils or chick peas. Even fruits find their way into the repertoire to offer a surprising counterpoint.

I have selected a few exciting mixed salads, all based on well-proven combinations of flavours and textures. I hope they will inspire you to create your own personal versions.

Salade aux Foies Chauds

GREEN TOSSED SALAD WITH SAUTÉED CHICKEN OR
DUCK LIVERS

Marie-Claude Gracia lives in Poudenas, a tiny village in the Gers, in a house fronted by a bed of fresh herbs and a large verbena. Surrounding the village are fields of corn, which is grown partly to feed the ducks and geese which are the pride of the region, next to fields of cows with thick, bent horns.

Marie-Claude prepares duck in every possible way: duck stew with crisp *Cruchade*, corn pudding; crunchy *Confit*; grilled pieces of duck carcass, *Demoiselles*; and *Frittons Pâtés*. Her desserts are equally interesting: luscious *Millas*, a custard flavoured with armagnac and prunes; silky *Pots à la Crème* flavoured with verbena leaves; and light crêpes flavoured with aniseed and bitter orange.

When I asked her for a truly simple dish she prepared the following recipe with gusto. Whether it is done with duck, goose or chicken livers it makes a delicious dish. Marie-Claude uses her own fragrant Prune Vinegar for the recipe. It is delicious and keeps indefinitely. The prunes can be used to accompany a stuffed, boiled chicken or a *pot au feu*.

Thin slivers of cured Bayonne ham or sliced duck breast can be added to the salad and walnut oil can be used instead of olive oil.

SERVES 4

FOR THE PRUNE VINEGAR
300 ml (10 fl oz) good red wine vinegar
100 g (4 oz) sugar
freshly grated nutmeg
a few peppercorns
a pinch of ground cinnamon
225 g (8 oz) prunes, stoned

FOR THE SALAD
8 chicken livers or 2 duck livers
1 tablespoon butter (optional)
salt and freshly ground black pepper
1 batavia or escarole lettuce
a few chervil leaves
1 tablespoon groundnut oil
1 pear, peeled, cored and thickly sliced
1 shallot, coarsely chopped
1 tablespoon armagnac
1 tablespoon Prune Vinegar or red wine vinegar
2 tablespoons olive oil

To make the Prune Vinegar, place all the ingredients in a pan and bring to the boil. Remove from the heat and leave to cool. Bring back to the boil 4 times. Strain the vinegar through a sieve into a screw-top bottle.

Trim the livers and pat them dry. If you are using duck livers, you do not need any fat. If you are using chicken livers, melt the butter in a frying-pan. Sauté the livers for 4–5 minutes, turning them gently with a wooden spoon until they are golden brown on all sides but remain pink inside. Remove from the heat and sprinkle with salt and coarsely ground pepper. Discard the fat.

Wash, trim and dry the lettuce and tear it into bite-sized pieces. Place little piles of lettuce on individual plates and sprinkle with chervil leaves.

Heat a frying-pan, add the groundnut oil and cook the pear slices for 1–2 minutes until soft. Add the shallot and the livers and cook for a further 2 minutes. Pour the armagnac into the pan and stir so that the livers are coated with the juices. Remove the livers from the pan, cut them into thick slices and arrange them on top of the greens. Arrange the pears around the edge and scatter the shallots on top. Add the prune or wine vinegar to the hot pan, stir well, then pour it over the salad. Sprinkle with the olive oil, salt and pepper and serve.

FOIE GRAS

In 2500 BC, Egyptians were already busy force-feeding geese with figs, and Ancient Romans, too, enjoyed fattened geese and their livers. But the idea of force-feeding is even older, geese preparing for their long migration flight south, have always eaten as much as they can gorge.

Force-fed ducks and geese are turned into Confit (see p.218), Magrets (see p.162), Grillons (see p.212), and mostly silky smooth and exquisite foie gras – duck or goose liver.

Regional Variations
Although the south-west and Alsace remain the centre of production for foie gras, it is preserved in different ways in different regions. In Alsace, they prefer to season goose liver with spices. In the south-west, they use duck liver and marinate it with salt, pepper and brandy – preferably armagnac – giving a sweeter and nuttier taste. Many other regions, such as Burgundy and the Auvergne, are now raising ducks and geese and preparing their own foie gras. Even in Brittany, where lambs used to nibble the left-over apples after the cider-making season, duck and geese have now taken their place.

Buying and Storing Foie Gras
In the last few years, foie gras has become immensely popular. It is sold uncooked (frais) and half-cooked (mi-cuit), but mostly preserved in sterilized jars (en conserve). It is expensive because breeding is a long process and because foie gras loses half of its weigh when it is cooked.

A foie gras cru, or frais, fresh uncooked liver, weighs about 450–675 g (1–1½ lb) for a goose, a little less for a duck, and may be sold vacuum packed. It can be refrigerated for 3 weeks.

A foie gras mi-cuit, or semi-conserve, barely cooked, is always of the finest quality and has been pasteurized at 200°C (400°F). It is sold vacuum packed, in a terrine or jar, or wrapped in foil and shaped as a roll. It can be refrigerated for up to 8 months.

Preserved foie gras can be prepared in a variety of ways, all governed by strict rules. A perfect slice of foie gras should be of a uniform colour since it must come from the same liver and must have been gently cooked. Today, foie gras is sold in a number of different categories which cover a range of both prices and quality. The labels must indicate all the ingredients and you should read them carefully so that you know what you are buying.

Foie gras d'oie on a label indicates that the jar contains liver from force-fed, fattened geese. It is a much finer quality of liver than foie d'oie which comes from ordinary goose livers.

Foie gras entier is a raw, whole force-fed goose liver – including both the large and small lobes of the liver in one piece – lightly seasoned and sold fresh or en conserve, preserved in a jar or a terrine. Only truffles may be added to this.

Foie gras de canard ou d'oie is 100 per cent liver made of agglomerated entire lobes of liver.

Bloc de foie gras is made of 50 per cent fattened duck liver or 35 per cent goose liver in chunks mixed with blended liver.

Parfait de foie is lesser quality, made with unfattened and imperfect livers. It is 50 per cent foie gras wrapped with forcemeat made with ordinary chicken, veal or pork liver.

Mousse or purée de foie are made with ordinary duck or goose livers rather than force-fed duck or goose livers.

Galantine, médaillon and pâté are prepared with veal, chicken or pork forcemeat wrapped around 35 per cent of real goose or duck liver, not necessarily liver from force-fed birds.

Serving Foie Gras
Cold foie gras can be sliced or cut into chunks and scattered over a green salad. Don't use plain red wine vinegar for a dressing as it will ruin the foie gras's delicate flavour. Make a fruit vinegar with a fine red wine vinegar, nutmeg, clove, sugar and fresh fruits all slowly reduced. It will taste sweet and just a little acid.

Preserved foie gras itself is traditionally served as a starter with warm toast, sliced brioche or baguette which should not be buttered. It is accompanied by a sweet dessert wine, a Pineau de Charentes or champagne. In the south-west, many people go against the grain and choose a vigorous Bordeaux red or a hearty Madiran wine, while in Alsace they like to serve a mellow Alsatian wine. Foie gras is the festive treat in France.

Salade de Poivrons Rouges aux Anchois

RED PEPPER AND ANCHOVY SALAD

Collioure is a pretty Catalan harbour town on the threshold of Spain. Surrounded by green hills, it boasts a beautiful castle, dark cliffs overlooking the sea and terraced vineyards sloping down towards the water. There are two factories where the freshly caught anchovies are cleaned and prepared in vinegar, brine or olive oil, hence most of the local dishes include anchovies in some form.

In Collioure, I met a family which symbolized the Catalan heritage. Monsieur Joseph Pous officiates at *Les Templiers*, a beautiful restaurant which was run by his parents before him. Monsieur Pous's son is a musician and plays the *sardane*, the slow local dance, while his wife runs a shop selling local crafts and also leads the *sardane* dance once a week. As I sat with him beneath the beamed ceiling of his beautiful bar, with a plate in front of us piled with sautéed *cèpes* and prawns, he recalled *pêle-mêle*, when Spanish Catalan resistance fighters walked across the border; the colony of painters, Matisse, Picasso, Dali, Marquet, Durain and Dufy, who lived in Collioure around the turn of the century; and mostly what it means in all aspects of life – politically, musically, gastronomically and emotionally – to be a Catalan today.

Later in the day we sat on his terrace overlooking the sea and ate this wonderful red pepper and anchovy salad. It was a lovely, warm evening and a couple of guitarists were playing and singing. They began with a native song, Charles Trénet's *sardane* about lazy evenings, then moved on to Gilbert Bécaud's song about Provençal marketplaces and finally to Louis Armstrong's melody about summertime in Dixieland. Somehow it all fitted together.

You can try adding a handful of sliced fennel bulb to this salad for a lovely texture.

SERVES 4

4 large fleshy red peppers
100 g (4 oz) fresh or tinned anchovy fillets in oil or vinegar
red wine vinegar or Banyuls wine vinegar (if using fresh anchovies)
2 hard-boiled eggs, peeled and quartered
8 black or green olives, stoned

FOR THE GARNISH

3 tablespoons finely chopped fresh flatleaf parsley
2 garlic cloves, crushed
3 teaspoons olive oil
2 teaspoons red wine vinegar
salt and freshly ground black pepper

Pre-heat the oven to 200°C/400°F/Gas 6.

Place the peppers on a baking sheet and cook in the oven for about 20 minutes, turning once or twice, until the skins are charred. Place in a plastic bag, close the top and leave for about 5 minutes. Remove from the bag, slide off the skins and remove the stem and seeds. Cut the flesh into triangles about 5 cm (2 in) wide and 7.5 cm (3 in) tall or into slivers.

If you are using fresh anchovies, marinate them in red wine vinegar or Banyuls wine vinegar for 24 hours. If you are using tinned fillets, drain, rinse and pat dry.

Arrange the anchovies and peppers on individual plates, alternating them so that they form a spiked pattern. Arrange the hard-boiled eggs and olives attractively on the plates.

To make the *persillade*, mix the parsley and garlic together, stir in the oil and wine vinegar and season with salt and pepper. Sprinkle over the salad and serve at room temperature with toasted bread.

OYSTERS

They have no mouth, no eyes, no nose. They start life as a male, turn female, then become male again if they live long enough. We have enjoyed these strange creatures for thousands of years. In 55 BC, after the Romans discovered the oysters in Brittany, they created oyster beds on the shores of Italy and offered as many as six dozen to each guest at their banquets. The latest record had the champion eating thirty-two dozen at one sitting.

The people of Brittany, Normandy, the Atlantic coast, Languedoc-Roussillon and Corsica have a love of oysters that has led to a prosperous oyster-farming industry in France, now Europe's foremost producer.

The quality of an oyster depends on where it flourishes, which is why oysters of a similar type often have different names, being called after the region from which they came. In fact, there are only two kinds of oyster: the round, flat Belon, which is by far the most exquisite today, and the hollow, craggier Portuguese or Japanese type. Bigger oysters are not tastier than small ones, yet they are priced according to their size. For cooking, it is better not to use the smaller ones since they will shrink a little under the heat.

Oyster Farms

It takes about four years of continuous care to develop a good oyster. The oyster farms are situated in calm waters where the sea bed is firm. Various supports made with shells, clay tiles and hollow tiles are created beneath the water so that the tiny spat, as small as a grain of sand, can cling to them and grow for about ten months into baby oysters. These are then stripped out and placed in basins where they are fed on plankton from the sea. Every year for four years they are moved to a new basin which supplies fresh water and protects them from predatory fish. During this time, each oyster filters from 7 to 9 litres (12 to 16 pints) of water a day. After four years the oysters are transferred to claires, huge clay oyster beds, from whence they are shipped to the markets. They can survive for about ten days out of water.

Choosing Oysters

Once, oysters were not eaten in the months without an 'r' – May to August, which is their breeding season. Summer oyster are now available, but they tend not to have much flavour.

Oysters are graded according to size. In France, Portuguese oysters are graded as P (petites, or small), M (moyennes, or medium), G (grosses, or large) and TG (très grosses, or very large) while flat Belon oysters are graded from 000 (the largest) to 6 (the smallest). Spéciales are rich, meaty oysters. Claires have been reared in clay basins. In Britain, they are graded from 1 (the largest) to 4 (the smallest); tiny ones are known as 'buttons'.

Opening Oysters

To open oysters, use an oyster knife or a strong, short, pointed knife. Hold the oyster in your left hand wrapped in a thick oven glove or cloth. Insert the point of the knife blade between the shells next to the hinge and twist to prise the shell open. Cut the muscle of the animal from the shell and discard the top shell. Use the knife to loosen the muscle in the lower hollow shell. If removing the meat, tip it, with the juice, into a bowl. If serving on the half shell, leave the oysters on the bottom shell.

Serving Oysters

If you are serving oysters raw, only open them fifteen minutes before you serve them and place them on a bed of ice sprinkled with coarse salt or seaweed to prevent them slipping. Pepper and buttered bread are the ideal accompaniments; vinegar or shallots will kill the delicate flavours.

LYON

Salade Lyonnaise

RICH MIXED SALAD FROM LYON

An excellent *Salade Lyonnaise* was served to me by the owner of one of Lyon's best-loved establishments, *Café des Fédérations*. Raymond Fulchiron explained that his *Salade* was the essence of simplicity: just salad, lardons, croûtons, vinaigrette and a perfectly poached egg. It can be enriched with chicken livers, Croûtons, shredded bacon, pieces of herring, anchovy fillets, beef tongue, country sausages, boiled potatoes, poached or hard-boiled eggs, pickled herrings or fresh herbs. An exuberant dish, it is always highly seasoned.

SERVES 4

6 handfuls of fresh greens such as curly endives, lamb's lettuce, young dandelion leaves, romaine lettuce
175 g (6oz) streaky bacon
2 slices country bread
2 garlic cloves, halved
1 tablespoon red wine vinegar
4 eggs

FOR THE VINAIGRETTE

2 tablespoons red wine vinegar
5 tablespoons olive oil
1 tablespoon Dijon mustard
1 tablespoon chopped fresh chives, tarragon, parsley or chervil
salt and freshly ground black pepper

Wash and trim the greens and tear them into bite-sized pieces.

Cut the bacon into pieces about 2.5 x 5 cm (1 x 2 in) and grill until crisp. Toast the bread then rub it lightly with the garlic on both sides and cut it into 2.5 cm (1 in) strips. Whisk all the vinaigrette ingredients until well blended.

Bring a pan of water with the wine vinegar to a rolling boil. Break the eggs into a bowl then carefully slide them into the boiling water so that the bubbles shape the whites neatly. Simmer for about 4 minutes so the whites are firm and the yolks still runny. Remove from the water and trim away an untidy bits of white.

Arrange the greens in a salad bowl, add the bacon and Croûtons, pour over the vinaigrette and toss. Arrange the eggs on top. Serve.

THROUGHOUT FRANCE

Les Salades Vertes

GREEN SALADS

The French eat a bowl of tossed green salad at least once a day throughout the year. Whether it is a simple lunch, an elegant dinner or a festive meal, a green salad is a healthy way of creating a pause after the main course to refresh the palate.

At home for an informal meal, the salad is often served on the same plate as the main meat or fish dish, or it may be served on a separate plate. Cheese usually comes later on its own plate. Recently, cheese and tossed lettuce are sometimes served together, although most people think the vinegar in the dressing kills the subtlety of the cheese.

The variety of salad leaves is vast, and often several kinds are chosen for one salad, Little Gem, Webb's Wonder, radicchio, escarole, romaine, oak leaf, lamb's or long-leafed cos; rocket, watercress, young dandelion leaves, endive, tender spinach leaves, young Swiss chard are all popular. With its tasty, fleshy leaves, purslaine has become very fashionable. When chicory leaves are used, they are cut into small slices, seasoned and arranged standing up round the dish so that the other greens can be placed in the centre.

Trim and carefully rinse the greens twice under cold water then tear them into bite-sized pieces (one never uses a knife to prepare salad leaves). Wrap them in a tea towel and store them at the bottom of the fridge until you are ready to use them. (If they are to be kept longer than a day, store them in a punctured plastic bag.)

Serve green salads in a large, wide glass or china bowl so that you can toss them easily without bruising the leaves. The dressing and its garnish are poured into the bottom of the bowl with the serving fork and spoon crossed on top and the salad leaves placed on top of them so that they do not touch the dressing. Bring the bowl to the table and toss lightly but thoroughly. We call this *fatiguer la salade*. A tossed salad cannot be kept for more than 30 minutes or it will turn soggy so discard any left-overs.

Dressings

In Provence, *mesclun*, a mixture of very young wild greens, is served with olive oil, vinegar and garlic *Chapons* (see p. 233). Bitter greens such as endive, rocket, tender spinach leaves and dandelion leaves are best seasoned with warm red wine vinegar, crisp bacon and *Chapons*. Single cream seasoned with lemon juice, salt and pepper makes a delicate dressing.

You will need a little more than a tablespoon of dressing per person. The most common dressing in France is Vinaigrette. It can be prepared using olive oil, groundnut oil or walnut oil and a variety of vinegars. There are also other popular dressings: olive oil, lemon juice, Dijon mustard and freshly minced herbs tastes delicious with endive, chicory or watercress.

Garnishes

Choose a few from this list:

1 tablespoon coarsely chopped walnut halves;
2 hard-boiled egg whites, minced;
2 hard-boiled egg yolks, crumbled;
4 anchovy fillets, crushed;
3 garlic cloves, crushed;
3 shallots, finely chopped;
3 teaspoons Dijon mustard;
3 teaspoons crumbled Roquefort;
3 teaspoons crumbled Roquefort mashed with a little brandy and 3 teaspoons single cream;
a few Chapons *(see p. 233) rubbed with garlic;*
Croûtons, oven-dried slivers of bread crust or bread rounds sprinkled with olive oil or fried in butter or oil and rubbed with garlic, if liked;
2 or 3 teaspoons of any of the following finely chopped fresh herb leaves: flatleaf parsley, basil, mint, coriander, chives, savory, chervil, tarragon, dill, fennel leaves;
if you only have dried herbs, mix them with oil and vinegar at least 30 minutes before serving.

With any salad dressing, proportions of vinegar, garlic and oil depend on personal taste.

THE LOIRE

Symphonie de Champignons de Couche

SYMPHONY OF CULTIVATED MUSHROOMS

Champignons de Paris, white mushrooms, acquired their name because they used to be cultivated in the Paris area. Now, a large proportion of them are grown deep in the dark, mysterious tunnels that connect the tufa caves scattered throughout the Loire valley.

Monsieur Robert Meyer of Meyerchampi in St Paterne Racan supplies one of the best restaurateurs in the region, who in turn created this dish in honour of the magestic fungi. Jean Bardet usually uses red oyster mushrooms as well as grey ones, but as they are not readily available, I've substituted chestnut mushrooms. The important thing is to have a variety of flavours and textures which contrast with the peppery taste of the rocket.

SERVES 6

225 g (8 oz) grey oyster mushrooms
225 g (8 oz) shiitake mushrooms
225 g (8 oz) chestnut mushrooms
225 g (8 oz) white mushrooms
100 g (4oz) butter
salt and freshly ground black pepper
2 shallots, finely chopped
200 ml (7 fl oz) chicken stock
1 handful small celery leaves, coarsely chopped
1 bunch of rocket

Wipe or wash the mushrooms carefully, making sure you do not soak them in water. Melt half the butter in a large frying-pan. When it starts to foam, throw in the mushrooms in the following order: oyster, shiitake, chestnut and finally white. Sauté them until golden, stirring continuously. Season with salt and pepper, add the shallots and stir until well coated.

Pour in the stock, bring to the boil then add the celery leaves. Reduce the heat and add the remaining butter a little at a time, making sure the sauce does not boil. Adjust the seasoning if necessary. Divide the rocket between individual plates, spoon the mushrooms and sauce over the top and serve warm.

BREAD AS A GARNISH

Chapons *are slivers of stale French bread crusts rubbed with cut garlic cloves until they are sticky and shiny and then drizzled with a little oil. They are served with salads, such as* Salade Niçoise, *or, as in the south-west, sautéed in duck, goose or chicken fat until golden then sprinkled over hot greens with chopped fresh herbs and tossed together gently.*

Panure *or* **Chapelure**, *breadcrumbs, are best made with 2–3 day old bread finely grated or chopped in a food processor. They can be used to top gratins, soups, stews or stuffed vegetables.*

Mouillettes *are long, narrow strips of fresh bread used to dip into poached eggs.*

Tartines *are rounds of bread, or baguettes cut lengthwise, buttered and spread with jam, honey or grated chocolate and served with hot chocolate or café au lait.*

To make perfect **Croûtons**, *pre-heat the oven to 200°C/400°F/Gas 6. Cut a baguette into 1 cm (½ in) slices. Quarter the slices if the loaf is large, or cut them into triangles for tiny croûtons. Arrange on a baking sheet and bake for 10–20 minutes until dried and lightly brown. Then sprinkle with a little oil or a dot of butter and bake for a further 1 minute.*

Salade au Chèvre

GOAT CHEESE SALAD

This salad is equally delicious with either fresh or marinated cheese.

SERVES 4

FOR THE MARINATED CHEESE

3 x 100 g (4 oz) small, round goat cheeses
3–5 dried red chilli peppers
2–3 garlic cloves, peeled
3 bay leaves
2 sprigs of fresh thyme
olive oil

FOR THE SALAD

4 handfuls of romaine, batavia, lamb's lettuce,
endive, chicory or watercress, or a mixture

FOR THE VINAIGRETTE

5 tablespoons olive or groundnut oil or a mixture of
walnut and groundnut oils
1 tablespoon red wine vinegar
salt and freshly ground black pepper

To marinate the cheese, place the rounds in a jar and sprinkle with the peppers, garlic, bay leaves and thyme. Cover with olive oil, seal the jar and keep in the fridge for a few days or 3 to 4 months, stirring once or twice to ensure that the herbs and oil completely coat the cheese.

To make the *Salade au Chèvre*, wash, trim and dry the greens, tear them into bite-sized pieces and arrange on individual serving plates.

Drain the marinated cheese, if using, and reserve the oil. Cut it horizontally into thick slices. Arrange on a buttered flameproof dish (or place on rounds of bread) and place under a hot grill for a few minutes or until soft.

Whisk together the vinaigrette ingredients. If using marinated cheese, stir in 1–2 tablespoons of the fragrant oil. Sprinkle the vinaigrette over the salad. Use a spatula to transfer the grilled cheese into the centre of the greens and serve.

Salade au Gruyère et aux Noix

GREEN SALAD WITH GRUYERE CHEESE AND WALNUTS

This lovely salad is from Savoie, where Gruyère cheese, cream, ham and walnuts abound.

SERVES 4

FOR THE DRESSING

2 tablespoons red wine vinegar
1 tablespoon Dijon mustard
4 tablespoons olive oil
2 tablespoons single cream
salt and freshly ground black pepper

FOR THE SALAD

450 g (1 lb) Gruyère cheese
1 curly endive, romaine, or escarole lettuce
4 shallots finely chopped
2 tablespoons chopped fresh flatleaf parsley, chives or
tarragon
8 walnuts, halved
75 g (3 oz) cured ham such as Bayonne or prosciutto,
slivered

Blend together the dressing ingredients in a bowl. Cut the cheese into thin sticks about 2.5 cm (1 in) long, add to the bowl, stir and leave to stand for 30 minutes.

Wash and trim the greens and tear them into bite sized pieces. Place in a large serving bowl and add the shallots, herbs, walnuts, ham, cheese and dressing. Toss well so that all the greens are well coated in the dressing. Serve with country bread.

Vegetables

LES LEGUMES

Vegetables are never indifferent participants or mere accompaniments on a table. Whether they are served as a starter or main course, vegetables stand on their own. They may be served raw, become the better part of a soup (*Vichyssoise* (see p.62), *Potage Crécy* (see p.72), *Soupe à l'Oignon* (see p.68), or the core of a stew (*Ratatouille* (see p.237). They may be used as a binding agent, become crisp gratins (*Gratin de Tomates, Courgettes et Oignons* (see p.254), fritters, croquettes, luscious timbales (see *Flans de légumes* p.241) elegant purées (see p.239) or careful counterpoints to a pork, fowl, fish or beef dish.

One fact, however, continues to surprise and puzzle. With such extravagant open air vegetable markets, lavish supermarket displays, with such a wide seasonal variety of vegetables served, why are there so few vegetarians in France?

Growing, choosing, cooking vegetables with respect and imagination are part of a tradition and goes without saying. But firstly it's a pleasure and then a way to improve one's health or waistline. So although everyone takes time to go once or twice a week to a supermarket stall or an open market to select the freshest and most flavourful vegetables, although everybody delights in eating an abundance of artichokes, chicory, celeriac and mushrooms, very few ever think of registering as *bona fide* card-carrying vegetarians: they are too busy enjoying their vegetables.

Eating fresh and fragrant vegetables is a joy. Although we all have already learned that flavour does not go necessarily with good looks. Something may be round, shiny and red like a tomato but not taste anything like a tomato. Better wait for the local product grown in a sunny field – even if it is more expensive – if you want a true tomato, otherwise a fine photograph on the dining table might be altogether more inspiring. The charm of seasonal cooking – for centuries a necessity – is being rediscovered now. Although an enormous quantity of vegetables come from overseas, most people still follow nature's calendar, because the seasonal produce is always sharp flavoured. French greengrocers are called 'merchants of the four seasons', and they are always ready to point out which local goods have just arrived on the stalls. The first radishes and asparagus mean spring is here; green beans and tomatoes announce summer, mushrooms that autumn has started. Each region has collected and practised from its past dozens of ways to use the large supplies of tomatoes, beans, pumpkin or chestnuts which were so abundant in season that monotony was a threat. What began as a necessity for cooking a vast supply of seasonal produce became, thanks to the cooks' imagination and talent, endless flavourful variations on a theme.

There has always been a hierarchy among vegetables. 'The smallest, the bestest', so went the saying. It is no longer true. Fashions come and go and mini-turnips and mini-carrots and fennel are yesterday's news. Fashion in vegetable is fickle: celeriac or garlic purée, lamb's lettuce, leeks, sorrel and chicory simmered in butter, Jerusalem artichokes, green-coloured cauliflower, edible flowers such as courgette blossoms, broccoli (quite unknown in France a decade or so ago) are less popular now. Red and green cabbage used as a counterpoint to delicate, expensive products like lobsters, *foie gras*, pheasant or chicken; pungent vegetables such as fennel and celeriac; tangy chicory; crisp purslane, dandelion, rocket, and summer spinach are in favour and so are sharp apples served as a vegetable.

And now with the golden rules to observe with vegetables:

1 Choose firm, fresh, ripe, crisp vegetables.

2 Peel and rinse vegetables many times, especially watercress, chicory and lettuce.

3 Don't overcook vegetables. The traditional way to keep green vegetables fresh and brightly coloured is to boil them in a great quantity of rapidly boiling water then plunge them in cold water, so they can be re-heated when needed. I prefer to steam them; it is easier. Steaming vegetables has become very popular in the last ten years as no precious salt is lost, they keep their texture and their colour, they don't overcook and they are ready to be added to the *Pot au Feu*, the *Blanquette*, the *Navarin*, the *Potée* crisp and firm, at the last moment when the main dish is ready.

4 A tablespoon of RAW vegetables (and fresh herbs) sprinkled on a few minutes before the end of the cooking will add a fresh flavour to the dish.

5 The days of thick sauces are gone. The flavour, colour and the texture of each vegetable must speak loud and clear. A drop of olive oil or knob of butter is most truly the only seasoning a fresh vegetable needs.

PROVENCE AND LANGUEDOC

Ratatouille

PROVENÇAL VEGETABLE STEW

The whole Mediterranean coast loves vegetables and each region in the South prepares a version of the celebrated vegetable stew *La Ratatouille*. Generally, throughout Provence the emphasis is on tomatoes, courgettes, aubergines and basil, whereas in Languedoc, mainly red, green and yellow peppers are used.

In some places, the vegetables are diced and remain firm, in others they are cooked with white wine until they all blend together; in St Tropez they are sliced, layered and baked with cheese; in the Vaucluse, aubergines and tomatoes are simmered and flavoured with crushed anchovy fillets.

I have eaten puréed *Ratatouille* flavoured with a tablespoon of *Tapenade* (see p.78), and I have sampled a most refined version of this stew – a warm garlic purée in which minuscule cubes of courgettes, tomatoes, and aubergine skins (skin only!) were briefly cooked. It looked like a Seurat painting. I have heard of an interesting variation – *Bohémienne* (gypsy) – so called because apparently gypsies, who meet in the South, cook the dish and add to it their favourite delicacy – hedgehog!

The following recipe can be cooked until it is firm or soft, and eaten warm or cold. It may be served with poached eggs on top, it may be used as a filling for an omelette, or as an accompaniment to fish or poultry. It may also be poured over warm spaghetti or noodles with a tablespoon of olive oil, or served cold with lemon juice and olive oil drizzled over. It reheats beautifully.

Some people grill the peppers then peel them, but I find this too time consuming. I don't peel the tomatoes either; once the dish is cooked the skins are not noticeable and they do add flavour.

SERVES 4

4–5 tablespoons olive oil or a mixture of olive oil and vegetable oil
2 medium onions, thinly sliced
2 red, green or yellow peppers, or a combination of colours, sliced vertically then sliced into 1 cm (½ in) wide strips
2 small aubergines, sliced vertically then sliced into 1 cm (½ in) wide strips
2 courgettes, sliced vertically then sliced into 1 cm (½ in) wide strips
3 tomatoes, seeded and coarsely chopped
2 garlic cloves, chopped
1 tablespoon chopped fresh thyme
1 bay leaf
salt and freshly ground black pepper
1 tablespoon chopped fresh basil
2 tablespoons chopped fresh parsley

Heat 2 tablespoons of oil in a wide frying-pan and cook the onions slowly, stirring occasionally, for about 5 minutes. Add the peppers and cook for 10 minutes. Using a slotted spoon, transfer the onions and peppers to a bowl. Add a little more oil to the pan and cook the aubergines, stirring frequently, for 10 minutes. Using a slotted spoon, add to the bowl. Add the courgettes and a little more oil to the pan and cook for 2–3 minutes. Transfer to the bowl, then put a lid on top of the bowl and pour off the cooking oil.

Put the cooked vegetables in a frying-pan that is as wide and shallow as possible so water from the vegetables can evaporate easily. Add the tomatoes, garlic, thyme and bay leaf, sprinkle with salt and pepper and cook over a moderate heat, stirring occasionally, for 20 minutes. If you prefer firm vegetables, sprinkle with basil and parsley, salt and pepper and serve. If you prefer a very soft *Ratatouille*, cook for a little longer. Discard excess juices and add a drizzle of olive oil just before serving.

Carottes Vichy

CARROTS GLAZED WITH BUTTER AND SUGAR

The water from the springs at Vichy, in central France, has a high bicarbonate of soda content which, when combined with the butter and parsley, give the characteristic flavour to this simple, light and delicious dish.

The carrots should be young, tender and fresh. If they are small, they can be cooked whole with 2.5 cm (1 in) of their green feathery tops, but larger ones should be cut into even-sized pieces, or sliced on the diagonal.

SERVES 4

450 g (1 lb) young carrots
a small pinch of bicarbonate of soda
25 g (1 oz) unsalted butter
2 teaspoons caster sugar
salt
1 tablespoon chopped fresh parsley

Leave the carrots whole, cut into even-sized pieces or slice on the diagonal, according to their size. Put them into a heavy saucepan, just cover with water and add the bicarbonate of soda. Bring to the boil, lower the heat and simmer, shaking the pan occasionally, until the carrots are tender and nearly all the water has evaporated. Add the butter, sugar and a small pinch of salt and continue to cook, tossing the pan frequently, until the carrots are lightly glazed. Sprinkle with parsley just before serving.

VARIATION

In Provence, oil replaces the butter and 2 garlic cloves are added – the dish is no longer *Carottes Vichy* but it is delicious.

Aubergines au Coulis de Tomates

AUBERGINES WITH TOMATO SAUCE

This dish from Provence reflects much of the culture, climate and food of the Mediterranean countries. It is delicious served hot or at room temperature as part of a summer buffet.

SERVES 4

750 g (1½ lb) aubergines, sliced lengthways
salt and freshly ground black pepper
5–6 tablespoons olive oil
6 small onions, cut lengthways into eight pieces
4 garlic cloves, lightly crushed
1 small red pepper, seeds removed, chopped
750 g (1½ lb) tomatoes, skinned, seeded, chopped
1 bunch of fresh basil
1–1½ tablespoons tomato purée

Place the aubergines in a colander and sprinkle generously with salt. Place the colander on a large plate and leave the aubergines for 30 minutes to 'degorge'; this reduces the amount of oil the aubergines absorb when fried, and removes the bitter flavour that some large aubergines have.

Meanwhile, heat 1½ tablespoons of oil in a frying-pan, add the onions and garlic to the pan and cook, stirring occasionally, until softened, about 4 minutes. Add the pepper, cook for 2–3 minutes, then stir in the tomatoes and basil and leave the sauce to simmer for about 20 minutes until lightly thickened.

While the sauce is cooking, rinse the aubergines well under cold running water to remove excess salt. Pat dry with kitchen paper. Heat the 3–4 tablespoons of oil in a large frying-pan over a moderately high heat and fry the aubergine slices in batches until browned, about 7 minutes. Transfer the cooked aubergines to kitchen paper towels to drain, then lay them in a serving dish.

Remove the basil from the sauce and add tomato purée and salt and pepper to taste. Pour over the aubergines. Serve warm or at room temperature.

THROUGHOUT FRANCE

Purées de Légumes
VEGETABLE PURÉES

A number of vegetable purées have been eaten for years – chestnut and cabbage purées traditionally accompany game, potato purée has been ever-present on our tables, and as a child I was given a lovely carrot and potato purée with a dribble of olive oil when I was ill. Then Nouvelle Cuisine chefs discovered that many vegetables could be turned into interesting purées. Unfortunately they over-used the idea and the large Nouvelle plates looking like the palettes of abstract painters became predictable. People grew bored with their monotony and with the dearth of crunchy, fragrant food. The basic idea of turning a wide variety of vegetables into purées is, however, a good one and worth following – in moderation. As well as being delicious in themselves, vegetable purées can be used to thicken soups and sauces instead of the conventional flour or cream, giving them a lighter texture and an interesting taste.

Almost any baked, boiled or steamed vegetable – courgettes, leeks, turnips, green beans, carrots, beetroot, celeriac, cauliflower – can be transformed into a light, fluffy purée with cream, butter or olive oil. The cooked vegetables do need to be drained, though, which is why steaming is a good method to use. However, if a vegetable is too moist after it has been puréed, before adding cream, butter or olive oil, heat it gently in a saucepan, stirring until excess moisture has evaporated. Then stir in the cream, butter or olive oil. Alternatively beat in a little mashed potato, or a handful of cooked rice. You can flavour a purée with plenty of parsley, or chopped onion or garlic and some fresh herbs.

These are the vegetable purées I use the most.

Chestnut and Potato Purée
Traditionally served with game and pork.

SERVES 4
450 g (1 lb) chestnuts
approximately 300 ml (10 fl oz) milk
450 g (1 lb) potatoes, sliced
salt and freshly ground black pepper

Cut a slash in the skin of each chestnut then cook in a pan of boiling water for about 5 minutes. Remove the pan from the heat. Lift a few chestnuts at a time from the water and peel off the outer skin and the thin inner one. When all the chestnuts have been peeled simmer them just covered by milk in a small saucepan for about 15–20 minutes or until tender. Meanwhile, steam the potatoes for about 6 minutes until tender then pass through a sieve into a pan.

Drain the chestnuts, reserving the milk. Pass the chestnuts through a coarse sieve into the pan with the potatoes. Place over a low heat and beat in the reserved milk until you have a fluffy, smooth mixture. Season with salt and pepper.

Haricot Bean Purée

Lovely with any roast beef, lamb or pork.

SERVES 4

350 g (12 oz) haricot beans, soaked overnight,
drained
1 onion, studded with 1 clove
2 garlic cloves
1 bay leaf
2 sprigs of fresh thyme
1 onion, chopped
25 g (1 oz) butter
2 tablespoons double cream
freshly grated nutmeg
salt and freshly ground black pepper

Put the beans in a pan, add the whole onion, garlic, bay leaf and thyme. Cover with cold water, boil for 10 minutes, then cover the pan and simmer for 1½ hours until the beans are tender.

While they are cooking, cook the chopped onion in the butter, stirring occasionally, for 4–5 minutes.

Drain the beans, discard the whole onion and the herbs, then purée in a food processor with the chopped onion. Transfer to a clean pan and re-heat gently, stirring in the cream. Add nutmeg, salt and pepper to taste.

Broccoli Purée

This is very good with most meats and poultry.

SERVES 4

750 g (1½ lb) broccoli
3 tablespoons double cream
salt and freshly ground black pepper

Chop the broccoli stalks then steam them with the florets for 5–8 minutes until tender. Purée in a food processor then transfer to a pan over a low heat. Stir in the cream, and salt and pepper to taste.

Fennel Purée

This is very good with any fish and with pork and game. Keep the feathery leaves from the fennel for garnish and to add flavour.

SERVES 4

550 g (1¼ lb) fennel, thinly sliced
1 potato, sliced
2 tablespoons double cream or 25 g (1 oz) butter
salt and freshly ground black pepper
1 tablespoon feathery fennel leaves, cut with scissors

Steam the fennel for about 10 minutes until tender. Purée in a food processor then pass through a sieve into a pan.

Steam the potato for about 6 minutes until tender. Pass through a sieve into the pan. Heat gently and stir in the cream or butter, and salt and pepper to taste. Serve sprinkled with fennel leaves.

Celeriac Purée

Wonderful with pork, fish and game.

SERVES 4

450 g (1 lb) celeriac, peeled and cut into chunks
2 potatoes, chopped
450–600ml (¾ pint) milk
3 tablespoons double cream or 25 g (1 oz) butter
salt and freshly ground black pepper

Put the celeriac and potatoes into a medium-sized pan. Add sufficient milk just to cover, cover the pan and simmer the vegetables for about 30 minutes until tender. Drain well then pass through a sieve into a clean pan. Re-heat gently, stirring with a wooden spoon to drive off excess moisture. Stir in the cream or the butter, and add salt and pepper to taste.

Cabbage Purée

Delicious with pork and game.

SERVES 4

1 head white cabbage weighing about 750 g (1½lb)
25 g (1 oz) butter
salt and freshly ground black pepper

Cut the cabbage into quarters then cut out the central core. Chop the cabbage and add to a large pan of boiling water. Return quickly to the boil, cover and cook for about 20 minutes. Drain. Purée the cabbage in a food processor. Re-heat gently in a clean pan then beat in the butter, and salt and pepper to taste.

NOTE

The vegetables can be frozen after puréeing or sieving, and preferably before the cream or butter is added. Thaw in the fridge then re-heat gently.

BRITTANY

Flans de Légumes
VEGETABLE TIMBALES

Flans de Légumes are one of the most elegant and flavourful accompaniments. Vegetables are cooked, puréed, enriched with cream and eggs, and flavoured then baked and served with fish, meat, poultry or game. In Brittany, where artichokes are so plentiful, I ate *Flan d'Artichaut*, created by Olivier Brignon, chef at the *Hôtel d'Europe* in Morlaix.

SERVES 4

4 globe artichokes, total weight about
1.6 kg (3¾ lb)
juice of 1 lemon
salt and freshly ground black pepper
50 ml (2 fl oz) single cream
2 eggs
4 teaspoons hazelnut oil
cooked artichoke leaves (optional)

Snap the stems off the artichokes and discard any damaged outer leaves. Pull the outer leaves outwards from the base, then pull them downwards and off the base. Continue until you reach the pale inner leaves. Using a stainless steel knife, trim the tops of the inner leaves by one to two thirds. Rub the cut edges with lemon juice. Pare away the dark, tough exterior of the base, working in a spiral from the stem. Pull out the central, hairy 'choke' and any remaining leaves. Bring a large pan of water to the boil, add salt and the lemon juice, then the artichokes. Cover the pan and boil the artichokes for about 15–20 minutes until tender. Drain, rinse under cold running water and leave upside-down to drain and cool.

Pre-heat the oven to 200°C/400°F/Gas 6. Butter 4 approximately 7.5 cm (3 in) ramekin dishes and place in a baking tin.

Break or chop the artichoke bottoms into pieces and put into a food processor. Add the cream, eggs and hazelnut oil. Process briefly until smooth then season with salt and pepper.

Divide the artichoke mixture between the dishes. Pour boiling water around them to come 2.5 cm (1 in) up the sides then cover loosely with greaseproof paper. Bake in the oven for about 30 minutes until just set in the centre. Remove the dishes from the baking tin and leave to stand for a few minutes before running the point of a knife around the edge of each dish and inverting the artichoke moulds on to a warmed plate. If liked, surround the moulds with cooked artichoke leaves.

Carrot Timbales

SERVES 6

300 g (10 oz) carrots, chopped
1 potato, chopped
1 garlic clove
4 tablespoons chopped flatleaf parsley
2 eggs
3 tablespoons single cream
a pinch of freshly grated nutmeg
salt and freshly ground black pepper
20 g (¾ oz) butter

Pre-heat the oven to 200°C/400°F/Gas 6. Butter 6 x 7.5 cm (3 in) ramekin dishes and place in a baking tin.

Keeping them separate, steam the carrots and potato until tender. Put the carrots, garlic, parsley, eggs and cream into a food processor and process briefly to mix. Pass the potato through a sieve into a bowl then stir in the carrot mixture. Add freshly grated nutmeg and salt and pepper to taste. Divide between the dishes, then pour boiling water around them to come 2.5 cm (1 in) up the sides. Cover the dishes with greaseproof paper and cook in the oven for about 30 minutes until lightly set in the centre. Leave to stand for a few minutes before unmoulding. Place a small knob of butter on each before serving.

Garlic Timbales

Lovely with lamb and pork.

SERVES 4

approximately 18 garlic cloves
150 ml (5 fl oz) single cream
2 eggs
salt and freshly ground black pepper
15 g (½ oz) unsalted butter

Pre-heat the oven to 200°C/400°F/Gas 6. Butter 4 x 6 cm (2½ in) ramekin dishes and place in a baking tin.

Boil the garlic cloves for about 3 minutes. Drain well then put into a food processor. Add the cream, eggs and seasoning and mix together. Divide between the ramekins then pour boiling water around them to come 2.5 cm (1 in) up the sides. Cover the dishes with foil and bake in the oven for 15–20 minutes until lightly set in the centre. Leave to stand for a few minutes before unmoulding. Place a small knob of butter on each before serving.

PROVENCE

Artichauts à la Barigoule

BRAISED STUFFED ARTICHOKES

In Provence, small purple artichokes are eaten raw or cooked in innumerable ways but this is my favourite recipe. It is a tasty, light dish that is perfect for a simple lunch, or a first course for a more substantial meal.

SERVES 4

8 small purple artichokes, or 4 small globe artichokes
juice of ½ lemon
4 tablespoons olive oil
2 onions, chopped
4 tablespoons chopped fresh parsley
2 slices lean streaky bacon, chopped
2 garlic cloves, crushed
salt and freshly ground black pepper
2 carrots, sliced
3 garlic cloves, unpeeled
1 bay leaf
1 sprig of fresh thyme
120 ml (4 fl oz) dry white wine
120 ml (4 fl oz) water

Snap the stems from the artichokes, and remove the tough outer leaves. Cut off the hard tips of the remaining leaves with strong kitchen scissors. If using globe artichokes, place them stalk-ends down in a large saucepan of salted, boiling water to which the lemon juice has been added, and boil for 5 minutes. Remove the artichokes from the water and place upside-down to drain.

Using a small spoon or a melon baller, remove the fuzzy choke from the centre of each artichoke, scraping the bottom vigorously to clean it as thoroughly as possible.

Heat 2 tablespoons of olive oil in a large frying-pan and gently cook a third of the onions for about 5 minutes, stirring occasionally. Remove from the heat and stir in the parsley, bacon, crushed garlic and salt and pepper.

Place the artichokes upside-down and press down with your fist to force the leaves apart. Divide onion mixture between the artichokes.

Place the carrots, remaining onions, the garlic cloves, and remaining olive oil in a heavy-based pan or casserole which the artichokes will just fit in a single layer. Place the artichokes upright on the vegetables and sprinkle with salt and pepper. Add the bay leaf and sprig of thyme, and cook over a moderate heat for 5–10 minutes. Add the wine, bring to the boil, then simmer for 3–5 minutes. Add the water, cover and simmer gently for 45 minutes until the artichokes are tender. Check to see whether you need to add a little more water. Place the artichokes in a warm shallow serving dish, cover and keep warm. Using a large spoon, force the carrots, onions and garlic through a sieve placed over the pan or casserole. Stir the purée back into the cooking juices and simmer for 3–5 minutes. Discard the bay leaf and sprig of thyme and pour over the artichokes. Serve at once.

PROVENCE AND LANGUEDOC

Gratin de Courgettes
COURGETTE, RICE, ONION AND CHEESE GRATIN

In summer when the tomatoes are firm and fleshly I place four tomato halves, cut side up and the seeds removed, on the courgettes, before sprinkling over the breadcrumbs. I serve this dish as a first course, or as an accompaniment to roast meat or poultry.

As a variation you can purée the vegetables with the rice and eggs then bake for 20–25 minutes.

SERVES 4

2 x 1 cm (½ in) thick slices lean, streaky bacon, finely diced
3 tablespoons olive oil
3 onions, thinly sliced
6 courgettes, diced
65 g (2½ oz) cooked rice
75 g (3 oz) Gruyère or Parmesan, grated
6 tablespoons chopped fresh flatleaf parsley
2 eggs, beaten
1 tablespoon chopped fresh thyme
salt and freshly ground black pepper
4 tablespoons fresh breadcrumbs

Pre-heat the oven to 190°C/375°F/Gas 5. Oil a gratin dish.

Gently cook the bacon in a large frying-pan for a few minutes, add 2 tablespoons of oil, then the onions, and cook, stirring occasionally, for about 4 minutes. Stir in the courgettes and cook over a low heat for 15 minutes, stirring from time to time.

Remove the pan from the heat and stir in the rice, cheese, parsley, eggs, thyme, and salt and pepper. Transfer to the dish, sprinkle with the breadcrumbs and drizzle over the remaining olive oil. Bake in the oven for 15 minutes until the top is crisp and golden.

Cèpes Sautés
SAUTÉED CEPS

Ceps can be very expensive, unless you've found them yourself, but this recipe is worth trying with ordinary field mushrooms.

When I was visiting the Comte and Comtesse Manoir de Juaye at their home, Château de Brie, in Limousin, some of their neighbours brought them the first ceps of the season. When sautéeing ceps the comtesse used lard instead of vegetable oil and butter, and sautéed 3 sliced garlic cloves before adding the ceps caps and stems; she omitted the shallots. Being an enthusiastic cook, she showed me how she preserves ceps for the winter. She makes the following recipe, minus the lemon juice, then packs the ceps into sterilized jars, which are tightly sealed before being cooked in simmering water for an hour.

Ceps should be covered with an even, deep-brown skin and be very firm and fresh. The best ones are medium-sized. Ceps are delicious stuffed, in omelettes and casseroles, or simply sautéed in butter.

SERVES 6
900 g (2 lb) very firm ceps
2–3 tablespoons vegetable oil
about 25 g (1 oz) butter
salt and freshly ground black pepper
2 shallots, finely chopped
juice of ½ lemon
2 tablespoons chopped fresh parsley

Do not wash the ceps – just wipe them dry with a damp cloth. Separate the stems from the caps. Keep only 2.5 cm (1 in) of the stems and discard the rest. Cut the caps into 1 cm (½ in) thick slices, and chop the reserved stems. Heat the oil in a deep frying-pan. When it is very hot, add the butter, wait for 1 minute, then add the sliced ceps and sprinkle with salt and pepper. Toss with a wooden spoon, then cook for about 4 minutes until golden. Lower the heat, cook for a further 5 minutes then increase the heat for 2 more minutes. Using a slotted spoon, transfer the ceps to a warmed serving dish and keep warm.

Add more butter and oil if necessary. Add the shallots and chopped ceps stems and sauté until golden. Add to the ceps caps, sprinkle with seasoning, lemon juice and parsley and serve on warm plates.

Endives Gratinées
CHICORY WITH CHEESE AND HAM

In England, what you refer to as chicory, we, in France, call *endives*. To confuse things further when I refer to a curly, green-leaved type of lettuce, I say '*chicorée*' and you say 'endive'. But, cooking is not about trying to clarify the oddities of language. It is about treating ingredients sympathetically so they become delicious dishes. Choose small or medium-sized chicory that is creamy white and closed at the tip.

Chicory is often boiled, drained, wrapped in a slice of ham, covered with a cheese sauce, and then baked until crisp, but I prefer this recipe as it is lighter. There is no heavy sauce, the chicory is lightly caramelized, which softens its bitter taste, and the ham and cheese are more of an accent. Serve with chicken, roast pork or grilled lamb chops.

SERVES 4

8 chicory heads
salt and freshly ground black pepper
4 tablespoons water
juice of 1 lemon
40 g (1½ oz) unsalted butter, diced
100 g (4 oz) cooked ham, finely
chopped
40 g (1½ oz) Gruyère, grated
pinch grated nutmeg

With a sharp knife, cut each head of chicory in half lengthways. Place the chicory, head to tail, in a single layer in a large, heavy-based frying-pan. Sprinkle with salt, add the water and lemon juice, cover and bring to the boil. Simmer gently for 15 minutes.

Pre-heat the oven to 220°C/425°F/Gas 7. Butter a shallow ovenproof dish that is large enough to hold the chicory in a single layer.

Using a fish slice, transfer the chicory to the dish. Dot the butter over the top and bake in the oven for about 25 minutes, basting a couple of times, until browned. Sprinkle the ham, cheese, nutmeg and a little pepper over the top and return to the oven for about 5 minutes.

NORD

Pain d'Endives

A FLEMISH CHICORY PANCAKE

Chicory is grown in Belgium and northern France and is at its best during the cool months of the year. It is served raw in a variety of cold salads, it is prepared as a savoury tart with ham or streaky bacon and in a creamy soup. It is also braised and enriched with Béchamel or Mornay Sauce. This delicate, slightly bitter *Pain d'Endive* can be served with any roast meat or fowl.

Always choose ivory-coloured or pale green chicory with tightly gathered leaves, and make sure they are all of the same size, preferably small or medium, for even cooking. Rinse quickly under cold water then remove a small cone from the base with a sharp knife to remove excess bitterness (although a little bitterness is a lovely thing). Make a generous amount as it will shrink by half as it cooks. It can be prepared in advance and re-heated at the last moment.

SERVES 4

675 g (1½ lb) chicory, trimmed
75 g (3 oz) unsalted butter
a pinch of freshly grated nutmeg
salt and freshly ground black pepper
juice of 1 lemon
1 tablespoon butter, softened

Pre-heat the oven to 150°C/300°F/Gas 2.

Rinse the chicory under cold water, trim, and discard the wilted leaves. Slice it very thinly and pat dry. Butter a shallow ovenproof dish and place the chicory in it. Place a piece of buttered paper on top then a lid, so it is tightly closed. Cook the chicory in the oven for 2 hours. When you remove the lid and paper, the chicory should have enough texture to unmould easily on to a warm dish. Discard any liquid, if any. Sprinkle the top with nutmeg, salt, pepper, lemon juice and softened butter and serve at once.

SOUTH-WEST

Croûte aux Champignons

AN OPEN MUSHROOM TART

A spring and autumn dish when wild mushrooms are abundant, this *croûte* (bread crust) was traditionally prepared with sautéed wild mushrooms served on slices of stale bread or in an oven-dried carved-out loaf of bread cut lengthways, leaving only 3 mm (¼ in) of crust.

In the following recipe I am using a pastry shell and either fresh, wild mushrooms or a mixture of dried ceps and French cultivated mushrooms, since ceps and wild mushrooms are not always easily available. If you use tinned ceps, drain them carefully before sautéeing them. *Croûte aux Champignons* may be served as the core of a lunch or an accompaniment to duck, goose or roast meat. It can be made in advance and re-heated for 15 minutes in a pre-heated oven at 190°C/375°F/Gas 5.

FOR THE PASTRY
100 g (4 oz) plain flour
50 g (2 oz) unsalted butter
1 large egg
a pinch of salt
1–2 tablespoons cold water or dry white wine

FOR THE FILLING
2 eggs
50 ml (2 fl oz) milk
salt and freshly ground black pepper
a pinch of freshly grated nutmeg
*350 g (12 oz) wild mushrooms or 25 g (1 oz)
dried ceps*
*450 g (1 lb) cultivated mushrooms, trimmed and
thickly sliced*
3 tablespoons butter and 3 tablespoons oil
2 garlic cloves, chopped

1 tablespoon water
3 shallots, chopped
juice of 1 lemon
1 tablespoon fresh flatleaf parsley, chopped

Place the flour in a bowl and make a well in the center. Add the remaining pastry ingredients and use your fingertips to blend them gradually into the flour. Knead gently until smooth then roll into a ball, cover with cling film and chill for at least 1 hour.

Prepare the filling. Pour the eggs, milk, salt and pepper into a bowl and beat for 1 minute. If you are using fresh mushrooms, trim, wash and dry them. Cut off the stalks and slice the caps. Heat the oil and butter and fry the chopped stalks and the garlic gently for a few minutes over a medium heat. Add the sliced caps and cook for another 15 minutes. Add the water and simmer for 5 minutes. Add the shallots then sprinkle with lemon juice and parsley and set aside.

If you use dried ceps and fresh cultivated mushrooms, soak the dry ceps in 2 cups of warm, salted water for 30 minutes, then lift and drain them delicately and blot them carefully. Pass the liquid through a muslin-lined sieve and keep for later use.

Wash, trim and dry the fresh mushrooms, then slice them in thick slices. Heat the butter and oil in a frying-pan until very hot, then add the drained ceps and cook for about 5 minutes. Stir with a wooden spoon. Add the shallots and garlic and add 1 tablespoon of the liquid in which the dry ceps were soaking through a sieve. Cook for another 10 minutes. Add a little oil and when it is very hot, sauté the cultivated mushrooms for 5 minutes until lightly brown and soft, tossing the pan from time to time. Sprinkle with lemon juice, parsley, salt and pepper. Keep aside for later use.

Pre-heat the oven to 190°C/375°F/Gas 5 and grease an 18 cm (7 in) flat tin. Roll the

chilled dough into a circle and use to line the prepared tin. Cover with greaseproof paper and fill with a handful of baking beans. Bake in the oven for about 15–20 minutes until the edges of the pastry begin to brown. Remove the paper and beans. Return to the hot oven for 1 minute and then leave to cool for at least 15 minutes. Scatter the mushrooms on top. Beat the eggs, milk, salt, pepper and nutmeg and pour on the mushrooms. Bake for 25 minutes until the top is golden. Serve warm.

CHAMPAGNE

Gratin de Navets à la Champenoise

TURNIP GRATIN

Ignored or ill-loved by most people, turnips were for a long time considered country cousins which only belonged to a stew, a soup or a *Pot au Feu*. More recently, however, their slightly bitter flavour and light texture have inspired many chefs. But in the north, where root vegetables are prevalent, white, purple or yellow turnips are a basic staple.

Tiny, tender, spring turnips, often sold with their leafy green tops still on, are simply prepared and steamed in navarins, but larger winter turnips should always be carefully peeled as their skins are thick. They should then be kept in cold water to prevent them from browning, and blanched to avoid too sharp a taste. This *Gratin de Navets* beautifully balances roast pork or duck. It can be prepared in advance.

SERVES 4

675 g (1 ½ 1b) tender turnips, peeled and thinly sliced
3 tablespoons unsalted butter
1 tablespoon ground-nut oil
100 g (4 oz) lean streaky bacon, diced or cut into slivers
1 large onion, sliced
2 teaspoons chopped fresh thyme, savory or rosemary
salt and freshly ground black pepper a pinch of sugar
450 ml (15 fl oz) chicken, vegetable or beef stock
3 tablespoons Gruyère, grated
2 tablespoons finely chopped fresh parsley

Pre-heat the oven to 190°C/375°F/Gas 5.

Plunge the turnips into a large pan of cold, salted water and leave to soak for 5 minutes. Drain well. Heat 2 tablespoons of butter with the oil and fry the bacon gently for about 5 minutes until crisp. Add the onion and cook for a few more minutes. Add the thyme, savoury or rosemary. Remove from the pan and stir into the pan of turnips. Add the salt, pepper and sugar and stir with a wooden spoon. Slide the mixture into a crockery or porcelain ovenproof dish, pour in the stock, sprinkle with the grated cheese and dot with the remaining butter. Bake in the oven for 45 minutes. Serve sprinkled with parsley.

NOTE

If you use larger, winter turnips, peel them and cook them in a pan of boiling water for a few minutes.

THROUGHOUT FRANCE

Gratin de Pommes de Terre

POTATOES BAKED WITH MILK OR CREAM, AND
CHEESE

The subject of potato gratins raises many questions and remains a cause of hot debate. Should cream or milk be used? Or broth, as is used when making *Gratin Savoyard*? Should an egg be added? Should the potatoes be cooked in milk first then baked with cheese and cream?

It is fool-hardy to claim to provide a final, or definitive recipe but the following, which has been adapted and tested over the years is, for me, the ultimate potato gratin. In its simplicity it has every virtue. It is easy to prepare, creamy inside, crisp outside. It can be inexpensive (I often replace cream or milk with undiluted, unsweetened evaporated milk), and it is versatile. I serve it with roast chicken, lamb or pork, fish baked with lemon and tomatoes, and a selection of cold meats and *charcuterie*. I also serve it with a tossed green salad for a simple lunch.

A potato gratin seems to be appropriate for almost any occasion, from a buffet for 30 people, to a small, quiet, just-family dinner in the kitchen, to a light-and-simple lunch for visiting friends.

SERVES 4–6

2 garlic cloves, crushed
50 g (2 oz) unsalted butter
750 g (1½ lb) potatoes, thinly sliced
4 shallots, chopped
salt and ground white pepper
freshly grated nutmeg
100 g (4 oz) Gruyère, grated
*450 ml (15 fl oz) single cream, milk or evaporated
milk*

Pre-heat the oven to 180°C/350°F/Gas 4.

Rub a large ovenproof dish with 1 of the garlic cloves then spread half of the butter over the inside of the dish. Layer the potatoes, shallots, salt, pepper, nutmeg, the remaining garlic clove, and two-thirds of the cheese in the dish.

Bring the cream, milk or evaporated milk to the boil and slowly pour over the potato mixture, allowing it to trickle through the layers. Sprinkle over the remaining cheese, dot with the remaining butter, cover lightly with a piece of lightly oiled foil and bake for 1 hour. Remove the foil and bake for a further 20 minutes until the inside is creamy and the top very crisp.

PÉRIGORD

Pommes de Terre à la Sarladaise

CRISP POTATOES FROM DORDOGNE

Most regions have their own version of a potato cake. Potatoes may be diced, grated, sliced, puréed and then flavoured with bacon, cheese or eggs before they are cooked in butter, olive oil or bacon fat. Here in Sarlat, the prettiest city on the Dordogne river, the secret weapon is the goose or duck fat. Although this is one of the truffle centres of France, only fancy three-starred chefs would ever add truffles to this dish. In Sarlat it is always the beloved *hachis* — an explosive combination of raw parsley and garlic — which is scattered on the hot cake.

Pommes de Terre à la Sarladaise is generally served with tossed greens and a crisp duck *magret*, but it is good accompaniment to any roast meat or poultry. Whenever I prepare a duck or goose, I keep the extra fat, chop it and cook it with a little water over a low heat for a few minutes. Then I store the fat in a jar and keep it chilled ready to use. But, of course, goose and duck fat is also available in Britain in tins or jars.

SERVES 4

750 g (1½ lb) potatoes (about 6 medium potatoes), peeled and thinly sliced
4 tablespoons duck or goose fat or ground-nut and olive oil or bacon fat
salt and freshly ground black pepper
3 large garlic cloves, finely chopped
3 tablespoons fresh flatleaf parsley, chopped

Dry the potatoes carefully with a towel but do not wash them. Wipe a 25 cm (10 in) wide frying-pan carefully to make sure it is smooth. Heat 2 tablespoons of the fat in the pan, scatter in the potatoes and sprinkle with a little salt and pepper. Cook for about 5 minutes on a high heat, turning them with a flat spatula so they are all coated with the fat and colour a little. Lower the heat to medium for another 10 minutes, shaking the pan from time to time to make sure the potatoes are not sticking. Press the surface with a spatula, place a lid on top and cook for another 15 minutes until a knife goes through the potatoes easily.

Then, with a decisive gesture and keeping the lid tightly over the potato cake, turn the pan and rest the cake on the lid while you add the remaining fat to the hot pan. Slide the cake gently back into the pan, golden side up, and cook for another 5 minutes, uncovered. Turn off the heat and leave to stand for 5 minutes. Slide the cake on to a warm serving dish, sprinkle with garlic, parsley, salt and pepper and serve at once.

NOTE

The chopped garlic can be added to the sliced potatoes at the beginning of the cooking for a milder taste.

PICARDY

Flamiche aux Poireaux
SAVOURY LEEK FLAN

Once a country dish made with bread dough throughout Picardy, this savoury tart is now prepared with a delicate pastry shell garnished with leeks (or pumpkin, endive, onions or Maroilles cheese) and served locally with beer. It is sometimes prepared as a *tourte* with a pastry top, but I find the following version lighter. Use just the white part of the leeks and save the tender green parts for a vegetable soup or *Pot au Feu*.

SERVES 4

FOR THE PASTRY
250 g (9 oz) plain flour
1 teaspoon salt
125 g (4½ oz) unsalted butter
1 egg yolk
5 tablespoons cold water

FOR THE FILLING
3 tablespoons unsalted butter
6 small to medium leeks, weighing about 675 g (1½ lb), split and thinly sliced
2 teaspoons water
1 teaspoon salt
freshly ground black pepper
3 tablespoons milk
4 tablespoons double cream
2 egg yolks, beaten
75 g (3 oz) Gruyère, grated
a pinch of freshly grated nutmeg

Place the flour and salt in a bowl and rub in the butter until the mixture resembles breadcrumbs. Mix in the egg yolk and enough water to mix to a smooth pastry. Roll out the pastry to about 5 mm (¼ in) thick and use to line a 30 cm (12 in) flan tin. Chill in the fridge for 1 hour.

Pre-heat the oven to 220°C/425°F/Gas 7. Prick the bottom of the pastry with a fork, line with greaseproof paper and baking beans and bake in the oven for 10 minutes. Remove the paper and beans and leave to cool. Reduce the oven temperature to 180°C/350°F/Gas 4.

To prepare the filling, melt the butter, add the leeks, sprinkle with water, salt and pepper, cover and cook over a gentle heat for 15–20 minutes until very soft but not browned. Pour in the milk and cream, stirring, then cover and simmer gently for a further 20 minutes.

Remove from the heat and stir in the beaten egg yolks. Sprinkle the bottom of the cooked shell with half the grated cheese, pour in the leek mixture and sprinkle with a little pepper and nutmeg. Sprinkle the remaining cheese on top and bake in the lower half of the oven for 35 minutes. Serve hot or at room temperature.

NOTE

If you have large leeks and fear their overpowering flavour, blanch them in salted water for 10 minutes, drain then cook with the cream. Thin strips of bacon can be added to the leek as it is cooking.

THROUGHOUT FRANCE

Pommes Frites
POTATO CHIPS

The French love sophisticated vegetables such as artichokes and asparagus, but when it comes to basic crowd-pleasing food, *frites*, potato chips, dry and crisp outside, soft inside and crunchy with salt, remain everyone's favourite. Whether they are cooked in lard, beef or goose-fat, groundnut or corn oil, whether they are cut into matchsticks, thicker *Pont Neuf*, traditional chips, or thin, round slices, a pile of piping-hot *frites* sprinkled around a roast chicken or a steak spells immediate carefree pleasure. Of course, anyone can serve soggy, pale, greasy chips, but perfect ones require a little knowledge. You have to use a firm, mature maincrop variety of potato, such as King Edward, Désirée or Maris Piper, and an oil that can be heated to a high temperature without burning – groundnut oil is the best, but you can also use sunflower or corn oil. The oil must be at the correct temperature when the potatoes are added, so a cooking thermometer is useful. If you do not have one, test the heat of the oil by dropping in a cube of bread: when it turns golden brown in 1 minute, the oil is ready.

SERVES 6
900 g (2lb) firm potatoes
groundnut or corn oil
salt and freshly ground black pepper

Peel, slice and cut the potatoes into sticks, keeping them all to the same size and shape. Leave them in a bowl of cold water for 30 minutes then dry them thoroughly with kitchen paper. Keep them wrapped until ready to use so they will not discolour.

Add sufficient oil to a deep-fat fryer so that it is only one-third full to avoid the danger of the oil frothing over when the chips are added. Heat the oil to 180°C (350°F). Using the chip basket lower the chips into the hot oil and raise the heat a little so the temperature will not be lowered too much. Shake the pan gently for a few minutes to let the moisture evaporate. After 6 minutes or so the chips will rise to the surface and float. Lift them from the pan in the chip basket and let them drain and cool for about 5 minutes.

Re-heat the oil to 190°C (375°F). Lower the chips into it when it is the correct temperature and cook for 1 or 2 minutes, so they will become crisp and golden.

Lift the chips out of the oil and scatter them on a dish lined with kitchen paper. Shake a little and discard the greasy papers. Sprinkle lightly with salt, toss and serve. Never cover potato chips as they will become soggy.

VARIATION

I sprinkle freshly ground pepper, a little crushed garlic and chopped parsley or fresh thyme on top of my *frites*, but that is the Provençal in me.

VENDEE

Mojettes au Jambon
HARICOT BEANS WITH HAM AND TOMATOES

Mojettes are a staple of the Vendée, once one of the poorest areas in France. Madame Gardot prepared them for us and her family for a weekday lunch, serving them in the traditional way with slices of local ham sautéed in butter to remove some of the salt. To serve the beans as an accompaniment to a main course, omit the bacon and ham from the following recipe.

SERVES 4

*350 g (12 oz) white haricot beans, soaked overnight,
drained and rinsed
1 onion studded with 1 clove
2 carrots, sliced
2 bay leaves
2 tablespoons vegetable oil, or 25 g (1 oz) margarine
4 shallots, sliced
100 g (4 oz) streaky bacon, diced
100 g (4 oz) ham, diced
4 tomatoes, skinned, seeded and quartered
2 garlic cloves, crushed
small bunch of fresh thyme
salt and freshly ground black pepper
1 tablespoon snipped fresh chives or parsley*

Put the beans in a pan, add the whole onion, carrots and bay leaves, cover with water, bring to the boil, boil for 10 minutes then cover and simmer for about 1½ hours until tender. The beans must remain covered with water as they cook, so add some more if necessary.

Meanwhile, heat the oil or margarine in a frying-pan, add the shallots and sauté for about 4 minutes until soft, stirring occasionally. Add the bacon and ham and cook for 5 minutes, stirring from time to time. Stir in the tomatoes, garlic and thyme, and cook for 5 minutes.

Drain the beans well, discard the whole onion and bay leaves then stir into the frying-pan. Simmer together for 20 minutes. Season with salt and pepper then sprinkle over the chives or parsley

AUVERGNE

Truffade
MASHED POTATO WITH CHEESE

Truffade comes from the hilly pastures of Auvergne, in the centre of France, where so many splendid cheeses are prepared.

After Monsieur Morin had spent a morning explaining to me about *Bleu d'Auvergne*, mellow *Saint Nectaire* and mature *Cantal* in his cold, humid cheese cellar in Aurillac, he invited me to his warm kitchen to taste a warming dish of potatoes beaten with cheese, which he called *Truffade*. Other versions of *Truffade* are made by adding cheese to a 'cake' of fried potato and bacon.

In Auvergne *Truffade* is prepared with fresh *tome*, but in Britain a combination of white Cheshire cheese and soured cream will produce an acceptable alternative as regards flavour, but the mixture will not form the 'strings' that occur when *tome* is used. Serve with either a green tossed salad, or with a roast meat.

SERVES 6

2 tablespoons pork fat or vegetable oil
900 g (2 lb) potatoes, sliced
salt and freshly ground black pepper
350 g (12 oz) white Cheshire cheese, cut into very
thin slices, or crumbled
175 ml (6 fl oz) soured cream
1–2 garlic cloves, crushed
2 tablespoons finely chopped fresh parsley

Heat the oil in a large heavy-based frying-pan and, when it is hot, add the potatoes and cook, covered, for about 25 minutes, stirring from time to time with a wooden spoon. Some potatoes will be soft, some will remain crisp.

Sprinkle with pepper and a little salt, cover briefly then remove from the heat and add the cheese. Cover again for a minute or so, then add the cream and beat well with a wooden spoon, lifting the mixture slightly. Add the garlic and parsley before serving.

PROVENCE

Gratin de Tomates, Courgettes et Oignons
TOMATO, COURGETTE AND ONION GRATIN

This dish is light, piquant, inexpensive and may be prepared and left to cook while you sit and chat. When you are ready, you just have to take the crisp gratin from the oven or let it rest in the cooling oven for a while.

The vegetables should be fresh; the courgettes should be firm and shiny, and the tomatoes should be plump and heavy. For the most piquant gratin, the olive oil should be 'virgin', fruity and fresh.

SERVES 4

4 tablespoons olive oil
2 large onions, thinly sliced
3 garlic cloves, sliced
750g (1½lb) courgettes, thickly sliced
750g (1½lb) firm, plump tomatoes, skinned, seeded
and sliced
3 bay leaves
1½ tablespoons chopped fresh thyme
4 tablespoons chopped fresh parsley or basil
salt and freshly ground black pepper
25g (1 oz) Gruyère or Parmesan, grated
1 tablespoon fresh breadcrumbs

Pre-heat the oven to 190°C/375°F/Gas 5. Oil a baking dish.

Heat 1½ tablespoons of oil in a frying-pan and sauté the onions for 5 minutes. Add the garlic, cook for 1–2 minutes, then add a little more oil and the courgettes. Sauté for 3 minutes, then add the tomatoes and cook for 5 minutes.

Layer the vegetables in the dish with the bay leaves, thyme, parsley or basil, and salt and pepper.

Mix together the cheese and breadcrumbs. Sprinkle evenly over the top of the vegetables, drizzle a little olive oil all over and bake in the oven for 15–20 minutes, until crisp and lightly browned. Serve warm or lukewarm.

Chou Farci

STUFFED CABBAGE

For *Chou Farci* the cabbage must be a dark green, thick-leaved Savoy, and the stuffing must contain pork in some form. Otherwise it's all according to tradition and personal choice.

Chou Farci is a hearty, warming dish and ideal for cold winter nights and large appetites. It is also a good way of transforming left-over ham or roast pork into a glorious creation. You may like to prepare the cabbage ahead of time. If so stuff and tie it into a ball, then cover and chill it until 1 hour before you want to cook it. Leave the cabbage at room temperature for 1 hour then proceed with the recipe.

SERVES 6

1 Savoy cabbage, weighing about 1.25 kg (2¼ lb)
25 g (1 oz) butter
1 tablespoon vegetable oil
1 large onion, coarsely chopped
175 g (6 oz) smoked lean streaky bacon, cut into 6 mm (¼ in) cubes
300 g (10 oz) cooked well-flavoured ham, chopped
3 garlic cloves, finely chopped
2 eggs, lightly beaten
75 g (3 oz) rice, cooked and drained
8 tablespoons chopped fresh parsley
1½ teaspoons freshly ground coriander
salt and freshly ground black pepper

FOR THE VEGETABLES

Choose as many as you wish.
2 long celery sticks, cut into 5 cm (2 in) lengths
2 courgettes, sliced lengthways and cut into 5 cm (2 in) pieces
2 fennel bulbs, halved lengthways
2–4 small turnips, depending on size, halved or quartered
2 carrots, halved lengthways, then cut into 5 cm (2 in) long pieces
2 large, fresh garlicky or very spicy sausages, pricked with a fork

FOR THE SAUCE

175 ml (6 fl oz) olive oil
salt and freshly ground black pepper
1 teaspoon freshly ground coriander
1 tablespoon chopped mixed fresh herbs such as thyme, majoram, chervil and parsley
2 large tomatoes, skinned, seeded and diced

TO GARNISH

chopped fresh herbs such as parsley, chives and tarragon

With a sharp knife, cut out most of the core of the cabbage and discard any straggly leaves. Bring a large pan of water to the boil, lower in the cabbage, stalk-end down, and boil for 10–15 minutes. Transfer the cabbage to a colander and refresh under cold, running water. When cool, peel off the leaves, cut away the coarse central veins from the outer leaves then drain the leaves on kitchen paper. Finely chop and reserve the heart.

Heat the butter and oil in a large frying-pan. Add the onion and cook, stirring occasionally for about 4 minutes, until soft. Add the bacon and cook for a further 5 minutes, stirring from time to time. Transfer to a large bowl then stir in the chopped cabbage heart, ham, garlic, eggs, rice, parsley, coriander and pepper. The stuffing should be rather coarse.

Line a bowl with a large piece of muslin, cheesecloth or a thin tea towel. Lay a few cabbage leaves on the cloth, overlapping them slightly so they line the bowl. (You may like to place a few thin slices of bacon on the cloth before adding the first layer of cabbage leaves.) Sprinkle the leaves with salt and pepper, then spread on a thin layer of stuffing. Cover with 2 or 3 cabbage leaves, another layer of stuffing and so on until you have used all the ingredients, except 2 cabbage leaves. Use these for a final covering. Gather up the edges of the cloth and tie together with string to make a neat ball.

Half-fill a large pan with water, add salt and bring to the boil. Place the stuffed cabbage in the boiling water, add more boiling water, if necessary, to cover the cabbage, lower the heat and simmer for 1¼–1½ hours. Add the vegetables and sausages and simmer for a further 30 minutes, until the vegetables are tender. Alternatively, the vegetables and sausages can be steamed in a basket, over the cabbage.

Meanwhile, prepare the sauce by mixing the olive oil, salt, pepper, coriander and herbs together in a bowl until thoroughly combined, then stir in the tomatoes. Stir again before serving.

Lift the cabbage from the pan and place in a colander. Cut open the string with scissors, loosen the cloth and carefully slip it from under the cabbage. Place a large, warm serving plate over the top of the colander and, holding on tight to the plate and colander, turn them together in a decisive gesture. Remove the colander. Sprinkle the cabbage with some of the chopped fresh herbs. Lift the sausages to a warm plate and slice them. Add the vegetables to the plate. Pour about 300 ml (½ pint) of the hot cooking broth in a warm serving bowl and sprinkle over the remaining fresh herbs. Take the cabbage, the vegetables and sausages and the bowls of sauce and broth to the table and serve at once.

ALSACE

Galettes de Pommes de Terre

CRISP POTATO, ONION AND HERB CAKES

What a joy to walk in Strasbourg with its decorated timber houses, cobbled streets, carved wooden balconies and numerous canals and rivers with their pretty covered bridges and watch the storks in their huge nests in the park. All this is seductive enough for a while, then one suddenly realizes that the key to the city's life is elsewhere – in the *winstubs*. A *winstub* is a sort of Alsatian bistro-café-inn where animated conversations, good food and energy prevail. Whether they have a plump porcelain stove, a brass grandfather clock and old beams, or a plainer setting, they are always cosy and lively, and consistently serve a rich variety of Alsace specialities along with Alsace wines and schnaps. Traditionally neither coffee nor beer are served. Marie-Claude Piéton and Thérèse Willer took me for a splendid luncheon in the *winstub 'Au Pont du Corbeau'*. We ate stuffed calves' hearts with red cabbage sautéed with onions, apples and chestnuts, and boiled beef with raw vegetables. But mostly we ate my favourite Alsatian dish, *Galettes de Pommes de Terre*, golden, crisp and irresistibly inviting potato cakes served with a bowl of fresh curd cheese and a crisp green salad. *Galettes* may be served as a light lunch dish or as an accompaniment to roast lamb or pork, or grilled steak. A dilemma: I have been unable to decide which of my two *galette* recipes I should choose for this book so I offer both. I am so taken by them I am often tempted to serve them both together to my potato-loving friends.

Recipe 1

This recipe makes one large, baked galette flavoured with bacon

SERVES 4

550 g (1¼) potatoes, peeled and thickly sliced
1 tablespoon groundnut oil
225 g (8 oz) lean streaky bacon, finely chopped
2 onions, chopped
2 teaspoons chopped fresh thyme
salt and freshly ground white pepper
25 g (1 oz) unsalted butter
1 tablespoon finely chopped fresh chervil, parsley or chives

Pre-heat the oven to 180°C/350°F/Gas 4. Grease an ovenproof dish.

Put the potatoes into a bowl. Heat the oil in a thick frying-pan, add the bacon and cook, stirring occasionally, for 2–3 minutes. Using a slotted spoon, transfer to the bowl with the potatoes. Add the onions to the pan, cook for 3–4 minutes, stirring from time to time, until beginning to colour and soften. Pour into the bowl with the thyme and salt and pepper. Toss all the ingredients together to coat the potatoes.

Transfer to the dish, press down hard on the top of the mixture with a fish slice then dot with the butter and bake for 30 minutes. Press firmly on the potatoes and cook for a further 30 minutes, pressing on the potatoes a couple of times more.

Run a knife around the inside edge of the potatoes to loosen, place a warmed plate on top, and unmould on a warm round serving dish. Sprinkle with chervil, parsley or chives.

Recipe 2

This makes thin galettes that are like potato pancakes. They are served with a selection of accompaniments – soft, cream cheese, very finely sliced onions and horseradish. Potatoes that are boiled before being fried remain much more crisp than if fried from raw.

SERVES 4

550 g (1¼ lb) small–medium sized potatoes
2 eggs, lightly beaten
1 onion, very finely chopped
2 teaspoons finely chopped fresh flat leafed parsley
1 teaspoon finely snipped fresh chives
a pinch of freshly grated nutmeg
salt and freshly ground black pepper
2 tablespoons groundnut oil
15 g (½ oz) butter

TO SERVE

curd cheese or a mixture of soured cream and drained, sieved cottage cheese
thinly sliced onions
horseradish sauce

Boil the potatoes for about 15 minutes until cooked but firm. Drain well, leave until they are cool enough to handle then grate them on a medium-sized grater into a bowl. Add the eggs, onion, herbs, nutmeg, salt, and pepper and stir thoroughly.

Heat the oil and the butter in a heavy-based frying-pan, spoon in half of the potato mixture to make a thin layer, press down then cook over a moderate heat for about 4 minutes on each side, turning over half-way through with a fish slice. Transfer to a warm plate and keep warm while frying the remaining mixture in the same way.

Sprinkle the *galettes* with pepper and serve piping hot with curd cheese, or soured cream mixed with drained, sieved cottage cheese, thinly sliced onions and horseradish sauce.

Cheese

LES FROMAGES

*W*its often like to muse over the fact that because France has more than 500 different kinds of cheese it must be a diverse and interesting country, and one which is sometimes quite difficult to govern. Lately, the rules imposed – or about to be imposed – by the new European market have created a great deal of anguish among the cheese-lovers of France. Would a bland industrial pasteurized type of cheese replace the vast range of cheeses made here for centuries? Fortunately, the same fear was shared by many traditional cheese-makers in Britain, Portugual, Spain, Italy and the Netherlands and diversity prevailed. The traditions of cheese-making remain strong, so although the many rules are strict, fine quality cheese-making will endure.

France is the world's premier producer of cheese with about 1 500 000 tons per year of cows', ewes' and goats' milk used either raw or pasteurized and turned into cheese by craftsmen on small farms, in co-operative dairies or large factories. Some of these cheeses are internationally famous, but others are not known outside their own region, being made by a lone farmer, given no registered name and consumed entirely on the spot.

The metamorphosis of milk into cheese starts with the processing of the milk through the separating and treatment of the curd, moves through the careful ageing of the cheese (*affinage*) which is probably the most important step, and finally on to the packaging. It is a varied and patient process, and produces cheeses that differ in taste, texture and appearance.

The most popular cheeses in France remain Camembert, goat cheeses and Roquefort, but everyone has one or two favourites that no one else has ever heard of, and true gourmets regularly canvas both their local cheese shop and the countryside looking for new products as well as savouring familiar ones.

For the sake of clarity, I will say that according to their origin, preparation and shape, cheeses can be grouped into nine main families.

Les Pâtes Molles à Croûtes Fleuries

'Soft, creamy cheese with soft downy crusts', these are made with raw or pasteurized cows' or goats' milk and have a fat content of between 20 and 75 per cent. They have a creamy texture and a white or golden mould crust. It is the penicillium spread on the surface of the curd which gives the famous white fuzz (downy like a beautiful woman's cheek) of Camembert. The cheese will then ripen and be cured in cellars for two to four weeks to acquire its celebrated soft texture and delicate flavour.

The most famous cheeses in this family are: Brie, first made around the eighth century and prepared both in Meaux and Melun; Camembert, developed during the Revolution and probably the most popular cheese in France, always sold in its round wooden box; Neufchâtel, shaped as hearts, logs or rounds; Chaource; Carré de l'Est and Coulommiers.

These cheeses are at their best in autumn, winter and the beginning of spring because the cows have grazed on fields of flowers and new buds. This type of cheese does not keep very well. In fact, in France most people only buy one portion of Brie or half a Camembert to make sure the texture is *à cœur*, uniformly ripe and fresh. A good cheese merchant will always inquire when you are going to serve this cheese – lunch today, dinner tomorrow – so that it will be perfect when it is needed. Make sure the crust does not become reddish or wrinkly and that when you cut the cheese it is ivory throughout and neither chalky white nor too runny. Curiously in Normandy, Camembert is served soft, totally ripe but still firm, whereas in Paris it must be aged a bit longer so that it is slightly runny.

Wrap the cheese carefully and store it at the bottom of the fridge. Serve it with bread, ripe pears or figs. Although pasteurized industrially-made Camemberts may be good, unpasteurized craftsman-made Camembert is better, and imitations made far away from Normandy and sold in portions wrapped in plastic should only be used in cooking.

Les Pâtes Molles à Croûte Lavée

'Soft cheeses with a washed crust' have a stronger taste. Their curd is cut, stirred, matured in cool, moist cellars for over a month, and turned twice a week. The crust is brushed and may be washed with salty water, beer, cider, brandy or wine. The cheeses must be stored in a moist place wrapped in a towel moistened with salty water or wine. Autumn and winter are the best time to eat them.

The most famous members of this family are: Livarot, a very ancient type of cheese from Normandy with a red crust and one of the most pungent; Maroilles; Pont l'Évêque, a square, golden cheese also from Normandy; Munster, the most famous Alsatian cheese made in the same valley since the seventh century and sold in a pretty wooden box; Époisses; and the glorious Vacherin Mont d'Or which is so creamy it must be eaten with a spoon.

Les Fromages de Chèvre

There are hundreds of types of goat cheeses made in Burgundy, Lyonnais, the Loire valley, Provence and the south-west. They come in all shapes: logs, tall cylinders, pyramids, tiny mounds. Apparently it was the Arab invasions of France during the eighth century which led to the breeding of goats in Poitou, hence the names of the most popular goat cheeses such as Chabichou and the tiny Chavignol which derive from the Arab word *chabli* for goat.

Goat cheeses are sold fresh, soft, dry, crumbly or very hard, and have either a bluish-white surface or are covered with ashes, herbs or spices. They may also be wrapped in a vine leaf, chestnut or plane leaves, or savory (*pèbre d'ail*). They may be sprinkled with white wine, olive oil or brandy.

The most famous goat cheeses are: Chevrotin which comes from different cities such as Chevrotin de Valençay, Chevrotin de Moulins; Chabichou; Chavignol; Picodon; Pouligny Saint Pierre; cylinder-shaped Sainte Maure from the Loire with a piece of straw in the centre; Selle sur Cher; Banon; Pélardon; and the tiny pungent *bouton de culotte*, the trouser button.

Serve goat cheeses from May to November when they are at their best. Fresh, as *fromage frais*, they are served soft and silky with a little cream and chives or with a drizzle of honey or marc brandy. When the texture is firmer, the taste becomes more intense and the crust begins to form and turn pale yellow. Then they are eaten for snacks or grilled on top of salad leaves

as a starter or served at the end of a meal. Later when the cheese becomes very dry, shrivelled and pungent, it may be kept in olive oil with herbs in a glass jar then eaten with bread, served with a tossed green salad or stored for longer soaked in white wine or brandy.

Pâtes Persillées

The so-called 'parsleyed cheeses' are rich ivory-coloured cheeses which have blue or greyish-green streaks of mould running through them. They are made with cows' or ewes' milk. The most famous of all these cheese are Roquefort; Fourme d'Ambert; Bleu d'Auvergne; and the newest one, the creamy Bleu de Bresse.

Roquefort is the most prestigious. It was already being made from ewes' milk around the year AD 800 and was the first cheese to be given a specific AOC label (see p.264) to protect its quality.

The curd is made with natural rennet which is cut, crumbled and salted, then placed in perforated moulds and sprinkled with powdered rye bread which has been left to mould for three months (or sometimes with liquid penicillium). It is left to rest in chilled well-ventilated rooms for a few days then removed from the moulds and salted with sea salt on each side for a further week. The next stage involves piercing the cheese with long needles 'to let the cheese breathe' and stimulate the growth of the blue moulds by allowing the air to circulate within the cheese. It is then matured slowly in chilly, moist limestone cellars situated deep beneath the village which impart its characteristic blue colour. Finally, each cylinder is wrapped in tin foil so that the blue mould can spread more slowly while it matures for four months until it is unctuous, high in flavour, pale ivory in colour with blue-green veins.

Handmade Roquefort is firmer while machine-made versions are softer, dry and tend to be crumbly.

Roquefort and most blue cheeses hate both the cold and the heat and must be tightly wrapped in foil and stored at the bottom of the fridge. Remove them from the fridge about three hours before serving with a choice of breads, a pot of unsalted butter, walnuts, figs, pears or grapes. A strong red wine used to be the classic accompaniment to Roquefort, but recently a sweet Sauterne or Monbazillac, or a good port have become more popular as they offer an interesting counterpoint. Roquefort is good all year round.

Fromages Frais, Fromages Blancs

These fresh cheeses are neither pressed nor brushed but are simply the curd of cows' or goats' milk, pasteurized or raw, skimmed, whole or enriched with cream. Cream, honey, sugar, orange blossom, salt, pepper, garlic, fresh herbs, cumin, olive oil and brandy can all be added to flavour the cheese.

Petit-Suisse, Neufchâtel Frais and Boursin are drained and matured for a very short time and can be served, like fromage frais, with herbs, spices, raisins, chopped walnuts, minced onions, sugar or salt. There are also regional fresh cheese specialities like Brousse (which is similar to Ricotta); Crémets; Jonchées. Fontainebleau is made with fromage frais and single cream which is whipped then lightly wrapped in white muslin.

Because they are light, not too rich and not salty, they are popular on their own or to replace cream in sauces and some desserts. They can be used instead of Gruyère in gratins. They can have 40 per cent, 20 per cent or 0 per cent fat content, so, of course, the 0 per cent has become the best friend of all 'lean cuisine' fans.

Les Pâtes Pressées non Cuites

These cheeses, prepared with raw pressed curd, were first made by the Romans, and the tradition was carried on by the monks who continued to produce them for centuries in their *abbayes*. In fact, there are still about twelve *abbayes* making cheese today. These cheeses are made with pasteurized or raw ewes' and cows' milk. The curd is cut into tiny pieces, washed in lukewarm water and placed under a press to mature for between two weeks and a year, while it is brushed, turned and washed regularly.

The main cheeses of this type are: Cantal; Laguiole; Ossau-Iraty, a ewes' milk cheese from the Pyrénées; Reblochon from the Alps; Saint Nectaire which smells like hazelnuts or mushrooms; Salers; Mimolette which is French and not Dutch, as is often thought; Morbier from the Jura; and Tommes of all kinds, mostly from Savoie.

Under the amber-coloured crust of their huge moulds, Cantal, Laguiole and Salers – three famous cheeses from the Cantal region – are quite different, although they are made in basically the same way. In the high plains of central France Salers and Aubrac cows feed throughout the year on fresh clover, liquorice, gentian and blueberries. Salers, a more pungent type of Cantal, is made exclusively with the milk from brown-coloured Salers cows, which graze on hilly slopes. The cheeses each weigh 55 kg (121 lb) and must age for about a year. Laguiole is made on the Aubrac hills, in the south of the Cantal region, with the milk of the long-eyelashed, grey-coloured Aubrac cows.

Les Pâtes Pressées Cuites

These great wheels of mature, hard cheese require an enormous amount of milk for their preparation and are an important source of protein and calcium during the winter months.

The milk is heated then cooled and mixed with rennet so that the milk quickly curdles. The curd is then sliced into tiny pieces, stirred and heated for between half an hour and an hour, then left to stand for about three weeks, while it is washed, brushed and turned over regularly. It is the carbon gas released during the process which makes the holes in the cheese. By knocking against the crust of the cheese with his fist when the top is sufficiently rounded, the cheese-maker can judge whether the cheese has matured sufficiently. It can then be transferred to cool cellars to stop the production of the gas and to finish maturing.

In this Gruyère family, the finest cheese is the Beaufort, a cheese without holes which was first made by the Romans. The Comté from the Jura is a slowly-aged, delicate, fruity cheese with pea-sized holes and a yellow crust; the Emmenthal has larger holes and is most often used for cooking.

The label *grand cru*, generally reserved for fine wines, is also used for cheeses if they have been made with raw milk produced by cows fed only on fresh grass.

Hard cheeses taste good throughout the year and keep well wrapped in a tea towel lightly moistened with salty water or dry white wine.

Fromages Fondus

Processed cheeses were first invented in the regions where *pâtes pressées cuites* like Gruyère are made. Often, Cantal, Emmenthal, Comté, Gruyère or even Roquefort and Bleus are used as the base for such cheeses which have become very popular, partly because they can be bought wrapped in individual portions.

They are prepared with a variety of crustless cheeses which are grated and mixed with milk, cream and sometimes spices, walnuts, ham, cumin, paprika or garlic. They can be spread on toast for snacks, cooked in gratins, used for *croque-monsieur* or cheese-burgers.

Les Fromages Forts

These fermented mixtures of cheese blended with local brandy or wine and flavoured with herbs or pepper are prepared in each region in a specific way. They are definitely an acquired taste. They offer a way to use left-over bits of cheese or cheeses which have hardened. They are strictly home-made products and need to be tasted with determination.

In the south, grated goats' cheese is moistened with brandy, pepper and herbs then aged in pots until it becomes the potent *Cachat* or *Brous*. In Burgundy, grated goats' and cows' cheeses are crushed and marinated with local marc brandy, thyme, bay leaves and vegetable broth then stored in a tightly-sealed crockery pot. Near Lyon, grated goats', cows' and Gruyère cheeses are mixed with fresh cheese, white wine and butter into a soft paste then kept for a fortnight before being spread on crisp toast or chicory leaves.

Appellation d'Origine Contrôlée

In a world where industrial products tend to prevail, supermarkets overflow with efficiently-packaged, inexpensive Danish-made Comté or Dutch-made Camembert, which may have their place in the market, but have nothing to do with the products prepared under the same name by skilled local craftsmen. So many countries chose to create a *marque* which a product could display to indicate and protect its origin and quality. Wine-growers, olive oil-makers, ham butchers and cheese-makers have therefore created their own *Appellation d'Origine Contrôlée*, and there are currently thirty-two cheeses able to boast the fact that they are AOC. For a cheese to qualify as AOC, it must conform to a specific series of quality controls relating to the region of origin, the soil, the climate, the type of animal, their breeding and feed, and the techniques of production. Each package of cheese must specify: the region from which the milk is collected; that the cheese is made from raw milk (although a few pasteurized cheeses are now accepted); that it is made by a precisely-defined traditional process; the size of each cheese; specific times spent draining and ageing the cheese before packaging; that it is wrapped where it is made; and the percentage of fat in each cheese.

Cooking with Cheese

Cheeses are wonderful served as a *Plateau de Fromages*, but that is just the beginning. Spectacular multi-coloured trays of tiny rectangles, triangles and circles of cheeses covered with fresh herbs, cumin, raisins, minced walnuts and chopped olives make a splendid starter. Cheese is also an essential element of many cooked dishes such as soups, quiches, soufflés, omelettes, pies, gratins, salads and tarts. Camembert, Roquefort or hard cheeses can be wrapped in flaky pastry to serve with drinks. Grilled goat cheese can be served sprinkled with thyme and savory. Gougères may be served plain or filled with Roquefort custard and pine nuts, or a nutmeg and Gruyère sauce.

Cheese is a last-minute helper in the kitchen: a dot of softened butter and cheese to top a sizzling steak, a spoonful of Camembert, parsley, mushroom and cream stirred into a bowl of hot pasta, make a simple meal into a sumptuous one. Sliced cheese dipped in egg yolk and breadcrumbs then fried in hot oil with bits of *Magrets* (see p.162) turn a tossed green salad into a proper meal. Baked tomatoes filled with herb-flavoured goat cheese make a lively accompaniment to a roast. Celery and fennel coated with a cheese Béchamel make a fragrant gratin. In Savoie, *concoillote*, fresh curds, butter, white wine and garlic, are melted together and spooned over potatoes, while in the Auvergne, potatoes and cheese are transformed into the luscious *Aligot* and the lively *Truffade* (see p.253), a mashed potato and cheese dish. To make baked potatoes into a nourishing lunch, scoop out the flesh and mix it with some rinded Cambembert, sprinkle with breadcrumbs and dot with butter before baking until hot.

There are also many interesting offerings for dessert: a delicate layer of puff pastry covered with fresh cheese and berries sprinkled with mint; a tangy rosemary, honey-fresh cheese ice-cream; or baked apples filled with almonds and marmalade served on a layer of fresh cheese.

Storing Cheeses

Apart from goat cheese or hard cheese like Gruyère, it is best to keep as little cheese as possible at home. Only buy what you need for two days. If you have a good cheese shop, buy only one or two pieces from a perfectly ripe cheese and serve it on the same day.

Wrap each cheese in its own paper and foil and leave it in the salad crisper at the bottom of the fridge. Add a piece of celery or the green leaves of a carrot to the package for extra moisture. Old-fashioned *gardemanger*, with their fine metal mesh, are wonderful for storing cheese in a cool, dark, well-ventilated place, and they can be found in specialist stores.

Gougère

A SAVOURY CHEESE CHOUX PASTRY

There are no serious wine tastings in Burgundy without its best *faire valoir*: Gougère. And the ritual would charm the hardest heart: splendid, vaulted cellars, rich Burgundy wine served in the *impitoyables* – the huge round glasses with their narrow rim to capture the wine's splendid bouquet – and lots of warm, fragrant, golden Gougère puffs to nibble.

Gougère will enhance almost any wine – potent red, dry white or cool rosé – but it is particularly lovely served as an apéritif with kir (see p.338). Served as a large, golden ring with a tossed green salad, it makes a delicate luncheon dish or a pretty starter, and it is perfect as part of a warm buffet spread.

Gougère can be made as a large ring or as separate individual puffs. Dicing the cheese will give a more interesting texture. Generally one does not fill a Gougère, but they can be stuffed with a Béchamel Sauce (see p.95) flavoured with cheese or with Roquefort and pine nut filling.

The only secret of making a fluffy Gougère is not to open the oven door before it is ready, and always to leave the Gougère in the oven for a few minutes after you have turned it off, so that it settles.

SERVES 4–6

250 ml (8 fl oz) milk
50 g (2 oz) butter
100 g (4 oz) plain flour, sifted
3 eggs
½ teaspoon salt
a pinch of freshly ground black pepper
a pinch of freshly grated nutmeg
50 g (2 oz) Gruyère, grated or finely diced
2 teaspoons Dijon mustard
a pinch of cayenne pepper (optional)

FOR THE TOPPING
2 tablespoons finely diced Gruyère

Pre-heat the oven to 200°C/400°F/Gas 6. Butter a baking sheet.

Put the milk and butter in a pan and heat until the butter has melted. Bring to the boil then shoot in the flour all at once and stir vigorously with a wooden spoon until the mixture comes away cleanly from the sides of the pan. Beat the eggs into the mixture one at a time then season with the salt, pepper and nutmeg. Add the cheese and mustard. The batter should be very smooth and shiny. Taste it, and add a pinch of cayenne pepper or salt if necessary. Drop teaspoonfuls of the batter on the baking sheet at least 5 cm (2 in) apart. Sprinkle with the topping cheese and bake in the oven for 20 minutes. Reduce the temperature to 180°C/350°F/Gas 4 and bake for a further 10 minutes until well risen and golden brown. Do not be tempted by the delicious aroma to open the oven door as the Gougère is cooking.

Turn off the oven and leave the oven door ajar for a few minutes to allow the Gougère to settle. Transfer the Gougère delicately to a serving platter.

NOTE

When I don't entertain friends from Burgundy, I often add a tablespoon or two of Parmesan cheese, dry goats' or ewes' cheese to the Gougère batter for added flavour.

Alternatively, you can make one large Gougère by spooning large teaspoonfuls of dough on to a greased baking sheet, piling them on top of each other to form a plump ring with at least a 5 cm (2 in) circle in the centre (you can sit a small tin cup in the centre of the ring so that you make a neat hole). Bake for 30 minutes at 200°C/400°F/Gas 6, then reduce the heat to 180°C/350°F/Gas 4 and bake for a further 20 minutes.

Fondue Savoyarde

CHEESE, WINE AND KIRSCH FONDUE

This mountain dish was always the core of the *veillées*, those long evenings filled with singing and chatting, peeling chestnuts and shelling walnuts in Savoy villages.

Now, fondue is served in all ski resorts every night. Whether it is prepared with an assortment of cheese or with just Gruyère, it is the most convivial of dishes. Cold water and a little kirsch *eau-de-vie* are generally the best friends of the fondue, and chilled white wine its most dangerous companion.

True Savoyards say that the authentic version of the fondue (which is originally a Swiss dish) is the *berthoud*. The master *fromager-affineur*, Daniel Boujon, from Thonon-les-Bains, showed me the crucial difference. A *berthoud* is made exclusively from the French cheese Abondance. It is mixed with either white wine or Madeira and is baked individually in small cast iron dishes. But when you prepare a fondue you will need long-handled forks as well as standard cutlery, and a tabletop heater to keep the fondue sauce warm in a flameproof dish.

SERVES 4

3 garlic cloves, crushed
3 tablespoons butter
750 g (1½ lb) Gruyère (without holes), shredded
600 ml (1 pint) dry white wine
3 teaspoons arrowroot
3 tablespoons kirsch
salt and freshly ground black pepper
a pinch of freshly grated nutmeg
1 teaspoon bicarbonate of soda
about 8 slices stale or oven-dried bread, diced into
2.5 cm (1 in) pieces

TO FINISH

3 egg yolks
1 tablespoon butter
a handful of diced bread

Rub a flameproof enamel or earthenware casserole dish with the crushed garlic cloves. Add 1 tablespoon of the butter then the cheese and about two-thirds of wine. Reserve the remaining butter and wine to add as the sauce is cooking. Cook on a low heat, stirring with a wooden fork or spoon and lifting the mixture until all the cheese has melted and the sauce begins to bubble. Blend together the arrowroot and kirsch and stir it into the mixture with the salt, pepper, nutmeg and bicarbonate of soda. The fondue should have the consistency of a thick custard. Stir in a little more butter or wine as it cooks to maintain the correct consistency.

To serve, each guest spears a long-handled fork into a cube of bread and dips it into the fondue so that it is well coated then transfers it to their plate. Use a standard fork to eat the coated bread or you will burn your lips. You may like to serve a tiny glass of kirsch in the middle of the meal to make the fondue more digestible.

When most of the sauce has been eaten, add the egg yolks, butter and diced bread to the dish and stir for a few minutes. Serve with a large spoon to each individual plate.

NOTE

You may like to serve the warm mixture over hot sliced boiled potatoes, or for a grand treat, add a few tablespoons of cream then sprinkle the top of the fondue with a few shredded truffles if some come your way. In some villages, the pieces of bread are lightly dipped into kirsch before dipping into the fondue.

Gratin Dauphinois

POTATOES BAKED IN CREAM AND CHEESE

Gratin Savoyard is traditionally prepared with potatoes, Beaufort cheese, a type of Gruyère, and meat broth, while *Gratin Dauphinois* uses milk or cream. Some add a layer of wild mushrooms, some a few thinly sliced turnips, some a piece of celeriac, or some sautéed leeks for an interesting texture.

Gratin Dauphinois is a splendid accompaniment, an easy way to be acclaimed for your culinary expertise with little effort. The potatoes should be served straight from the cooking dish when they are soft but not mushy.

SERVES 4

2 garlic cloves, crushed
1 tablespoon butter
5 large firm, fleshy potatoes, thinly sliced
a pinch of freshly grated nutmeg
salt and freshly ground black pepper
75 g (3 oz) Beaumont or Gruyère, grated
300 ml (10 fl oz) single cream, warmed

Pre-heat the oven to 190°C/375°F/Gas 5.

Rub an ovenproof dish with some of the garlic and butter. Pat the potatoes dry with kitchen paper or a towel but don't rinse off the starch. Season the potatoes with nutmeg, salt and pepper and mix with half the cheese and the remaining garlic. Spread the mixture in the ovenproof dish, pour over the warm cream and stir so that every potato is well coated with cream. Sprinkle with the remaining cheese and dot with the remaining butter. Bake in the oven for 1 hour. Place a loose piece of oiled foil on top to prevent the dish from becoming too brown and return to the oven for a further 30 minutes. Serve straight from the dish.

NOTE

I sometimes cook the potatoes and cream on top of the oven for 30 minutes then bake them in the oven for 30 minutes until crisp. Unsweetened condensed milk can be used instead of single cream.

Cervelle de Canut

FRESH CHEESE DESSERT

Cervelle de Canut is a lovely way to conclude a meal, something between a cheese and a pudding. You will need a rich type of fromage frais (Sainsbury's and Waitrose are good). The seasoning and herbs are very much a matter of personal taste.

SERVES 4

450 g (1 lb) grainy fromage frais (20 per cent fat) or
curd cheese
1 tablespoon cottage cheese
2 tablespoons olive oil
2 teaspoons red wine vinegar
2 tablespoons dry white wine
1 teaspoon marc brandy
salt and freshly ground black pepper
1 tablespoon chopped fresh flatleaf parsley
1 tablespoon snipped fresh chives
1 teaspoon chopped fresh tarragon
2 garlic cloves, crushed
1 shallot or small onion, finely chopped
300 ml (10 fl oz) single cream

Beat the fromage frais or curd cheese and cottage cheese together then add the remaining ingredients and beat gently with a fork until well blended. The mixture should not be too smooth. Serve with crisp toasted bread.

Plateau de Fromages

CHEESE BOARD

A cheese board can be the most exuberant of displays or the most discreet of offerings. Everything depends on timing, situation, budget and which cheeses are in season. For most people, cheese is a blessing after a simple meal of soup, salad or omelette. When faced with a large family Sunday dinner (especially one which follows a large family lunch), I often arrange on the dining room table a large bowl of tossed green salad, a big platter of tiny steamed potatoes, a pot of unsalted butter, a pot of Brittany lightly salted butter, a basket of baguette, walnut, rye and wholewheat country breads, and as the core of the meal a sumptuous *Plateau de Fromages*. But at the end of a formal meal, if I decide to serve a cheese course, it will be either one splendid Vacherin in its large, round, wooden box, top crust removed, served with a spoon and spread on thin crisp slices of bread, or one large, single piece of Roquefort cheese served with walnuts, white grapes, rye bread, a sweet dessert wine or a mature port. For an informal dinner *en famille*, I serve a tiny *plateau* with two or three cheeses, a bowl of fruit and a pot of butter. If I am entertaining I'll prepare a formal *Plateau de Fromages*, offering a great diversity of choice.

Most restaurants offer a cheese board, but the best quality restaurants tend to have two-tier trolleys, *chariot de fromages*, or immense wicker trays covered with a huge variety of cheeses, usually including an extravagant display of local seasonal produce. It is an overwhelming sight. Most good restaurateurs deal with a reliable network of producers and maintain close ties with neighbouring cheese-makers who deliver perfectly mature products daily.

At home, a cheese board should include at least Camembert, Brie, Livarot and Roquefort. A formal *Plateau de Fromages* should offer at least one, preferably two or three, cheeses of each type (one Roquefort, two Bleus, a soft, a semi-dry and a pungent *chèvre*, for example), accompanied by at least two different wines and offered after the meat and salad courses and before the dessert. The fashion of serving cheese on the same plate as a tossed salad is not yet acceptable; the salad dressing is hard on the delicate flavour of the cheese.

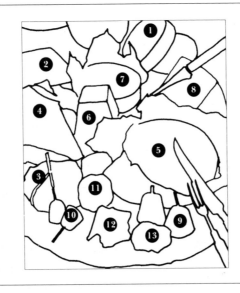

PLATEAU DE FROMAGES

1 Liverot
2 Pont Lévèque
3 Banon *(Vine Leaf Chèvre)*
4 Brie
5 Reblochon
6 Ash Chèvre
7 Camembert
8 Roquefort
9 Fresh Young Boutin de Coulotte
10 Dried Boutin de Coulotte
11 Chèvre Crottin
12 Cebecóu
13 Chèvre Cou *(Chèvre without chestnut leaf)*

The cheeses should be removed from the fridge and unwrapped at least an hour before serving and arranged on vine or fig leaves or a plain paper doiley on a platter or flat wicker tray. Place a fork on the tray to hold the cheese, at least two cheese knives and a thin, warmed knife for serving Roquefort and Bleu cheeses.

Cut a cheese in such a way that every guest has a share of the crust, which they may eat or not according to taste. I think it is often the tastiest part. Cut soft, creamy cheese in triangles, goat cheese in slices, tiny goat mounds in halves. Start with the mildest of the cheeses then move on to the strongest, most pungent one. Accompany the cheese with a variety of good breads, a pot of quality unsalted butter, cider, a hearty red wine, dry white wine or a sweet dessert wine for your guests to choose.

THROUGHOUT FRANCE

Soufflé au Fromage

CHEESE SOUFFLÉ

Contrary to its reputation, *Soufflé au Fromage* is not a temperamental creature. Prepared with a solid base which gives it flavour and body, and egg whites which provide the magical air bubbles, it is a reliable dish but it does need to be understood and respected. The egg whites must be at room temperature and be stiffly beaten until truly glossy then folded into the base a little at a time, and you must not open the oven while it is cooking. Once you know the nature of the beast, taming it is child's play.

CAFES

The French spend a great deal of time in cafés. We sit outdoors and sip a diabolo menthe, *a refreshing mixture of sparkling water and mint syrup, to get a bit of sun after a long day in the office. We sit indoors to savour a* thé citron, *lemon tea, and three croissants after a long walk through the rainy streets. We run to a café when we want to finish a book or when we feel at a loss and want to observe how others live, dress, quarrel. We go there to meet a daughter after school so she can complain, wonder and giggle over a foamy hot chocolate and a croque-madame, a slice of bread topped with ham, grated cheese and egg and grilled until bubbling.*

People talk and read and show off in cafés. Young executives indulge themselves with un sérieux, *a draught beer, and read their faxes. Students spend the afternoon over* petits noirs, *espresso or filter coffee, and intense conversation. Tourists ask for* café crème, *and once more wonder where the cream is when they are presented with a pot of espresso and a pot of warm milk, while the waiter declares once more that's the way it has always been. Local shopkeepers come for a quick break, a* grand crème, *double espresso, warm milk, and a pile of* tartines, *slices of buttered baguettes. Pampered grandmothers sit and chat over madeleines and* liégois, *chocolate or coffee topped with whipped cream. Exotic beauties order* citron pressé, *made with fresh lemon juice. Lovers order* double express *and ignore it to continue their dreams, their anguish, their bliss, their discoveries. Elderly men sip their bitter* Suze *and feel nothing changes. The French spend a great deal of time in cafés.*

SERVES 4

75 g (3 oz) Gruyère, Gruyère and Parmesan or
Gruyère and Pecorino, finely grated
300 ml (10 fl oz) milk
50 g (2 oz) butter
50 g (2 oz) plain flour
salt
cayenne pepper
a pinch of freshly grated nutmeg
4 egg yolks
5 egg whites

Grate the cheese an hour or so before making the soufflé so that it is slightly dry.

Pre-heat the oven to 200°C/400°F/Gas 6 and butter a 1.5 litre (2½ pint) soufflé dish. Sprinkle with 2 tablespoons of the cheese. The egg whites must be at room temperature.

To prepare the sauce, bring the milk to the boil. Melt the butter over a low heat, stir in the flour with a wooden spoon and cook for 2 minutes, stirring continuously. Remove from the heat, gradually pour in the hot milk and stir until blended. Return to the heat and whisk vigorously for about 2 minutes until thickened. Season to taste with salt, cayenne pepper and nutmeg. The mixture should be quite thick and leave the sides of the pan. Remove from the heat and beat in the egg yolks one at a time. Mix in three-quarters of the remaining cheese. The sauce should be lukewarm. If it is too warm when the cheese is added, the cheese will melt too much.

Beat the egg whites with a pinch of salt until they hold soft peaks. Add 1 tablespoon of the whites to the pan to loosen the mixture. Delicately fold in half the remaining egg whites, cutting down and up towards the sides of the pan using a metal spoon or spatula. Add the remaining cheese then fold in the remaining egg whites.

Pour the mixture into the soufflé dish; it should be about three-quarters full. Smooth the top with a spatula. Reduce the oven temperature to 190°C/375°F/Gas 5. Place the soufflé in the lower third of the oven and bake for about 25–30 minutes. Push a thin skewer into the centre and if it comes out clean, the soufflé is ready to serve at once.

Desserts

LES DESSERTS

*I*t is along the Loire valley, in Alsace and in Normandy where desserts are taken the most seriously. But of course, every region has its own distinctive tastes. In Provence, it may be for a fresh goat cheese flavoured with honey; in Brittany a more substantial *far breton*; in Auvergne, a handful of fresh walnuts served with a piece of Cantal cheese; in the southwest a dish of pears, berries and prunes simmered in Sauternes wine and peppercorns.

Cakes, tarts and custards are definitely not everyday fare in France. During the week, most people tend to enjoy a platter of cheese and fruit at the end of a meal since we all know here that when dessert arrives on the table, one is no longer hungry and it is generally believed that a good meal does not need a rich ending. So dessert is either very light and fresh, or else it must stand out and be truly memorable.

On festive days and on Sunday, however, a stop at the pastry shop remains both an adventure and a must. Even if their *éclairs*, *mille feuilles* and *brioche mousseline* are not necessarily as airy as those in Paris, the smallest provincial town has bakers and pastry shops which offer staggering displays of local specialities as well as classic, highly elaborate cakes. So much so that few home cooks in

France dare challenge such professional creations. They would rather stick to *Gâteau de Savoie* (see p. 318), *Teurgoule* or *Gâteau Basque* (see p. 320) because they can prepare them with their eyes closed. They can count on the seductive aroma drifting through the house and memories of past delights being summoned at the first bite. It is a known fact that with a *gâteau maison*, there is more than meets the eye.

Because elaborate desserts, considered the domain of the professional pastry chefs, and home or regional desserts are so very far apart, making pastry is no joking matter in a French home. It is a sensual way to evoke childhood pleasures, to show off, to make a grand statement, but it is not a casual activity like tossing a salad or making a *Daube*. So if you like Tante Cécile, you had better praise and finish her *Bavarois*, even if you think it a bit of an *étouffe-chrétien*, a 'Christian smotherer'.

But times change and in the last decade, desserts at home and in restaurants have come back into the limelight. They help to balance the 'light food' which prevails in some circles and is still lingering in many starred restaurants. Whether it is called a *farandole* (a Provençal dance) of pastries, a 'dessert trolley', or '*le palais de Dame Tartine*' (a palace of goodies), an extravaganza of custards, sorbets, cakes and mousses concludes most restaurant menus. And because there is nostalgia for real flavours, for the taste of good butter, honey, fresh eggs and sharp, familiar fragrances, they tend to include many regional specialities and home desserts.

Now that industrially-made pastry, frozen and packed, is available everywhere in supermarkets and from the lorries that bring regular supplies even to the most remote of French villages, great, but simple, home-made desserts like *Clafoutis*, *Oeufs à la Neige* (see p. 305), *Madeleines* (see p. 333) and the like are seductive again. A festive meal at home may offer a medley of chocolate mousse and *Pots à la Crème* but it may also have a *Pithiviers* (see p. 316) or a plump *Baba au Rhum* (see p. 322).

Making pastry alone in one's kitchen remains a true challenge and the result must be worth the effort. The following recipes have been my trustworthy companions for the last few years.

Sweet wines and champagne are served with dessert, but coffee is taken after the meal, never with dessert and seldom at the dining room table. Chocolates and petits fours are sometimes served with the coffee or after-dinner herb teas in restaurants or at home after an elegant dinner.

Pâte Brisée

PASTRY

Use this pastry for tartlet or *barquette* shells.

1 QUANTITY

This quantity makes enough pastry for 1 x 23 cm (9 in) tart or 12 x 7.5 cm (3 in) tartlets

225 g (8 oz) plain flour
1 egg
1 egg white
½ teaspoon salt
3 tablespoons water
100 g (4 oz) butter, cut into pieces

Place the flour in a bowl and make a well in the centre. Add the remaining ingredients using the fingertips to blend them into the flour. Knead gently until smooth, roll into a ball, cover with cling film and chill for at least 2 hours.

Grease the moulds with a little butter and arrange on a baking sheet. Add a little flour to the dough if it is too sticky. Roll out the pastry on a lightly floured surface or between 2 sheets of baking parchment to about 5mm (¼ in) thick. Cut pieces slightly larger than the moulds, remove and discard the paper, if using. Lift the pieces on your rolling pin and unroll over the moulds. Fit the pastry into the moulds, pushing gently with the fingertips, then trim excess pastry from the edges. Decorate the edge, pushing the blunt side of a knife or the back of a spoon against the dough.

For unfilled, fully-baked shells: refrigerate the baking sheet and filled moulds for 1–2 hours so that the edges will not collapse as they cook.

Pre-heat the oven to 180°C/350°F/Gas 4.

Prick the bottom of the pastry with a fork then bake the shells for about 10 minutes.

Prick the bases again and push the dough back up with the back of a spoon if it has collapsed. Bake for a further 10–15 minutes until the shells have shrunk a little from the moulds and are lightly browned. Leave to cool then carefully remove from the moulds using a spatula.

For partially-cooked, filled shells: refrigerate the baking sheet and filled moulds for 1–2 hours.

Pre-heat the oven to 190°C/375°F/Gas 5.

Prick the bottom of the pastry with a fork. Line the tartlets with a piece of buttered baking parchment or kitchen foil and fill with handfuls of baking beans, lentils or rice. Bake just below the centre of the oven for about 15 minutes. If the sides tend to collapse during baking, push them against the sides with the back of a spoon. The shell will shrink a little from the mould and brown lightly on the edges. Remove the baking beans and paper then return the moulds to the oven for a further minute. Leave to cool.

Pâte Feuilletée

PUFF PASTRY

Make sure your flour, butter, rolling pin and pastry board are chilled before you start. To chill your work surface stand a roasting tin filled with ice on it until you are ready to work.

Wrapped in a plastic bag or kept in a plastic container, puff pastry freezes well.

1 QUANTITY

This quantity makes enough for 1 x 23 cm (9 in) tart or 12 x 7.5 cm (3 in) tartlets

225 g (8 oz) plain flour
225 g (8 oz) butter, softened
1 teaspoon salt
120 m (4 fl oz) cold water

Place the flour in a bowl and make a well in the centre. Blend in 2 tablespoons of the softened butter. Add the salt and cold water and blend for 15 minutes until the dough is smooth and elastic. If the room is very warm, chill the dough for 15 minutes.

Roll out the dough on a lightly floured surface to a rectangle 20 x 38 cm (8 x 15 in). Gently shape the remaining butter into a 10 cm (4 in) square and place it on the centre of the dough. Fold the top third of the dough down over the butter, pressing the edges with your fingers. Fold the bottom third of the dough up over the butter, again pressing the edges with your fingers, to make a 13 x 20 cm (5 x 8 in) rectangle of butter tightly enclosed in pastry. Turn the dough 90° to bring the seam to your left. Roll it out again, fold it and turn it in the same way, making sure the butter does not come through the dough as you roll it. Roll out and fold once again. Wrap the pastry in cling film and chill for 30 minutes.

Each rolling and folding of the dough is called a 'turn'. Make 2 more turns then chill for a further 30 minutes. Continue in this way until you have completed 8 turns in all.

Roll out the pastry on a lightly floured surface to about 3 mm (⅛ in) thick. Cut into circles or rectangles slightly larger than the moulds. Gently press the pastry into the moulds and trim the edges. Chill for 30 minutes.

Pre-heat the oven to 230°C/450°F/Gas 8 for 15 minutes.

Reduce the oven temperature to 180°C/350°F/Gas 4. Bake the pastry moulds for about 15 minutes.

VARIATION

Flaky pastry, which is often used for *Pithiviers* (see p. 316), only requires 4 turns.

(see p. 316)

THROUGHOUT FRANCE

Pâte Sablée

SWEET PASTRY

With its crunchy, buttery texture, *Pâte Sablée*, also known as *Pâte Sucrée*, is my favourite for *barquettes* and *tartelettes*. Even if it is a little more brittle and fragile than *Pâte Brisée*, it is well worth it. I use partially-baked tartlets for peaches, pears or custard and fully-baked shells for softer fruits such as strawberries.

1 QUANTITY
*This quantity makes enough for 1 x 9 tart or
12 x 7.5 cm (3 in) tartlets*

*225 g (8 oz) plain flour
50 g (2 oz) caster sugar
½ teaspoons salt
finely grated rind of 1 lemon
150 g (5 oz) butter, cut into pieces
2 egg yolks*

Place the flour in a bowl and make a well in the centre. Add the remaining ingredients using the fingertips to blend them into the flour. Knead gently until smooth, roll into a ball, cover with cling film and chill for at least 2 hours.

Grease the tartlet moulds with a little butter and arrange them on a baking sheet. Roll out the pastry on a lightly floured surface or between 2 sheets of baking parchment to about 5 mm (¼ in) thick. Cut round or oval pieces 2.5 cm (1 in) larger than the moulds, remove and discard the paper, if using. Lift the pieces on your rolling pin and unroll over the moulds. Fit the pastry into the moulds, pushing gently with the fingertips, then trim excess pastry from the edges. Decorate the edge, pushing the blunt side of a knife or the back of a spoon against the dough.

See *Pâte Brisée* on p. 276 for baking instructions.

See *Pâte Brisée* on p. 276 for baking instructions.

THROUGHOUT FRANCE

Crème Patissière

PASTRY CREAM

This thick custard sauce is the traditional filling for most pastries. It must be made a day in advance, and it will keep in the fridge for two days. It can be flavoured with chocolate, coffee, lemon or orange liqueur. It is perfect for éclairs and *Choux à la Crème* (see p. 304) and can be used to coat the pastry crust in a tart or to fill a puff pastry cake such as *Pithiviers* (see p. 316).

MAKES 600 ML (1 PINT)
600 ml (1 pint) milk
1 vanilla pod, cut in half lengthways
5 egg yolks
100 g (4 oz) caster sugar
a pinch of salt
2 tablespoons plain flour
1 tablespoon cornflour
2 tablespoons Grand Marnier, cognac, kirsch, orange blossom water, coffee, chocolate, vanilla essence, almond essence, anise, rum or liqueur, or to taste
1 teaspoon butter, melted, or cream
3 tablespoons single cream (optional)

Place the milk and vanilla pod in a pan and bring to the boil. Remove from the heat, cover and keep warm.

Meanwhile, whisk the egg yolks, sugar and salt for about 5 minutes until the mixture turns frothy and pale yellow. Blend in the flour and cornflour. Discard the vanilla pod and gradually pour the hot milk into the egg mixture, stirring constantly. Return the mixture to the pan over a medium heat and gradually bring to the boil, stirring continuously so that the custard does not stick to the bottom of the pan. When it reaches boiling point, lower the heat and beat vigorously for 2 minutes then remove from the heat and continue to beat for a few seconds.

Stir in the liqueur or flavouring, pass through a sieve into a bowl and keep stirring until the custard has cooled. Add the melted butter or cream on the top to prevent a skin forming. Chill until required. You can stir in the tablespoonfuls of cream if the custard is too thick.

THROUGHOUT FRANCE

Crème Anglaise

VANILLA CUSTARD

This light custard sauce requires a little patience, and should be prepared a day in advance. It will keep for several days in the fridge. It is used as a base for *Oeufs à la Neige* (see p.305), ice-cream, or to accompany *Gâteau de Savoie* (see p.318), *Marquise* (see p.306) or *Bavarois* (see p.310). It can be flavoured with vanilla, caramel, coffee, chocolate, orange, lemon, ginger, aniseed or a fruit liqueur. It should be made in a stainless steel pan.

MAKES 600 ML (1 PINT)
600 ml (1 pint) milk
1 vanilla pod, cut in half lengthways (optional)
6 egg yolks
150 g (5 oz) caster sugar
a pinch of salt
2 tablespoons butter
finely grated rind of 1 orange or lemon, or to taste, or 3 teaspoons orange blossom water, strong coffee or cocoa powder or 3 tablespoons brandy, rum, Grand Marnier or kirsch

Place the milk, vanilla pod and seeds, if using, in a heavy-based pan, bring to the boil then remove from the heat, cover and keep warm.

Place the egg yolks in a bowl and gradually work in the sugar and salt, whisking vigorously for about 5 minutes until the mixture is smooth and pale yellow. Gradually stir in the hot milk then return to the pan over a low heat and stir gently for 6–10 minutes without allowing the custard to reach simmering point. All the froth will disappear and the custard will be thick enough to coat the back of a spoon.

Remove from the heat, add the butter and chosen flavouring and continue to stir for a few minutes. Strain into a cold bowl and stir until the custard is cool, standing the bowl over a pan of ice cubes to speed up the process, if necessary. Cover and chill until ready to serve. If lumps appear, process in a blender.

THROUGHOUT FRANCE

Crème Chantilly

WHIPPED CREAM FLAVOURED WITH BRANDY, CHOCOLATE, COFFEE OR ORANGE

Chantilly is famous for lace, china and its horse racing track but most of all for Chantilly cream. My mother learnt how to make Chantilly cream the day before her wedding, and decided to serve green salads and bowls of Chantilly cream at every meal. It was only after a month that she reluctantly introduced an omelette into her menu.

Chantilly is festive, versatile and easy to prepare. It can be flavoured with vanilla, cocoa powder, brandy, rum, coffee, candied ginger or orange peel. Seasoned with salt, it is used as a garnish for soups, or served with asparagus, steamed fish, or fish terrines.

Chantilly cream must be prepared at least one hour in advance and you must make sure all the ingredients are very cold. It will keep for about a day if it is covered and chilled. Discard the drops of liquid in the bowl as you serve.

MAKES 600 ML (1 PINT)
300 ml (10 fl oz) double cream, chilled
4 tablespoons cold milk
2 tablespoons icing sugar, sifted
1 teaspoon vanilla essence
1 tablespoon iced water
1 tablespoon rum or brandy liqueur or 75 g (3 oz) plain chocolate melted with 1 tablespoon water or 1 tablespoon instant coffee powder or 1 tablespoon finely shredded candied ginger or orange peel

It is much better to use a hand wire whisk since it will take no more than 3 minutes. If you use an electric whisk or a blender, start at a low speed and increase the speed after 1 minute.

Mix the cream and milk in a large, cold bowl as the mixture will double in volume. Whip the cream, moving the whisk around the bowl and lifting as you whisk to add as much air as possible, until the cream forms soft peaks. Add the sugar, vanilla essence and water and continue to whisk until very stiff. Stir in your chosen flavouring, cover and chill for 1 hour.

Salade de Fruits

FRESH FRUIT SALAD

A fresh fruit salad is one of the most refreshing ways to end a meal; it is ideal after a *Coq au Vin* (see p. 154) or a *Choucroute Garnie* (see p. 197).

Choose a mixture of cherries, raspberries, peaches, apricots, pears, apples, plums, figs, strawberries, mangoes, melons, oranges, kumquats, tangerines, pineapple or bananas, according to availability. Then add blueberries, blackcurrants, redcurrants, grapes or fresh almonds as an accent.

SERVES 4

about 550–750 g (1¼–1½ lb) fruit
juice of 1 lemon
juice of 2 oranges
4 tablespoons brandy, rum, kirsch, Cointreau or
Grand Marnier (optional)
about 50–75 g (2–3 oz) sugar
75 g (3 oz) blueberries, blackcurrants, redcurrants or
grapes, or 50 g (2 oz) fresh almonds

TO SERVE

finely diced candied orange or grapefruit peel
finely chopped crystallized stem ginger or fresh ginger
small mint leaves
Tuiles (see p. 329)

Peel, core or stone the fruit. Half, slice or dice as appropriate. Place in a shallow dish, individual dishes or glasses. Pour over the lemon and orange juices and the brandy, rum, kirsch or liqueur, if using, and gently stir in sugar to taste. Cover and chill for at least 1 hour.

Just before serving, add blueberries, blackcurrants, redcurrants, grapes or nuts and scatter over candied orange or grapefruit peel, or ginger, or both, toss, sprinkle over small mint leaves and serve.

VARIATIONS

- For a special occasion, pour Champagne, or other sparkling white wine, over just before serving; do not toss but serve at once.
- Purée together 2 ripe peaches or 1 large mango, and the juice of 3 oranges then pour over the fruit.

Tarte aux Pruneaux

PRUNE TART

Throughout France, prunes are used in a variety of savoury as well as sweet dishes, but this tart is one of the most delectable sweet recipes I know.

SERVES 4

100 g (4 oz) plain flour
a pinch of salt
50 g (2 oz) unsalted butter, softened
cold water
icing sugar for sprinkling

FOR THE FILLING

350 g (12oz) large prunes
4 tablespoons apricot jam
4 tablespoons cognac, prune brandy or armagnac

Soak the prunes in tea or water for at least 2 hours.

Place the flour and salt in a bowl, toss in the butter then rub into the flour until the mixture resembles breadcrumbs. Rapidly stir in the water to make a soft but not sticky dough and form into a ball. Cover, and place in the fridge for 30 minutes.

Pre-heat the oven to 200°C/400°F/Gas 6. Butter a 20 cm (8 in) flan tin.

Drain the prunes and remove the stones. Put

the prunes into a bowl, crush them coarsely with a fork, then mix in the apricot preserve and half the brandy.

Roll out the dough on a lightly floured surface to a circle about 25 cm (10 in) in diameter. Fold the dough back over the rolling pin and carefully transfer to the flan tin. Pass the rolling pin over the flan tin to remove excess pastry. Prick the base with the tip of a knife or a fork.

Spread the prune mixture into the pastry shell and bake in the oven for about 35–40 minutes.

Remove the tart from the oven and transfer to a wire rack. Sprinkle with the remaining brandy and leave to cool slightly. Sprinkle with icing sugar just before serving warm or lukewarm.

THROUGHOUT FRANCE

Compote de Fruits
POACHED FRESH FRUIT

This is a refreshing, light compote with clear, sharp fruit flavours. To make a good compote, you don't need exotic or perfect-looking fruit; fruit that is too ripe, not ripe enough, or too blemished to be acceptable in a basket of fresh fruit can be used. You can use just one type of fruit or a mixture but allow five to six pieces of fruit for four people.

The compote can be served in so many different ways, either lukewarm or cold: on plain yoghurt for breakfast, as a filling for *crêpes* and sweet omelettes, with *Gâteau Breton* (see p. 315), *Kugelhopf* (see p. 321), *Pain d'Épices* (see p. 325) or warm *Madeleines* (see p. 333).

SERVES 4

1 lemon
5–6 pears, peaches, apricots or apples, or a mixture
50 g (2 oz) sugar
300 ml (10 fl oz) water
75 g (3 oz) green or black grapes (optional)
1 tablespoon brandy or calvados (optional)
chopped mint to serve (optional)

Pare 2 x 7.5 cm (3 in) strips of rind from the lemon, then squeeze the juice. Peel the fruit, cut in half and discard the cores or stones, as appropriate, then quarter or slice the fruit.

Put the lemon rind and juice, sugar and water in a medium pan, and bring to the boil. Add the fruit, lower the heat, cover and simmer gently for 8–15 minutes until just tender; turn the pieces over half-way through.

Remove the fruit with a slotted spoon and put in a shallow bowl to cool. Boil the cooking liquid until lightly thickened, then pour over the fruit. Add the grapes and brandy or calvados if you wish. Cover and chill. Serve sprinkled with chopped mint leaves if you like.

Poires, Pruneaux, et Oranges au Vin Rouge et aux Épices

PEARS, PRUNES AND ORANGES COOKED IN RED
WINE WITH SPICES

Serve with *Gâteau Breton* (see p. 315), warm *Madeleines* (see p. 333), *Pain d'Épices* (see p. 325), or Tuiles (see p. 329).

SERVES 6

4 oz (100 g) plump raisins
6 large prunes, stoned
1 lemon
3 oranges
6 firm but ripe pears with stems
600 ml (1 pint) full-bodied red wine
175 g (6 oz) sugar
4 teaspoons black peppercorns
a pinch of freshly grated nutmeg
1 cinnamon stick
1 teaspoon coriander seeds
1 clove
2 bay leaves
1 tablespoon finely chopped fresh ginger

Place the raisins and prunes in a bowl, pour over boiling water and leave for 1–2 hours. Using a potato peeler, pare 2 large strips of rind from the lemon and 1 of the oranges, then squeeze the juice from the lemon and orange. Finely grate the rind from 1 of the remaining oranges, then peel and thinly slice them both; reserve the grated rind and orange slices.

Peel the pears and place stem up, in a pan that they just fit. Add the wine, sugar, spices, bay leaves, strips of orange and lemon rind and the lemon and orange juices. Bring to the boil then cover, using a dome of foil if necessary to avoid crushing the pear stems, and simmer gently for 10 minutes. Drain the prunes and raisins, add to the pan and simmer for a further 15 minutes. Add the reserved orange slices, turn off the heat and leave the fruit to cool in the poaching liquid.

Transfer the prunes and raisins to a glass or china serving bowl and place the pears, stems up, on top. Put the orange slices round the edge.

Boil the poaching liquid over a high heat until slightly syrupy. Add the reserved grated orange rind and the ginger. Check the taste and add more ginger if needed. Discard the peppercorns, cinnamon, clove, orange and lemon rind. Leave the syrup to cool then pour, with the bay leaves, over the fruit. Serve when cold, or cover and chill.

VARIATION

In Burgundy a few tablespoons of *crème de cassis* are often stirred into the wine syrup just before serving (if you do this, reduce the amount of sugar you add to the pears to about 100 g (4 oz).

THROUGHOUT FRANCE

Charlotte aux Poires

PEAR CHARLOTTE

Foods have highs and lows. Once upon a time no special Sunday lunch, and no grand 'cousin Georges is back from Africa' dinner was complete without a Charlotte. These were extravaganzas of custard, gelatine, whipped cream and brandy encased in sponge fingers. They looked and tasted rich so cooks felt better people for serving them. Today fashions and tastes have changed. We want fresher flavours, we want textures, we shun gelatine, so the only Charlottes I serve now are packed with fruit, and the jacket is made of thin slices of bread. I use peaches, pears, apples or apricots for the filling and enhance the fruit flavour with lemon juice. The result is tangy, crunchy and utterly delicious whether it is served lukewarm or cold.

The secrets of a successful fruit Charlotte are cooking the fruit until it becomes very thick, filling the mould to the very top since during the cooking the fruit will settle, and using an apricot jam that is very sharp (add a little lemon juice if it is not). If the Charlotte becomes whimsical and does not unmould easily, don't complain, don't explain, don't panic; gather everything as well as possible, pour the warm apricot jam on top, sprinkle with a little icing sugar and serve your guests yourself. At the first bite, everyone will be conquered.

I serve the Charlotte with a light vanilla, or kirsch flavoured custard, or a raspberry or strawberry purée.

SERVES 4

900 g (2 lb) ripe pears
grated rind and juice of 1 lemon
100 g (4 oz) unsalted butter
3 tablespoons apricot jam
8 slices firm bread, crusts removed

FOR THE GLAZE

2 tablespoons sieved apricot jam
1 tablespoon lemon juice

TO SERVE (OPTIONAL)

icing sugar

Pre-heat the oven to 200°C/400°F/Gas 6.

Peel, core and roughly chop the pears. Put into a heavy-based pan, add the lemon rind and 25 g (1 oz) butter and cook over a low heat until the mixture is very thick. This may take between 20 and 35 minutes according to the quality of the fruit. Stir in the apricot jam and lemon juice.

Cut 2 circles from the bread, 1 to fit the bottom of a 15 cm (6 in) charlotte mould and 1 for the top. Cut the remaining bread into strips. Melt the remaining butter then brush 1 side of each piece of bread completely with the butter. Line the mould with the bread (except the circle for the top), buttered side outwards and overlapping the pieces slightly to make sure there are no gaps.

Carefully pour the pear mixture into the mould; the mould should be filled to the top. Cover with the remaining bread, buttered side up. Bake for about 35 minutes until the top is crisp and brown. Allow the Charlotte to settle for 5–10 minutes after removing from the oven then place a plate on top and, holding the mould and plate firmly together, invert them, and give a sharp shake. Carefully lift off the mould.

For the glaze, gently heat the apricot jam and

lemon juice together in a small saucepan until melted. Brush over the Charlotte. Sift over a little icing sugar, if liked, and serve warm.

VARIATIONS

- A handful of hazelnuts or raisins can be added to the pears just before stirring in the apricot jam, to provide extra texture, as well as flavour.
- To serve the Charlotte cold, unmould but do not glaze it. Leave it to cool completely then place in the fridge for about 4 hours. Brush with the glaze before serving.

AUVERGNE

Poires à la Fourme d'Ambert

PEARS WITH BLUE CHEESE

Blue cheese has a great affinity with pears, which the charming Michel Mioche at the *Hotel Radio*, Chamalières, showed to good effect in a simple, elegant dessert containing one of the great cheeses of his native Auvergne, *Fourme d'Ambert*. This has quite a rich, tangy flavour and looks like a tall, slim Stilton. The other Auvergnat blue cheese, *bleu d'Auvergne*, or even Roquefort or Stilton can be used in place of *Fourme d'Ambert*. When selecting the pears, make sure that they have a good, definite taste – Comice and Williams are best – and that they are ripe. If you suspect the pears are not quite good enough, poach them before proceeding with the recipe.

SERVES 6

3 large ripe pears
½ lemon
100 g (4 oz) caster sugar (optional)
6 slices brioche, each about 5 mm (¼ in) thick
250 g (8 oz) Fourme d'Ambert or any strong blue cheese, cut into 6 slices
2 tablespoons pink or black peppercorns (optional)
1 tablespoon icing sugar (optional)

Peel the pears and rub them with the cut side of the lemon. If necessary, poach them in a pan which is just large enough to hold them, with the sugar and sufficient water to cover, until tender but not too soft. Halve, core and cut each pear into 8 slices.

Pre-heat the grill.

If you have a heart-shaped biscuit cutter, cut hearts from the brioche slices, otherwise, cut 6 circles. Cut the brioche trimmings into small cubes. Toast the brioche shapes until golden brown on both sides.

Scatter the brioche cubes evenly in 6 small gratin or small, shallow heatproof dishes. Place 4 slices of pear on top of the cubes then cover with a slice of cheese. Scatter over the peppercorns, if using. Place under the grill until the cheese has melted. Place a brioche heart or circle on top, sift over icing sugar, if using, and serve immediately.

Gratin de Fruits au Sabayon

SABAYON AND FRUIT GRATIN

Raspberries, redcurrants or cherries, orange, grapefruit or tangerine are essential to the dish for their sharp flavour and their juices. All fruit must be fresh and ripe, but you can use frozen berries. When I have a good variety of red fruits I use orange juice. If the fruits lack flavour, I simmer a sweet wine for twenty minutes, then sprinkle the fruits with grated orange or lemon rind.

SERVES 4–6

FOR THE FRUIT

225 g (8 oz) raspberries
1 large orange
1 juicy pear
2 apricots or 1 peach or 2 plums or 1 additional pear
225 g (8 oz) strawberries, halved
juice of ½ lemon
a few mint leaves, finely chopped

FOR THE SABAYON

3 egg yolks
a pinch of salt
3 tablespoons caster sugar
8 tablespoons orange juice, Marsala, Champagne, dry white wine or sweet white wine
juice of 1 lemon
1 tablespoon demerara sugar
2 tablespoons flaked almonds (optional)

Spread the raspberries in the bottom of the individual ramekins or gratin dish. Peel and remove all the pith and membrane from the orange. Peel and core the pear. Peel and stone the other fruits. Cut the fruit into thick slices. Scatter the fruit in the dishes and sprinkle with the lemon juice and mint. Place the egg yolks, salt, sugar and orange juice or wine and lemon juice in the top of a double boiler or in a heavy bowl placed over a large pan of simmering water. Whisk the mixture vigorously for at least 10 minutes until it is thick and frothy. It should be creamy and warm to the touch and double its size. Pour over the fruit. Sprinkle with the demerara sugar, and flaked almonds, if using, and grill for about 3 minutes until golden brown on top. Serve with fresh berries or sorbet.

Beignets de Pommes au Rhum

APPLE FRITTERS WITH RAISINS AND RUM

Raisins marinated in rum turn simple apple fritters into a sumptuous dessert. I like to serve *Compote de Fruits* (see p. 281), redcurrant jelly and blackcurrant jelly, or a fruit sorbet with the fritters.

SERVES 4

40 g (1½ oz) raisins
2 tablespoons rum
5 crisp apples
vegetable oil for deep frying
caster sugar for sprinkling

FOR THE BATTER

2 eggs, separated
75 ml (3 fl oz) light-flavoured beer
75 g (3 oz) flour
a pinch of salt
½ teaspoon groundnut oil
grated rind of 1 lemon

Put the raisins in a bowl, stir in the rum and leave to stand for 2½ hours. Peel, core and thinly slice the apples, stir into the bowl and leave for about 30 minutes.

Meanwhile, make the batter. Slowly stir the egg yolks and beer into the flour and salt, then beat in the oil to make a smooth batter. Leave in a warm place for 1 hour.

Pre-heat the oven to 150°C/300°F/Gas 2. Half-fill a deep fat frying-pan with vegetable oil and heat to 190°C (375°F).

Drain the rum from the apples into the batter and stir in lightly. Whisk the egg whites until stiff but not dry then, using a large metal spoon, gently fold into the batter. Add the apples, raisins and lemon rind to the batter. Using a dessert spoon, scoop up individual slices of apple with a raisin or two, and drop into the hot oil. Fry for about 3 minutes until golden on both sides, turning them over with a large spoon half-way through. Remove with a slotted spoon and drain on kitchen paper. Keep the fritters warm on plates lined with paper towels, in the warm oven. When all are cooked, sprinkle with caster sugar and serve warm.

Tarte Tatin

WARM CARAMELIZED APPLE UPSIDE-DOWN TART

The two *demoiselles* Tatin who ran the *Hôtel Terminus* in Lamotte-Beuvron near the Loire river had both determination and imagination. One version of the legend behind their famous tart is that one day, by mistake, one of the sisters put the apples she had cooked for a tart into the dish before she had lined it with pastry. Instead of tipping the apples out and starting again, she put the pastry on top and inverted the tart after cooking. The alternative story is that similar upside-down tarts had been made for years throughout France but the sisters' version must have been especially good and because their customers included many travellers and people who were visiting the area for the excellent hunting, the fame and reputation of their tart quickly spread. There is a rumour that *Maxim's*, the temple of chic cookery in Paris, sent a spy disguised as a gardener to Lamotte-Beuvron to learn their 'secret'.

Nowadays, pears only or a mixture of pears, apples and sometimes quinces often replace the plain apples used in the original recipe.

I have prepared this splendid tart many times and like to serve it with well chilled, lightly sweetened whipped cream. Sometimes I add chopped crystallized ginger, grated lemon rind, rum, calvados, cognac or Grand Marnier to the cream.

SERVES 6

FOR THE PASTRY

150 g (5 oz) plain flour
1½ tablespoons caster sugar
1 teaspoon salt
75 g (3 oz) butter, chilled
2 tablespoons vegetable oil
3–5 tablespoons cold water

FOR THE FILLING

1.5 kg (3 lb) firm apples, such as Granny Smith or
450 g (1 lb) apples and 750 g (1½ lb ripe but firm
Comice pears
75 g (3 oz) unsalted butter
175 g (6 oz) sugar
juice of 2 lemons
finely grated rind of 1 lemon

TO SERVE

lightly sweetened whipped cream, chilled

Place the flour, sugar and salt in a large bowl. Toss in the butter then rub into the flour until the mixture resembles coarse sand. Rapidly stir in the oil and cold water and press into a ball. Place on a floured work surface, then pressing the dough with the heel of your hand, push a little at a time away from you in a quick motion. When all the ingredients are well blended, gather the dough into a ball and knead for 1 second. Sprinkle with flour, wrap in cling film and place in the fridge for about 40 minutes to become firm.

Pre-heat the oven to 220°C/425°F/Gas 7. Butter a 23 cm (9 in) loose-bottomed cake tin.

For the filling, peel, core and quarter the apples. Heat the butter in a heavy-based frying-pan, add the sugar and stir with a wooden spoon for about 3 minutes until it bubbles and becomes golden. Pack the apples into the pan, sprinkle with lemon juice and lemon rind and cook over a high heat for about 20 minutes, shaking the pan occasionally, until the fruit is a rich golden colour, and rendered most of its juices. Transfer to the cake tin.

Remove the pastry from the fridge, place it on a floured work surface and beat it with a rolling pin if it is too hard to handle. Knead it for a few minutes then form into a ball. Place a rolling pin in the centre of the ball and roll back and forth firmly. Lift the dough, turn it once and continue rolling until you have a circle about 28 cm (11 in) in diameter. Fold the dough back over the rolling pin, lift it carefully then unroll it over the cooked apples. Tuck the edge of the dough between the fruit and the side of the dish. With the tip of a knife cut a few holes in the dough so the steam can escape.

Place the tart in the oven and bake for about 30 minutes until the pastry turns brown. Place a wide plate on top of the tart, hold the edges of the tin and the plate firmly together then quickly turn the tart upside down. Give a sharp punch on the bottom of the tin with the palm of your hand covered with an oven glove, and let the tart unmould itself slowly. Serve warm with the sweetened cream.

NOTE

A *Tarte Tatin* that has been cooked but not unmoulded can be re-heated in an oven pre-heated to 190°C/375°F/Gas 5 for about 10 minutes. If it has been unmoulded, place it under a hot grill until the topping is bubbling and the fruit warm. Of course, neither will be as good as a freshly baked tart.

NORMANDY

Tarte aux Pommes Normande

RUSTIC NORMANDY APPLE TART

Monique Piat's beautiful half-timbered auberge overlooking the Valley d'Auge in the heart of Normandy is surrounded by a rich variety of apple trees. We prepared this apple tart, which seems to be the original apple tart Eve intended to offer to Adam. No custard, no compote, no glaze, just lots of apples standing straight and close together, 'like a group of little soldiers', said Monique. We used twenty apples for a tart prepared for about eight people. This tart is often called *Bourdelot* locally (although the term is also used for an apple wrapped in pastry and baked whole). You can serve the warm tart with a bowl of double cream.

SERVES 4

½ quantity Pâte Sablée (see p. 277)
900 g (2 lb) firm, tart apples
juice of 1 lemon
1 egg white
1 tablespoon brown sugar

Prepare the pastry then chill for 1 hour. Core and quarter the apples, leaving them unpeeled. Sprinkle with the lemon juice to prevent them from browning. Pre-heat the oven to 220°C/425°F/Gas 7. Butter a 23 cm (9 in) shallow cake tin.

Roll out the pastry on a lightly floured surface to a circle slightly larger than the tin and use to line the base of the prepared cake tin, leaving a little pastry up the sides. Brush the base with the egg white. Reserve a few of the apple pieces. Arrange the remaining apples in concentric circles round the tart on one of their cut sides and pressed tightly against each other so they stand firmly. Slice the reserved apples and insert the slices between the gaps so that the cooked apples will remain in a tight mass. The apples will stand about 5 cm (2 in) above the pastry shell. Sprinkle with the brown sugar. Fold the sides of the pastry in and gently fold into a neat, plump roll around the edges. Bake in the oven for 40–50 minutes until the apples are soft and golden. Serve lukewarm.

BRITTANY

Omelette aux Pommes

SOUFFLÉ OMELETTE FILLED WITH APPLES
FLAVOURED WITH RUM

Whether filled with Fruit Compotes (see p. 281), preserves or ice-cream, soufflé omelettes are easy to prepare, inexpensive and remain an unusual dessert. This light *Omelette aux Pommes* could be served with a bowl of soured cream or whipped cream.

SERVES 4

2 crisp, firm, not too-sweet apples such as Granny Smith
4 tablespoons dark rum
75 g (3 oz) butter
5 eggs, separated
70 g (2½ oz) caster sugar
icing sugar, for sprinkling

TO SERVE

soured cream or whipping cream, whipped

Peel and core the apples then cut into 5 mm (¼ in) thick slices. Place in a bowl, pour over the rum and leave for 1 hour.

Using a slotted spoon, remove the apple slices from the bowl. Melt 40 g (1½ oz) butter in a medium-sized frying-pan, add the apple slices

and cook over a low heat for 10 minutes, turning the slices over half-way through this time.

In a bowl, whisk together the egg yolks, sugar and rum marinade until frothy. In another, clean, dry bowl, whisk the egg whites until stiff but not dry. Gently fold into the egg yolk mixture.

Melt half of the remaining butter in an 18 cm (7 in) omelette pan over moderate heat. Pour in half of the egg mixture. Cook for 5 minutes. Hold a plate over the pan, invert the omelette on to the plate, then slide it back into the pan for a further 2 minutes. Slide the omelette on to a warm serving plate. Repeat with the remaining egg mixture.

Place half of the cooked apples in the centre of each omelette and fold the omelette over them. Sprinkle the tops with icing sugar and serve at once with soured cream or whipped cream.

THROUGHOUT FRANCE

Tarte aux Pommes

CLASSIC APPLE TART

Tarte aux Pommes is eaten everywhere in France and there are many different approaches to making it. Most of the tarts are open, but the apples may be diced, quartered or sliced; they may be cooked on a pastry shell sprinkled with sugar or sliced almonds, or spread on a layer of thick apple sauce. Sometimes it is made with a paper-thin, flat layer of pastry covered with apples. It is served warm and feels more like the evocation of a tart than the real thing.

The following recipe makes a classic apple tart. The pastry is partially cooked so that it is set and does not become soggy. The apple sauce is then spread over the pastry case and topped with a pretty concentric arrangement of sliced apples. If you use cooking apples,

make sure you choose a variety that remain firm when cooked. If you like to try different variations, you can use twice as much apple sauce for a mellow texture, replace the apricot jam with Seville marmalade for a sharper flavour, or add toasted almond flakes on top before you cook it. Serve at room temperature or barely warm, never chilled.

SERVES 4–6

1 quantity Pâte Brisée (see p. 276)

FOR THE FILLING

750 g (1½ lb) cooking apples such as Bramleys
4 tablespoons butter
150 g (5 oz) caster sugar
3 tablespoons apricot jam
1 tablespoon calvados or rum
grated rind (optional) and juice of 1 lemon
750 g (1½ lb) dessert apples such as Cox's

FOR THE GLAZE

4 tablespoons apricot jam, sieved
2 tablespoons caster sugar

TO SERVE

bowl of Crème Chantilly *(see p. 279) or double cream.*

Pre-heat the oven to 180°C/350°F/Gas 4. Butter a 25 cm (10 in) flan ring.

Roll out the prepared pastry on a lightly floured surface and use to line the flan ring. Prick the base with a fork. Bake in the oven for about 5 minutes then leave to cool.

Peel and core the cooking apples and chop them coarsely. Place them in a pan with 1 tablespoon of the butter and simmer over a low heat for about 15 minutes, stirring occasionally, until soft. Add 75g (3 oz) of the sugar, the apricot jam, calvados or rum and 2 tablespoons of the butter and stir until well blended. Taste and add a little of the lemon juice or a little more jam or calvados, if necessary, and the lemon rind, if using.

Peel and core the dessert apples and slice them thinly. Toss with the lemon juice then sprinkle with half the remaining sugar.

To make the glaze, warm the sieved apricot jam with the sugar over a low heat for about 3 minutes, stirring gently until melted. Remove from the heat.

Spread a little of the warm glaze on the base of the cold shell. Cover the remainder and keep it warm for later use. Spoon the apple purée into the pastry shell and arrange the raw apples in concentric circles on the top, starting in the centre and overlapping the slices as you go. Sprinkle with the remaining sugar and dot with the remaining butter.

Bake in the oven for 20 minutes. Lower the oven temperature to 160°C/325°F/Gas 3 and bake for another 20 minutes until the apples are soft and lightly browned. Place on a rack to cool and spoon the reserved warm glaze over the top. Serve with the Chantilly or double cream.

SOUTH-WEST

Croustade

FILO PASTRY WITH APPLE FILLING FLAVOURED
WITH ARMAGNAC

This famous dessert from south-western France is filled with apples or prunes flavoured with armagnac. It is prepared in many ways and has many names – *Croustade, Pastis, Tourtière* – and was clearly inspired by the Arab tradition still evident in the region.

At her lovely auberge in St Martin d'Armagnac, I helped Pierrette Sarran make this exquisite *Croustade* for us and I found the process memorable but quite awesome as she whispered, 'Mireille, the dough must be as thin as a bride's veil'. Pierrette kneaded 900 g (2 lb)

of flour, 3 eggs, 150 ml (5 fl oz) of water and a pinch of salt to a dough which she chilled overnight. Then she expertly stretched the dough over a huge table swathed in a cotton cloth until it was paper thin.

As Pierrette also told me that it takes at least thirty or so attempts to make a perfect dough, I strongly recommend that you use frozen filo pastry, although I would never dare to mention this to Pierrette; it could be the end of a friend-ship.

The pastry is always cut with sharp scissors rather than a knife. Prunes marinated in arma-gnac (see p. 330) or poached quinces can be added to the sliced apples, if you wish.

SERVES 8

FOR THE FILLING

1 large apple, peeled and thinly sliced
3 tablespoons armagnac

FOR THE PASTRY

275 g (10 oz) filo pastry, thawed
100 g (4 oz) butter
50 g (2 oz) caster sugar

Marinate the apple in the armagnac for a few hours. Alternatively, you can sprinkle the apple with armagnac as you assemble the pastry.

Pre-heat the oven to 200°C/400°F/Gas 6. Butter a baking sheet.

Unroll the pastry and keep the sheets covered with a damp tea towel to prevent it from drying out while you are working with the rest of the pastry. Melt the butter and add the sugar. Lay one sheet of pastry on the baking sheet and brush generously with the butter and sugar mixture. Lay a second sheet on top, brush with butter and sugar then lay a third sheet on top and brush again. Arrange the apple slices in a thin layer over the pastry, avoiding the corners. Lay another sheet of pastry on top at an angle so that it creates a star shape. Brush it with butter and sugar, then lay two more sheets directly on top, brushing each time. Don't press the pastry as the sheets will stick together as they bake. Bake in the oven for about 10 minutes until crisp and golden brown. Serve lukewarm cut into wedges with sharp scissors.

NOTE

Sometimes, orange blossom water is added to the armagnac.

THROUGHOUT FRANCE

Tarte au Citron et à l'Orange

LEMON, ORANGE AND ALMOND TART

Topped with pieces of fruit, *Tarte au Citron* has a refreshing texture and flavour, and the combination of crisp pastry shell and light, sharp custard topped by a layer of orange and lemon pieces covered with marmalade and toasted almonds is irresistible.

SERVES 8

FOR THE PASTRY
175 g (6 oz) plain flour
90 g (3½ oz) butter
2 egg yolks
a pinch of salt
75 g (3 oz) icing sugar
2 tablespoons very cold water

FOR THE FILLING
3 lemons
2 oranges
75 g (3 oz) caster sugar
70 g (2½ oz) unsalted butter
2 eggs

4 tablespoons sieved orange marmalade
25 g (1 oz) flaked almonds
icing sugar, for dusting

Sift the flour on to the work surface and form a well in the centre. Place the butter, egg yolks, salt, sugar and water in the well and gradually work in the flour using the fingertips to make a soft dough; add a little flour if it is too sticky or add a little water if it is too dry. Form the dough into a ball. Push the dough away from you with the heel of one hand. Gather it up again using a metal palette knife or pastry scraper and repeat for 1–2 minutes. Form into a ball, cover with cling film and chill for 45 minutes.

Pre-heat the oven to 200°C/400°C/Gas 6. Butter a 23 cm (9 in) loose-bottomed flan tin.

Using a rolling pin, flatten the dough, then roll it out to a circle about 27 cm (11 in) in diameter. Fold the dough back over the rolling pin and carefully lift it over the flan tin. Press the dough into the shape of the tin, allowing the excess to hang over the rim. Pass the rolling pin across the top of the rim to cut off the dough neatly. With the thumb of one hand, push the edge of the pastry inwards gently, then, with a finger of the other hand, pinch the pastry pushed up initially to crimp it. Continue around the edge of the pastry shell. Prick the bottom of the pastry shell with a fork. Place in the fridge for 15–30 minutes.

Lower the oven temperature to 190°C/375°F/Gas 5. Line the pastry shell with greaseproof paper, fill with baking beans and place the flan tin on a baking sheet. Bake for 15 minutes until set and lightly browned. Remove the baking beans and greaseproof paper and bake the pastry for a further 5 minutes. Leave to cool.

Grate the rind from 1 of the lemons and ½ an orange. Squeeze the juice from 2 lemons. Beat together the sugar, butter and orange and

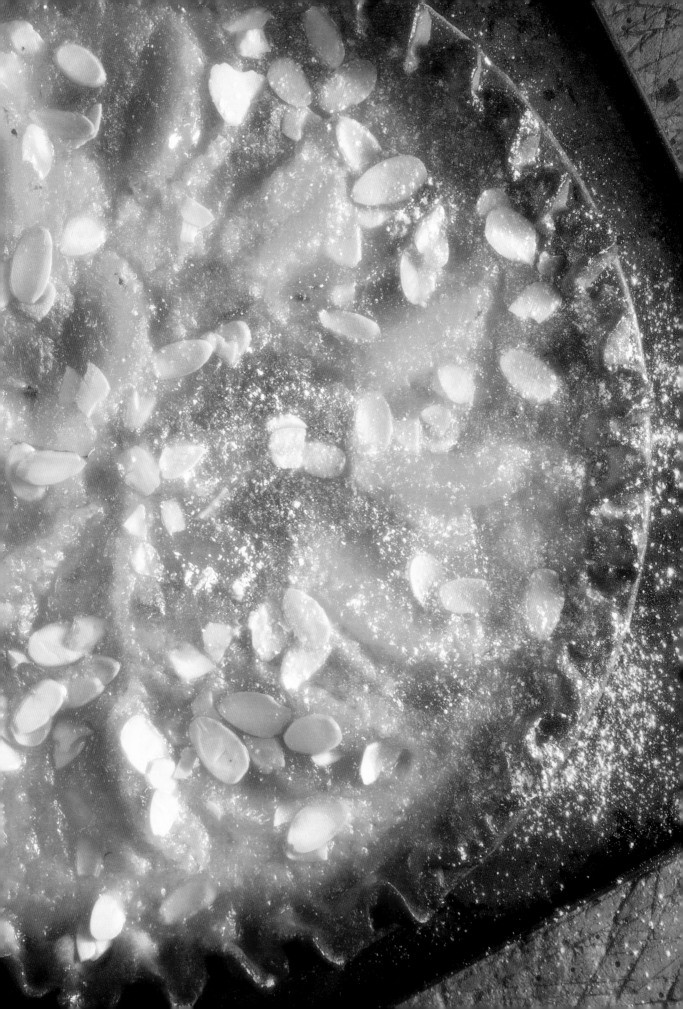

lemon rinds until light and fluffy. Gradually beat in the eggs. Slowly stir in the lemon juice.

Peel both oranges and the remaining lemon as you would in order to eat them, then using a sharp knife carefully scrape off the pith. Holding the fruit over a bowl to catch any drips, cut down between the membrane and the fruit to remove the segments. Add any juice collected in the bowl to the butter mixture then spread in the pastry case. Place the lemon and orange segments on top, pressing them down lightly.

Warm the marmalade in a small saucepan over a low heat. Carefully brush over the orange and lemon segments then sprinkle with the almonds. Bake in the oven for 15 minutes. Leave to cool for 10 minutes then transfer to a wire rack to cool completely. Dust with icing sugar just before serving the tart.

ALSACE

Tarte aux Quetsches
PLUM TART

Purple *quetsches* are Alsace's favourite cooking plum. They can be bought raw, cooked, dried and lately frozen, and can be used in a variety of desserts, including many different versions of *Tarte aux Quetsches*. This is my favourite recipe because it is light and allows the sharp, clear flavour of the fruit to stand out better.

Be sure to place the halved plums cut side up so the juices do not make the pastry soggy.

SERVES 6

FOR THE PATE SUCREE
175 g (6 oz) plain flour
a pinch of salt
90 g (3½) unsalted butter, softened and diced
50 g (2 oz) caster sugar
2 large egg yolks

FOR THE FILLING
120 ml (4 fl oz) milk
120 ml (4 fl oz) double cream
½ vanilla pod
3 eggs
about 75 g (3 oz) caster sugar, depending on the sharpness of the plums
½ teaspoon plain flour
550 g (1¼ lb) quetsches, or other sharp but well-flavoured plums, halved and stoned
caster or icing sugar for sprinkling

To make the pastry, butter a 23 cm (9 in) fluted flan tin, about 2.5 cm (1 in) high, and preferably loose-bottomed.

Sift the flour and salt on to the work surface and form a well in the centre. Put the butter, sugar and egg yolks into the well, then, using your fingertips, lightly 'peck' these ingredients together until they resemble coarse scrambled eggs. Still using the fingers, gradually draw in the flour until large crumbs are formed. Using a pastry scraper or metal palette knife, quickly gather the crumbs to form a ball and knead gently by pushing the dough away from you with the heel of one hand, then gathering up the dough with the pastry scraper or palette knife and repeating for a minute or so until the dough peels easily away from the work surface. Form into a ball, wrap in cling film and place in the fridge for 30 minutes.

On a lightly floured surface and using a lightly floured rolling pin, roll out the pastry to a circle about 23 cm (9 in) diameter. Fold the pastry backwards over the rolling pin, then lift it and lay it centrally over the flan tin. Lift the edge of the pastry and gently ease it into the shape of the tin, making sure it fits well into the flutes and the angle between the base and the sides. Roll the pin firmly over the top to remove surplus pastry, then, with your finger, press the dough evenly up the sides. Use your finger and thumb to neatly crimp the edge.

Prick the base lightly with a fork and place the pastry case in the fridge for at least 15 minutes until firm.

Pre-heat the oven to 220°C/425°F/Gas 7. Lay a sheet of greaseproof paper in the base of the pastry case and cover with baking beans. Bake in the oven for about 12 minutes, then carefully lift away the greaseproof paper and baking beans. Return the pastry to the oven and bake for a further 3–4 minutes. Remove from the oven. Lower the oven temperature to 200°C/400°F/Gas 6.

For the filling, pour the milk and cream into a pan, add the vanilla pod and bring to the boil.

Whisk the eggs and sugar together until light and frothy, then quickly whisk in the flour. Remove the vanilla pod from the saucepan. Slowly pour the boiling liquids on to the egg mixture, whisking constantly, to make a smooth custard. Leave to cool, stirring occasionally to prevent a skin forming.

Arrange the plums, cut-side uppermost, in the base of the pastry case then pour the custard around them. Place in the oven and bake for about 20–25 minutes until lightly set in the centre and golden brown.

Transfer the flan tin to a cooling rack and leave until the tart is lukewarm. Remove the outer ring of the tin if a loose-bottomed tin has been used, sprinkle the filling with caster or icing sugar and serve the tart, preferably while it is still warm.

THROUGHOUT FRANCE

Barquettes de Fruits

FRUIT TARTS

Nothing is more inspiring than a platter of glittering fruit tartlets. The oval moulds are called *barquettes* because they look like little boats. The round *moules à flan* with a loose base are my favourite as they unmould easily.

The tartlets can be made with *Pâte Brisée* or *Pâte Sablée*, which I prefer even though it is a little more fragile. The *Crème Patissière* can be omitted and the pastry brushed with glaze or sprinkled with sugar and biscuit crumbs with fruits on top. For strawberries, grapes, raspberries, cherries, pineapple, oranges or lemons, tart shells should be totally cooked to avoid soggy crusts. For poached fruits such as pears, apricots, plums, peaches or for custard, they should be partially cooked (see p. 276).

Frozen or tinned fruits must be properly drained. The fruits can be whole, halved or sliced and arranged in slightly overlapping circles. Well-drained cooked fruit should be arranged cut side down, but fresh fruit cut side up so the base doesn't become soggy.

Apricot glaze is used for apricots, pears and peaches while redcurrant glaze is traditionally reserved for red berries. I often use them interchangeably. Allow one or two tartlets per person.

SERVES 4–6

1 quantity Pâte Sablée *(see p. 277) or* Pâte Brisée
(see p. 276)

150 ml (5 fl oz) Crème Patissière *(see p. 278)*
*flavoured with 2 tablespoons brandy, orange blossom
water or fruit liqueur*

300 ml (10 fl oz) redcurrant jelly or apricot jam

1 tablespoon sugar

1 tablespoon kirsch (optional)

750 g (1½ lb) strawberries, hulled and halved

Prepare the pastry and let it cool. Prepare the pastry cream, stir in your chosen flavouring and let it cool.

Butter the individual tartlet moulds and arrange them on a baking sheet.

Roll out the pastry on a lightly floured surface or between 2 sheets of baking parchment to about 5 mm (¼ in) thick. Cut round or oval pieces 2.5 mm (1 in) larger than the moulds, remove and discard the paper, if using. Lift the pieces on your rolling pin and unroll over the moulds. Fit the pastry on the bottom and edges of the moulds, pushing gently with the fingertips, then trim off any excess pastry around the edges.

Make a pretty design along the edge, pushing the blunt side of a knife or the back of a spoon against the dough. Chill the baking sheet and filled moulds for 1–2 hours so that the edges will not collapse as they cook.

Pre-heat the oven to 180°C/350°F/Gas 4.

Prick the bottom of the pastry with a fork then bake the shells in the oven for about 10 minutes. Prick the bases again and push the dough back up with the back of a spoon if it has collapsed. Bake for a further 10–15 minutes until the shells have shrunk a little from the moulds and are lightly browned. Leave to cool then carefully remove from the moulds using a spatula. (Remember that some fruits only need the shells to be partially cooked, see p. 297).

To prepare the glaze, pour the jelly or jam into a saucepan, add the sugar and stir over a low heat until the mixture begins to froth and turn sticky and smooth. Stir in the kirsch, if using. Paint a little glaze on the inside of the pastry shells and reserve the rest.

Just before the meal, spread about 1 cm (½ in) of *Crème Patissière* in the pastry shells and arrange the strawberries, stem down with the largest fruit in the centre and the smallest ones at the edges. Warm the reserved glaze to lukewarm and spoon it delicately over the fruit. Serve at once or chill for an hour or so. Sprinkle with a little icing sugar before serving, if liked, or let them shine in their glaze.

NOTE

If you are using pears, apricots, cherries or plums, poach them in a sweet syrup for about 5 minutes then leave them to cool in the liquid. Drain them carefully. Use partially-cooked pastry shells, glazed and filled with *Crème Patissière*. Top with the sliced fruit and brush with the remaining glaze. Bake for a further 5 minutes.

Crêpes Normandes

THIN CREPES FILLED WITH APPLES AND

FLAVOURED WITH CALVADOS

Crêpes offer the simplest and cheapest of desserts – but surely one of the most delicious. Every region of France prepares crêpes in its own individual way. The batter may be flavoured with aniseed, lemon, rum, armagnac, or orange blossom water, as in Roussillon; the crêpes may be spread with local salted butter, as in Brittany, or filled with a variety of jams, honeys, walnuts or whipped cream. But whether they are served at the end of a meal or as a mid-afternoon snack, they seem to be the ultimate crowd-pleaser for all ages.

For me, *Crêpes Normandes* served with a sharp local cider or a sweet dessert wine are the top of my list of favourites. They can be prepared in advance and – a wonderful point for a hostess – heated a few minutes before serving.

SERVES 4–6

FOR THE CREPES

100 g (4 oz) plain flour

2 eggs

¼ teaspoon salt

120 ml (4 fl oz) milk or beer

120 ml (4 fl oz) water

2 tablespoons butter, melted, or 1 tablespoon oil and 1 tablespoon butter, or a piece of pork fat to cook the crêpes

FOR THE FILLING

750 g (1½ lb) crisp, sharp apples such as Granny Smith

50 g (2 oz) soft brown sugar

1 tablespoon butter

1 tablespoon lemon juice

grated rind of 1 lemon

TO DECORATE

4 tablespoons redcurrant jelly

4 tablespoons water

juice of 1 lemon

1 tablespoon calvados

Pour the flour into a bowl and make a well in the centre. Beat the eggs lightly then add the salt. Blend the eggs into the flour then whisk in the milk or beer and water and the melted butter or oil. The mixture does not have to be perfectly smooth. Cover and leave to rest for at least 1 hour.

Peel, core, and slice the apples and place in a pan with the sugar, butter, lemon juice and lemon rind. Cover and simmer over a low heat for about 20 minutes until soft, stirring occasionally.

When you are ready to cook the crêpes, stir the batter well; it should be smooth like custard. For quicker results, you can use two small pancake pans about 13 cm (5 in) in diameter. Grease the pans before cooking each crêpe by adding a little piece of butter, or by rubbing the pan with a piece of muslin dipped in oil and wrapped round a fork, or with a piece of pork fat on a fork. Very little fat is needed after you have cooked the first few crêpes.

Heat and grease the pan. Pour in 2 or 3 tablespoons of batter, turning the pan so that the base is evenly coated in batter. After 1 minute, the edges of the crêpe will begin to brown and detach from the pan. Shake the pan gently to detach the crêpe, then toss it or turn it with a spatula and cook the other side for 1 minute. Stack the cooked crêpes on top of each other on a platter as you cook them.

Butter a shallow baking dish.

When all the crêpes are cooked, place a tablespoon of cooked apple in the centre of each crêpe and roll it like a fat cigar. Place the crêpes side by side in the baking dish in a single layer. Dot with a little butter and cover with kitchen foil. You can prepare to this point in advance and chill.

Pre-heat the oven to 180°C/350°F/Gas 4 about 30 minutes before serving.

Re-heat the crêpes in the oven for 20 minutes.

Mix the redcurrant jelly, water and lemon juice in a small pan and stir over a medium heat for a few minutes until blended. Remove the foil from the crêpes and pour half the mixture over them. Return to the oven for a further 5 minutes. Remove from the oven, sprinkle with the calvados and pour over the remaining redcurrant sauce. Serve directly from the baking dish with a spatula and a large spoon.

NOTE

Some regions have interesting versions such as crêpes stuffed with sliced, poached pears or quince which are flavoured then flambéed with pear liqueur or pear brandy.

PARIS AND THROUGHOUT FRANCE

Crêpes Suzette

ORANGE BUTTER CREPES FLAMBEED IN BRANDY

Long live the Suzette who inspired such a glorious dish. Although the finished dessert is theatrical, it follows a simple process; crêpes are made in advance, flavoured with orange butter, sprinkled with warm liqueur, ignited and served. It is better if the crêpes and the orange butter are prepared, covered and chilled overnight. This makes the crêpes easier to handle and the orange butter more piquant. You must make sure the sauce in the chafing dish is very hot when you add the crêpes and that they are thoroughly heated before serving them.

This is a very rich and heady dish not intended for children or timid souls. I allow two or three crêpes per person and I never prepare more than ten or twelve crêpes at a time as the dish cannot be made properly and with the necessary dramatic quality for a larger group.

SERVES 4

FOR THE CREPES

100 g (4 oz) plain flour
¼ teaspoon salt
2 eggs
300 ml (10 fl oz) milk, beer or water
1 tablespoon butter or oil
butter or oil to cook the crêpes

FOR THE ORANGE BUTTER

grated rind of 1 lemon
grated rind of 1 orange
3 tablespoons icing sugar, sieved
2 tablespoons orange juice
100 g (4 oz) butter, softened
2 tablespoons Grand Marnier, Cointreau or Curaçao

FOR THE SAUCE

3 tablespoons butter
3 tablespoons caster sugar
juice of 1 orange
2 tablespoons cognac
2 tablespoons Grand Marnier or Cointreau

To make the batter, mix together the flour, salt, eggs, milk, beer or water and butter or oil and stir for a few minutes until thoroughly blended. Cover and leave to stand for at least 1 hour so the batter has the consistency of a light custard.

To make the orange butter, place the lemon and orange rinds in a bowl and sprinkle with the sugar and orange juice. Blend in the butter and liqueur with a fork to make a soft paste. Cover and chill.

Heat and grease a pancake pan. Pour in 2 or 3 tablespoons of batter, turning the pan so that the base is evenly coated in batter. After 1 minute, the edges of the crêpe will begin to brown and detach from the pan. Shake the pan gently to detach the crêpe, then toss it or turn it with a spatula and cook the other side for 1 minute. Stack the cooked crêpes on top of each other on a platter as you cook them, putting greaseproof paper between each one. Cover and chill overnight.

Remove the crêpes and orange butter from the fridge an hour before serving. Spread each crêpe with a small teaspoon of orange butter. Roll them or fold them in quarters into triangles.

Depending on the size of your pan, you may need to cook the crêpes in 2 batches, so use a proportion of the ingredients, if necessary. Heat the butter for the sauce in a large chafing dish or frying-pan, sprinkle with the sugar and let it brown slightly. When the bottom is coated with a light caramelized sauce, add the orange juice and stir until hot. Start heating the rolled or folded crêpes, adding them two or three at a time, turning them in the sauce with a spatula and a pair of tongs and pushing them to the outside of the dish when they are ready. Sprinkle with the cognac and Grand Marnier or Cointreau. Ignite, if you wish, basting the pancakes until the flame dies, although you do not have to go through this dramatic gesture. Holding each folded crêpe with two spoons or spatulas, turn it delicately in the warm sauce. Serve the crêpes on warm dessert plates and spoon a little hot sauce over them.

NOTE

Originally *Crêpes Suzettes* were made with tangerines instead of oranges; it's worth trying.

PERIGORD

Tarte aux Noix
WALNUT TART

In Périgord, walnuts are used to prepare aperitif wine, salads, sauces, custards, cakes, and the local fragrant walnut oil. *Tarte aux Noix* is more of a confection than a dessert, and I serve it in small slices with a bowl of apple compote or a pear sorbet.

Walnuts should be left for a few minutes in a hot oven to be at their best before cooking them. The tart is better prepared in advance, wrapped in foil and kept for a week.

SERVES 8–10
275 g (10 oz) plain flour
1 teaspoon salt
2 tablespoons caster sugar
125 g (4½ oz) unsalted butter, diced
7–9 tablespoons water
1 egg

FOR THE FILLING
150 ml (5 fl oz) single cream
135 ml (4½ fl oz) water
300 g (11 oz) caster sugar
200 g (7 oz) walnuts, halved
4 tablespoons unsalted butter
2 tablespoons sugar

Place the flour, salt and sugar on a work surface, add the butter and mix lightly between thumb and fingertips to form light flakes. Add a little water at a time until the dough binds together. Add the egg, knead lightly then shape into a ball, wrap in a plastic bag and chill overnight if possible.

Grease a 23 cm (9 in) loose-bottomed flan tin. Roll out the pastry between 2 sheets of greaseproof paper and use to line the prepared tin. Chill for 1–2 hours.

Pre-heat the oven to 220°C/425°F/Gas 7. Heat the cream. Pour the water and sugar into a heavy-based pan and cook on a high heat for about 10 minutes, shaking the pan so that the syrup heats evenly. The bubbles will turn a deep brown and the mixture will become syrupy. Remove from the heat and leave to cool for 2 minutes. Carefully pour in the hot cream, whisking vigorously. It will become frothy. Add the walnuts and butter and return to a very low heat for 1–2 minutes, stirring continuously. Pour into the chilled pastry case and bake in the oven for 25 minutes. sprinkle the sugar on top then lower the oven temperature to 160°C/325°F/Gas 3 and bake for a further 15 minutes, checking to make sure that the top does not become too brown. Place on a wire rack to cool.

THROUGHOUT FRANCE

Choux à la Crème

CHOUX BUNS WITH PASTRY CREAM FILLING

Lovers call each other *mon petit chou*, mothers call their babies *mon chou à la crème*. Choux pastry is probably France's most beloved pastry. It may be served plain, without a filling or topping, when it will be *chouquette* in Paris and *bijoux* (jewels) in Provence, or it may be filled with pastry cream (*Crème Patissière*), whipped cream, or a mixture of the two, as in this recipe, or with ice-cream.

Small balls of choux pastry covered with hot chocolate sauce are called *profiteroles*; if the pastry is shaped like tiny cabbages it is a *chou*; if the pastry is finger-shaped it becomes an *éclair*; if cooked in a large ring a *Gâteau Paris Brest*; little choux puffs piled in conical shape on a sweet pastry base and stuck together with caramel, make a spectacular *Croquembouche*.

Unfilled choux pastry shapes can be kept in an air-tight container in a cool place or the fridge, frozen for about 1 month. Defrost in the refrigerator for 24 hours. If necessary, crisp-up the choux pastry in the oven before serving. Always allow to cool before filling. Choux pastry shapes filled with ice-cream or cream must be served at once, but if pastry cream has been used they can be kept for a little while.

MAKES 30–35 SMALL BUNS

FOR THE CHOUX PASTRY
250 ml (8 fl oz) mixed milk and water
1 teaspoon sugar
a pinch of salt
75 g (3 oz) unsalted butter, diced
150 g (5 oz) plain flour
4 eggs, beaten
1 egg, beaten with 1 teaspoon water, to glaze

FOR THE PASTRY CREAM FILLING (CREME PATISSIERE)
6 egg yolks
100 g (4 oz) caster sugar
40 g (1½ oz) plain flour
a pinch of salt
450 ml (15 fl oz) milk
1–2 tablespoons brandy, kirsch, Grand Marnier, rum or orange flower water
15 g (½ oz) unsalted butter
50 ml (2 fl oz) double or whipping cream, whipped (optional)

TO FINISH
sifted icing sugar

Pre-heat the oven to 200°C/400°F/Gas 6. Butter 2 baking sheets.

To make the choux pastry, pour the milk, water, sugar, salt and butter into a saucepan. Heat gently until the butter melts then bring quickly to the boil. Remove from the heat and quickly add all the flour in one go. Beat very vigorously with a wooden spoon for 1 minute then return the pan to a moderate heat and stir until the dough comes away from the sides of the pan. Leave to cool slightly then beat in the eggs a little at a time, making sure all the egg has been incorporated before adding any more. Continue adding egg until the mixture is thick, smooth and glossy. Place teaspoonfuls of the mixture, spaced well apart, on the baking sheets, and brush the tops with the egg glaze.

Bake in the oven for about 10 minutes, then increase the oven temperature to 220°C/425°F/Gas 7 and bake for a further 15–20 minutes until well-risen, golden and crisp. Pierce a small hole in the bottom of each bun to allow the steam to escape then return to the oven with the heat switched OFF and the door propped open with a wooden spoon, for a few minutes so the pastry dries inside. Transfer to a wire rack to cool.

To make the filling, whisk the egg yolks and sugar together until thick and pale yellow, then stir in the flour and salt. Bring the milk to the boil in a heavy-based pan previously rinsed with cold water, then slowly pour into the egg yolk mixture, stirring constantly. Pour back into the pan and cook over a low heat, stirring constantly, until the mixture thickens. Continue to cook, still stirring, for 2 minutes but do not allow to boil. Remove from the heat and stir in the brandy, kirsch, Grand Marnier, rum or orange flower water, and the butter. Leave to cool, stirring occasionally to prevent a skin forming. If you want to make the filling a little lighter, gently fold in the whipped cream if using, when the pastry cream is cold.

Increase the size of the hole in the bottom of each choux bun with the tip of a sharp knife then either pipe, or use a small spoon to fill them with the pastry cream. Sprinkle the tops with icing sugar.

THROUGHOUT FRANCE

Oeufs à la Neige
SNOW EGGS OR FLOATING ISLANDS

The most festive of desserts, a pile of snowball meringues floating on pale-yellow custard, *Oeufs à la Neige* spells happiness at first sight.

SERVES 4

FOR THE MERINGUES
4 egg whites
225 g (8 oz) caster sugar

FOR THE CUSTARD
600 ml (1 pint) milk
6 egg yolks
50 g (2 oz) caster sugar
2–3 tablespoons Grand Marnier, rum or orange flower water

TO SERVE
cocoa or finely chopped candied orange peel or grated plain chocolate or caramel – 75g (3 oz) caster sugar and 2 tablespoons water and a few drops lemon juice

To make the 'snowball' meringues, bring a wide frying-pan or pan of salted water to the boil. Meanwhile, in a clean, dry bowl whisk the egg whites until stiff but not dry. Gradually whisk in the sugar until stiff and shiny. Lower the heat beneath the pan so the water is barely simmering. Slide the egg whites, spoonful by spoonful on to the hot water but do not crowd them, and poach for 2–3 minutes depending on size, turning the balls over half-way through. Using a skimmer or slotted spoon, remove them from the water and place in a wide tray tilted gently, so they drain. You will have to cook the meringues in several batches.

Then on with the custard. Rinse a pan with cold water, leaving a few drops of water in the bottom to avoid scorching. Pour in the milk and bring quickly to the boil. Meanwhile, whisk the egg yolks and sugar until thick and pale yellow. Stir in a few spoonfuls of hot milk. Lower the heat beneath the pan then, using a wooden spoon, stir the egg yolk mixture into the pan. Continue to stir over a low heat until the custard is thick enough to leave a fine coating on the spoon; do not allow it to boil at any time. Remove the pan from the heat and leave the custard to cool, stirring occasionally. Add the Grand Marnier, rum or orange flower water.

When you are almost ready to serve, pile the meringues on each other. If you are in a hurry, sprinkle a little cocoa on top. If you have a minute, chop some candied peel or grate some plain chocolate and sprinkle over the meringues. If you have another 5 minutes, make a caramel by gently heating the sugar and water in a small heavy-based pan for 2–3 minutes. Add the lemon juice and continue to heat until golden. Immediately remove from the heat and trickle in a criss-cross pattern over the meringues and the chocolate shavings; it will harden at once. Slide the pile of meringues into the centre of a wide shallow dish and pour the custard around, or serve the meringues and custard in separate bowls. This dish may be kept in the fridge for a day, but the caramel will melt.

VARIATION

The meringues may be served with a raspberry coulis, made by sieving 450 g (1 lb) fresh or frozen raspberries and sweetening to taste.

THROUGHOUT FRANCE

Marquise au Chocolat
A LIGHT, MOIST CHOCOLATE DESSERT

This sumptuous dessert – which is, in fact, a glorified chocolate mousse, is easy to prepare and requires no baking. It is always served sliced on individual plates which have been coated with Chantilly cream, apricot purée or a custard flavoured with coffee, lemon, bitter chocolate, pistachio, aniseed or orange. Restaurants find it so very fashionable that in France it hardly seems worth serving it at home, although the range of colours and flavours in this recipe make it worthwhile. It must always be chilled for twenty-four hours before serving. The dark chocolate should be as bitter as possible; Sainsbury's or Waitrose Continental are good brands as they have 78 and 72 per cent cacao respectively.

SERVES 4–6

FOR THE MOUSSE
225 g (8 oz) plain unsweetened chocolate
1–2 tablespoons strong black coffee
175 g (6 oz) butter, cut into pieces
3 eggs, separated
100 g (4 oz) icing sugar
a pinch of salt
grated rind of 1 orange or 1 piece thinly slivered candied orange rind

TO DECORATE
1 quantity Crème Anglaise *(see p. 278) flavoured with 2 tablespoons Grand Marnier and grated rind of 1 orange*
2 tablespoons thinly slivered candied orange rind (optional)

Line a 450 g (1 lb) loaf tin with cling film.
Break the chocolate into small pieces. Place the chocolate and coffee in the top of a double

boiler or in a bowl over a pan of gently simmering water. Leave to melt, stirring occasionally. Remove from the heat. Add the butter, egg yolks, icing sugar, salt and orange rind then return to the heat until the butter has melted. Leave to cool slightly. Taste to check and correct the flavour, if necessary.

Beat the egg whites until they hold soft peaks. Delicately fold half of them into the chocolate mixture, then fold in the remainder until the mixture is smooth. Pour the mixture into the prepared tin, cover with kitchen foil and chill for at least 24 hours.

Prepare the *Crème Anglaise* and stir in the liqueur and grated orange rind. Leave to cool then chill.

Half an hour before serving, remove the *Marquise* and custard from the fridge. Dip the loaf tin into a bowl of hot water for a second, cover the top with a flat plate and unmould the mousse with one decisive movement.

Use a long, warm knife to slice the *marquise* into 1 cm (½ in) slices and arrange them in the centre of dessert plates. Spoon a little *Crème Anglaise* around the *Marquise* and garnish with the slivers of candied orange rind. Alternatively, unmould the *Marquise* whole on to a serving dish and surround with the *Crème Anglaise*.

NOTE

For a more chocolatey flavour, I often add 2 tablespoons of cocoa powder to the melted chocolate.

THROUGHOUT FRANCE

Mousse au Chocolat

CHOCOLATE MOUSSE FLAVOURED WITH COFFEE
AND ORANGE

Chocolate mousse is a must in any cook's repertoire, as it is easy to make and always popular with everyone. Serve with thin biscuits, sliced oranges and sliced grapefruit sprinkled with honey, vanilla-flavoured custard, or whipped cream mixed with a little soured cream.

SERVES 6–8

175 g (6oz) plain chocolate, chopped
15 g (½ oz) unsalted butter
2 tablespoons instant coffee powder
4 eggs, separated
40 g (1½ oz) caster sugar
2–3 teaspoons grated orange rind
1 tablespoon finely chopped candied
orange peel (optional)
2 tablespoons Grand Marnier or Cointreau
3 tablespoons whipping cream, chilled
1 egg white

TO DECORATE

grated plain chocolate or cocoa powder

Place the chocolate, butter and coffee powder in a bowl, place over a pan of hot, not boiling, water and leave until the chocolate has melted, stirring occasionally. Remove the bowl from the pan and leave to cool.

Meanwhile, whisk the egg yolks with 1 tablespoon sugar until thick and pale yellow. Using a tablespoon, stir in the chocolate and coffee mixture, the orange rind and peel, if using, and the Grand Marnier or Cointreau.

Lightly whip the cream and fold into the chocolate mixture. Whisk all the egg whites until stiff but not dry, then gradually whisk in the remaining sugar. Using a large metal spoon, gently fold into the chocolate mixture in 3 or 4 batches. Pour into a large pretty serving bowl or individual dishes. Cover and place in the fridge for 2–3 hours.

Decorate the top with grated plain chocolate or sieved cocoa powder, before serving.

VARIATION

The mousse can also be served frozen. Pour the prepared mixture into a lightly oiled charlotte mould, or similar freezer-proof mould, tin or dish. Cover with foil and freeze for 24 hours. To unmould, dip the bottom of the mould, tin or dish into a bowl of hot water for a few seconds, place a large serving plate over the mould, tin or dish and, holding tightly to the side of the mould and the edge of the plate, turn them over in a decisive movement and give a sharp shake. Sprinkle the grated chocolate or cocoa powder over the top and serve.

ALSACE

Mousse au Kirsch
KIRSCH MOUSSE

René de Miscault produces a wide variety of *eaux-de-vie*, some made from wild berries of the Vosges mountains, others from more exotic ingredients, such as fresh ginger. But France's most popular *eau-de-vie* is cherry flavoured kirsch, which Madame de Miscault uses in this very rich but easy dessert.

SERVES 4
5 egg yolks
150 g (5oz) caster sugar
5–6 tablespoons kirsch
250 ml (8fl oz) crème fraîche or whipping cream

FOR THE GARNISH (OPTIONAL)
cherries marinated in kirsch

Using a wooden spatula, beat the egg yolks with the sugar in a bowl placed over a pan of hot, but not boiling, water for about 10 minutes until thick and light.

Remove the bowl from the heat, stir in the kirsch and continue to beat until the mixture is cold.

In a separate bowl, beat the crème fraîche or cream until soft peaks form, then, using a large metal spoon, gently fold into the egg yolk mixture. Pour into individual glasses and chill for a few hours. Serve garnished with cherries marinated in kirsch, if liked.

THROUGHOUT FRANCE

Bavarois à l'Orange

MOULDED CREAM DESSERT FLAVOURED WITH
ORANGE LIQUEUR

A royal dessert served on grand occasions, this is nevertheless quite easy to prepare at home. In fact, it is a mixture of *Crème Anglaise*, *Crème Chantilly* and gelatine blended together and chilled until firm so that it can be unmoulded. In cold weather, you may need less gelatine than in summer. A ring mould with a hole in the centre – whether it is plain or fluted – is necessary to ensure an even cooling of the mixture and for a homogeneous texture.

A Bavarois can be flavoured with orange, hazelnuts, almonds or fresh fruit purée, and these will also add texture to the custard. It is served with *Crème Chantilly* (see p. 279), *Crème Anglaise* (see p. 278), *coulis de fruits*, fruit purée, or fresh fruit.

SERVES 6
almond or groundnut oil for greasing
600 ml (1 pint) milk
5 egg yolks
100 g (4 oz) caster sugar
a pinch of salt
1 teaspoon cornflour
10 g (¼ oz) gelatine
100 ml (3½ fl oz) orange juice
3 tablespoons orange liqueur
2 tablespoons grated orange rind
600 ml (1 pint) whipping cream, chilled

TO SERVE
3 oranges, thinly sliced
1 candied orange rind, cut into thin slivers
300 ml (10 fl oz) double or whipping cream,
whipped, or fruit purée

Grease a 25 cm (10 in), 5 cm (2 in) deep ring mould with almond or groundnut oil.

Heat the milk in a pan. Place the egg yolks in a bowl and gradually work in the sugar and salt, whisking vigorously for about 5 minutes until the mixture is smooth and pale yellow. Gradually stir in the hot milk then return to the pan over a low heat and stir gently for 6 to 10 minutes without allowing the custard to reach simmering point. All the froth will disappear and the custard will be thick enough to coat the back of a spoon. Remove from the heat and stir in the cornflour.

Soak the gelatine in the orange juice for 10 minutes. Stir into the warm custard with the orange liqueur and orange rind until well blended. If it is not smooth enough, rub through a sieve then leave to cool.

Whip the cream until stiff. When the custard is cool but not cold, place the whipped cream on top and, using a large spoon or spatula, gently lift the custard on top of the cream. Continue to lift and fold the mixture, turning the bowl with your left hand so that it is evenly blended.

Spoon the mixture into the prepared mould and cover with a piece of kitchen foil. Holding it with both hands, tap the mould lightly on a table to make sure it is tightly packed. Place in the coldest part of the fridge overnight or for at least 4 hours.

Dip the mould in a bowl of hot water for a second or dip a tea towel in hot water, wring it out then wrap it around the mould. Run a sharp knife round the edge. Place a plate on top of the mould and turn it over to unmould the Bavarois with a decisive movement. Arrange the sliced oranges around the edges and the candied orange on top. You may offer a bowl of whipped cream or a bowl of fruit purée with the Bavarois. An unmoulded Bavarois can be chilled for a few hours.

Soufflé au Chocolat

CHOCOLATE SOUFFLE

A soufflé spells luxury, excitement and happiness yet this superstar is very easy to make. There is a base which gives flavour, and whisked egg whites for lightness and drama. Cooking for the right length of time in a pre-heated oven is important.

I like to serve the Soufflé with a bowl of whipped cream or, for a lighter, fresher dessert, a dish of sliced pears or peaches sprinkled with lemon juice.

SERVES 4–6

90 g (3½ oz) plain chocolate, chopped
50 g (2 oz) caster sugar, plus extra for coating
2 tablespoons plain flour
250 ml (8 fl oz) milk
15 g (½ oz) butter
3 whole eggs, separated
1 extra egg white
2 tablespoons strong coffee
icing sugar for dusting

Pre-heat the oven to 200°C/400°F/Gas 6. Butter an 18 cm (7 in) soufflé dish and then sprinkle caster sugar in an even layer over the bottom and around the sides.

Place the chocolate in a heatproof bowl, and place the bowl over a pan of hot water. Cover the bowl and leave the chocolate to melt, stirring twice.

Meanwhile, stir the flour and 3 tablespoons milk together in a bowl. Bring the remaining milk to the boil in a heavy-based pan then slowly stir into the bowl. Pour back into the pan and cook over a medium heat, stirring constantly, until the sauce boils and thickens. Simmer for 2–3 minutes. Remove from the heat, add the butter and leave to cool for a few minutes. Stir in the yolks one at a time, then stir in the chocolate mixture and the coffee.

In a clean, dry bowl, whisk the egg whites until you see soft peaks standing in the bowl, then gradually whisk in the sugar until you have shiny firm peaks and all the sugar is absorbed. Slowly pour the chocolate mixture all around the edges of the bowl and fold the two mixtures together, lifting delicately but quickly using a tablespoon.

Pour into the soufflé dish, run the point of a knife around the edge of the mixture then place the dish in the oven. Lower the temperature to 180°C/350°F/Gas 4. After 45 minutes gently open the oven door and pull the soufflé towards you, quickly dust the top with icing sugar. Slide the dish back into the oven and bake for a further 5 minutes. By then the soufflé will have puffed up and browned, and be lightly set in the centre.

As soon as the soufflé is ready take it to the table. Plunge 2 large spoons straight down into the soufflé in one decisive move to break the crust before you serve it.

Flans Caramel

CARAMEL CUSTARDS

These light, caramel-coated custards are one of the quickest, easiest, inexpensive of desserts, yet remain one of the most popular. *Flans Caramels* can be kept for 1–2 hours in an oven with the heat turned off and served lukewarm for the lightest, most exquisite texture. They can also be cooked in advance and chilled, but they must be returned to room temperature at least 30–45 minutes before serving as they should never be served cold. However, chilling the custards does tend to make them more compact.

For a special occasion, serve a platter with a variety of *Flans Caramel* (see p.312) and *Mousse au Chocolat* (see p. 308), and *Tuiles* (see p. 329) or warm *Madeleines* (see p. 333).

SERVES 4

75 g (1½ oz) caster sugar
2 eggs, beaten
2 egg yolks
600 ml (1 pint) milk
1 tablespoon finely chopped candied orange peel, or
very finely grated fresh orange rind (optional)

FOR THE CARAMEL

75 g (3 oz) caster sugar
1 tablespoon water
7 g (¼ oz) butter

Pre-heat the over to 180° C/350° F/Gas 4. To make the caramel, gently heat the sugar and water in a small, heavy-based pan , swirling the pan, until the sugar has dissolved. Bring to the boil, then lower the heat and leave to develop an amber colour; do not stir. Immediately remove from the heat, swirl in the butter then quickly pour into individual heatproof dishes.

Without delay, turn the dishes in all directions so the caramel coats the bottoms and sides before it hardens. Leave to cool.

Whisk the sugar, eggs and egg yolks together until pale.

Pour the milk into a heavy-based pan previously rinsed with cold water and bring to the boil. Slowly pour into the eggs, stirring constantly, then pour into the dishes.

Place the dishes in a large baking tin and pour in hot water to come half-way up the sides of the dishes. Bake in the oven for 20 minutes, until lightly set in the centre.

Remove the baking tin from the oven and lift the dishes from the water. Sprinkle candied orange peel or grated orange rind on top of each custard, if you wish.

VARIATION

If you would like to unmould the custards, cook for another 5 minutes. Remove the dishes from the baking tin and leave for a few minutes. Run a knife round the edges of the dishes and place a flat plate on top of each dish. One at a time, hold each dish and plate firmly together and give a decisive shake so the custard slides from the dish.

Flan à l'Armagnac

ARMAGNAC AND PEAR *POTS DE CREME*

We can apply the age-old question of the problem of the chicken and the egg to who started *pots de crème*, Paris or the provinces, and who improved it most. In Provence they add liquorice and rosemary honey, in Paris they prefer green herb tea or chocolate, and in Roussillon it is the explosive saffron-anisseed-cinnamon combination. But in Périgord they have the most satisfying version one could wish following a rich meal. It is prepared in minutes and in advance so no panic at the last moment, and it is best served at room temperature.

SERVES 4–6

2 large pears, peeled, cored and thinly sliced in
slivers
juice of 1 lemon
2 tablespoons water
175 g (6 oz) caster sugar
600 ml (1 pint) milk
2 eggs
2 eggs yolks
salt
3 tablespoons armagnac (or to taste)
a pinch of icing sugar

Prepare the pears, place them in a pan, sprinkle them with the lemon juice, and add half the water. Cover and cook them briefly until tender over a low heat.

Prepare the caramel: melt half the sugar and remaining water in a heavy-based pan until it dissolves then cook over a medium heat until it turns into a thick brown syrup. Do not stir but swirl the pan, holding the sides with an oven glove. Pour the hot caramel into the bottom of ramekins or of an ovenproof dish, tilting on all sides to coat the bottom and the sides evenly. Leave to cool.

Pre-heat the oven to 180°C/350°F/Gas 4.

Bring the milk to the boil. Beat the eggs and egg yolks vigorously in a bowl with the remaining sugar, then slowly pour in the hot milk, stirring constantly. Stir in the armagnac. Taste to make sure the custard has enough flavour and correct if needed. Place the caramelized pots in a baking tin and add enough hot water to come half-way up the ramekins or dish. Add a few slivers of pears in the bottom of each pot, then cover with the egg and milk mixture. Bake in the oven for 15–20 minutes for ramekins or 30–35 minutes for one dish until the centre remains soft. Do not chill. Dust with a light cloud of icing sugar on the top. Serve at room temperature, never too cold.

THROUGHOUT FRANCE

Crème Brûlée

CREAMY CUSTARD TOPPED WITH CRISP CARAMEL

An all-time favourite, this unctuous, delicate dish is easy to serve as it is presented in its cooking dish. Its origin is uncertain, with claims that it comes from either the French West Indies or the Catalan region of from. It can be prepared in one dish or in individual ramekins. At the *Mère Poularde* restaurant in Normandy, I sampled a predictably rich version using twelve egg yolks to a litre of cream.

SERVES 4–6

600 ml (1 pint) double cream
100 ml (3½ fl oz) milk
2 vanilla pods, halved
5 egg yolks
100 g (4 oz) caster sugar
2 teaspoons cornflour
2 tablespoons grated orange rind or finely chopped candied orange rind
75 g (3 oz) demerara sugar

Pre-heat the oven to 150°C/300°F/Gas 2. Butter a large ovenproof dish or individual ramekins.

Bring the cream, milk and vanilla pods to the boil in a pan. Remove from the heat, discard the vanilla pods, cover and keep to one side. Blend the egg yolks, sugar, cornflour and orange rind. Stir in the hot cream and whisk vigorously. Pour the mixture into the prepared dish or dishes; it should only be about 2.5 cm (1 in) deep. Place the dish or dishes in a roasting tin filled with water to come about 2.5 cm (1 in) up the sides. Bake in the oven for 30 minutes until the cream is set but not too firm. Leave to cool then chill for 2 hours.

Pre-heat the grill. Sprinkle the cream with the demerara sugar and grill for a few seconds so the top is covered with a golden crust. Serve lukewarm or cold.

NOTE

You may like to add a few raspberries, sliced strawberries or 2 Seville orange slices to the bottom of the dish before pouring in the custard.

NORMANDY AND LOIRE

Les Crémets

FRESH CREAM HEARTS

These are as popular in Normandy as they are in the Loire. They are made in heart-shaped moulds with draining holes or in a plain colander lined with a piece of muslin. They should be prepared a day in advance and served coated with fresh cream or with a purée of fruits.

SERVES 4

600 ml (1 pint) double cream
200 ml (7 fl oz) soured cream
1 tablespoon finely grated lemon rind
1 teaspoon caster sugar
4 egg whites

TO DECORATE

275 g (10 oz) fresh or frozen berries
75 g (3 oz) caster sugar
juice of 1 lemon
2 tablespoons single cream
225 g (8 oz) raspberries or strawberries

Line individual perforated moulds or a colander with a piece of muslin.

Whisk the cream until it forms soft peaks then gently stir in the soured cream, lemon rind and sugar. Whisk the egg whites until stiff then fold them into the cream mixture. Pour the mixture into the prepared moulds and stand them in a deep plate so that they can drain. Chill overnight.

Purée the fruit, sugar and lemon juice in a food processor, adding a little more sugar or lemon juice to taste.

When you are ready to serve, invert the *Crémets* on to individual plates, top with single cream and spoon a little fruit purée around them. Serve the fresh berries on a flat platter and the rest of the fruit purée in a sauce boat.

NOTE

I sometimes use a mixture of cream cheese, cottage cheese, and double cream for *Crémets*, choosing the proportions to make a pleasing texture.

BRITTANY

Gâteau Breton

BUTTER CAKE

What gives all Breton pastries and cakes their unique flavour is the mixture of sugar and good quality, fresh, lightly salted butter that is used to make them. This Breton cake seems everyone's favourite at tea time or after a light meal, when it is served with cooked fruits, such as *Compote de Fruits* (see p. 281) or Pears Cooked in Red Wine (see p. 282).

This recipe was given to me by one of Brittany's superwomen, Madame Sylvie Kersabiec. She runs the large manor house that has been in her family for ten centuries, is the elected mayor of her village, Moustoir-ac, helps with her husband and son's flock of sheep, smokes two packets of *Gitanes* a day and is an attentive grandmother of eight. Quite appropriately, her family motto is *Mieux vaut penser que rire* – it's more worthwhile to think than to laugh.

SERVES 6–8

6 egg yolks, lightly beaten
2 teaspoons milk
275 g (9 oz) plain flour
175 g (6 oz) caster sugar
200 g (7 oz) lightly salted butter, diced

Pre-heat the oven to 180°C/350°F/Gas 4. Butter a 23 cm (9 in) springform cake tin or loose-bottomed flan tin.

Place about half an egg yolk in a small bowl and mix with the milk. Reserve for later. Put the flour into a large bowl, stir in the sugar then form a well in the centre. Add the butter and remaining egg yolks. Using your finger tips mix them together, then work in the flour to make a smooth, but sticky, dough.

Sprinkle your hands with flour. Place the dough in the tin or ring and pat it out to fill the tin or ring. Using a fork, score criss-cross lines on the top, brush with the egg yolk and milk mixture then bake in the oven for about 1 hour until firm to the touch. Cool slightly, then carefully transfer to a wire rack.

VARIATION

Layer thinly sliced raw apple or stoned and chopped, cooked prunes between two layers of the cake mixture before baking.

Pithiviers

FLAKY PASTRY CAKE WITH ALMOND CREAM

FILLING

This cake originated in the city of Pithiviers but is now offered in most *patisseries* throughout France. According to Madame Jacqueline Pilloy, winner of the 1992 Confrérie du Gâteau Pithiviers' competition, the original confection was a sweet, dense sponge cake made with ground almonds and decorated with glacé cherries and angelica strips (see p.341). In time this recipe was to be overshadowed by the more elabrate flaky pastry version which follows.

There are several stages to preparing this recipe, observe them closely for a perfect *Pithiviers*.

SERVES 8

FOR THE PASTRY

200 g (7 oz) plain flour
175 g (6 oz) butter, softened
1½ teaspoons salt
5 tablespoons cold water
150 g (5 oz) butter, chilled

FOR THE CRÈME À PITHIVIERS

150 g (5 oz) ground almonds
100 g (4 oz) caster sugar
2 egg yolks
75 g (3 oz) butter
2 tablespoons rum

FOR THE GLAZE

1 small egg, beaten
2 tablespoons icing sugar
juice of 1 lemon

First, prepare the pastry. Place the flour and softened butter in a food processor and process at low speed for 1 minute. Add the salt and cold water and blend for a second then transfer to a bowl and knead for 1 minute until the pastry is smooth. Shape into a ball, cover and chill for 1 hour.

Place the cold butter between two sheets of waxed paper and tap it with a rolling pin to soften it a little. Flour the dough and the work surface. Roll out the pastry to a rectangle 15 x 46 cm (6 x 18 in). Dot the top two-thirds of the pastry with pieces of butter. Fold the bottom unbuttered third up over the butter, pressing the edges with your fingers. Fold the top third of the pastry down, again pressing the edges with your fingers. Turn the pastry 90° to bring the seam to your left. Roll it out again, fold it and turn it in the same way, making sure the butter does not come through the pastry as you roll it and sprinkling with a little flour to prevent it sticking. Roll out and fold once again. Wrap the pastry in cling film and chill for 30 minutes.

Make 2 more turns then chill for a further 30 minutes.

For the *Crème à Pithiviers*, mix together the ground almonds, sugar and egg yolks with a wooden spoon then blend in the butter and rum to a smooth paste. Chill until ready to use.

Butter a baking sheet.

Remove the pastry from the fridge and roll it into 2 x 20 cm (8 in) circles. Place one circle on the baking sheet and brush the edges with beaten egg. Spoon the *Crème à Pithiviers* into the centre. Place the other circle of dough on the top and press the edges together firmly. Scallop the edges with the back of a knife and brush the top with beaten egg. Puncture a few holes in the crust to let the steam escape during baking. Chill in the fridge for 30 minutes.

Pre-heat the oven to 200°C/400°F/Gas 6 for 10 minutes.

Brush the surface of the cake with a little beaten egg. Reduce the oven temperature to 190°C/375°F/Gas 5 and bake for 15 minutes. Reduce the temperature again to 180°C/350°F/Gas 4 and bake for a further 15 minutes.

Mix together the icing sugar and lemon juice and brush it over the top of the cake. Bake for a further 5 minutes until glazed and golden brown, reducing the oven temperature again if it browns too quickly.

THE LOIRE

Le 'Vrai' Gâteau Pithiviers

ALMOND SPONGE CAKE

In the following recipe which comes from Madame Jacqueline Pilloy, she uses a professional bitter almond essence to intensify the flavour, but if you can't find it, the normal almond essence will do. The traditional decoration of glacé cherries and angelica strips is absolutely *de rigueur* for the authentic version.

SERVES 6

200 g (7 oz) caster sugar
4 eggs
100 g (4 oz) unsalted butter, softened
200 g (7 oz) ground almonds
1 teaspoon almond essence (or 1 drop if using the professional variety)
150 g (5 oz) icing sugar, sifted
1 tablespoon water
angelica strips and glacé cherries to decorate

Pre-heat the oven to 180°C/350°F/Gas 4. Grease and line a 20cm (8 in) cake tin.

Beat the sugar and eggs together in a large bowl until pale and doubled in size; it is easier if you use a hand mixer. Add the butter and mix thoroughly. Add the almonds and almond essence and mix again. Pour into the prepared tin and bake in the oven for about 45 minutes until the top is golden and a knife inserted in the centre comes out clean. Turn out and allow to cool completely.

Sift the icing sugar into a small bowl and add the water very gradually, using just enough to make the icing stiff but spreadable. Ice the cake thinly and decorate with the cherries and angelica.

Gâteau de Savoie

LIGHT SPONGE CAKE

This dome-shaped cake is served as a dessert or a tea-time *goûter*, or snack. It is often sliced and may be offered with stewed fruits, tangerines or prunes preserved in armagnac (see p.330), ice-cream, sorbets, light custard, fruit purée or a warm chocolate sauce. The cake is best prepared in a fairly large quantity in a 2.25 litre (4 pint) dome-shaped mould, and made a day in advance.

SERVES 8

225 g (8 oz) caster sugar
7 eggs, separated
150 g (5 oz) plain flour
100 g (4 oz) cornflour, arrowroot or potato flour
1 teaspoon grated lemon rind
1 tablespoon lemon juice or orange blossom water
1 teaspoon icing sugar

Pre-heat the oven to 180°C/350°F/Gas 4. Butter a 2.25 litre (4 pint) dome-shaped mould and dust with a little flour.

Reserve 2 tablespoons of the sugar. Beat the egg yolks and gradually add the remaining sugar until the mixture is pale yellow and frothy. Whisk the egg whites until they form soft peaks then add the reserved sugar and whisk again until stiff. Blend the flour with the cornflour, arrowroot or potato flour. Fold a tablespoon of the egg whites and a tablespoon of the flours alternately into the egg yolks, lifting to let as much air as possible into the mixture. Fold in the lemon rind, the juice or orange blossom water. Pour the batter into the prepared mould; it should only be three-quarters full. Sprinkle with the icing sugar. Place it on a baking sheet and bake in the oven for 40–50 minutes until a skewer inserted into the centre comes out clean. If the top of the cake reaches the top of the mould and begins to brown, cover it with a moist piece of kitchen paper. Remove from the oven and leave to cool in the mould for 10 minutes before turning out. Leave to cool before slicing. If you do not use it at once, store the cake wrapped in kitchen foil; or it freezes perfectly.

Gâteau aux Marrons

CHESTNUT, CHOCOLATE AND BRANDY CAKE

This recipe is indispensable in more ways than one: it is easy to remember as the proportions of the main ingredients are the same, it is easy to make, does not require baking, and is irresistibly good. Generations of heartbroken, exam-weary teenagers have survived thanks to this cake. I serve it with pear or lemon sorbet, unsweetened cooked pears or a light vanilla-flavoured custard. Canned unsweetened chestnut purée is perfectly acceptable for this cake.

SERVES 6–8

225 g (8 oz) plain chocolate, chopped
225 g (8 oz) butter, softened
225 g (8 oz) unsweetened chestnut purée
225 g (8 oz) caster sugar
1–2 tablespoons brandy

TO DECORATE

grated plain chocolate, or cocoa powder and icing sugar

Place the chocolate in a bowl then put the bowl over a pan of hot, not boiling, water and leave until the chocolate starts to melt. Stir the chocolate until it is smooth, then remove from the heat.

In another bowl, beat together all the remaining

ingredients, except the grated chocolate or cocoa powder and icing sugar. Stir in the chocolate then spoon into a loaf tin or a ring mould. Cover and leave in the fridge overnight.

To serve dip the tin or mould briefly in hot water, place a plate over the tin or mould then, holding the tin or mould and the plate firmly together turn them over and give a sharp shake. Lift the tin or mould away. Sprinkle grated chocolate or cocoa powder and icing sugar over the top and serve sliced.

VARIATION

This cake, adorned with tiny meringue-mushrooms and marzipan pixies is sometimes served as a *Bûche de Noël*. One bite of it and anyone will believe in Father Christmas.

THROUGHOUT FRANCE

Gâteau au Chocolat

BITTER CHOCOLATE CAKE

This is a deliciously moist, creamy cake with a soft crust on the top. Add only the mininum amount of sugar for the best flavour. I sometimes add two tablespoons of cocoa and a tablespoon of strong coffee for a more powerful flavour. Serve with a bowl of thinly sliced oranges or with a lemon-flavoured *Crème Anglaise* (see p.278).

225 g (8 oz) plain unsweetened chocolate
1½ tablespoons water
6 eggs, separated
225 g (8 oz) caster sugar
225 g (8 oz) butter, softened
40 g (1½ oz) plain flour
2 tablespoons Grand Marnier (optional) or 1 tablespoon finely grated orange rind
1 teaspoon cocoa
1 tablespoon thinly shredded candied orange rind

Break the chocolate into small pieces and place it in a heatproof bowl with the water over a pan of gently simmering water. Leave to melt for 20 minutes without stirring.

Pre-heat the oven to 150°C/300°F/Gas 2. Butter a 25 cm (10 in) cake tin, sprinkle with a little caster sugar then shake off any excess.

Whisk the egg yolks and sugar until pale yellow and the mixture trails off the whisk in ribbons. Add the lukewarm, melted chocolate then blend in the softened butter and the flour. Add the Grand Marnier, if using, or orange rind. Beat the egg whites until stiff then delicately fold them into the mixture with a metal spoon, lifting the mixture as much as possible. Pour into the prepared tin and bake in the centre of the oven for about 1½ hours. The cake will be about 5 cm (2 in) high and as you touch it, it should feel very soft, almost runny, under a light crust. Remove from the oven and leave to cool in the tin. Turn out only when it is thoroughly cold as it will have become firmer and be easy to cut with a warm, sharp knife. Serve sprinkled with the cocoa and scattered with the shredded candied orange rind.

BASQUE COUNTRY

Gâteau Basque

RICH PASTRY CAKE WITH BITTER CHERRY OR
CREME PATISSIERE FILLING

Biarritz may boast about its grand palaces and its bold and graceful surfers, but for me *Gâteau Basque* remains its ultimate claim to fame. *Gâteau Basque* is considered both a pie and a cake and it comes in many versions. It may be filled either with cherry jam, prune purée, a brandy-flavoured *Crème Patissière* or with a mixture of cherry preserve and *Crème Patissière*. My favourite filling is bitter cherry jam flavoured with a spoonful of kirsch and the juice of a lemon.

SERVES 4–6

FOR THE PASTRY
275 g (10 oz) plain flour
1 egg
1 egg yolk
½ teaspoon salt
150 g (5 oz) caster sugar
finely grated rind of 1 lemon
150 g (5 oz) butter, cut into pieces

FOR THE FILLING
6 tablespoons bitter cherry jam
juice of 1 small lemon
1 tablespoon kirsch

FOR THE ALTERNATIVE CREAM FILLING
1 quality Crème Patissière *(see p. 278) flavoured
with orange blossom water, rum or brandy*

FOR THE ALTERNATIVE PRUNE FILLING
350 g (12 oz) prunes, stoned
300 ml (10 fl oz) strong tea

FOR THE GLAZE
1 egg yolk, beaten
1 teaspoon milk

First, make the pastry. Place the flour in a large bowl and make a well in the centre. Add the egg, egg yolk, salt, sugar, lemon rind and butter. Gradually blend the flour into the other ingredients until the pastry is soft and smooth. Dust with a little flour, cover and chill for a few hours or overnight.

Select your filling. For the cherry filling, mix together the cherry jam, lemon juice and kirsch. For the custard filling, prepare the *Crème Patissière* and leave it to cool. For a custard and jam filling, prepare half quantities of these two fillings. For a prune filling, simmer the prunes in the tea for about 30 minutes until soft. Strain and purée the prunes, add a little of the tea to make the desired consistency.

Butter a 20 cm (8 in) cake tin.

Divide the pastry into two, one part slightly larger than the other. Roll out or pat the largest piece of pastry into a 23 cm (9 in) circle and use it to line the bottom and sides of the prepared cake tin. Spoon your chosen filling into the centre. Roll or pat the second piece of pastry into a 20 cm (8 in) circle. Place it over the filling and fold the edges of the large circle over the top, pressing all round with your fingers to seal the pastry and prevent the filling from leaking out. Beat the egg and milk and brush over the top. Make light criss-cross lines on the top with the tines of a fork and make 2 incisions with a sharp knife to let the steam escape as it cooks. It is a rustic-looking cake. Chill in the fridge for 30 minutes.

Pre-heat the oven to 220°C/425°F/Gas 7 for a few minutes then lower the temperature to 190°C/375°F/Gas 5.

Bake the cake in the oven for 40–45 minutes until golden brown. Run a sharp knife around the edge then let it cool in the tin for 15 minutes. Carefully remove from the tin and finish cooling on a wire rack. It will become a little firmer as it cools. Lift delicately and place on a serving platter.

Kugelhopf

RICH YEAST CAKE WITH SULTANAS

In Ribeauvillé, they make splendid hand-printed fabrics, they have geranium-covered balconies, beautiful timber houses and a splendid bell-tower. But the town is most well known for its annual festival celebrating Alsace's most beloved cake – *Kugelhopf*. During the festival there are horse-drawn carriages, little girls with wide red skirts, and huge red or black bows on their heads, men wearing black felt hats, black trousers and red jackets, joyful sounds of bells ringing and brass bands playing and everywhere streets lined with tables covered with piles of *Kugelhopf* cakes, both large and small, all equally golden, plump and fragrant. I thought I had eaten my share of this cake in Colmar's beautiful baker's shop, *Helmstetter*, and Strasbourg's splendid pastry shop, *Christian*, comparing the flavour of the fresh, sweet *Kugelhopf* with the more buttery taste of traditional French brioches. But in Ribeauville we had an absolute *Kugelhopf* orgy. At breakfast, lunch, tea and dinner we ate *Kugelhopf*. By the end of the day we felt like Walking *Kugelhopfs* ourselves – and we probably looked like them too.

The name comes from *Kugel*, which means a ball, and *hopf*, the name for beer yeast. *Kugelhopfs* can be either slightly sweet and flavoured with almonds and raisins, or slightly salty with streaky bacon. *Kugelhopfs* are baked in fluted brown, glazed earthenware ring moulds, which make them look like a medieval merchant's hat. Metal moulds will do if you cannot find the real thing, but earthenware does give more even baking. The flavour of *Kugelhopfs* develops if they are baked a day in advance. They also freeze well.

SERVES 8

100 g (4 oz) sultanas
3 tablespoons kirsch or rum
400 g (13 oz) strong plain flour
1 packet easy-blend yeast
a pinch of salt
75 g (3 oz) sugar
3 eggs, beaten
150 ml (5 fl oz) warm milk
175 g (6 oz) unsalted butter, softened
100 g (4 oz) almonds, slivered
caster sugar for sprinkling
icing sugar for dusting

Put the sultanas into a bowl, stir in the kirsch or rum and leave to marinate while making the dough.

Put the flour into a bowl, stir in the yeast, salt and sugar then make a well in the centre. Pour the eggs into the well and start drawing the flour mixture into the eggs, and gradually pour in the milk. Work all the ingredients together to make a smooth dough then beat until it comes away from the sides of the bowl. Turn on to a lightly floured surface and knead for 10–15 minutes, stretching the dough with your hands, until it becomes very elastic. Lightly work in the butter. Place the dough in an oiled bowl, cover with a damp towel, and leave to rise for 2 hours at room temperature until doubled in volume.

Butter a 23–25 cm (9–10 in) fluted ring mould, strew it with the almonds and sprinkle with a little caster sugar.

Turn the dough on to a floured surface, punch it down, and stretch it a few times with your hands. Drain the sultanas then knead briefly into the dough. Place in the mould and leave to rise to the top of the mould - about 1 hour.

Pre-heat the oven to 200°C/400°F/Gas 6.

Bake the *Kugelhopf* for 40–45 minutes until well browned and a skewer inserted in the centre comes out clean. If the top becomes too brown cover with foil and lower the temperature to 180°C/350°F/Gas 4. Remove from the oven, allow to cool for a few minutes then turn on to a wire rack to cool completely. Dust liberally with icing sugar.

VARIATION

Serve sprinkled with kirsch or rum and topped with whipped cream or with fruit compote.

NOTE

To use dried yeast measure 4 tablespoons of lukewarm milk into a small bowl, stir in 1 teaspoon of the sugar, sprinkle over 4 teaspoons of dried yeast, stir once and leave until there is a good head of froth, about 10–15 minutes. Pour into the flour with the eggs. Use only 75 ml (3 fl oz) milk for the recipe.

To use fresh yeast, heat the milk in the recipe until it is lukewarm, pour into a small bowl and crumble over 35 g (1¼ oz) fresh yeast, stir together with a teaspoon then add to the flour after the eggs, as instructed for the milk.

THROUGHOUT FRANCE

Baba au Rhum

MOIST, PLUMP CAKE FLAVOURED WITH SYRUP
AND BRANDY AND FILLED WITH FRUIT OR CREAM

All we know about this cake is that it was invented and brought to France by Louis XV's father-in-law. It is one of the most popular desserts in France. Small, plump Babas oozing with rum and syrup are part of every bistro's dessert offering; and wrapped in their little pleated paper cases, they are a staple of every *patisserie* window display.

When the dough is baked in the shape of a large ring, the cake is called a Savarin in memory of the famous gourmet Brillat Savarin. A few raisins steeped in Malaga wine or rum, diced candied fruits or a few drops of orange blossom water may be added to the dough. Choose a light custard, fresh fruit or fruit compote to fill the centre of a Savarin, if you wish. This recipe makes enough for 1 Savarin or about 8 Babas. Savarins and Babas freeze well. If you are making a Savarin, choose either the fruit or the orange filling. You will not need a filling for the Babas.

SERVES 6

FOR THE BABAS OR SAVARIN

25 g (1 oz) fresh or 15 g (½ oz) dried yeast
6 tablespoons warm milk
225 g (8 oz) strong plain flour
a pinch of salt
2 tablespoons caster sugar
2 eggs, lightly beaten
4 tablespoons melted butter

FOR THE SYRUP

250 ml (8 fl oz) water
juice of 1 lemon or 1 orange
150 g (5 oz) caster sugar
4 tablespoons rum, kirsch or Grand Marnier

FOR THE FRUIT FILLING ALTERNATIVE

2 apples, peeled, cored and sliced
2 pears, peeled, cored and sliced
juice of 1 lemon

FOR THE ORANGE FILLING ALTERNATIVE

4 oranges, peeled and thinly sliced
2 tablespoons Grand Marnier
1 tablespoon lemon juice
2 tablespoons sugar

FOR THE GLAZE
4 tablespoons apricot jam, sieved
1 tablespoon sugar
juice of 1 lemon

TO DECORATE
4 glacé cherries
1 quantity Crème Chantilly *(see p. 279)*
glacé fruits
a few slivers of angelica
a few flaked almonds

To make the dough, blend the yeast and milk together with 2 tablespoons of the flour and leave to stand in a warm place until frothy. Place the remaining flour in a bowl with the salt and sugar and make a well in the centre. Pour in the yeast mixture, blend in the flour and knead for a few minutes. Knead in the eggs, one at a time, then the melted butter. Knead well for about 10 minutes until the dough is soft, elastic and sticky like a thick batter. Cover with a damp tea towel and leave to rise in a warm, turned-off oven for about 20 minutes until doubled in size.

Lightly butter a ring mould or individual moulds.

Punch down the dough and place it in the mould or divide it between the individual moulds so that they are about half full. Leave in a warm place to rise for 40 minutes.

Pre-heat the oven to 190°C/375°F/Gas 5.

Bake in the oven for about 25 minutes for a Savarin or 15 minutes for Babas until a knife or thin skewer inserted into the centre comes out clean. Leave to cool on a rack for a few minutes then unmould and leave to cool. If the cake sticks to the mould, wrap it in a piece of kitchen foil for a few minutes. The steam produced will make it easy to turn out.

To make the syrup, bring the water, lemon or orange juice and sugar to the boil and boil for about 3 minutes until thick. Leave to cool then add the liqueur. Prick the top of the Savarin with a fork and slowly spoon the syrup over the cake so that the cake is fully impregnated. Baste the cake until most or all of the syrup has been absorbed. It should be very moist but not totally soggy. Just before serving, remove excess syrup with a spoon or bulb baster. If you are preparing individual Babas, you can immerse them in syrup then drain them on a rack.

For the fruit filling, simmer the apples, pears and lemon juice over a low heat until soft. Reserve.

For the orange filling, place the orange slices in a bowl and sprinkle with the Grand Marnier, lemon juice and sugar. Cover and reserve.

To prepare the glaze, heat the apricot jam, sugar and lemon juice in a small saucepan for about 1 minute, stirring until smooth and liquid.

Spoon the glaze over the tops of the Babas or Savarin. Place a glacé cherry or a dot of *Crème Chantilly* on top of each Baba, or decorate the top of a Savarin with glacé fruits, slivers of angelica and flaked almonds. Press them down gently then brush with another light coating of glaze. Spoon the chosen filling into the centre of the Savarin and serve with the *Crème Chantilly*. If you have chosen a fruit filling, you may like to decorate the top of the Savarin with fresh berries.

NOTE

I sometimes use strong tea instead of water to prepare a more fragrant syrup. Before being soaked in syrup, the cake can be wrapped in foil and chilled for 2 weeks or frozen for even longer. Thaw the cake thoroughly then warm it for 5 minutes in a moderate oven before pouring over the lukewarm syrup.

Génoise

ICED SPONGE CAKE WITH CREAM FILLING

This glorious sponge cake is generally cut in half, filled with butter cream, spread on top with a thin layer of apricot jam then covered with a rich icing or a garnish of candied fruits. Génoise cake also makes the most versatile of bases and can be cut into small squares or triangles and covered with icing to become *petits fours*.

I like Génoise covered with a light icing, slivered almonds or bitter chocolate shavings. I fill it with a layer of *Crème Bourdaloue*, jam, or a light chocolate mousse.

Tightly wrapped in foil, it will keep in the refrigerator for a week. It also freezes well, but must be thawed slowly.

MAKES 1 X 9 INCH (23 CM) CAKE

FOR THE CAKE
5 eggs
150 g (5 oz) caster sugar
75 g (3 oz) butter, melted
150 g (5 oz) plain flour
1 teaspoon grated lemon rind

FOR THE CRÈME BOURDALOUE FILLING
300 ml (10 fl oz) milk
1 egg
2 egg yolks
150 g (5 oz) caster sugar
50 g (2 oz) rice flour or arrowroot
100 g (4 oz) ground almonds
50 g (2 oz) butter
1 tablespoon kirsch

FOR THE GLAZE
3 tablespoons apricot jam
1 tablespoon rum
6 tablespoons water

FOR THE ICING
150 g (5 oz) icing sugar, sifted
1 egg white

TO DECORATE
2 squares plain chocolate, scraped to make shavings

Pre-heat the oven to 180°C/350°F/Gas 4. Butter a 23 cm (9 in) cake tin then dust with a little flour and shake off the excess. The eggs should be at room temperature and the melted butter lukewarm when you begin.

To make the cake, place the eggs and sugar in a bowl and whisk for about 5 minutes until very fluffy and pale yellow and the mixture trails off the whisk in ribbons. Alternatively you can use a food processor. Don't overbeat the mixture or it will become dry.

Bring a pan of water to the boil. Place the bowl containing the egg mixture over the water and beat the mixture vigorously for a few minutes until the mixture is warm to the touch. Remove from the heat and continue to whisk for about 3 minutes until cool, thick and pale yellow. It should double in bulk. Stir in the melted butter, then whisk in the flour and lemon rind a little at a time, lifting the batter upwards so that it is smooth and homogeneous. Pour the mixture into the prepared cake tin and bake it in the centre of the oven for 25–35 minutes until golden brown. A finger pressed on the surface will not leave a print or a knife inserted into the centre will come out clean. The cake will only rise by one-third. Remove from the oven and leave to cool for 10 minutes before unmoulding upside-down on to a rack to cool completely. The bottom of the cake will become the top and provide a smooth surface which will be easy to ice.

To make the *Crème Bourdaloue* filling, heat the milk in a pan. Beat the egg, egg yolks and sugar in a bowl then slowly stir in the flour or arrowroot and ground almonds. Pour in the hot milk and mix well then pour the mixture into the pan. Bring to the boil, stirring, then reduce the heat and simmer for about 2 minutes, stirring until the mixture is very thick. Remove from the heat and stir in the butter and kirsch. Leave to cool.

To make the glaze, simmer the jam, rum and water in a small saucepan for a few minutes until thick then rub through a sieve.

To make the icing, place the icing sugar in a small bowl and make a well in the centre. Gradually blend in the egg white, a little at a time, until the mixture is thick, smooth and soft.

Slice the cake in half horizontally, fill with the *Crème Bourdaloue* and sandwich together. Spread a thin layer of glaze over the top and sides of the cake and leave to dry for a few minutes. Pour the icing delicately over the cake and allow it to spread gracefully like butter on hot toast. Leave it to dry. Sprinkle with the chocolate shavings.

BURGUNDY

Pain d'Épices

SPICE BREAD

Both returning Crusaders and merchants trading in the Middle East and the Orient are credited with introducing *Pain d'Epices* to France. Many regions developed their own versions, and Burgundy was no exception. From the fourteenth century the recipe developed in Dijon was considered the best in the dukedom and was served at the court as a festive dessert. It was (and still is) also believed to have therapeutic properties. By the eighteenth century, egg yolks, rye flour, richly flavoured honey and 10 spices were declared compulsory. Today, *Pain d'Epices* may be made with wheat flour, which gives a lighter, softer, crumbly texture, or rye flour, which produces a more dense, heavy cake, or a combination of the two flours. The mixture may be flavoured with just lemon and aniseed, or with many other spices such as cloves, coriander and cinnamon.

Pain d'Epices remains a beloved cake in Burgundy. It may be sold as a pretty crown decorated with candied fruits, or as iced fancy shapes, such as donkeys, fish, pigs, rabbits or hearts, often with initials on the icing. *Nonnettes*, once prepared in convents, hence the name, and *Duchesses* are small *pain d'épices* filled with blackcurrant jelly, apricot, quince, plum or tangerine jam, and covered with a thin layer of icing or chocolate. Made as a 6.75 kg (15 lb) loaf called *pavé d'epice de santé*, 'health cake', it is thinly sliced and lightly buttered as part of the afternoon tea or the children's *goûter* when they return home from school. Dipped into a glass of sweetened red wine it is served as a tonic to the elderly and the sick. With the current popularity of sweet-savoury flavour combinations it is served in thin, toasted slices with goose or duck liver. *Pain d'Epices* may also replace bread or sponge fingers as a lining for a charlotte, and it can be blended with a rich custard to make a delicious ice-cream, or combined with cream, rum and raisins to become a traditional pudding.

SERVES 6–8

225 g (8 oz) fragrant honey
120 ml (4 fl oz) water
300 g (10 oz) light rye flour
1 teaspoon coriander seeds, crushed
½ teaspoon ground cinnamon
1 tablespoon aniseeds, chopped
½ teaspoon ground cloves
1 teaspoon freshly grated nutmeg
finely grated rind and juice of 1 lemon
2 tablespoons finely diced candied orange peel
2 teaspoons baking powder
2 egg yolks
2 teaspoons milk

TO SERVE

warm, poached peaches or pears, ice-cream or custard

Gently heat together the honey and water, stirring until the honey has melted. Remove from the heat. In a mixing bowl stir together the flour, spices, lemon rind and candied orange peel, then slowly pour in the honey and water, stirring constantly. Beat in the lemon juice, cover and leave at room temperature for 2 hours.

Pre-heat the oven to 150°C/300°F/Gas 2. Generously butter an approximately 20 x 10 cm (8 x 4 in) loaf tin.

Stir together the baking powder and egg yolks then stir into the cake mixture, which should be very soft and smooth; add a little water to soften it if necessary. Pour the cake mixture into the loaf tin and bake for 1 hour. Transfer the loaf to a wire rack, brush the top with milk and leave to cool. Wrap tightly in greaseproof paper and foil and leave for 3 days to allow the flavour to develop. Always keep the cake tightly wrapped as it is quite dry and quickly dries out further if left unwrapped. Serve sliced with warm, poached peaches or pears, ice-cream, or custard.

VARIATIONS

• In Alsace, *Pains d'Epices* are spicy biscuits which are baked in many different fancy shapes and decorated with coloured icings. They are hung on Christmas trees, included in children's Christmas stockings or given as presents, with initials piped on them.

NORMANDY

Sorbet au Calvados
CALVADOS SORBET

Calvados is the brandy that is distilled from cider, in the same way as brandy is made from wine. This sorbet is a light and refreshing way of clearing the palate and digestion. It can also be served as a dessert with *Tuiles* (see p. 329), in a large *Tulipe* (see *Tuiles*), with *Madeleines* (see p. 333), or with a scoop of Chocolate Mousse (see p. 308) and a tablespoonful of an apple Compote (see p. 281).

SERVES 4

175 g (6 oz) sugar
475 ml (16 fl oz) water
pared rind and juice of 1 large lemon
½ egg white
2 tablespoons calvados

FOR DECORATION

mint leaves

Gently heat the sugar and the water in a saucepan, stirring with a wooden spoon until the sugar has dissolved. Add the lemon rind and bring to the boil. Boil hard for 2 minutes then cover and leave to cool.

Remove the lemon rind from the saucepan and strain in the lemon juice. Pour the liquid into a large ice-cube tray, then put in the freezer and leave for about 30 minutes until beginning to freeze at the edges.

Whisk the egg white until stiff. Tip the partially frozen mixture into a cold bowl and whisk briefly to break up the ice crystals. Add the calvados and gently fold in the egg white using a cold metal spoon. Return to the ice-cube tray and place in the freezer and freeze until firm. Serve scooped into a cold bowl or individual glasses and decorate with mint leaves.

ALSACE

Tarte aux Cerises à la Frangipane

BITTER CHERRY AND HAZELNUT CUSTARD TART

Tarte aux Cerises à la Frangipane is a spirited dessert, especially when the custard is made with hazelnuts rather than almonds. When using fresh cherries, they must be stoned, a delicate job, then poached in a wide saucepan so most of their juice evaporates. I think frozen or tinned *griottes* or *bing* cherries are the best for this recipe as they are ready-stoned and have a strong, pungent taste, but you can try it with any well-flavoured sour cherries.

SERVES 4–6

1 quantity Pâte Sablée *(see p. 277) or* Pâte Brisée
(see p. 276)
900 g (2 lb) sour cherries, stoned

FOR THE FILLING
100 g (4 oz) hazelnuts or almonds
4 tablespoons butter
50 g (2 oz) caster sugar
2 eggs

FOR THE GLAZE
3 tablespoons redcurrant jelly
1 tablespoon icing sugar
1 tablespoon kirsch

Butter a 25 cm (10 in) loose-bottomed flan ring.

Prepare and chill the pastry. Roll it out on a lightly-floured board. Line the flan ring, prick the base with a fork then chill for 1–2 hours. Pre-heat the oven to 180°/350°F/Gas 4. Bake the dough in the oven for about 20 minutes until golden. Leave to cool on a rack.

If you are using fresh fruit, place them in a wide pan with a little water and simmer for a few minutes until most of the juices have evaporated. Remove them from the pan with a slotted spoon and leave to drain, reserving the juice. If you use frozen, tinned or bottled cherries, drain them thoroughly and reserve the juice.

To prepare the filling, finely grind the nuts in a food processor. Add the butter and sugar and process for 1 minute. Add the eggs and process for a few seconds until blended.

Pre-heat the oven to 190°/375°F/Gas 5.

Place the redcurrant jelly, icing sugar and cherry juices in a pan, bring to the boil and simmer, uncovered, until thick, stirring occasionally. Add the kirsch and simmer for another minute. Spread a thin coating of the warm glaze on the bottom of the cooked shell. Spoon in the cool filling. Arrange the cherries on top of the custard, stem sides down. Brush the remaining glaze over the top. Place in the oven for about 15 minutes until the cherries have softened a little. The custard will pop up around them and the glaze will shine evenly on top. Cool on a wire rack. Serve with a wide spatula and large spoon.

Sablés à l'Armagnac

ARMAGNAC BISCUITS

When Madame Lydie Dèche of the Domaine de Millais made these biscuits, all the ingredients came from the family's farm and armagnac production. But I have successfully prepared these at home without home-made Armagnac and cream from my own herd of dairy cows.

MAKES ABOUT 36
300 ml (10 fl oz) double cream
225 g (8 oz) caster sugar
225 g (8 oz) plain flour
3 tablespoons armagnac

Pre-heat the oven to 220°C/425°F/Gas 7. Butter a baking sheet.

Mix together all the ingredients until the mixture is smooth and fairly stiff. Place teaspoonfuls of the mixture on the prepared baking sheet 7.5 cm (3 in) apart since the biscuits will spread as they cook. Turn the oven temperature down to 190°C/375°F/Gas 5. Place the biscuits in the centre of the oven and bake for about 10–15 minutes until golden. Remove from the oven and cool on a wire rack. Store in an air-tight tin.

NOTE

A few raisins marinated in armagnac for a few hours and drained can be placed on top of each little *sablé* before baking.

Tuiles

CRISP ALMOND BISCUITS

These delicate biscuits shaped like dainty tiles have always been popular, but lately the same mixture has been used to make cup-shaped *tulipes* and *aumonières* (children's purses), which are filled with ice-cream, sorbets or diced fresh fruit. Pine nuts can be used instead of almonds.

MAKES ABOUT 30
100 g (4 oz) flaked almonds
50 g (2 oz) blanched whole almonds
50 g (2 oz) butter at room temperature
100 g (4 oz) caster sugar
2 egg whites
50 g (2 oz) plain flour
a pinch of salt

Pre-heat the grill. Place all the almonds under the grill and toast for a few minutes, turning frequently, until evenly browned. Leave to cool then crush the flaked almonds and cut the whole almonds into slivers.

Cream the butter and sugar until the mixture is light and fluffy. Stir in the egg whites and blend well. Lightly stir in the flour, crushed almonds and salt to make a very soft mixture. Cover and leave in the fridge for 1–1½ hours.

Pre-heat the oven to 200°C/400°F/Gas 6. Butter 2 large baking sheets and oil a rolling pin.

Drop teaspoons of the almond mixture on 1 baking sheet, spacing them well apart. Flatten lightly with a fork dipped in cold milk, then sprinkle with the slivered almonds. Lower the oven temperature to 190°C/375°F/Gas 5, and bake for 5–8 minutes until the edges turn light brown. Meanwhile, fill the second baking sheet in the same way.

To make Tulipes, mould the warm biscuits around a small orange or the base of a small bowl.

Immediately the biscuits are removed from the oven, lift them one at a time from the baking sheet with a spatula, and quickly roll around the rolling pin to shape it. If the biscuits cool and harden before you have shaped them, return to the oven for a few minutes to soften. Bake the second batch while the first are being shaped. Continue in this way until all the mixture has been cooked. Leave to cool on wire racks or on a cold surface. When cold, store in an air-tight container for up to 1 week.

GASCONY

Glace à l'Armagnac et aux Pruneaux

PRUNE ICE-CREAM FLAVOURED WITH ARMAGNAC

The area around Agen in south-west France is renowned for its succulent prunes, which are puréed for desserts, stuffed for sweetmeats, served with roast meat and macerated in the other local product, armagnac.

In Auch, capital of Gascony, the celebrated chef of the *Hôtel de France*, André Daguin, made this luscious dessert for us with the ease and vigour of a true musketeer. He topped it with a marinated prune on a dessert plate coated with a light vanilla custard.

I would advise you to prepare the Prunes in Armagnac at once, since they need to marinate for several weeks. You will use them also with cakes, on stewed fruits, in fruit omelettes, or in tiny glasses as a mid-afternoon snack or to complete a meal. They will keep for a year. Remember to use a wooden spoon to remove the prunes and to close the jar tightly after each use. For the fastidious gourmand, Bas-Armagnac is the best.

SERVES 4–8

FOR THE PRUNES

300 ml (10 fl oz) strong tea
75 g (3 oz) sugar
350 g (12 oz) extra-large prunes, stoned
600 ml (1 pint) armagnac
1 clove

FOR THE CUSTARD

1 litre (1¾ pints) milk
10 egg yolks
275 g (10 oz) caster sugar

Prepare the tea, stir in the sugar then leave to cool. Soak the prunes overnight in the tea then drain them carefully. Place the prunes in a glass jar, cover with the armagnac, add the clove and stir. The prunes should not rise to the surface. If they do, add a little more armagnac. Close the jar tightly, turn it upside down and keep it in a cool, dark place for at least 4 weeks.

Place the milk in a heavy-based pan, bring almost to the boil then remove from the heat, cover and keep warm.

Place the egg yolks in a bowl and gradually work in the sugar, whisking vigorously for about 5 minutes until the mixture is smooth and pale yellow. Gradually stir in the hot milk then return to the pan over a low heat and stir gently for 6–10 minutes without allowing the custard to reach simmering point. All the froth will disappear and the custard will be thick enough to coat the back of a spoon. Remove from the heat, cover with a piece of grease-proof paper and leave to cool.

Measure 300 ml (10 fl oz) of prunes and armagnac and coarsely chop the prunes to make a moist mixture. Stir this into the cold custard. Pour the mixture into an ice-cream maker and process until firm and creamy. Alternatively, pour into a freezer tray and freeze until firm,

removing from the freezer and whisking several times during freezing. Unmould on to a platter lined with a folded napkin so that it will not slip as you cut it. Garnish each serving with a prune in armagnac.

NOTE

The proportions of armagnac and prunes can obviously be altered to suit personal taste.

BURGUNDY

Les Sablés aux Pommes et au Cassis

RICH SHORTBREAD BISCUITS WITH APPLES, AND BLACKCURRANT SAUCE

Today, ambitious young chefs search and try, and search and try new ways to serve dishes which suit current tastes yet remain close to the traditional cooking of their area.

One of the most successful in this quest is Bernard Loiseau, chef-patron of one of France's most celebrated three-star restaurants in Burgundy, the *Côte d'Or*, in Saulieu. This is one of his recipes, which he cooked for me and it was very, very good.

SERVES 4

FOR THE BISCUITS
175 g (6 oz) plain flour
100 g (4 oz) unsalted butter, diced
50 g (2 oz) icing sugar
1 egg yolk

FOR THE BLACKCURRANT SAUCE
600 ml (1 pint) red wine
2 tablespoons Crème de Cassis *(see p. 337)*
50 g (2 oz) sugar
150 g (5 oz) fresh or frozen blackcurrants (optional)

FOR THE APPLE
1 large apple, peeled and diced
15 g (½ oz) unsalted butter
2 tablespoons sugar
8 walnut halves

To make the biscuits, place the flour in a bowl, add the pieces of butter, sugar and half of the egg yolk. Using your fingertips, mix together lightly for a few minutes, then turn on to a lightly floured surface, form into a ball then knead by pushing portions of the dough away from you with the heel of your hand. Gather the dough into a ball again then repeat for 1–2 minutes. Cover and place in the fridge for 30 minutes.

To make the blackcurrant sauce, bring the wine to the boil with the *Crème de Cassis* then add the sugar. Simmer for 15 minutes or until reduced by just over half. Add the blackcurrants, if using, and simmer gently for 3–4 minutes. Keep aside for later.

Pre-heat the oven to 190°C/375°F/Gas 5.

Roll out the dough on a lightly floured surface using a lightly floured rolling pin until it is very thin. Using a 7.5 cm (3 in) fluted biscuit cutter or a wide glass, stamp out 8 circles. Carefully transfer to a baking sheet. Using the point of a sharp knife, mark a lattice pattern on the top of 4 circles. Beat the remaining half egg yolk and brush over the top of the marked circles to glaze. Bake for about 7 minutes until lightly browned. Leave to cool briefly before transferring to a wire rack to cool completely.

For the apple, heat the butter in a small frying-pan, add the apple and cook, stirring occasionally, for about 4 minutes. Sprinkle over the sugar, add the nuts, stir and sauté for 1 minute.

Divide the blackcurrant sauce between 4 dessert plates. Place an unglazed biscuit in the centre of each plate, then top with apple and walnuts. Cover with a glazed biscuit to make a pretty golden sandwich on a pool of blackcurrant.

LORRAINE

Madeleines

MADELEINE CAKES

These delicate, shell-shaped cakes evoke nostalgic memories for most French people and are associated with leisurely moments. Madeleines have never been out of fashion, but today we tend to serve them lukewarm because this is when they taste best and are at their most moist, with just the right touch of crispiness around the edges. There is also a trend, especially in restaurants, to make them in different sizes and flavoured with pistachios, almonds, honey, jam or chocolate. But, in spite of all the renewed attention to their plump selves, Madeleines remain steadfastly part of Sunday *goûters* (afternoon teas), dinners and picnics, served with cooked fruit, Chocolate Mousse (see p. 184), sorbets or just a glass of chilled sweet wine or a flute of Champagne. Madeleines are also what we put in the pockets of our brave four-year-olds when they start nursery school, to remind them there is life beyond such hardship.

Madeleines are baked in special shell-shaped tins and I have found that (7.5 cm) 3 in ones produce the best results. The cakes are often flavoured with orange flower water; lemon is also a popular flavouring, and I add another one by browning the butter. They are baked at a high temperature so the traditional dome will form.

MAKES ABOUT 20 CAKES

90 g (3½) unsalted butter, diced
3 eggs, separated
90 g (3½ oz) caster sugar
90 g (3½ oz) plain flour
scant teaspoon baking powder
a pinch of salt
grated rind of 1 large lemon
1½ tablespoons lemon juice
icing sugar for dusting

TO SERVE

a bowl of sliced oranges marinated in orange liqueur
and a little lemon juice
a bowl of Fruit Compote (see p. 281)
a bowl of Mousse au Chocolat (see p. 308)
a bowl of whipped cream flavoured with diced
crystallized ginger

Heat the butter in a small pan until it turns brown. Remove from the heat and cool slightly. Whisk the egg yolks and sugar together until pale yellow and thick, then slowly stir in the melted butter.

Whisk the egg whites until stiff but not dry. Using a large metal spoon, fold the egg whites, spoonful by spoonful, into the yolk mixture, alternating with spoonfuls of flour and the baking powder and salt. Finally, gently fold in the lemon rind and juice. Chill the mixture for about 30 minutes.

Meanwhile, pre-heat the oven to 220°C/425°F/Gas 7. Butter and flour the Madeleine moulds thoroughly.

Spoon the cake mixture into the moulds so they are two-thirds full then bake for about 7 minutes, until domed, then lower the oven temperature to 190°C/375°F/Gas 5 and bake for a further 7 minutes or so until pale golden brown on top and slightly darker brown around the edges.

Run the tip of a knife around the edge of each Madeleine and unmould on to a wire rack. Dust with icing sugar and serve lukewarm.

NOTE

- Madeleines can be kept in an air-tight container for 2–3 days, or in a freezer for 1 month.
- To warm Madeleines, place them on a baking sheet, cover lightly with foil and re-heat in an oven pre-heated to 180°C/350°F/Gas 4 for 5–8 minutes.

Truffes

Home-made chocolate truffles are delicious. They are perfect as a gift for anyone. Enjoy truffles in small quantities as they have a very powerful chocolate flavour. Use a good quality bitter chocolate such as Sainsbury's or Waitrose's Continental Chocolate which have 78 and 72 per cent cacao respectively.

MAKES ABOUT 70 TRUFFLES
2 egg yolks
100 g (4 oz) icing sugar, sieved
120 ml (4 fl oz) double cream
50 g (2 oz) butter, softened
450 g (1 lb) plain unsweetened chocolate, grated
3 tablespoons calvados or cognac (optional)

FOR THE COATING
225 g (8 oz) plain unsweetened chocolate, grated
1 tablespoon strong black coffee
1–2 tablespoons cocoa

Place the egg yolks and half the sugar in a bowl and beat until pale yellow. In a separate pan, beat the cream, butter and remaining sugar over a low heat and bring to the boil. Place the bowl containing the egg and sugar mixture over a pan of gently simmering water, stir in the warm cream and grated chocolate and stir until smooth. Add the brandy, if using, remove from the heat and whisk until lukewarm.

Line a small baking tin with baking parchment. Pour in the cool chocolate mixture, fold the parchment over the top and chill for 4 hours. Dust your hands with a little sieved icing sugar and roll the chocolate mixture into small walnut-sized balls. Chill again until firm.

Place the unsweetened chocolate and the coffee in a bowl over a pan of simmering water and stir. Lightly roll each truffle in the melted chocolate then in cocoa. Chill for 48 hours and store them in an airtight tin.

**WHERE
DO YOU STAND?**

A gourmand *eats well but a little too much.*

A gourmet *is a delicate expert.*

A goinfre *eats with avidity.*

A glouton *eats excessively.*

A goulu *eats too quickly.*

Home Beverages

BOISSONS DE MENAGE

Many people still love to boast about the wine or the liqueur they prepare at home. It is economical, you know exactly what goes into it, and there is that magical element of witchcraft in the making which is so exciting. Not only that, but these concoctions of fennel, thyme, sage, coriander seeds, juniper, fruits, brandy and wine are always supposed to have some medicinal virtues.

Cold wine beverages have always been popular in France. *Vin cuit*, a traditional spiced wine, used to be served in Provence on Christmas night with the 'thirteen desserts', including nuts and oranges, and for Epiphany with the *Gâteau des Rois*. It was made with the fresh must of crushed muscat grapes boiled rapidly to one-third of their volume and flavoured with coriander, cloves and orange rind then enhanced by a small glass of brandy. Today, as must is not readily available, *vin cuit* has been replaced by *Vin d'Orange* (see p. 264), port or a sweet dessert wine.

PROVENCE AND THROUGHOUT FRANCE

Vin Chaud

HOT SPICED WINE

Mulled wine, *Vin Chaud*, is a favourite in most homes in all regions of France. It is recommended in winter after a bracing walk – or before one. It is the best thing to prevent a cold, to cure a cold and to forget a cold.

SERVES 6
6 oranges
225 (8 oz) sugar
3 tablespoons boiling water
1.2 litres (2 pints) good red wine
2 bay leaves

Peel the rinds carefully from the oranges so that no pith is attached and place them in a bowl. Sprinkle with the sugar and pour over the boiling water. Stir well, cover and leave to stand for 40 minutes. Extract the orange juice.

Place the wine and bay leaves in the top of a double boiler or in a pan and heat gently. When the wine is warm, stir in the orange rinds and syrup then discard the orange rinds and bay leaves. Add the orange juice and continue to heat until very hot.

SOUTH

Vin d'Orange

ORANGE WINE

Orange wine is very popular in the south of France. It is generally prepared in February when the bitter Seville oranges are in season. If bitter oranges are unavailable, you can make it more fragrant by adding the juice of a lemon and the rind of an orange. It is served chilled as an apéritif or as a dessert wine.

MAKES ABOUT 5.5 LITRES (10 PINTS)
5 Seville oranges or 7 oranges and the rind of
1 oven-dried orange
rind of 1 lemon
1.2 litres (2 pints) brandy (45% alcohol content)
3.4 litres (6 pints) red or rosé wine
900 g (2 lb) sugar
2 vanilla pods, split in half

Wash the fruits and cut them into small pieces, discarding only the pips. Place them in a large glass jar with the lemon rind, brandy, wine, sugar and vanilla pods, close tightly and leave in a cool, dark place for about 6 weeks, stirring every few days. Strain, pour into bottles and store in a dark cupboard.

BURGUNDY

Crème de Cassis

BLACKCURRANT LIQUEUR

Blackcurrant berries and leaves were traditionally infused in herb teas to cure fever, plague and lingering digestive problems. Today, blackcurrants are made into jams, sweets, fruit purées, syrups, liqueur and Crème. Although it is prepared commercially, it is very easy to make at home. It is also easy to use at home, in Kir drinks, sorbets, in fruit purées, salads, and compotes.

MAKES ABOUT 1.75 LITRES (3 PINTS)
750 g (1½ lb) ripe blackcurrants
1.2 litres (2 pints) good red wine
900 g (2 lb) sugar
300 ml (10 fl oz) brandy

Rinse the berries under cold water, crush them coarsely and place them in a large glass jar. Pour in the wine, cover and leave to stand for 2 days.

Rub through a sieve into a saucepan and add the sugar. Bring to the boil, stirring with a wooden spoon, and simmer for 5 minutes. Leave to cool, strain again and stir in the brandy. Pour into bottles, seal and store in a cool place. It will keep for years.

SOUTH

Ratafia d'Oranges
SPICED ORANGE LIQUEUR

Ratafia, Riquiqui, Carthagène, Pineau – all these superb home drinks were, and often still are, prepared just after the *vendange*, the grape harvest, with the must newly crushed and blended with local cognac, armagnac or marc brandy and stored for at least a year in wooden barrels. They are the *vignerons'* treasures.

However, there is a Ratafia which is easier for us to prepare. It is also made with armagnac, cognac or marc brandy, but it can be flavoured with cherries, muscatel grapes, apricots, orange blossom, juniper, jasmine flowers, angelica, pomegranates, apricot and peach stones or aniseed.

In Provence and in the south-west, where they love the bitter taste of Seville oranges, they prepare the following version.

MAKES ABOUT 1.5 LITRES (2{1/2} PINTS)
6 oranges or 2 Seville and 4 sweet oranges
rind of 1 lemon
175 g (6 oz) sugar
3 cinnamon sticks
1.2 litres (2 pints) marc brandy, armagnac or cognac

Peel the rinds carefully from the oranges and the lemon so that no pith is attached. Cut it into thin strips and place in a pan. Extract the orange juice; you should have about 300 ml (10 fl oz). Pour over the rinds, bring to the boil for

a few seconds then remove from the heat and leave to cool.

Add the sugar, cinnamon and brandy and stir until the sugar has dissolved. Pour into glass jars, close tightly and store in a cool, dark place for 2 months. Strain the Ratafia and discard the rinds. Return to clean bottles, seal and store for a further month before tasting.

NOTE

If the oranges do not yield 300 ml (10 fl oz) of juice, you can add extra orange juice.

BURGUNDY AND THROUGHOUT FRANCE

Kir
WINE AND BLACKCURRENT APÉRITIF

The drinking of kir (*blanc cassé*) began decades ago when city workers started the day with an invigorating glass of white wine and added a little Crème de cassis to sweeten it. Blackcurrants grow alongside the vineyards in Burgundy, and in the 1950s the formidable Canon and Mayor of Dijon turned both into a national fashion and gave his name, *le Kir*, to the old *blanc cassé*.

The best wine for kir is a Bourgogne Blanc Aligoté, but you can also prepare it with champagne for a 'Royal'. Prepared with red wine it is a 'Cardinal'. Variations on the kir theme are made with blackberry, raspberry or strawberry and even peach liqueurs.

SERVES 1
1 glass dry white wine, chilled
1 teaspoon Crème de Cassis *(see p. 265)*

Mix together the wine and cassis and serve chilled.

LA RESERVE

Whether it is a simple family meal or a more elaborate one, it is always better to prepare most of it ahead of time. If possible serve two cold dishes and only one warm dish (which can also be prepared and just re-heated when required).

The list of ingredients can be long, forbidding, discouraging as one starts reading a recipe. And yet the same ingredients reappear over and over in most of this book's recipes. Of course you must take into account the time to shop for some last-minute fresh products, but if you have a well-stocked store cupboard you will save a great deal of time, anxiety and money.

Your store cupboard does not need to include all of the following items, but try to get as many as you can as they all keep.

Dry Goods

A jar of Dijon mustard (keep refrigerated once opened)
Red wine vinegar (preferably aged in wood)
White wine vinegar
Virgin olive oil (in a dark bottle away from the light)
Groundnut oil
Nutmeg
Coriander seeds
Peppercorns
Cayenne pepper
Dried thyme (kept in a dark container)
Dried savoury (kept in a dark container)
Dried rosemary (kept in a dark container)
Dried bay-leaves
Curry powder
Olives, black and green in brine

Anchovies tinned in oil (or brine or vinegar)
Fennel seed or aniseeds
A piece of dried orange rind
Caster and icing sugar
Plain flour
Yeast
Bitter chocolate
A jar of apricot jam
Almonds (keep frozen)
Walnuts (keep frozen)
Large prunes
A jar of honey
A bottle of Armagnac, or cognac or calvados brandy (or preferably one of each)
A bottle of dry white wine
A bottle of hearty red wine

Fresh Products

It is also a good idea to have a reserve of a few fresh ingredients.

In the fridge:
Eggs
Butter
A piece of Gruyère cheese
A thick slice of lean streaky bacon

In a cool part of the kitchen:
Apples
Lemons
Onions and shallots
Parsley
Carrots
Potatoes
A bunch of flat parsley or whatever fresh herbs you can find kept in a glass of cold water
Garlic (kept in a dry, dark, well-ventilated place)

Prepared-ahead Ingredients

Remember that fresh herbs, onions and shallots may be trimmed, peeled and chopped in the morning and then kept in closed containers ready for evening cooking.

Salad greens, leeks, courgettes, spinach, fennel, chicory may be washed, trimmed, wrapped in a kitchen towel and kept in a fridge overnight. Peeled potatoes will keep for a few hours in a bowl of cold water.

Soups, broths, cooked vegetables and grated cheese will keep chilled in closed containers for up to three days. Stews and pâtés will improve as they are kept in the fridge.

Equipment

I use very few utensils and most French kitchens are quite simple. Two sharp knives, a pair of kitchen scissors, a long-handled wooden spoon, a whisk, a large flat fish slice or spatula, a thick cast-iron frying-pan, two large saucepans, a cast-iron casserole, two ovenproof gratin dishes, a steamer, a sieve, a colander, a glass measuring jug with volume marked on the side, and finally a food processor are my most useful tools. I seldom need anything more sophisticated.

MENUS

Three Quick-to-prepare Menus

The great, reliable dishes to prepare quickly are *salades composées* (see p.225) and omelettes (see p.110). The following menus are the next best.

Menu 1

Céleri Rémoulade (see p.81)
or
Moules Marinières (see p.143)

ooooooo

Agneau aux Herbes and *Mesclun salad*
(see pp. 170 and 232)

ooooooo

Crêpes (see p.117) with honey and lemon juice
or
Poires à la Fourme d'Ambert (see p.285)

Menu 2

Aïgo Bouïdo (see p.64)
or
Piperade (see p.107)

ooooooo

Entrecôte Bordelaise and a watercress tossed salad
(see pp.183 and 231)

ooooooo

Salade de Fruits (see p.280)
or
Crème Chantilly with candied ginger (see p.279)

Menu 3

Pissenlit aux Lardons et à la Vinaigrette (see p.79)
or
Salade Niçoise (see p.80)

ooooooo

Sole Meunière and steamed potatoes (see p.128)

ooooooo

Omelette aux Pommes (see p.291)
or
Compote de Fruits (see p.281)

Two Buffet Menus

Assiette de Fruits de Mer (see p.137), *Plateau de Charcuterie* (see p.212), *Plateau de Fromages* (see p.270) and a basket of seasonal fruits are always welcome in a buffet display, but you may also like to choose from the following suggestions.

WINTER MENU

Flamiche aux Poireaux (see p.250)
Gougère (see p.266)

ooooooo

Daube aux Olives (see p.188)
Poulet au Fromage (see p.152)

ooooooo

Endives Gratinées (see p.244)
Endive, chicory or watercress seasoned with
vinaigrette and mustard

ooooooo

Cheese board (see p.270)

ooooooo

Poires, Pruneaux, et Oranges au Vin Rouge et aux Épices (see p.282)
Mousse au Chocolat (see p.308)
Flans Caramel (see p.312)
Tarte aux Noix (see p. 302)
Salade de Fruits (see p.280)
Crème Chantilly flavoured with orange rind and liqueur (see p.279)
Truffes (see p.335)

SUMMER MENU

Pissaladière (see p.87)
Crudités with a selection of sauces (see p.76)
Petits Farcis (see p.85)
Salade de Poivrons Rouges aux Anchois (see p.228)
Fromage de Chèvre à l'Huile d'Olive (see p.79)

ooooooo

Jambon Persillé (see p.222)
Poche de Veau Farcie (see p.180)

ooooooo

Mesclun or tossed green salad (see pp.232 and 231) season with a vinaigrette (see p.76), herbs and *chapons* (see p.233)

ooooooo

Cervelle de Canut (see p.269)
Mousse au Kirsch (see p.309)
Tarte au Citron et à l'Orange (see p.294)
Basket of fresh fruit

Two Family Celebration Menus

A family celebration requires the grand gesture of a sumptuous menu to match the occasion. These two menus will be suitable for a large gathering of family and, indeed, friends.

Menu 1

Bouillabaisse (see p.125)
or
Marmite Dieppoise (see p.123)

ooooooo

Épaule d'Agneau Farcie aux Légumes et aux Fruits (see p.174)
Watercress salad (see p.231)

ooooooo

Cheese board (see p.270) or one perfect Brie (optional)

ooooooo

Sorbet au Calvados with *Tuiles* (see pp.326 and 329)
or
Oeufs à la Neige (see p.305)

Menu 2

Gougère (see p.266)
or
Soupe à l'Oignon (see p.68)

ooooooo

Poule au Pot Farcie (see p.152)
Chicory salad (see p.231)

ooooooo

Cheese board (see p.270) or one perfect piece of Roquefort cheese with a bowl of walnuts or grapes (optional)

ooooooo

Glace à l'Armagnac et aux Pruneaux with *Sablés à l'Armagnac* (see p.330 and 329)

or

Baba au Rhum with fresh orange slices (see p.322) and a glass of *Ratafia d'Oranges* (see p.338)

Three Prepared-ahead Menus

Every hostesses dream is to be able to prepare an impressive dinner ahead of time so that she can enjoy the company of her guests and not be left frantically preparing the meal in the kitchen.

Soups are an ideal contribution to any meal that is prepared ahead as it keeps well and is usually quick and easy to prepare.

Menu 1

Soupe au Pistou (see p.65)

or

Petits Farcis (see p.85)

oooooooo

Paupiettes de Boeuf (see p.184)
Gratin de Tomates, Courgettes et Oignons (see p.254)

oooooooo

Cheese board (see p.270) or one perfect *Coulommiers* (optional)

oooooooo

Gâteau Basque (see p.320)

or

Tarte aux Quetsches (see p.296)

Menu 2

Poireaux Vinaigrette (see p.81)

or

Endives Gratinées (see p.244)

oooooooo

Boeuf Bourguignon with buttered pasta

or

steamed potatoes (see p.191)

oooooooo

Cheese board (see p.270)

or

three different types of goats' cheese (optional)

oooooooo

Crêpes Normandes (see p.300)

or

Tarte au Citron et à l'Orange (see p.294)

Menu 3

Terrine de Canard (see p.216)

or

Rillettes (see p.219) (with toast and gherkins)

oooooooo

Navarin d'Agneau with steamed vegetables (see p.178)

oooooooo

Cheese board (see p.270) (optional)

oooooooo

Marquise au Chocolat (see p.306)

or

Barquettes de Fruits (see p.297)

Children's Snack Menu: 'les Goûters'

EVERDAY FARE FOR AN AFTER-SCHOOL *GOUTER*

Tartines: sliced baguette buttered and sprinkled with grated chocolate (OR jam, honey, pâté or sliced saucisson)

ooooooo

Pain d'épices: thinly sliced (see p.325)

ooooooo

Sliced country bread covered with thinly sliced radishes and a sprinkle of olive oil

ooooooo

Sliced toasted bread rubbed with a garlic clove, sprinkled with olive oil and eaten with fresh grapes

ooooooo

Pan bagnat (made with a small hamburger bun if no small bread round is available)

ooooooo

Croque-monsieur (sliced bread covered with a thin slice of ham, grated cheese, grilled to crisp and cut into four triangles)

WHEN MANY CHILDREN GATHER AT
HOME FOR A *GRAND GOUTER*

Madeleines (see p.333) served with ice-cream or fruit compote (see p.281).

ooooooo

Kugelhopf (see p.321), *Gâteau Breton* (see p.315), *Gâteau de Savoie* (see p.318) or *Tarte aux Pommes* (see p.292), thinly sliced.

ooooooo

A bowl of dried fruits.

ooooooo

A basket of fresh tangerines, grapes and small apples. Avoid large fruits and red berries.

ooooooo

And, of course, every child's absolute favourite: a pile of hot crêpes served with brown sugar or an assortment of jams and honey. Each child will fill his crêpe and roll or fold it (see p.117)

TO DRINK

Hot chocolate

ooooooo

Café au lait

ooooooo

Sweet cider

ooooooo

Apple or grape juices

ooooooo

Mineral water or plain water flavoured with fruit syrups (mint, orange, pomegranate, lemon)

ooooooo

Cold milk with or without cocoa or commercial sodas

Agneau à l'Ail 169
Agneau aux Herbes 170, **171**
Aïgo Bouïdo 64
Aioli 76
Anchoïade 78
Artichauts à la Barigoule 242–3
Assiette de Fruits de Mer 137–8
Aubergines au Coulis de Tomates 238–9

Baba au Rhum 322–3
Baeckeoffe 202, **203**
Bagna Cauda 78
Bar au Vin Rouge 135
Barquettes de Fruits 297–8, **299**
Bavarois à l'Orange 310
Beignets de Courgettes 83
Beignets de Pommes au Rhum 288
Beurre Blanc 127–8
Beurre Mainé 100
Bisque de Crabes 66, **67**, 68
Blanquette de Veau 179–80
Boeuf à la Ficelle 186, **187**, 188
Boeuf Bourguignon 191
Bouillabaisse 125
Bourride 121
Brandade 136
Brouillade aux Cèpes 113

Cailles au Genièvre et au Cognac 160–1
Caillettes 221–2
Canard aux Pruneaux et à l'Armagnac 164–5
Caneton Rôti et sa Farce 158, **159**, 160
Carbonade de Boeuf 192
Carottes Vichy 238
Cassoulet 204–6
Céleri Rémoulade 81
Cèpes Sautés 244
Cervelle de Canut 269
Chapons 233
Charlotte aux Poires 284–5
Chevreuil en Ragôut 206–7
Chou Farci 256–7
Choucroute Garni 197–8
Choux à la Crème 304–5
Compote de Fruits 281

Confit de Canard 218–19
Consommé de Viande 72–3
Coq au Vin 154–6
Coulis de Tomates 99
Crabes à la Mayonnaise 144–5
Crème Anglaise 278–9
Crème Brûlée 314
Crème Chantilly 279
Crème de Cassis 337–8
Crème Patissière 278
Crèmets, Les 314–15
Crêpes 116, 117
Crêpes Normandes 300–1
Crêpes Suzette 301–2
Croustade 293–4
Crôute aux Champignons 246, **247**, 248
Crudités 76

Daube aux Olives 188–9
Daube en Gelée 189
Daurade au Four 133
Dindonneau aux Marrons 161–2

Endives Gratinées 244–5
Entrecôte Bordelaise 183–4
Epaule d'Agneau Farcie aux Légumes et aux Fruits 174, **175**, 176
Escalopes Vallée d'Auge 182
Escargots à la Bourguignonne 147

Flamiche aux Poireaux 250, **251**, 252
Flan à l'Armagnac 313
Flans Caramel 312
Flans de Légumes 241–2
Foie de Veau à la Moutarde 182–3
Foie Gras 227
Fondue Savoyarde 268
Fromage de Chèvre à l'Huile d'Olive 79

Galettes 116–17
Galettes de Pommes de Terre 257–8, **259**
Garbure, La 62–3
Gâteau au Chocolat 319
Gâteau aux Marrons 318–19
Gâteau Basque 320

Gâteau Breton 315–16
Gâteau de Foies de Volailles 108–9
Gâteau de Savoie 318
Gâteau Pithiviers, Le 'Vrai' 317
Génoise 324–5
Gigot Rôti aux Haricots Blancs 172–3
Glace à l'Armagnac et aux Pruneaux 330, **331**, 332
Gougère 266, **267**
Gratin Dauphinois 269
Gratin de Courgettes 243
Gratin de Fruits au Sabayon 286, **287**
Gratin de Navets à la Champenoise 248
Gratin de Pommes de Terre 249
Gratin de Tomates, Courgettes et Oignons 254, **255**
Grillons 212

Hachis Parmentier 190
Harengs Saurs 83–4
Hûitres Chaudes 145–6

Jambon à la Crème 201
Jambon Persillé 222, **223**, 224

Kir 338
Kugelhopf 321–2

Lapin à la Moutarde 209
Lapin en Civet 208–9
Légumes Secs en Salade 82
Lotte à l'Armoricaine 138, **139**

Madeleines 333
Magrets de Canard 162, **163**, 164
Marmite Dieppoise **122**, 123–4
Marquise au Chocolat 306, **307**, 308
Mayonnaise 101
Mojettes au Jambon 253
Morue, La 132
Mouclade **70**, 71
Moules et Palourdes Farcies 140–1
Moules Marinières 143–4
Mousse au Chocolat 308–9
Mousse au Kirsch 309

Navarin d'Agneau 178–9

Oeufs à la Neige 305–6
Oeufs Brouillés 105
Oeufs en Cocotte 109
Oeufs en Meurette 108
Oeufs Frits 104
Oeufs Miroir 105
Oeufs Mollets 104
Oeufs Pochés 104
Oie aux Pommes et aux Pruneaux
    165–6
Omelette aux Fines Herbes 111
Omelette aux Pommes 291–2
Omelettes de Campagne 111–13

Pain d'Endives 245
Pain d'Epices 325–6
Pâte Brisée 276
Pâté Chaud Familial 214–15
Pâte Feuilletée 276–7
Pâte Sablée 277
Pauchouse, La 120
Paupiettes de Boeuf 184–5
Petites Courgettes et Tomates
    Farcies 84
Petits Farcis 85
Pigeonneaux aux Olives 157
Pintade au Porto, Pommes et Poires
    156–7
Piperade **106**, 107
Pissaladière **86**, 87–8
Pissenlit aux Lardons et à la
    Vinaigrette 79
Pistou 77
Pithiviers 316–17
Plateau de Charcuterie 211
Plateau de Fromages 270, **271**, 272
Poche de Veau Farcie 180–1
Poireaux Vinaigrette 81–2
Poires, Pruneaux, et Oranges au Vin
    Rouge et aux Epices 282, **283**
Poires à la Fourme d'Ambert 285
Poisson au Court Bouillon 125–6
Pommes de Terre à la Sarladaise
    249–50
Pommes Frites 252–3
Porc aux Herbes et aux Légumes
    196–7
Pot au Feu 198, **199**, 200
Potage à l'Oseille 58
Potage au Cresson 58–9
Potage aux Champignons 59

Potage Crécy 72
Potée 194–5
Poule au Pot Farcie 152–4
Poulet à la Crème et aux Morilles
    150–1
Poulet au Fromage 152
Poulet au Vinaigre 151
Purées de Légumes 239–41

Quiche Lorraine **114**, 115

Ratafia d'Oranges 338
Ratatouille 237
Rillettes 219–21
Rôti de Porc aux Pommes 193–4
Rougets Grillés aux Feuilles de
    Vigne 129–30
Rouille 77

Sablés à l'Armagnac 329
Sables aux Pommes et aux Cassis
    332
Saint Pierre à l'Oseille 132–3
Salade au Chèvre 234, **Title Page**
Salade au Gruyère et aux Noix 234
Salade aux Foies Chauds 226
Salade de Coquilles St Jacques
    146–7
Salade de Fruits 280
Salade de Poivrons Rouges aux
    Anchois 228
Salade Lyonnaise **230**, 231
Salade Niçoise 80
Salades Vertes 231–2
Sardines en Brochettes **142**, 143
Sauce Aillade 98
Sauce Béarnaise 97–8
Sauce Béchamel 95
Sauce Bordelaise 93
Sauce de Sorges 98
Sauce Fleurette à l'Estragon 100
Sauce Gribiche 101
Sauce Hollandaise 91–2
Sauce Meurette 94, 108
Sauce Mornay 96
Sauce Mousseline 92
Sauce Parisienne 95
Sauce Poulette 95
Sauce Raïto 93–4
Sauce Ravigote 101
Sauce Rémoulade 102

Sauce Soubise 96
Sauce Verte 102
Saumon au Beurre Blanc 127–8
Saumon aux Lentilles 130, **131**, 132
Sole Meunière 128–9
Sorbet au Calvados 326, **327**, 328
Soufflé au Chocolat 311
Soufflé au Fromage 272
Soupe à l'Ail 63–4
Soupe à l'Oignon 68–9
Soupe au Pistou 65–6
Soupe aux Légumes 60
Soupe aux Lentilles 60–1
Soupe aux Pois Chiches 61
Soupe d'Asperges Vertes à l'Oseille
    57
Soupe de Pêcheurs 124–5
Suppions Farcis 140
Symphonie de Champignons de
    Couche 232–3

Tagine d'Agneau aux Oignons
    176–7
Tapenade 78
Tarte au Citron et à l'Orange 294,
    295, 296
Tarte aux Cerises à la Frangipane
    328
Tarte aux Noix 302, **303**, 304
Tarte aux Pommes 292–3
Tarte aux Pommes Normande **290**,
    291
Tarte aux Pruneaux 280–1
Tarte aux Quetsches 296–7
Tarte Flamée 88–9
Tarte Tatin 288–9
Terrine de Campagne 213–14
Terrine de Canard 216–17
Terrine de Foies de Volaille 215–16
Tourain, Le 64
Truffade 253–4
Truffes **334**, 335
Truite au Bleu 127
Tuiles 329–30

Vichyssoise 62
Vin Chaud 337
Vin d'Orange 337

Numbers in **bold** denote illustrations
Numbers in *italic* denote boxed features

Aïoli 76
    in Bourride 121
almond
    biscuits 329–30
    cream, in flaky pastry cake
        316–17
    sponge cake 317
Alsace Pizza 88–9
anchovies
    Anchoïade 78
    mayonnaise flavoured with 102
    and onion tart **86**, 87–8
    and red pepper salad 228
    in Salade Niçoise 80
    in Tapenade 78
apple(s)
    in crêpes, flavoured with calvados
        300–1
    in Croustade 293–4
    fritters with raisins and rum 288
    with guinea fowl braised in port
        156–7
    and prune stuffing, with roast
        goose 165–6
    with roast pork, wine and spices
        193–4
    with shortbread biscuits and
        blackcurrant sauce 332
    in soufflé omelette 291–2
    tart, classic 292–3
    tart, Normandy **290**, 291
    Tarte Tatin 288–9
armagnac
    biscuits 329
    in Croustade 293–4
    with duck and prunes 164–5
    flavoured prune ice-cream 330,
        331, 332
    and pear custard 313
artichoke(s)
    braised, stuffed 242–3
    timbales 241
asparagus soup with sorrel 57
aspic
    ham, parsley, garlic and vinegar in
        222, **223**, 224
aubergines
    stuffed 85
    with tomato sauce 238–9

bacon
    in Alsace Pizza 88–9
    and tomato and herb stuffing for
        mussels and clams 141
    in warm dandelion and endive
        salad 79
baked eggs 109
basil
    pistou 77
        in vegetable soup 65–6
Basque Pepper Omelette 107
beans, haricot
    in cabbage soup 62–3
    in cassoulet 204–6
    with ham and tomatoes 253
    and pork stew 194–5
    purée 240
    with roast leg of lamb, tomatoes
        and shallots 172–3
    in vegetable soup with pistou
        65–6
    warm salad of 82
Béarnaise sauce 97–8
Béchamel sauce 95
beef
    Bourguignon 191
    Carbonade 192
    consommé 72–3
    jellied stew 189
    and parsley and garlic potato
        gratin 190
    poached 186, **187**, 188
    slices stuffed with vegetables and
        herbs 184–5
    steak with marrow, shallots and
        wine 183–4
    stew with olives 188–9
beverages 336–8
biscuits
    almond 329–30
    armagnac 329
    shortbread, with apples and
        blackcurrant sauce 332
blackcurrant
    kir 338
    liqueur 337–8
    sauce, with shortbread biscuits
        332
blue cheese with pears 285

Bourride 121
brandy
    and chestnut and chocolate cake
        318–19
    with quails, thyme and juniper
        berries 160
bread
    as a garnish *233*
    spice 325–6
    types of *69*
breadcrumbs *233*
bream, baked with fennel, lemon
    and herbs 133
broccoli purée 240
butter
    in Beurre Blanc sauce 127–8
    cake 315
    clarifying 129
    orange, with Crêpes Suzette
        301–2
    parsley and garlic 147
    in Sauce Béarnaise 97–8
    in Sauce Hollandaise 91–2
    and shallot and herb stuffing 143
    used for thickening sauces 100

cabbage
    purée 241
    soup 62–3
    stuffed 256–7
cafes *273*
cakes
    almond sponge 317
    Basque 320
    bitter chocolate 319
    butter 315
    chestnut, chocolate and brandy
        318–19
    Génoise 324–5
    Kugelhopf 321–2
    light sponge 318
    Madeleine 333
    Pithiviers 316–17
    Rum Babas 322–3
    spice bread 325–6
calvados sorbet 326, **327**, 328
calves liver with mustard and wine
    sauce 182–3
capers
    in Tapenade 78

caramel custards 312

carrot(s)
glazed with butter and sugar 238
soup 72
timbales 242

celeriac
purée 240
salad 81

ceps, sautéed 244
Chantilly cream 279
chapons *233*
charcuterie 210–11
Charlotte, pear 284–5

cheese 260–5, 266–72
in Alsace Pizza 88–9
board 270, **271**, 272
with chicken, wine and vegetables
(gruyère) 152
with chicory and ham (gruyère)
244–5
choux pastry 266, **267**
cooking with 265
and cream stuffing, for mussels
and clams (gruyère) 141
dessert 269
fondue (gruyère) 268
goats' cheese marinated in olive
oil   79
goat cheese salad 234, **Title Page**
with green salad and walnuts
(gruyère) 234
marinating 79, 234
with mashed potato 253–4
Mornay sauce 96
with pears (blue cheese) 285
soufflé 272
storing 265
types of 261–5

cherries, bitter
in Gâteau Basque 320
and hazelnut custard tart 328

chestnut
and chocolate and brandy cake
318–19
and mushroom and olive stuffing,
with roast turkey 161–2
and potato purée 239

chick pea
soup 61
warm salad of 82

chicken 148–9
with cheese, wine and vegetables
152
Coq au Vin 154–5
with cream and morel mushrooms
150–1
with cucumber in vinegar and
cream sauce 151
poached stuffed 152–4

chicken liver(s)
custard 108–9
sautéed, in green tossed salad 226
terrine 215–16

chicory
with cheese and ham 244–5
pancake 245

chocolate
cake 319
and chestnut and brandy cake
318–19
dessert 306, **307**, 308
mousse 308–9
soufflé 311
truffles **334**, 335

choucroute and pork 197–8
choux buns with pastry cream filling
304–5

clams
in seafood platter 137–8
stuffed 140–1, 143

cockles
in seafood platter 137–8
consommé, beef 72–3
Coq au Vin 154–6
Coulis 99

courgette(s)
fritters 83
gratin 243
omelette 112
stuffed 84, 85
and tomato and onion gratin 254,
255

Court Bouillon 125–6

crab
bisque 66, **67**, 68
mayonnaise 144–5

crackling 212

cream
dressing 81
hearts, fresh 269

Crème Brûlée 314

Crème Patissière 278
in choux buns 304–5
in Gâteau Basque 320

crêpes 116–17
filled with apples, flavoured with
calvados 300–1
Suzette 301–2

crôutons *233*
cucumber with chicken in vinegar
and cream sauce 151

curry
with creamy mixed fish and
seafood **122**, 123–4
mayonnaise 101

custard
armagnac and pear 313
caramel 312
chicken liver 108–9
Crème Brûlée 314
Crème patissière 278
hazelnut, in bitter cherry tart 328
with snowball meringues 305–6
vanilla 278–9

dandelion and endive salad with
bacon 79

desserts 274–5, 276–335
apple fritters with raisins and rum
288
apple tart, classic 292–3
apple tart, Normandy **290**, 291
armagnac and pear custard 313
Bavarois à l'Orange 310
bitter cherry and hazelnut custard
tart 328
calvados sorbet 326, **327**, 328
caramel custards 312
chocolate 306, **307**, 308
chocolate mousse flavoured with
coffee and orange 308–9
chocolate soufflé 311
choux buns with pastry cream
filling 304–5
Crème Brûlée 314
Crème Chantilly 279
Crème Patissière 278
crêpes filled with apples,
flavoured with calvados 300–1
Crêpes Suzette 301–2
Croustade 293–4
fresh cheese 269

fresh cream hearts 314–15
fresh fruit salad 280
fruit tartlets 297–8, **299**
kirsch mousse 309
lemon, orange and almond tart 294, **295**, 296
pear Charlotte 284–5
pears, prunes and oranges cooked in red wine 282, **283**
pears with blue cheese 285
plum tart 296–7
poached fresh fruit 281
prune ice cream flavoured with armagnac 330, **331**, 332
prune tart 280–1
rich shortbread biscuits with apples and blackcurrant sauce 332
sabayon and fruit gratin 286, **287**
snow eggs 305–6
soufflé omelette filled with apples flavoured with rum, 291–2
Tarte Tatin 288–9
vanilla custard 278–9
walnut tart 302, **303**, 304
dips 76–8
duck 149
breasts 162, **163**, 164
in Cassoulet 204–6
confit 218–19
crackling 212
with prunes and armagnac 164–5
Rillettes 219
roast, with spinach stuffing 158, **159**, 160
terrine 216–17
duck livers, sautéed, in green tossed salad 226

eggs 103, 104–17
baked 109
fried 104
hard boiled in mayonnaise 101
mollets 104
poached 104
scrambled 105
creamy mushroom scrambled, 113
shirred 105
in wine sauce 108
see also crêpes; custard; omelettes
equipment 340

fennel
with baked bream, lemon and herbs 133
purée 240
filo pastry with apple filling flavoured with armagnac 293–4
fish 118–19, 120–47
poached in Court Bouillon 125–6
see also individual names
fish soups
Bouillabaisse 125
Bourride 121
Marmite Dieppoise **122**, 123–4
Pauchouse 120
provence-style 124–5
flaky pastry cake with almond cream filling 316–17
foie gras *227*
fondue 268
fritters
apple, with raisins and rum 288
courgette 83
fruit
poached fresh 281
in Rum Babas 322–3
and sabayon gratin 286, **287**
salad 280
tartlets 297–8, **299**
see also individual names

galettes 116–17
garlic
Aïoli 76
in beef, parsley and potato gratin 190
with lamb and herbs 170, **171**
and parsley butter 147
Pistou 65–6, 77
Rouille 77
soups 63–4
timbales 242
and walnut sauce 98
and wine sauce, with roast lamb 169
goats' cheese 262
marinated in olive oil 79
salad 234, **Title Page**
goose roast, with apple and prune stuffing 165–6
gratin

beef, parsley and garlic potato 190
courgette 243
Dauphinois 269
potato 249
sabayon and fruit 286, **287**
tomato, courgette and onion 254, **255**
turnip 248
green mayonnaise 102
gruyère cheese *see* cheese
guinea fowl brasied in port, with apples and pears 156–7

ham
with chicory and cheese 244–5
in duck terrine 216–17
with haricot beans and tomatoes 253
in parsley, garlic and vinegar aspic 222, **223**, 224
slices baked in fragrant sauce with mushrooms and shallots 201
haricot beans *see* beans
hazelnut custard, and bitter cherry tart 328
herring fillets, marinated 83–4
Hollandaise sauce 91–2

ice cream
prune, flavoured with armagnac 330, **331**, 332
ingredients, storage of 339–40

Jellied Beef Stew 189
John Dory with sorrel 132–3
juniper berries
with quails, thyme and brandy 160

kipper fillets, marinated 83–4
kir 338
kirsch mousse 309
Kugelhopf 321

lamb
in Cassoulet 204–6
with herbs and garlic 170, **171**
and onion stew 176–7
roast, with creamy garlic and wine sauce 169
roast leg, with haricot beans,

tomatoes and shallots 172–3
stuffed breast 180–1
stuffed shoulder 174, **175**, 176
and vegetable stew 178–9
leek(s)
with oysters 146
and potato soup 62
savoury flan 250, **251**, 252
warm salad of 81–2
lemon
with baked bream, fennel and
herbs 133–4
mayonnaise 101
with crab 145
and orange tart 294, **295**, 296
with sole 128
lentil(s)
with salmon 130, **131**, 132
soup 60–1
livers
calves, with mustard and wine
sauce 182–3
duck, sautéed with green tossed
salad 226
foie gras *227*
see also chicken livers; terrines

Madeleine cakes 333
marrow
bone in Pot au Feu 198, **199**, 200
with steak, shallots and wine
183–4
mayonnaise 101
crab 144–5
curry 101
flavoured with anchovies, shallots
and herbs 102
green 102
herb 101
lemon 101
mustard-flavoured 81
piquant hard-boiled eggs 101
meat 167–8, 169–209
Baeckeoffe 202, **203**
Cassoulet 204–6
Pot au Feu 198, **199**, 200
Rillettes 219–21
sausages 211, 221–2
Terrine de Campagne 213–14
see also individual names

meringues 305–6
monkfish with tomato, herb, garlic
and wine sauce 138, **139**
Mornay sauce 96
mousse
chocolate 308–9
kirsch 309
mullet, red
barbecued 129–30
mushroom(s)
and chestnut and olive stuffing,
with roast turkey 161–2
with chicken and cream 150–1
with creamy scrambled eggs 113
in Jambon à la Crème 201
open tart 246, **247**, 248
sautéed ceps 244
soup 59
symphony of 232–3
in veal casserole with pearl onions
and cream 179–80
with veal escalopes, wine and
cream 182
mussels
cooked in white wine and herbs
143–4
creamy soup **70**, 71
in seafood platter 137–8
stuffed 140–1, 143
mustard
croquettes 186, 188
flavoured mayonnaise 81
with sautéed rabbit, wine and
herbs 209
and wine sauce, with calves liver
182–3

olive oil
goats' cheese marinated in 79
olive(s)
in beef stew 188–9
and mushroom and chestnut
stuffing, with roast turkey
161–2
with pigeon 157
in Salade Niçoise
In Tapenade 78
omelettes 110
Basque pepper 107
flat 111
courgette 112

onion 113
potato 113
spinach 111–12
tomato 112
rolled 110
herb 111
soufflé, filled with apples,
flavoured with rum 291–2
stuffings for 110
onion(s)
in Alsace Pizza 88–9
and anchovy tart **86**, 87–8
and lamb stew 176–7
omelette 113
sauce 96
soup 68–9
stuffed 85
and tomato and courgette gratin
254, **255**
orange(s)
butter, with Crêpes Suzette
301–2
and lemon tart 294, **295**, 296
with pears and prunes cooked in
red wine 282, **283**
spiced, liqueur 338
wine 337
oysters 229
with cream and chives 145–6

pancakes 116–17
chicory 245
see also crêpes
parsley and garlic butter 147
pastry
cake, with filling 320
choux 304–5
savoury cheese 266, **267**
flaky 316–17
Pâte Brisée 276
Pâte Feuilletée (puff) 276–7
Pâte Sablée (sweet) 277
pâtés 213, 215
veal, in a crust 214–15
sea also terrines
pear(s)
and armagnac custard 313
with blue cheese 285
Charlotte 284–5
with guinea fowl braised in port,

156–7
with prunes and oranges cooked in red wine 282, **283**

peppers
in Basque omelette 107
red, and anchovy salad 228
and sardine brochettes **142**, 143
pigeon with olives 157
pistou 77
in vegetable soup 65–6
plum tart 296–7

poached
beef 186, **187**, 188
eggs 104
fish in Court Bouillon 125–6
fruit 281
salmon with white butter sauce 127–8
stuffed chicken 152–3
trout 127

pork 210–11
and bean stew 194–5
crackling *212*
platter of cooked meats 212
Rillettes 219–20
roast, with apples, wine and spices 193–4
roast, seasoned with herbs and vegetables 196–7
and sauerkraut 197–8

potato(s)
and beef, parsley and garlic gratin 190
cakes 249–50
and chestnut purée 239
chips 252–3
and cold leek soup 62
galettes 257–8, **259**
gratin 249
gratin Dauphinois 269
mashed, with cheese 253–4
mustard croquettes 186, 188
omelette 113
and salt cod purée 136

poultry 148–9 *see also* individual names

prawns
in seafood platter 137–8
preserving 218

prune(s)
and apple stuffing, with roast

goose 165–6
with duck and armagnac 164–5
in Gâteau Basque 320
ice cream flavoured with armagnac 330, **331**, 332
with pear and oranges cooked in red wine 282, **283**
tart 280–1
vinegar 226
purées, vegetable 239–41

quails with thyme, juniper berries and brandy 160
Quiche Lorraine **114**, 115

rabbit 168
jugged, in herbs and red wine 208–9
Rillettes 219–21
sautéed, seasoned with mustard, wine and herbs 209
raisins
with apple fritters and rum 288
Ratatouille 237
red mullet, barbecued 129–30
red peppers *see* peppers
rice
in Gratin de Courgettes 243
Rillettes 219–21
Rouille 77
roux 100
Rum Babas 322–3

Sabayon and fruit gratin 286, **287**
salads 225
celeriac 81
goat cheese 234
green 231–2
green, with gruyère cheese and walnuts 234
salads (continued)
green tossed, with sautéed chicken/duck livers 226
Lyonnaise **230**, 231
Niçoise 80
red pepper and anchovy 228
scallop 146–7
symphony of mushrooms 232–3
warm chick pea or haricot bean 82
warm dandelion, or spinach, and

endive with bacon 79
warm leek 81–2

salmon
with lentils 130, **131**, 132
poached with white butter sauce 127–8
salt *177*
salt cod, dried *132*
and potato purée, 136
sardine and pepper brochettes **142**, 143

sauces 90, 91–102
Aïoli 76
Anchoïade 77
Bagna Cauda 78
Béarnaise 97–8
Béchamel 95
Beurre Blanc 127–8
cooked egg, with shallots and herbs 98
cream dressing 81
Hollandaise 91–2
Mornay 96
Mousseline 92
onion 96
Pistou 65–6, 77
Ravigote 101
Rouille 77
Tapenade 78
tarragon cream 100
thickening of 100
tomato 99
vinaigrette dressing 81
walnut and garlic 98
wine 94
wine, herb and shallot 93
wine, tomato and herb 93–4
see also mayonnaise
sauerkraut and pork 197–8
sausages 211, 221–2
scallop salad 146–7
scrambled eggs 105
creamy mushroom 113
sea bass with red wine sauce 135
seafood platter 137–8
shellfish 118–19
in Marmite Dieppoise **122**, 123–4
in seafood platter 137–8
see also individual names
snails with parsley and garlic butter 147

snow eggs 305–6
Sole Meunière 128–9
sorbet, calvados 326, **327**, 328
sorrel
  with asparagus soup 57
  with John Dory 132–3
  soup 58
soufflé
  cheese 272
  chocolate 311
soups 55–6, 57–73
  asparagus, with sorrel 57
  beef consommé 72–3
  cabbage 62–3
  carrot 72
  chick pea 61
  crab bisque 66, **67**, 68
  creamy mussel **70**, 71
  garlic 63–4
  lentil 60–1
  mushroom 59
  onion 68–9
  sorrel 58
  vegetable 60
  vegetable, with pistou 65–6
  Vichyssoise 62
  watercress 58–9
  see also fish soups
spice bread 325–6
spiced orange liqueur 138
spinach
  and endive salad with bacon 79
  in green mayonnaise 102
  omelette 111–12
  in stuffed squid 140
  stuffing with roast duck 158, **159**, 160
squid, stuffed 140
strawberry tartlets 298, **299**
stuffed
  artichokes 242–3
  cabbage 256–7
  lamb shoulder 174, **175**, 176
  mussels and clams 140–1, 143
  veal breast 180–1
  vegetables 84, 85
sultanas
  in Kugelhopf 321

Tapenade 78

tarragon cream sauce 100
Tartines 233
tarts
  apple, classic 292–3
  apple, Normandy **290**, 291
  bitter cherry and hazelnut custard 328
  fruit 297–8, **299**
  lemon, orange and almond 294, **295**, 296
  onion and anchovy **86**, 87–8
  open mushroom 246, **247**, 248
  plum 296–7
  prune 280–1
  Quiche Lorraine **114**, 115
  savoury leek 250, **251**, 252
  Tatin 288–9
  walnut 302, **303**, 304
terrine(s)
  chicken liver 215–16
  de Campagne 213–14
  duck, ham and liver 216–17
timbales, vegetable 241–2
tomto(es)
  and bacon and herb stuffing for mussels and clams 141
  in Basque pepper omelette 107
  and courgette and onion gratin 254, **255**
  with haricot beans and ham 253
  and herb, garlic and wine sauce, with monkfish 138, **139**
  omelette 112
  with roast leg of lamb, haricot beans and shallots 172–3
  sauce 99
    with aubergines 238–9
  stuffed 84, 85
  and wine and herb sauce 93–4
trout, poached 127
turkey
  roast, with mushroom, chestnut and olive stuffing 161–2
turnip gratin 248
truffles 44
  chocolate **334**, 335

vanilla custard 278–9
veal
  casserole with mushrooms, pearl onions and cream 179–80

escalopes with mushrooms, wine and cream 182
  pâté in a crust 214–15
  stuffed breast of 180–1
vegetable(s) 235–6, 237–59
  in Pot au Feu 198, **199**, 200
  Baeckeoffe 202, **203**
  beef slices stuffed with 184–5
  Crudités, with dips 76–8
  and lamb stew 178–9
  and meat sausages 221–2
  purées 239–41
  Ratatouille 237
  timbales 241–2
  soup 60
  soup with pistou 65–6
  stuffed 85
  with chicken, cheese and wine 152
  with roast pork 196–7
  with stuffed chicken 152–4
  see also individual names
venison casserole 206–7
Vinaigrette 76, 232
  dressing 81
  for goat cheese salad 234
  for Salade Lyonnaise 231
vinegar
  in Court Bouillon 126
  and cream sauce, with chicken and cucumber 151
  prune 226

walnut(s)
  and garlic sauce 98
  in green salad with gruyère cheese 234
  tart 302, **303**, 304
watercress soup 58–9
wine (beverages)
  hot spiced 337
  Kir 338
  orange 337